Happy ... day ...

Flyfisher's Guide to™

Freshwater
Florida

I know??

You like Flyfishing

So Ya here

Hope Ya like it!!

Titles Available in This Series

Flyfisher's Guide to™
Freshwater
Florida

Larry Kinder

Wilderness
Adventures
Press, Inc.™

Belgrade, Montana

This book was made with an easy-open, lay-flat binding.

© 2003

Cover photograph: © 2003 Larry Kinder
Photographs contained herein © 2002 Larry Kinder
Fish description artwork © 2003 Duane Raver
© 2003 Wilderness Adventures Press, Inc.

Flyfisher's Guide to™

Published by Wilderness Adventures Press
45 Buckskin Road
Belgrade, MT 59714
800-925-3339
Website: www.wildadv.com
email: books@wildadv.com

10   9   8   7   6   5   4   3   2   1

Library of Congress Cataloging-in-Publication Data

Kinder, Larry, 1949-
  Flyfisher's guide to freshwater Florida / by Larry Kinder.
      p. cm.
  ISBN 1-885106-97-1 (pbk. : alk. paper)
  1. Fly fishing--Florida--Guidebooks. 2. Freshwater fishes--Florida--
Guidebooks. 3. Florida--Guidebooks. I. Title.
  SH456 .K43 2002
  799.1'24'09759--dc21
                              2002153184

Table of Contents

Region 2—North-Central Florida

Region 3—Central and South Florida

Capt. Brian Clancey, a saltwater guide on Mosquito Lagoon, uses a square-backed canoe with a small motor to fish coastal streams on days that he does not have charters.

Acknowledgments

I first want to recognize my wife, Joan, and acknowledge that without her support this and my other writing endeavors would not be possible. Among my fishing buddies, my two daughters, Michelle and Katie, stand out for having fished with me throughout their entire lives. Their presence contributed to fishless days still being counted as successful days on the water.

I want to thank Pete Elkins for mentoring me as I began to write. He has taught me most of what I know about writing and fishing. I have evolved with time and experience so that I now use styles for each that work best for me, but I remain grateful for his many years of assistance.

The editors of numerous magazines have given me the opportunity to write for them and I am most appreciative. I especially want to thank Karl Wickstrom (publisher) and Jeff Weakley (editor) of *Florida Sportsman*, however, for encouraging me to expand both my fishing and writing and then share it with others.

In the preparation of this guidebook, I had to do substantial research and found the contributions of Herb Allen, Bob Wattendorf, Mart Trainor, and Paul Shafland to the Florida Fish and Wildlife Commission website to be most helpful and informative.

I also want to thank the boat and tackle manufacturers who have provided support in varying degrees to me and other writers. I would like to acknowledge John Brazleton at Redington, Kelli Threatt at Watermark Boat Division, and Steve Peet at Confluence Watersports Company for equipment used in obtaining photographs for this guidebook. I will continue to use their fine products for many years to come.

Good fishing partners are to be cherished and I want to recognize Dan Limbaugh, with whom I have fished for more than 25 years, as one of the finest there could ever be. I also have had substantial help from Brian Penrose, Ken Bay, Suzie Reihl, Brian Maloney, Matt Socha, Dan McKinley, Glen McKinley, Capt. Brian Clancey and Capt. James Hillman in the preparation of this guidebook.

The list goes on, but space does not permit me to recognize everyone. Many others have made contributions through the years that have assisted me in acquiring the experience and expertise necessary to write this guidebook. I am indebted to all of you.

*The author casts toward some snags on the deeper,
outside bend of a stream.*

Introduction

Fishing is my passion. I began tossing wiggling worms into root wads on an Ozark stream when I was a very small child and I have continued to fish at every opportunity. As a teenager, I would drive several hours late on Friday nights after a date so that I could join friends and float for the weekend on the same streams I had fished as a child. College took me to West Point and then law school, and as I traveled across the country as an Army officer, I fished wherever I could find water in every conceivable way possible. Like so many others, I retired to Florida where I have fished over 200 days a year for more than a decade. In order to justify the time I spent on the water, I bought a camera and computer and tried my hand at writing on days I could not fish. You are reading the product of much of that effort for the past year.

Most freshwater fish in Florida, and they are numerous, have never seen a fly. This is a state where an angler who is fishing with a cane pole in the county of his residence does not need a fishing license. Fishermen and fisherwomen come from all over the country to fish for Florida's fabled largemouth bass, but few bring a fly rod. In late winter and early spring, another group comes from up north to catch our large and tasty crappie. Bream, that group of panfish including stumpknockers, pumpkinseeds, redbreasts, redears, and bluegills, are favored by locals throughout the year. Very few of these fish are caught by flyfishers, however. I hope in some small way to change that because just about anywhere in the state, at any time of the year, freshwater fish can be caught using a fly rod. The opportunities are nearly limitless.

I urge you to come see our beautiful state and sample our freshwater fishing while here. If you do, I hope that you will bring your fly rods and enjoy yourself. The purpose of this guidebook is to help you get to productive waters where you can catch freshwater fish and point out some helpful hints about how to do so with a fly rod.

I feel privileged to have prepared this guidebook and hope that you find it to be helpful.

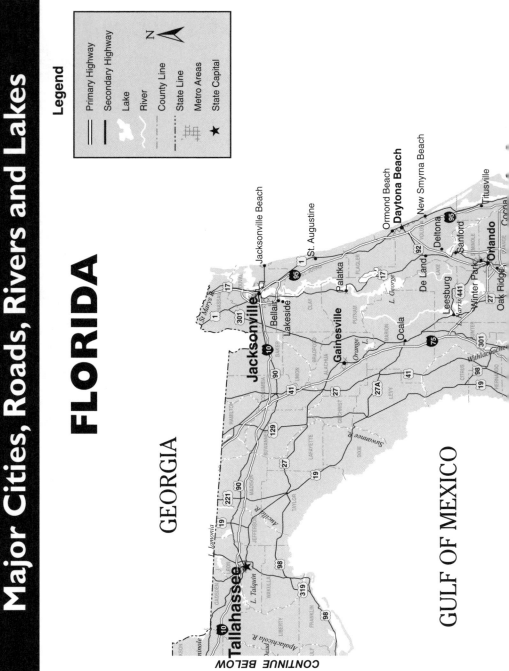

Major Cities, Roads, Rivers and Lakes

FLORIDA

Legend

— Primary Highway
— Secondary Highway
Lake
River
County Line
State Line
Metro Areas
★ State Capital

N

GEORGIA

GULF OF MEXICO

Tallahassee
Jacksonville
Gainesville
Orlando
Daytona Beach

Jacksonville Beach
St. Augustine
Ormond Beach
New Smyrna Beach
Titusville
Cocoa
Deltona
Sanford
Winter Park
Oak Ridge
De Land
Leesburg
Ocala
Palatka
Bellair
Lakeside

CONTINUE BELOW

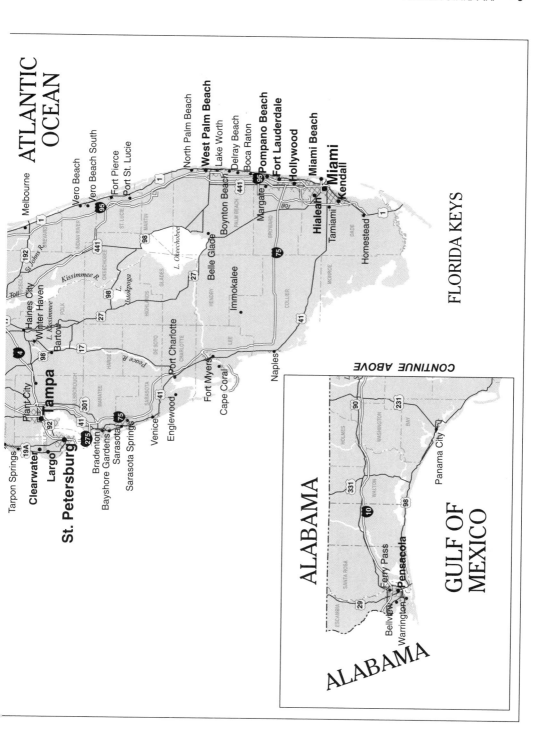

Road Signs Revised

In January 2002, the Florida Department of Transportation (FDOT) began changing exit numbers along Florida's Interstate Highway System. The exit numbers will be changed from consecutive exit numbers to milepost numbers and the new exit numbers will match the numbers on the mile markers along the highway. The advance guide signs and the exit direction signs will display both the old and new exit numbers for two years (ending in June 2005) so that everyone can get used to the new numbers.

To be consistent, I have used the old sequential numbering system that was in place when I began writing this guidebook. As indicated above, these exit numbers will continue to be posted (as a small, square green sign usually attached to the upper right side of the new exit signs) until mid-2005. I have included conversion tables for the major interstate highways showing both the old and new exit numbers to give readers a point of reference.

Exit signs are being changed from sequential exits to numbers that match the mile markers.

Florida's New
Interstate Exit Numbers

TRAVELING I-4	OLD NUMBER	NEW NUMBER	INTERSECTING ROADWAY
East & West	1	1	SR 585
East & West	2	2	40th St.
East & West	3	3	US 41
East & West	4	5	SR 574
East	5	6	Orient Rd.
East & West	6	7	US 301
East & West	7	9	I-75
East & West	8	10	CR 579
East & West	9	14	McIntosh Rd.
East & West	10	17	Branch Forbes Rd.
East & West	11	19	SR 566
East & West	13	21	SR 39 (Alexander St.)
East & West	14	22	SR 553
East & West	15	25	County Line Rd.
East & West	15A	27	SR 570 (Polk Pkwy.) West
East	16	28	SR 546 (Memorial Blvd.)
East & West	17	31	SR 539 (Kathleen Rd.)
East & West	18	32	US 98
East & West	19	33	SR 33/CR 582 (Socrum Loop)
East & West	20	38	SR 33
East & West	20A	41	SR 570 (Polk Pkwy.) East
East & West	21	44	SR 559
East & West	22	48	CR 557
East & West	23	55	US 27
East & West	24	58	CR 532
East & West	None	60	SR 429 (Future Interchange)
East & West	24C	62	World Dr. South
East & West	24D	62	World Dr. North
East	24E	62	SR 417 (Southern Connector)
East & West	25A	64A	US 192 East
East & West	25B	64B	US 192 West
East	26C	65	Osceola Pkwy.
West	26C	65	Osceola Pkwy. East
West	26D	65	Osceola Pkwy. West
East	26A	67	SR 536 East
West	26B	67	SR 536 West
East & West	27	68	SR 535
East	27A	71	Central Florida Pkwy.
East & West	28	72	SR 528 (Bee Line Exwy.)
East	29	74A	SR 482 (Sand Lake Rd.)
West	29A	74A	SR 482 (Sand Lake Rd.)
West	29B	74B	Universal
East	30A	75A	Universal/International Dr. & to SR 435 South
West	30A	75A	SR 435 South

TRAVELING I-4	OLD NUMBER	NEW NUMBER	INTERSECTING ROADWAY
East & West	30B	75B	SR 435 North (Kirkman Rd.)
East & West	31	77	Florida's Turnpike
East & West	31A	78	Conroy Rd.
East & West	32	79	John Young Pkwy.
West	33	80	US 17/92/441
East	33A	80A	US 17/92/441 South
East	33B	80B	US 17/92/441 North
West	34	81A	Michigan St.
West	35A	81B	Kaley Ave. East
West	35B	81C	Kaley Ave. West
East	35	81BC	Kaley Ave. East and West
East & West	36	82A	SR 408 (East-West Exwy.)
West	37	82B	Gore Ave.
East & West	38	82C	Anderson St.
West	39	83	South St.
East	40	83A	SR 526 (Robinson St.)
East	41	83B	SR 50 (Colonial Dr.), US 17/92 (Amelia St.)
West	41	84	SR 50 (Colonial Dr.)
East & West	42	84	Ivanhoe Blvd.
East & West	43	85	Princeton St.
East	44	86	Par Ave.
East & West	45	87	SR 426 (Fairbanks Ave.)
East & West	46	88	SR 423 (Lee Rd.)
West	47	90	SR 414 (Maitland Blvd.)
East	47A	90A	SR 414 (Maitland Blvd.) East
East	47B	90B	SR 414 (Maitland Blvd.) West
East & West	48	92	SR 436 (Semoran Blvd.)
East & West	49	94	SR 434
East & West	50	98	Lake Mary Blvd.
East	51A	101A	CR 46A
East	None	101BC	SR 417 (Under Construction) and SR 46
West	None	101AB	CR 46A and SR 417 (Under Construction)
West	51	101C	SR 46
East & West	52	104	Orange Blvd./US 17/92
East & West	53	108	Dirksen Dr.
West	53CA-CB	111	Saxon Blvd.
East	53CA	111A	Saxon Blvd. East
East	53CB	111B	Saxon Blvd. West
East & West	54	114	SR 472
East & West	55	116	Lake Helen/Orange Camp Rd.
East & West	56	118	SR 44
East	57	129	US 92 East
East	58	132	SR 400 East

TRAVELING I-10	OLD NUMBER	NEW NUMBER	INTERSECTING ROADWAY
East & West	1	5	US 90 Alt.
West	2	7	SR 297
East	2A	7A	SR 297 South

East	2B	7B	SR 297 North
East & West	3	10A	US 29 South
East & West	3	10B	US 29 North
East & West	4	12	I-110
East & West	5	13	SR 291
East & West	6	17	US 90
East & West	7	22	SR 281 (Avalon Blvd.)
East & West	8	26	CR 191
East & West	9	28	CR 89 (Ward Basin)
East & West	10	31	SR 87
East & West	11	45	SR 189 (Holt)
East & West	12	56	SR 85
East & West	13	70	SR 285
East & West	14	85	US 331
East & West	15	96	SR 81
East & West	16	104	CR 279
East & West	17	112	SR 79
East & West	18	120	SR 77
East & West	19	130	US 231
East & West	20	136	SR 276
East & West	21	142	SR 71
East & West	22	152	SR 69
East & West	23	158	CR 286
East & West	24	166	CR 270-A
East & West	25	174	SR 12
East & West	26	181	SR 267
East & West	27	192	US 90
East & West	28	196	SR 263 (Capital Circle)
East & West	29	199	US 27
East & West	30	203	SR 61 (Thomasville Rd.)
East & West	31	209A	US 90 West
East & West	31	209B	US 90 East
East & West	32	217	SR 59
East & West	33	225	US 19
East & West	34	233	CR 257
East & West	35	241	US 221
East & West	36	251	SR 14
East & West	37	258	SR 53
East & West	38	262	CR 255
East & West	39	275	US 90
East & West	40	283	US 129
East & West	41	292	CR 137
East & West	42A	296A	I-75 South
East & West	42B	296B	I-75 North
East & West	43	301	US 41
East & West	44	303	US 441
East & West	45	324	US 90
East & West	46	327	CR 229
East & West	47	333	CR 125
East & West	48	335	SR 121
East & West	49	336	SR 228

East & West	50	343	US 301
East & West	51	351	SR 115-C (Chaffee Rd.)
East & West	52	355	Marietta
East & West	53	356	I-295
East & West	54	357	SR 103 (Lane Ave.)
East & West	55	358	SR 111 (Cassat Ave.)
West	56	359	Lenox Ave./Edgewood Ave.
East & West	57	360	SR 129 (McDuff Ave.)
West	58	361	US 17 (Roosevelt Blvd.) South
East & West	59	362	Stockton St.

TRAVELING I-75	OLD NUMBER	NEW NUMBER	INTERSECTING ROADWAY
North & South	1B	1A	Palmetto Exwy. North
North & South	1A	1B	Palmetto Exwy. South
North & South	2	2	NW 138th St./Graham Dairy Rd.
North & South	3A	4	Miami Gardens Dr.
South	3B	5	Florida's Turnpike South
North & South	4A	7A	Miramar Pkwy. East
North & South	4B	7B	Miramar Pkwy. West
North & South	5A	9A	SR 820 (Pine Blvd.) East
North & South	5B	9B	SR 820 (Pine Blvd.) West
North & South	6A	11A	Sheridan St. East
North & South	6B	11B	Sheridan St. West
North & South	7A	13A	Griffin Rd. East
North & South	7B	13B	Griffin Rd. West
North & South	8	15	Arvida Pkwy.
North & South	10	19	I-595 (Sawgrass Exwy.)/SR 869
North	11	21	SR 84 (NW 184th Ave./Indian Trace)
North & South	12	22	NW 196th Ave./Arvida Pkwy.
North & South	13A	23	SR 25/US 27 North
North & South	13B	23	SR 25/US 27 South
North & South	14	49	Government Rd./Snake Rd.
North & South	14A	80	SR 29
North & South	15	101	CR 951 (Collier Blvd.)
North & South	16	107	CR 896 (Pine Ridge Rd.)
North & South	17	111	CR 846 (Immokalee Rd.)
North & South	18	116	Bonita Beach Rd.
North & South	19	123	Corkscrew Rd.
North & South	20	128	Alico Rd.
North & South	21	131	Daniels Pkwy.
North & South	22	136	SR 884 (Colonial Blvd.)
North & South	23	138	SR 82 (Dr. Martin Luther King Jr. Blvd.)
North & South	24	139	Luckett Rd.
North & South	25	141	SR 80
North & South	26	143	SR 78
North & South	27	158	Tuckers Grade
North & South	28	161	N. Jones Loop Rd.
North & South	29	164	US 17
North & South	30	167	Harbor View Rd.
North & South	31	170	Kings Hwy.

North & South	32	179	Toledo Blade Blvd.
North & South	33	182	Sumter Blvd.
North & South	34	191	CR 777 (River Rd.)
North & South	35	193	Jacaranda Blvd.
North & South	35A	195	Laurel Rd.
South	36	200	SR 681
North & South	37	205	SR 72
North & South	38	207	SR 758 (Bee Ridge Rd.)
North & South	39	210	SR 780 (Fruitville Rd.)
North & South	40	213	University Pkwy.
South	41	217	SR 70
North	41A	217A	SR 70 East
North	41B	217B	SR 70 West
South	42	220	SR 64
North	42A	220A	SR 64 East
North	42B	220B	SR 64 West
North & South	43	224	US 301
North & South	44	228	I-275 North
North & South	45	229	CR 6 (Moccasin Wallow Rd.)
North	46	240	SR 674
South	46B	240A	SR 674 East
South	46A	240B	SR 674 West
North & South	47	246	CR 672 (Big Bend Rd.)
North & South	48	250	Gibsonton Dr.
North & South	49	254	US 301
North & South	50	256	Lee Roy Selmon Exwy.
North & South	51	257	SR 60
South	52	260	SR 574 (Martin Luther King Blvd.)
North	52A	260A	SR 574 (Martin Luther King Blvd.) East
North	52B	260B	SR 574 (Martin Luther King Blvd.) West
North & South	53	261	I-4
North & South	54	265	SR 582 (Fowler Ave.)
North & South	55	266	CR 582-A (Fletcher Ave.)
North & South	56	270	CR 581 (Bruce B. Downs Blvd.)
South	57	274	I-275 South
North & South	57A	275	SR 56
North & South	58	279	SR 54
North & South	59	285	SR 52
North & South	60	293	CR 41
North & South	61	301	US 98
North & South	62	309	CR 476
North & South	63	314	SR 48
North & South	64	321	CR 470
South	65	328	Florida's Turnpike
North & South	66	329	SR 44
North & South	67	341	CR 484
North & South	68	350	SR 200
North & South	69	352	SR 40
North & South	70	354	US 27
North & South	71	358	SR 326
North & South	72	368	CR 318

North & South	73	374	CR 234
North & South	74	382	SR 121
North & South	75	384	SR 24
North & South	76	387	SR 26
North & South	77	390	SR 222
North & South	78	399	US 441
North & South	79	404	CR 236
North & South	80	414	US 41/US 441
North & South	81	423	SR 47
North & South	82	427	US 90
North & South	83	435	I-10
North & South	84	439	SR 136
North & South	85	451	US 129
North & South	86	460	SR 6
North & South	87	467	SR 143

TRAVELING I-95	OLD NUMBER	NEW NUMBER	INTERSECTING ROADWAY
South	1	1A	Rickenbacker Causeway
North & South	2	1B	SW 8th St./SW 7th St.
North & South	3	2A	US 1
North	4	2B	NW 2nd St.
South	3A	2C	Miami Ave.
North & South	5	2D	I-395
North & South	6	3A	SR 836 West
South	5A	3B	NW 8th St.
South	7	4	I-195 and SR 112
North	7	4A	I-195
North	7	4B	I-195 and SR 112
North & South	8	6A	SR 944 (NW 62nd St./NW 54th St.)
South	9A	6B	NW 69th St.
North & South	9	7	SR 934 (NW 79th St./NW 81st St.)
North & South	10	8A	NW 95th St.
North & South	11	8B	SR 932 (NW 103rd St.)
North	12	9	SR 924 (NW 119th St.)
North & South	13	10A	NW 125th St.
North & South	14	10B	SR 916 (Opa Locka Blvd.)
North	15	11	NW 151st St.
North	16	12A	SR 826 West/Florida's Turnpike
North	17	12B	SR 826 East
North	18	12C	US 441
South	18	12	US 441 (SR 826/Florida's Turnpike/ SR 9)
North & South	19	14	SR 860 (Miami Gardens Dr.)
North & South	20	16	Ives Dairy Rd.
North & South	21	18	SR 858 (Hallandale Beach Blvd.)
North & South	22	19	SR 824 (Pembroke Rd.)
North & South	23	20	SR 820 (Hollywood Blvd.)
North & South	24	21	SR 822 (Sheridan St.)
North & South	25	22	SR 848 (Stirling Rd.)
North & South	26	23	SR 818 (Griffin Rd.)
North	26A	24	I-595 West

North	26B	24	I-595 East
North & South	27	25	SR 84 (SW 24th St.)
South	26C	26	I-595 East
South	26D	26	I-595 West
North & South	28	26	SR 736 (Davie Blvd.)
North & South	29	27	SR 842 (Broward Blvd.)
South	30	29	SR 838 (Sunrise Blvd.)
North	30A	29A	SR 838 (Sunrise Blvd.) East
North	30B	29B	SR 838 (Sunrise Blvd.) West
South	31	31	SR 816 (Oakland Park Blvd.)
North	31A	31A	SR 816 (Oakland Park Blvd.) East
North	31B	31B	SR 816 (Oakland Park Blvd.) West
North & South	32	32	SR 870 (Commercial Blvd.)
South	33	33	SR 840 (Cypress Creek Rd.)
North	33A	33A	SR 840 (Cypress Creek Rd.) East
North	33B	33B	SR 840 (Cypress Creek Rd.) West
North	34	36	SR 814 (Atlantic Blvd.)
South	34A	36A	SR 814 (Atlantic Blvd.) East
South	34B	36B	SR 814 (Atlantic Blvd.) West
North	35	38	Copans Rd.
South	35A	38A	Copans Rd. East
South	35B	38B	Copans Rd. West
North & South	36	39	SR 834 (Sample Rd.)
North & South	36C	41	SR 869 (SW 10th St.)
North	37	42A	SR 810 (Hillsborough Blvd.) East
North & South	37B	42B	SR 810 (Hillsborough Blvd.) West
North & South	38	44	CR 798 (Palmetto Park Rd.)
North & South	39	45	SR 808 (Glades Rd.)
South	40	48	SR 794 (Yamato Rd.)
North	40A	48A	SR 794 (Yamato Rd.) East
North	40B	48B	SR 794 (Yamato Rd.) West
North & South	40C	50	Congress Ave.
North & South	41	51	CR 782 (Linton Blvd.)
North	42	52	SR 806 (Atlantic Ave.)
South	42A	52A	SR 806 (Atlantic Ave.) East
South	42B	52B	SR 806 (Atlantic Ave.) West
North & South	43	56	Woolbright Rd.
North & South	44	57	SR 804 (Boynton Beach Blvd.)
North & South	44C	59	Gateway Blvd./NW 22nd Ave.
North & South	45	60	Hypoluxo Rd.
North & South	46	61	CR 812 (Lantana Rd.)
North & South	47	63	6th Ave. South
North & South	48	64	10th Ave. North
North & South	49	66	SR 882 (Forest Hill Blvd.)
North & South	50	68	US 98 (Southern Blvd.)
North & South	51	69	Belvedere Rd.
North & South	52A	70A	SR 704 (Okeechobee Blvd.) East
North & South	52B	70B	SR 704 (Okeechobee Blvd.) West
North & South	53	71	Palm Beach Lakes Blvd.
North & South	54	74	CR 702 (45th St.)
North & South	55	76	SR 708 (Blue Heron Blvd.)

North & South	56	77	CR 850 (Northlake Blvd.)
North	57A	79A	SR 786 (PGA Blvd.) East
North	57B	79B	SR 786 (PGA Blvd.) West
South	57	79AB	SR 786 (PGA Blvd.)
South	57C	79C	Military Trail South
North & South	58	83	Donald Ross Rd.
North & South	59A	87A	SR 706 (Indiantown Rd.) East
North & South	59B	87B	SR 706 (Indiantown Rd.) West
North & South	60	96	CR 708
North & South	61	101	SR 76 (Kanner Hwy.)
North & South	61C	102	CR 713 (High Meadows Rd.)
North & South	62	110	SR 714 (Martin Hwy.)
North & South	63	118	Gatlin Blvd.
North & South	63C	121	St. Lucie West Blvd.
North & South	64	126	CR 712 (Midway Rd.)
North & South	65	129	SR 70 (Okeechobee Rd.)
North & South	66A	131A	SR 68 (Orange Ave.) East
North & South	66B	131B	SR 68 (Orange Ave.) West
North & South	67	138	SR 614 (Indrio Rd.)
North & South	68	147	SR 60 (Osceola Blvd.)
North & South	69	156	CR 512 (Fellsmere Rd.)
North & South	70	173	SR 514
North & South	70A	176	CR 516
North & South	71	180	US 192
North & South	72	183	SR 518
North & South	73	191	CR 509
North & South	74	195	SR 519
North & South	75	201	SR 520
North & South	76	202	SR 524
North & South	77A	205	SR 528 (Bee Line Exwy.) East
North & South	77B	205	SR 528 (Bee Line Exwy.) West
North & South	77C	208	Port St. John Rd.
North & South	78	212	SR 407
North & South	79	215	SR 50
North & South	80	220	SR 406
North & South	81	223	SR 46
North & South	82	231	CR 5A
North & South	83	244	SR 442
North	84	249	SR 44
South	84A	249A	SR 44 East
South	84B	249B	SR 44 West
North & South	85	256	SR 421
North & South	86A	260A	SR 400 East
North & South	86B	260B	I-4 West
North	87	261	US 92
South	87A	261A	US 92 East
South	87B	261B	US 92 West
North & South	87C	265	LPGA Blvd.
North & South	88	268	SR 40
North & South	89	273	US 1
North & South	90	278	Old Dixie Hwy.
North & South	91	284	SR 100

North & South	91C	289	Palm Coast Pkwy.
North & South	92	298	US 1
North & South	93	305	SR 206
North & South	94	311	SR 207
North & South	95	318	SR 16
North & South	95A	323	International Golf Pkwy.
North & South	96	329	CR 210
North & South	97	337	I-295 North
North & South	98	339	US 1 (Phillips Hwy.)
North	99	340	SR 115 (Southside Blvd.)
North & South	100	341	SR 152 (Baymeadows Rd.)
North & South	101	344	SR 202 (J. Turner Butler Blvd.)
North	102	345	Bowden Rd. to SR 109/University Blvd.
South	103A	346A	SR 109 (University Blvd.) East
South	103B	346B	SR 109 (University Blvd.) West
North & South	104	347	Alt. US 1 (SR 126/Emerson St.)
South	105	348	US 1 (Phillips Hwy.)
South	106	349	US 90 East
North	107	350A	US 1 (Prudential Dr.)
South	108	350B	SR 13 (San Marco Blvd.)
North	109	351A	Park St.
North	111	351B	I-10 West
South	112	351C	Margaret St.
South	113	351D	Stockton St.
North	114	352A	Myrtle Ave.
North	114A	352B	Forsyth St.
North	115	352C	Monroe St.
North & South	116	353A	Church St./Myrtle Ave./Forsyth St.
North & South	117	353B	US 90 Alt. (Union St.)
North & South	118	353C	US 23 (Kings Rd.)
North & South	119	353D	SR 114 (8th St.)
North & South	120A	354A	US 1 South/MLK Jr. Pkwy. East
North & South	120B	354B	US 1 North/MLK Jr. Pkwy. West
North & South	121	355	SR 122 (Golfair Blvd.)
South	122	356	SR 117 (Norwood Ave.)/SR 115 (Lem Turner Rd.)
North	122A	356A	SR 117 (Norwood Ave.)
North	122B	356B	SR 115 (Lem Turner Rd.)
North & South	123	357	SR 111 (Edgewood Ave.)
North & South	124A	358A	SR 105 (Heckscher Dr.)
North & South	124B	358B	Broward Rd.
North & South	125	360	SR 104 (Dunn Ave., Busch Dr.)
North & South	126A	362A	SR 9A
North & South	126B	362B	I-295
South	127	363	Duval Rd. (Jacksonville Int.. Airport)
North	127A	363A	Duval Rd. East
North	127B	363B	Duval Rd. W (Jacksonville Int. Airport)
North & South	128	366	Pecan Park Rd.
North & South	129	373	SR 200/SR A1A
North & South	130	380	US 17

Florida Facts

Florida is a large peninsula in the extreme southeastern corner of the United States that separates the Atlantic Ocean from the Gulf of Mexico. The horizontal distance across the northern part of the state above the Panhandle is more than 350 miles. Across most of the state, however, the width is usually no more than 100 miles. The vertical distance from top to bottom is even greater, stretching more than 500 miles. If you were to drive from Pensacola near the northwest border to Key West at the extreme southern end, you would travel more than 800 miles. From your starting point in Pensacola, you are actually closer to Chicago than Key West.

As you travel around the state, you will encounter a wide variety of wildlife and vegetation, which changes from one locale to another, differing with soil type, rainfall, and average temperature.

Florida's climate is described as being mostly humid subtropical, except for the extreme southern portion, which is tropical. Rainfall amounts vary, but they are greatest from June through October, corresponding to the period of tropical storms. The following table shows the average monthly temperature for various cities in Florida, and a comfort index that has been adjusted to account for humidity.

The blue heron is among the many tropical birds that can be seen while on the water in Florida.

TEMPERATURES AND COMFORT INDEX
FOR SELECTED CITIES

Comfort Index (C/I): -2 cool to cold; 1 comfortable to cool; 0 comfortable; 1 warm; 2 hot; 3 hot and humid.

Tallahassee	JAN	FEB	MAR	APR	MAY	JUN	JUL	AUG	SEP	OCT	NOV	DEC
High Temp	63	66	74	80	86	91	91	91	89	82	73	66
Low Temp	38	40	47	52	61	69	71	71	68	56	46	40
C/I	-1	-1	0	1	1	3	3	3	3	1	1	0

Jacksonville	JAN	FEB	MAR	APR	MAY	JUN	JUL	AUG	SEP	OCT	NOV	DEC
High Temp	64	67	73	79	85	89	91	91	87	80	74	67
Low Temp	40	43	49	55	62	69	72	72	69	59	50	43
C/I	-1	0	0	1	1	3	3	3	3	1	0	-1

Orlando	JAN	FEB	MAR	APR	MAY	JUN	JUL	AUG	SEP	OCT	NOV	DEC
High Temp	71	73	78	83	88	91	92	92	90	85	78	73
Low Temp	49	50	55	59	66	72	73	73	72	66	58	51
C/I	0	0	0	1	2	3	3	3	3	1	0	0

Tampa	JAN	FEB	MAR	APR	MAY	JUN	JUL	AUG	SEP	OCT	NOV	DEC
High Temp	70	71	77	82	87	89	90	90	89	84	78	72
Low Temp	50	52	56	61	67	73	74	74	73	65	57	52
C/I	0	0	0	1	2	3	3	3	3	1	0	0

Miami	JAN	FEB	MAR	APR	MAY	JUN	JUL	AUG	SEP	OCT	NOV	DEC
High Temp	75	76	79	82	85	88	89	89	88	85	80	77
Low Temp	59	60	64	68	72	75	76	77	76	72	67	62
C/I	0	0	1	1	2	3	3	3	3	3	1	1

The largest concentration of people, as well as projected growth in population, is in southeastern Florida. However, all along the coastline, as well as in central Florida near Orlando, you will find populated and well-developed areas. More recently, areas along interstate highways have also seen substantial growth.

Florida has a wonderfully unique collection of native animals. These include manatees, dolphins, otters, birds (including eagles, blue herons, osprey, flamingos), alligators, panther, turtles (including loggerheads and leathernecks), bear; deer, turkeys, as well as colorful tree snails and lizards.

The foliage is similarly remarkable. So much so that when Ponce de Leon discovered the area, he named the lush peninsula "Florida" for the Spanish "feast of flowers." From pines in the panhandle to mangroves in the Keys, with assorted palms and stunning flowering plants in between, you will undoubtedly encounter a kaleidoscope of color brought to you compliments of Mother Nature.

Back to the reason you came to Florida…freshwater fly fishing. There are over 3 million acres of water on the more than 7,700 named lakes and reservoirs, as well as more than 12,000 miles of streams (with an additional 1,200 miles of coastline). More than 250 species of freshwater fish have been collected from interior waters. The 1.14 million freshwater anglers take 16.5 million fishing trips a year and generate more than $1.4 billion in economic output. As a result of freshwater fishing, over $37.4 million in taxes is now generated each year and 18,873 jobs have been created. Freshwater fishing is big business, with Florida the world's number one recreational fishing destination. (The economic contribution of saltwater fishing is substantially more than even these amounts.) Florida has good reason to call itself the "Fishing Capital of the World."

The Florida Fish and Wildlife Commission (FWC) stocks nearly 4 million fish each year into more than 100 different bodies of water, primarily the Fish Management Areas. In addition, the FWC maintains more than 300 ramps statewide and 44 fishing piers, most of which are accessible to the physically challenged. The most sought-after freshwater species, the largemouth (black) bass, reaches legendary sizes in Florida and attracts professional, tournament, and recreational anglers from all over the world.

Fly fishing has only recently become popular in Florida. Even now, however, it is primarily done in coastal areas for tarpon, bonefish, and other inshore species like snook, seatrout, and redfish. Consequently, most fly fishing shops are located along the coast, primarily stocked with flies intended for these saltwater species.

The following charts reflect the peak fishing periods for selected species of freshwater game fish by region.

Peak Periods of Fishing

(+++ = excellent, ++ = good, + = fair)

Region 1	Jan	Feb	Mar	Apr	May	Jun	Jul	Aug	Sep	Oct	Nov	Dec
Black Bass	+	++	+++	+++	+++	++	+	+	++	++	+	+
Bream	+	+	++	+++	+++	+++	+++	+++	++	++	+	+
Crappie	+++	+++	+++	++	++	++	++	++	++	++	++	+++
Stripers	+++	+++	++	++	++	++	++	++	++	++	++	+++
Am. Shad	+++	+++	++	+							+	++

Region 2	Jan	Feb	Mar	Apr	May	Jun	Jul	Aug	Sep	Oct	Nov	Dec
Black Bass	+	++	+++	+++	+++	++	+	+	++	++	+	+
Bream	+	+	++	++	+++	+++	+++	+++	++	++	+	+
Crappie	+++	+++	++	++	++	++	++	++	++	++	++	++
Stripers	+++	+++	++	++	++	++	++	++	++	+++	+++	+++

Region 3	Jan	Feb	Mar	Apr	May	Jun	Jul	Aug	Sep	Oct	Nov	Dec
Black Bass	++	+++	+++	+++	+++	++	++	++	+++	+++	+++	+++
Bream	+	++	+++	+++	+++	+++	+++	+++	+++	+++	++	+
Crappie	+++	+++	+++	++	+	+	+	+	++	++	++	+++
Stripers	+++	+++	++	++	+	+	+	+	++	++	++	+++
Peacock Bass*	+	+	++	++	+++	+++	+++	+++	++	++	++	+

*Peacock bass fishing is only successful during daylight hours.

When should you come and what should you bring? Come any and every time that you can. There will be quality freshwater fly fishing available for the informed angler at a variety of places throughout the state. This guidebook should be helpful to you in selecting and getting to your destination of choice. For helpful hints on what to bring, see the section entitled "Getting in Gear."

Florida Regions

North Central
Florida

Region 2

St. Johns
River
System

Region 1

Central and
South Florida

Region 3

Everglades

Tips on Using This Guidebook

I am not going to be able to cover in sufficient detail all of the 12,000 miles of rivers flowing in and about Florida, all of which have fish of one type or another. Nor will this guidebook detail fishing opportunities on every one of the more than 7,700 lakes, ponds, pits, and puddles that can be found in one locale or another. I will attempt, however, to provide specific information on those bodies of water with desirable fish and suggest which fly patterns are most likely to work after you have arrived.

To accomplish this goal in a logical manner, I have divided the freshwater areas of Florida into three regions. Region 1 covers east-central and northeast Florida. I have referred to this geographical area as "The St. Johns River System" because nearly all the lakes in this region are just wide spots in the north-flowing St. Johns River. I have noted a couple of exceptions for lakes that are not part of this river system at the end of Region 1.

Region 2 is the large geographical area that makes up west Florida and north-central Florida. All of the rivers in this region of the state, and there are several, meander southward toward the Gulf of Mexico. In addition to these rivers, numerous lakes have been created by their impoundment. Additionally, there are many other lakes in the region that are free-standing and independent of any river system. I have started Region 2 in the far western portion of the Panhandle and moved easterly across the state.

Region 3 is made up of the waters in central and south Florida. The area is characterized by an interconnected series of lakes in central Florida with water that moves toward the "Big O," Lake Okeechobee. Again, the area also has numerous other lakes that stand alone, a few rivers, and hundreds of reclaimed phosphate pits, especially in Polk County.

Millions of fish are raised in hatchery ponds
to be stocked in Florida's lakes and rivers.

I have attempted to include all lakes that have boat ramps for public use. There will certainly be other ramps on these lakes maintained by fish camps, as well as by local municipalities. You will have enough information, however, to get you to a launch site in the area of good fishing. Just a reminder, the Florida Department of Transportation recently decided that it would be a good time to change all interstate road signs from sequential exits to a numbering system that corresponds with the mile-marker system. To be consistent, this guidebook uses the old sequential system that was in place when I began writing. I have included tables that list both old and new numbers for every exit on the interstate system. (See "Road Signs Revised" at the front of this book.)

Florida lakes do not readily lend themselves to flyfishers who want to wade. A few lakes have sandy bottoms, but most are choked with weeds and sediment that has settled to the bottom, forming a soft muck that can be thigh deep at times. In addition, most of the lakes have alligators residing along the shorelines (I am hard-pressed to think of many that do not). Snakes may also make wading uncomfortable. As a result, you will be doing most of your fishing from a boat, making a launch site necessary.

Numerous lakes covered do not have public ramps. These lakes are often accessible by canal or by moving upstream or downstream a short distance from a lake that does have a public ramp. They are included because they offer significant fishing opportunities and can be accessed by canoe or kayak, but not a motorized boat.

The fish are pretty much captive in their lake environment. While they may move from deep water (a relative term when talking about Florida lakes) to shoreline cover to spawn in the spring, or even on a daily basis to feed under the cover of darkness, they do not come and go from within the lake with the changing seasons or fluctuations in water temperature. The primary exception is the run of American shad upriver on the St. Johns River in winter and early spring. In addition, striped bass in the rivers can move over a broad range during the course of a year.

Florida does not have significant insect hatches (unless you count mosquitoes) that will affect fishing. Hence, there are no hatch charts in this guidebook. Most fly patterns will imitate baitfish, crustaceans, and amphibians that live in the water and terrestrials that have fallen into the water. The size and profile of any fly you select should still match the predominant forage in the area, though.

After discussing the more significant bodies of water, I attempt to "cull" the many wonderful waters in this state down to a top-10 list ("Florida's Top Ten Freshwater Fisheries"). The selection process was difficult, and I found that I also had to include one additional body of water from each region that represented the best-of-the-best.

I next included a section on important fly patterns for assorted species that should be included on a "sampler" trip of Florida freshwater fishing. If you are unable to bring these patterns with you, I have also included a list of fly shops around the state near the end of the guidebook. Recall, however, that not a lot of fly fishing is freshwater and that most tackle shops will be located in coastal areas. While they are geared for coastal fishing, most do have a limited selection of freshwater flies.

A section entitled "Florida Freshwater Game Fish" follows and it covers the freshwater species available and their movements over the course of a year. For this detailed information, I thank the Florida Fish and Wildlife Conservation Commission (Division of Fisheries) for permission to copy material from their website.

My recommendations for appropriate Florida fly fishing gear for a trip lasting more than a few hours follows these topics. Fishing in Florida can be significantly different from fishing elsewhere, and I urge you to consider these suggestions seriously.

I give some tips on traveling to Florida in the next section. Many of them are discussed elsewhere in the book in more detail, but the most important are compiled together in this section. Flyfishers are a varied lot, and in addition to the hub city recommendations at the end of each section, I have included a brief discussion of Florida's award-winning state park system where you can find significant opportunities for the entire family or group with whom you may be traveling. Next, there is a section regarding "drawdowns," in which I explain why it is necessary to have them and why they make some lakes "hot" for a period of several years.

There is an obligatory summary of most of the freshwater fishing regulations and I have included a website for a complete listing of all Florida Fish and Wildlife Commission rules and regulations pertaining to freshwater fishing. I have also added a subsection pertaining to the state's Fish Management Areas (FMA) that sets forth an additional set of regulations (in addition to the general regulations) unique to those particular bodies of water. Many of the FMA lakes and ponds are quite small and do not have a ramp or launch site, and because of that, are not discussed in the regional description of bodies of freshwater. Nonetheless, they are included to let you know that they are out there and fishable with special rules and regulations.

After listing fly shops and guides that are available, I conclude this guidebook with a list of other resources that you may also find helpful.

Alligators are present throughout Florida. While they attempt to avoid human contact, you should give them a wide berth.

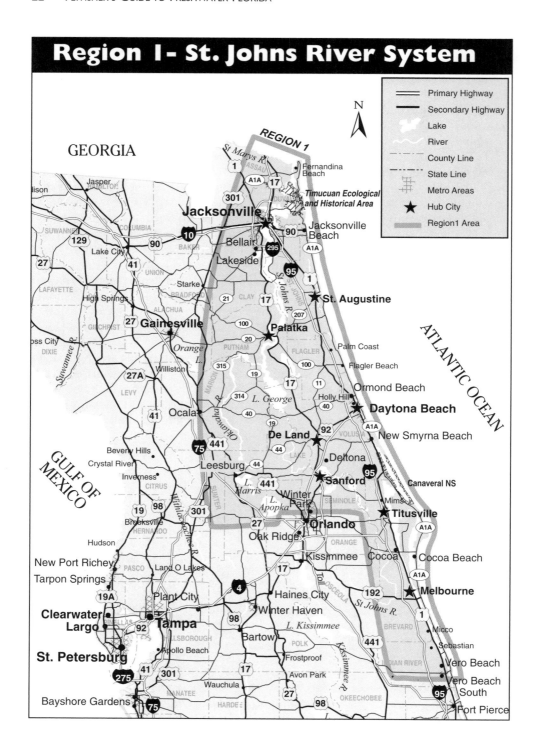

Region 1- St. Johns River System

Region 1

The St. Johns River System

A decade or so ago we'd have been hard-pressed to observe a flyrodder plying any stretch of this long, meandering river. But, today, seeing fly casters making sensational catches on anything that swims is a common sight everywhere. Heck, even some old-timey, die-hard "Crackers" are trading in their baitcasters, spinners and cane poles in favor of fly sticks.

Herb Allen, from the Division of Fisheries "Fishing Updates" in June 1999.

The St. Johns River system is a world-class fishery whose waters are home to bodacious largemouth bass and myriad other species of fish that are sure to test the mettle of even the best freshwater flyfishers.

The St. Johns is the longest river in Florida and unique in that it is one of the few rivers in the United States flowing north. From its marshy headwaters in east-central Florida, it meanders 310 miles through northeast Florida before emptying into the Atlantic Ocean at Mayport Inlet near Jacksonville.

Water flow could be generously considered as "slow" along the St. Johns River because the drop in elevation from the headwaters to the river's mouth is less than 30 feet, or about one inch per mile. During dry periods, and the resulting low water, salt water from the Atlantic Ocean will enter the St. Johns River at the inlet and can cause a reverse flow all the way to Lake Monroe in central Florida, a river distance in excess of 150 miles!

The presence of salt water, however, adds incredible variety to a scenic and already marvelous fishery. Renowned for largemouth bass, crappie, and bream in the freshwater portion, the St. Johns River offers a smorgasbord of game fish for the flyfisher when it becomes brackish with the addition of Atlantic salt water. Redfish can be caught 100 miles upriver from the inlet. Snook, spotted seatrout, and crappie can be taken from the same dock pilings south of Jacksonville. A noteworthy early spring run of American shad extends for more than 150 miles upriver from Jacksonville, and much of this same area is noted for its striped bass and sunshine bass. Bridges in the Jacksonville area even hold tarpon during the warmer months.

The St. Johns River drains three major land areas, known as drainage basins or watersheds, and its width varies greatly along its course. Because of its northward flow, the names of these basins may at first seem backwards. The Upper Basin is the

Suzie Reihl ponders
which fly to try.

broad, low-lying marsh located at the southern headwaters. In this area, the river is narrow and not well defined as it moves through the marsh. The Middle Basin is a series of lakes (wide, slow-moving portions of the river) renowned for their trophy-sized largemouth bass, bream, and crappie. By the time the St. Johns has reached the Lower Basin above Palatka, it has widened substantially and the large volume of brackish water holds a host of game fish.

The major tributaries flowing into the St. Johns River are the Econlockhatchee River (draining south-central Florida below Orlando and entering the headwaters from the west near State Road 46), the Wekiva River (draining central Florida from Orlando eastward and entering the St. Johns near Sanford), Alexander Springs (draining central Florida east of the Ocala National Forest and entering the St. Johns north of Deland), and the Oklawaha River (draining central Florida northward and entering south of Palatka). The Oklawaha River is over 100 miles long, has many significant lakes formed by a series of dams (locks permit boat travel), and has forever been impacted by the failed Cross-Florida Barge Canal. These tributary rivers each add millions of gallons of water to the St. Johns River.

Because of the variety of fish available, one fly rod and reel will not be enough. In the Upper Basin, you will probably need nothing more than a 6-weight outfit. In the Lower Basin, you will want to add something heavier. Bring along an extra spool for each fly reel, too. You will likely need a weight-forward floating line and an intermediate sink-tip. Forget the waders—too many 'gators. You are going to be fishing from a boat. Like the fly rod, the size of the boat will also increase as you move northward.

A camera should be included with the rest of your gear, as the scenery, waterfowl, and wildlife along the St. Johns River are spectacular (and you might just catch the largest freshwater fish of your life). You will be able to see century-old southern plantations, forts that date back to the Seminole Indian Wars, pioneer settlements, and ancient Indian burial mounds dotting the banks of this historic river. These banks were home to Native Americans, including the Timucuans and Seminoles, for some 7,500 years.

Much of Florida's ancient history is also revealed along the river. Fossils of sabertooth cats, mastodons, and giant sloths tell a tale of long-extinct mammals living in a land much different from what we know today. Sharks teeth boil up in springs from underlying limestone and remind us of an even earlier time when Florida was covered by the sea.

Fishing, as we know it today, is still affected by this period. Geological findings show that when sea levels dropped eons ago and the water receded, the area between Lake Harney and Lake George in central Florida was an inland arm of the Atlantic Ocean. With thousands of years of rain, the water became predominantly fresh, but salt deposits slowly settled to the bottom. Today, remaining salt deposits in the ground cause rainwater runoff and springs to bring a degree of salinity to the water in this portion of the Middle Basin. As a result, these waters are able to support a permanent population of mullet and striped bass that do not migrate to and from the sea.

The salinity found in this central region also serves as a barrier to the movement of some species. For example, the Florida Game and Freshwater Commission has found that largemouth bass do not migrate from the northern sections of the river into the southern sections past Lake Harney. As a result, the southern headwaters are dependent upon the success of yearly spawning to sustain bass populations. When there are good conditions for spawning, there will be good catches of yearling bass in a couple of years. After periods of poor spawning the catch rate will be down. Consequently, fishing will be good some years and not so good in other years in the Upper Basin, depending on how good the spawn was two and three years previous.

The salinity has a good side, too. The portion of the river between Lake Harney and Lake Monroe is the spawning ground for tremendous numbers of American shad. These game fighters make a long journey from the Atlantic Ocean, and in the winter months between December and March, flyfishers casting small shad darts will have a blast.

Before we begin our 330-mile trek up the St. Johns River, let's take a look at the weather that we are likely to encounter. Region 1 parallels about 300 miles of the Atlantic coast in northeastern Florida and the nearby ocean plays a significant role in the weather. There are only three seasons (spring, summer, and fall), although some cold fronts do dip as far down as the Middle Basin in January and February.

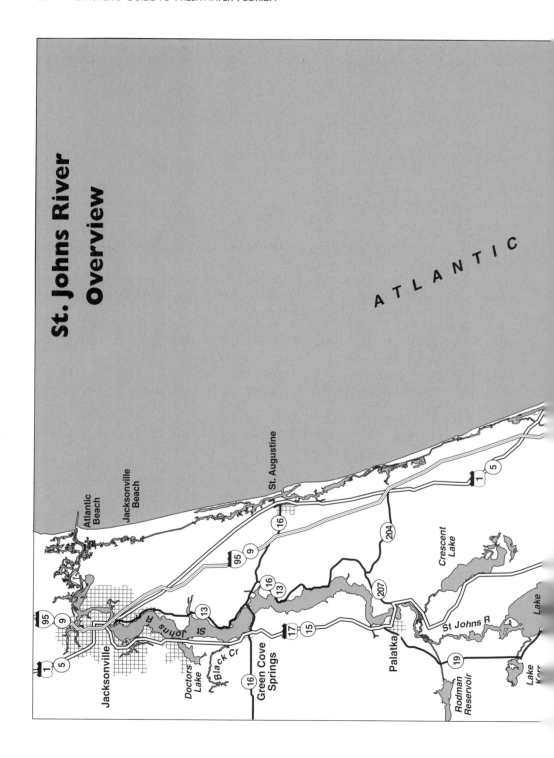

St. Johns River Overview

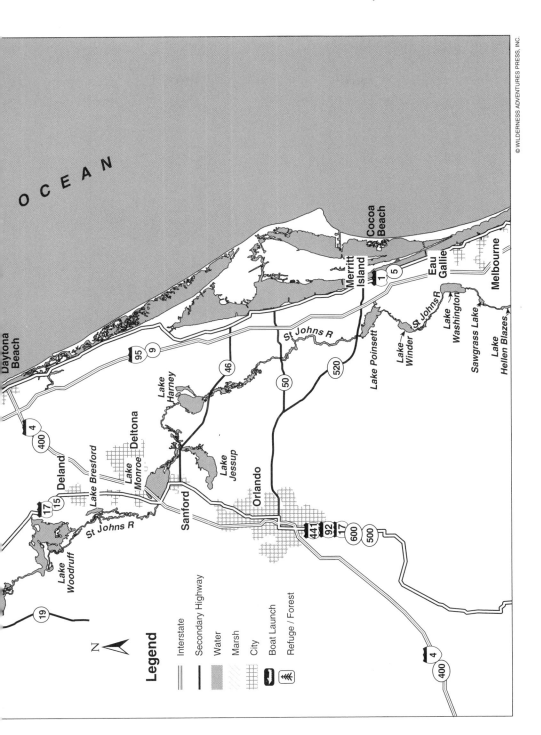

American shad migrate from Canada and move more than 200 miles up the St. Johns River.

In the spring (February, March, April, and May), waters begin to warm as a result of the rising air temperatures. These air temperatures of the Middle Basin will be about 40 degrees at night and in the mid-50s during the day at their coolest in February. (The Lower Basin will be about 5 degrees cooler, while the Upper Basin will be about 5 degrees warmer. Also, allow as much as 10 degrees cooler for a severe cold front.)

There will be very little rain during the spring, and largemouth bass will be shallow and aggressive. The biggest bass of the year will be caught in early spring on large, deer-hair poppers. The run of American shad is in progress, and crappie are in vegetation that rims the river's lakes. Bream (redbreasts, bluegills, stumpknockers, shellcrackers, and warmouths) will be spawning on the full moon in late spring also near the shoreline. Striped bass and sunshine bass will be looking to spawn as well. Look for them in and near the mouths of feeder creeks and streams.

In the summer months (June, July, August, and September), air temperatures will reach a high of about 90 degrees. (Again, allow 3 or 4 degrees variation for the Upper and Lower Basins.) The days typically begin with a period of morning calm, followed by light winds from the west. These winds taper off in mid-morning only to pick back up again from the east in the afternoon as convection forces take over. These onshore breezes bring cool, moist air that invariably causes rain, sometimes quite heavy and often accompanied by bolts of ground-seeking lightning. The storms come from the west and are fueled by the light, onshore breezes. (Upper atmosphere winds remain from the west, while moist lower-level breezes come from the east. The air gets warmed over the hotter mainland and rises before being rapidly cooled.) You can usually see the storms as they approach, and they are frequently very localized. It may rain on one side of a lake and not the other. Just because it is not raining where you are fishing does not mean that you are safe from nearby lightning. This is not a time to be on the water with a long, graphite fly rod high above your head. The leading edge of the storm frequently has strong winds and will often be accompanied by tornadoes. This typically happens late in the afternoon.

The tracks of tropical storms, which develop near the equator in late summer and early fall, can take them near or over Florida. Pay close attention to weather advisories. The anticipated path of these storms is forecast several days in advance and local residents are well prepared to evacuate with several days of supplies when necessary. As a tropical storm or hurricane gets closer, its path is more certain. A direct "hit" is not necessary for severe weather, however, as the band of showers extends for several hundred miles. The best advice is to pay close attention to weather warnings and have flexible travel plans. These tropical storms can leave lakes in the Middle Basin high, and they often flood low-lying areas and cover many of the small one-lane ramps.

Try fishing in the morning from first light (5:30 a.m.), and take a break in the heat of the afternoon. Go back out in the early evening and fish until dusk (8:30 p.m.). You will be on the water during the prime daylight conditions and you are not likely to encounter bad weather. Largemouth bass move from deeper water to feed in the shallows under limited and low-light conditions. Bream can still be caught shallow,

Much of the Upper Basin of the St. Johns River is a low-lying marsh.

but crappie are down in the deepest water. Striped bass and sunshine bass will often school in open water.

The fall and winter months (October, November, December, and January) are quite pleasant in Region 1. Water temperatures cool from midsummer highs and fish become more active. Air temperatures vary from mid-40s in the late-fall evenings to the 60s during the day. There are occasional rains, but the tropical storm season is over by the end of October, and the chance of severe weather is limited.

Fish may feed anytime during the day and schooling activity in open water can often be observed. Largemouth bass are moving about and can be found in both open water and near shoreline cover, while crappie move higher in the water column over river channels. Bream move away from shorelines out toward deeper water. Striped bass and sunshine bass often come to the surface to feed late in the day, especially when it is overcast.

Florida has suffered several years of less than normal rain. As a result, many of the lakes in central Florida have water tables that are substantially lower than at any time in the recent past. Many of the ramps giving access to the lakes in the Orlando area are out of the water and many bass boats hang high and dry. This condition affects some of the lakes in the upper portion of the Oklawaha River (the Harris Chain of Lakes and the Clermont Chain of Lakes). This also concentrates fish for the time being, however, while allowing new grasses and vegetation to grow along exposed shorelines. Fishing is very good, and it will soon be even better.

Let's begin looking at these fly fishing opportunities at the headwaters of the St. Johns River and continue northward with the wandering and widening ways of this beautiful river.

Ken Bay caught this American shad near the SR 46 Bridge in winter.

THE UPPER (SOUTHERN) BASIN

Beginning just 25 miles north of Florida's famed Lake Okeechobee and draining an area in excess of 900 square miles in northern St. Lucie, Indian River, and Brevard Counties that is known as the St. John's Marsh, the St. Johns River is no more than a series of narrow waterways inching their way to the north through a broad, flat wetland area in east-central Florida. The waterways in the extreme upper portion can be navigated only by kayak or airboat in late spring when there has been little rain for several months. After the rains of early summer, however, this area may have an additional five feet of water.

As a result of drainage modifications to the marsh and runoff from farming operations, sediment has settled in the river, and the channel, to the extent that there is a channel, has become a muck-filled mess. In addition, because of the increased fertility of the water, there is often rampant vegetation growth in and on the water. Restoration efforts are underway to make the area more navigable.

The waterways have, for the most part, merged coming out of Lake Poinsett and on into Brevard County and enough slow-moving water is usually present for a boater to move from place to place. Between State Road 50 and State Road 46 (west of Titusville), in an area known as the Saint Johns National Wildlife Refuge, the river is a marshy maze. With no discernible channel, there are dozens of small lakes and ponds, as well as numerous side channels to the river located within the refuge. Only a few of the lakes have ramps and airboats are frequently used to navigate the shallow, marshy waters in this area.

Continuing northward, with the addition of the Econlockhatchee River, the St. Johns River gains volume, moves out of the low-lying marsh and begins to take on river-like qualities. Because of the slow flow, even in its headwaters, natural lakes have formed in numerous wide spots along the river. Assorted styles of bass boats and johnboats can be used to navigate and fish the waters north of State Road 46. The GFC ramp at SR 46 is well used and often crowded. It provides access to Lake Harney to the north, Puzzle Lake to the south, and a take-out for those floating the lower portion of the Econlockhatchee River.

Even though many of the small lakes in the headwaters area have hard bottoms and can be waded, the marsh around them is filled with alligators and flyfishers will want to stay safely in their boats. Vast numbers of largemouth bass, most of them smaller than those found in the two more northern basins, but a few of significant size, and assorted members of the bream family will be of primary interest to anglers plying these upper waters. Low water levels will cause these fish to move out of the seemingly endless marsh and hang on the edge of the river channel and in deeper holes. The sheer numbers of fish that can be caught is staggering at times.

American shad that have migrated from Canada down along the East Coast and entered the St. Johns make it all the way to Lake Harney and the lower portion of the headwaters to spawn. They are a wonderful addition for flyfishers during winter months. Although you are barely 30 miles from the Atlantic Ocean as the crow (or sea

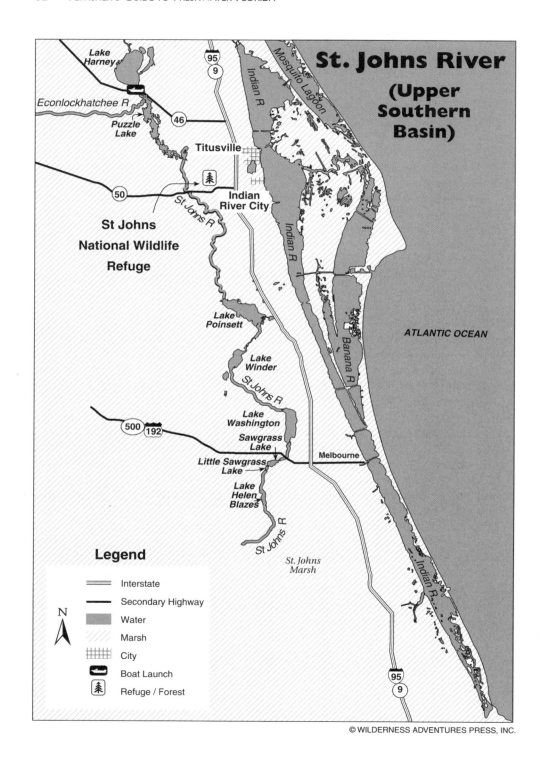

St. Johns River
(Upper Southern Basin)

Lake Harney

Econlockhatchee R

Puzzle Lake

Titusville

Indian River City

St Johns National Wildlife Refuge

Indian R

Mosquito Lagoon

Indian R

St Johns R

Lake Poinsett

ATLANTIC OCEAN

Lake Winder

St Johns R

Banana R

Lake Washington

Sawgrass Lake

Melbourne

Little Sawgrass Lake

Lake Helen Blazes

St Johns R

St. Johns Marsh

Indian R

Legend

N

Interstate
Secondary Highway
Water
Marsh
City
Boat Launch
Refuge / Forest

© WILDERNESS ADVENTURES PRESS, INC.

gull) flies, you are almost 300 miles from the ocean by waterway. Nonetheless, a salt-water license is required to take the American shad.

Gather your fly fishing gear and mosquito repellant and let's see how to get to each of the lakes having public boat ramps from Interstate 95, the main artery moving traffic up and down the east coast of Florida. All the roads are paved and well maintained unless otherwise indicated. If you want to check on water conditions before departing, call the local Fish and Wildlife Conservation Commission (FWC) office at 321-752-3115.

Lake Hellen Blazes and Sawgrass Lake

As tannin-stained water from the St. Johns Marsh inches northward in upper St. Lucie and on through Indian River County, it begins to form a small channel that gathers like fingers joining a hand. By Brevard County, however, the river has a clearly identifiable course. The first two natural lakes to appear along what is now the St. Johns River are Lake Hellen Blazes (381 acres) and Sawgrass Lake (407 acres) to the north. Neither of these two small lakes is presently fishable, however, in that they are almost completely covered with hydrilla. The FWC is considering efforts to restore both lakes and time will tell if their efforts, if undertaken, will be successful. No ramps are available at either lake and access is gained from Lake Washington to the north and boating south on the St. Johns River.

Lake Washington

Lake Washington (4,600 acres) just west of Melbourne is the first of many large lakes that are naturally formed by the St. Johns River as it slowly moves northward seeking its release to the sea. Lake Washington has a long history of bass fishing, but it also yields excellent stringers of black crappie (locally known as speckled perch), large bluegill, and shellcrackers.

Largemouth bass tend to gather around the shoreline bulrush, with spring the best season. Try this same area early and late in the day during the summer and fall, as well. Poppers (chartreuse, size 2 or 4) and topwater flies made of deer hair (brown or olive, size 1-4) are the local favorites. There are still a few lunkers around, although not as many as in years long past.

The bluegill and shellcrackers like small poppers (black, brown, chartreuse or yellow, size 6-10) or terrestrials (black or brown, size 8-12). Many of these bream get to be the size of large man's hand and can be testy as they run in circles at the end of your line. Like the largemouth bass, they are near the bulrush from spring to fall.

Crappie are most easily taken by fly in the spring when they move near Lake Washington's shoreline bulrush to spawn. A Clouser (chartreuse/white or yellow/white, size 1-4) pattern will take these tasty panfish, which weigh up to two pounds.

There is a public ramp available on the east side of Lake Washington. From I-95

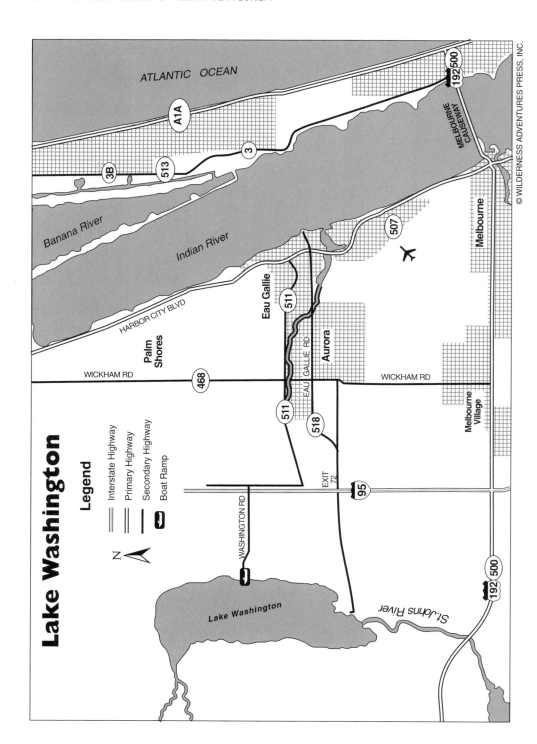

just north of Melbourne, take exit number 72 east onto Eau Gallie Blvd. (State Road 518), and go 2.2 miles to Wickham Road. Turn left onto Wickham Road (State Road 509) and go north 1.3 miles. Turn left onto Lake Washington Road and go west 4.6 miles (going under I-95 along the way) to the ramp at the end of the road.

Lake Winder

The next lake on the St. Johns River system is Lake Winder, an 1,800-acre lake with an average depth of six feet. Hydrilla frequently covers the water.

Largemouth bass will be suspended in the vegetation, but for the most part they will be inaccessible to flyfishers because of the extensive hydrilla. When open water is available, look for bass along the shoreline. Lake Winder also an excellent bluegill and shellcracker lake when open water is present.

There is no ramp on the lake, and to get there requires a five-mile run south from Lake Poinsett. In late fall and winter, crappie are frequently found at the end of the run just before entering Lake Winder.

Lake Poinsett

Lake Poinsett, at just over 5,000 acres, is a large, shallow lake west of the city of Cocoa. It is regarded by many anglers as the best bass fishing lake in the southern half of the St. Johns River chain. Seldom more than five feet deep, the lake is about six miles long and just over two miles wide.

Much of Lake Poinsett's open water has hydrilla, which makes it difficult for fly-fishers to work the water. Don't despair. The shoreline has bulrush and offers excellent cover for both largemouth bass and bream. Look especially hard at coves that have maidencane and lily pads, as these harbor some of Lake Poinsett's bigger bass. Bream will also be present along shorelines from spring to fall, and crappie move into the shallows to spawn in early spring.

Access to Lake Poinsett is from State Road 520. Take Exit 75 off I-95 and go west on State Road 520 for 4.5 miles. The ramp is at the James G. Bourdeau Memorial Park on the south side of the bridge where SR 520 crosses the St. Johns River. Lake Poinsett is upriver, a half-mile run to the south.

Lake Cone

This small, shallow lake lies in the marsh west of the St. Johns River and north of State Road 50. To access Lake Cone, take Exit 79 from I-95 and go 4.7 miles west on SR 50. The ramp is on the south side of the bridge crossing SR 50. Upon launching, the lake is downstream, one mile after going under the bridge. Many airboats frequent this area and the lake is of little interest to flyfishers.

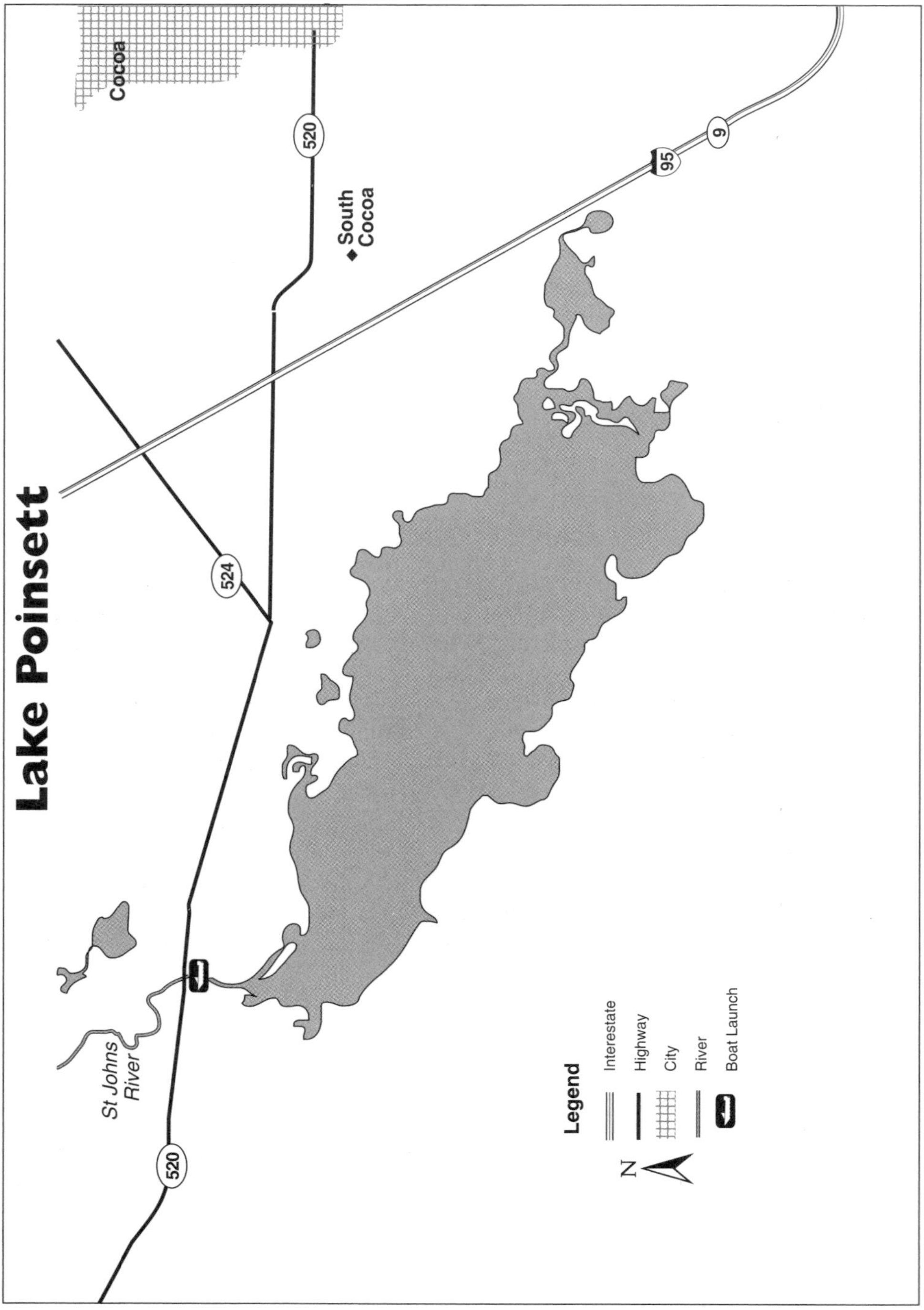

Lake Poinsett

© WILDERNESS ADVENTURES PRESS, INC.

Cocoa

520

South
Cocoa

95

9

524

St Johns
River

520

Legend

Interstate

Highway

City

River

Boat Launch

N

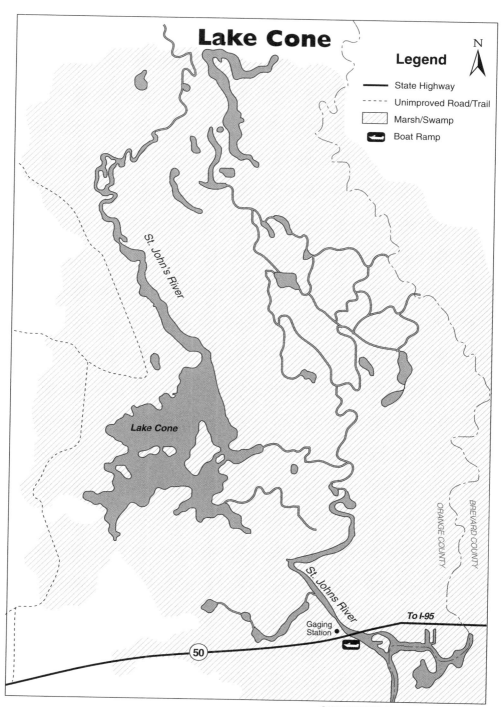

Lake Cone

Legend

N

— State Highway
- - - Unimproved Road/Trail
▨ Marsh/Swamp
⬛ Boat Ramp

St. John's River

Lake Cone

St. Johns River

ORANGE COUNTY

BREVARD COUNTY

To I-95

Gaging
Station •

50

© WILDERNESS ADVENTURES PRESS, INC.

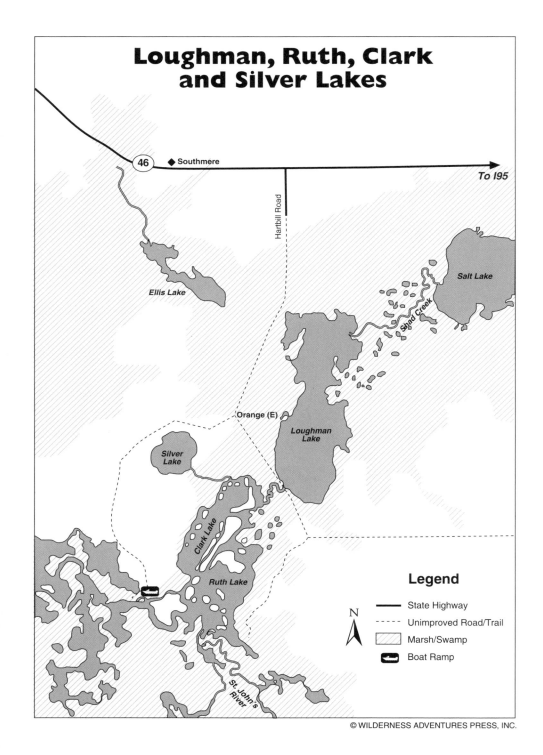

Loughman, Ruth, Clark and Silver Lakes

Southmere

46

To I95

Hartbill Road

Ellis Lake

Salt Lake

Shad Creek

Orange (E)

Loughman Lake

Silver Lake

Clark Lake

Ruth Lake

St. John's River

Legend

N

—— State Highway

- - - - Unimproved Road/Trail

Marsh/Swamp

Boat Ramp

© WILDERNESS ADVENTURES PRESS, INC.

Loughman Lake, Ruth Lake, Clark Lake, and Silver Lake

These four connected lakes lying at the northern edge of Brevard County are only 5 feet above mean sea level and average about four feet deep. Loughman Lake (600 acres) is the most interesting of the four. This very shallow lake is fed both by the St. Johns River and by saltwater springs.

As a result of Lake Loughman's mixed freshwater and saltwater sources, flyfishers can catch all the freshwater fish common to the area, as well as flounder and even shad on occasion. On the freshwater side, members of the bream family are most common, along with some largemouth bass around structure and vegetation. Flies such as those used on other area lakes for bream and bass will work here, too.

For the flounder, a small Clouser (white or yellow, size 2-6) needs to be worked slowly along the bottom. This area is also about the upstream limit for American and hickory shad. If winds push high, upstream tide to their southernmost extreme in the early spring, flyfishers can find shad and take them on flies.

Access to the four lakes is gained off State Road 46. From I-95, take Exit 81 and go west on SR 46 for 4.2 miles. Turn left onto Hartbill Road (it becomes a dirt road after the first mile) and go 5.2 miles. The ramp is at Hartbill Park at the end of the road. Be careful with a trailer as the ramp is very steep and has not been well maintained. Since you will need to use a small, light craft in this area, consider launching from the river's edge two hundred yards to the south in the area used to launch airboats. There is unimproved parking that will accommodate 100 vehicles. This area is unusable at times because of high water.

Upon launching, the St. Johns River is to your right and Ruth Lake and Clark Lake are to your left (east). At the northern end of Clark Lake, one can gain access to Silver Lake (west) and Loughman Lake (east) through small feeder creeks.

Airboats can be launched from the shoreline at Hartbill Park near Ruth Lake.

ELLIS LAKE

Ellis Lake is a small, very shallow lake in the marsh northwest of Loughman, Ruth, Clark, and Silver Lakes. There is no ramp or paved road leading to Ellis Lake and it is of little significance to flyfishers.

SALT LAKE

Salt Lake is a very shallow 300-acre lake lying in the extreme eastern edge of the grassy marsh. Salt Lake has a good population of bream and small bass, but flyfishers will not find it worth the effort necessary to get there when there are so many other lakes in the area with much greater potential.

Salt Lake is about five miles east of the St. Johns River and access can be had by airboat or canoe from State Road 44. Take Exit 81 from I-95 and go 2.5 miles west to the ramp. Look for a sign indicating "boat ramp" on the right side of SR 46, as the small, paved ramp at the launch site known as 6-Mile Creek is not easily seen from the road. Salt Lake is a mile to the south through the canal in the grassy marsh.

PUZZLE LAKE

Puzzle Lake is a 1,300-acre maze along the St. Johns River and its side channels.

During periods of low water, the marshy area between the ramp and Puzzle Lake is quite shallow and the rivers channel is not well defined. Between January and April, American shad making their spawning run upriver can be caught by flyfishers using shad flies. Largemouth bass can be taken with poppers and deer-hair flies from the vegetation along the various channels and Puzzle Lake's irregular shoreline.

To access Puzzle Lake, go 11.7 miles west on State Road 46 from I-95 Exit 81. There is a GFC ramp with ample parking on the west side of the bridge where SR 46 crosses the St. Johns River. You will motor to your right upon launching and Puzzle Lake is about three miles to the south.

BUCK LAKE AND FRESHWATER LAKE

These lakes, lying east of Puzzle Lake and State Road 46, are not accessible by anything other than an airboat. They are of no significance to flyfishers.

THE ECONLOCKHATCHEE RIVER

With its headwaters only 30 minutes east of Orlando, the dark, unspoiled waters of the "Econ," as it is known locally, wind 18 miles through a mixture of wetlands, swamps, pasture, and a flatland forest of giant oaks and cypress before merging with the St. Johns River. An 8-mile float can be made between the bridge at State Road 419 and the bridge at Snowhill Road. From Orlando, take State Road 50 east to SR 419 and then north on SR 419 for 8.2 miles. You can put in at the SR 419 Bridge. In this narrow, upper region of the river, high sandy banks are lined with oaks and cabbage palms along sharp turns and water flowing 2-3 miles per hour. This is a good area to fly fish

Salt Lake

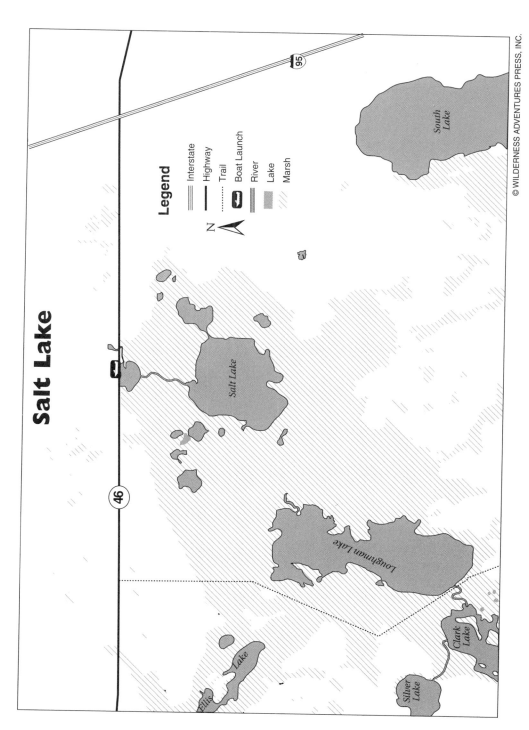

Legend

≡ Interstate
— Highway
⋯ Trail
▣ Boat Launch
River
Lake
Marsh

N

South Lake

Salt Lake

Loughman Lake

Silver Lake

Clark Lake

Lake

Ellis

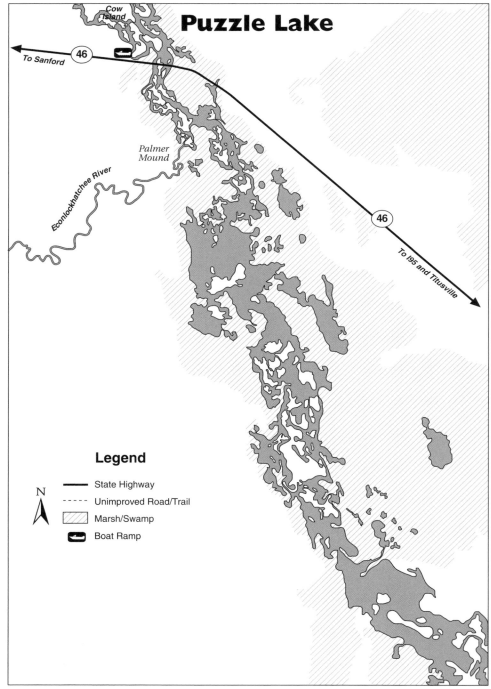

© WILDERNESS ADVENTURES PRESS, INC.

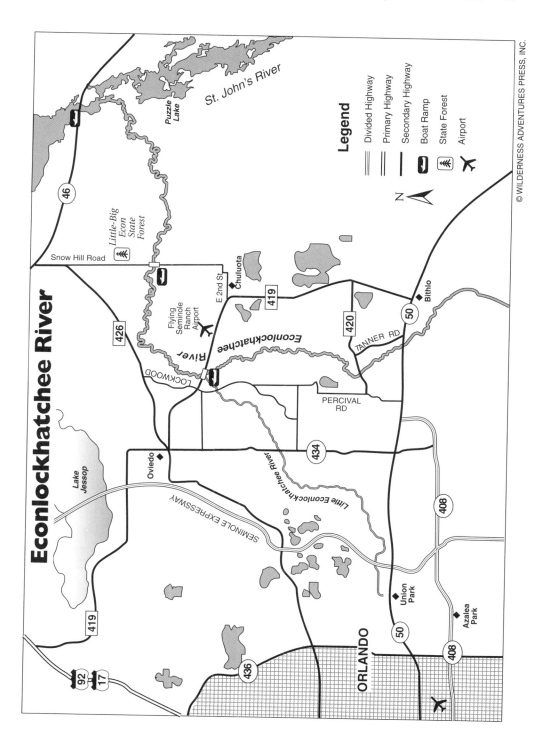

Econlockhatchee River

during windy conditions, as the high banks offer protection. Dark-colored bass averaging one to two pounds readily rise to poppers cast next to fallen trees along the shoreline.

The middle and lower sections of the Econ have slower moving water. Starting at the Snowhill Road Bridge, it is a 10-mile float to the St. Johns River and an additional mile and a half to the take-out point north on the St. Johns at State Road 46. Take State Road 426 from Oviedo east for 6.8 miles to Snowhill Road. Turn south and go 2.9 miles to the bridge. The middle portion of the river has lower banks with cypress trees and cabbage palms. As one approaches the St. Johns River, the lower Econ becomes wider with gentle curves as it moves slowly through pastureland and on into the marshes along the St. Johns. Topwater flies such as soft- and hard-bodied poppers fished early and late in the day around structure along the shoreline often result in good catches of bream and largemouth bass up to four and five pounds.

*The C. S. Lee Park on the west side of the SR 46 Bridge
gives access to Lake Harney.*

Lake Harney

Lake Harney (6,058 acres) averages about seven feet deep, and it is the first large lake formed by the widening waters of the St. Johns River. A few miles beyond the lake to the north, the grassy marsh associated with the headwaters begins to yield to higher ground. In early spring, Lake Harney is an excellent largemouth bass and black crappie lake. Later in the spring and on into the summer, the lake continues to offer very good bream fishing.

In cold weather (January and February), crappie will be suspended over the river channel and a sinking fly line will be necessary. A small Clouser Minnow (chartreuse or yellow, size 6-10) would be an excellent choice. Crappie up to two pounds are common in Lake Harney. When the crappie move to shorelines to spawn, an intermediate sink-tip line, again with a small Clouser Minnow, would be an excellent choice.

Largemouth bass can be caught along shoreline floating vegetation with poppers and deer-haired flies. Early and late in the day offer the best opportunities to take Lake Harney's bass. As the waters warm, bream fishing heats up along the shoreline, especially on a full moon, with flyfishers using small poppers and assorted terrestrials. Many fly fishermen choose to use a fly with a monofilament weedguard that shields the hook from floating vegetation near the shoreline. I have not found the weedguards to make a fly completely weedless, but it sure helps. Whether or not hooksets are impeded is a subject about which opinions differ greatly.

Access to Lake Harney is from the GFC ramp at C. S. Lee Park off State Road 46. Take Exit 81 off I-95 and go west on SR 46 for 11.7 miles. The double ramp is on the north side of the west end of the bridge crossing SR 46. There is plenty of paved parking, but this ramp is frequently busy, especially on weekends in early spring when crappie fishing is hot.

Go left upon launching, and Lake Harney is about a mile to the north. Be careful! This is the first opportunity for anglers with anything other than canoes, small johnboats, and airboats to launch on the St. Johns River. You might very well encounter a 150-hp bass boat running wide open as you make one of several turns on the 50-foot-wide river snaking its way toward Lake Harney. On this one-mile run, you will also encounter bank fishermen for the first time.

Lake Ashby

Lake Ashby (1,200 acres) is nine miles northwest of Lake Harney and offers good largemouth bass and excellent bream fishing. A small canal and creek that can be navigated only by airboat and canoe when it is not choked with growth runs through the marsh leading back to Lake Harney.

Like other area lakes, there is quite a bit of vegetation growing up to the surface and floating on Lake Ashby. The bass suspend in the shade created by the lily pads and bonnets and will come to the surface to take a popper or deer-hair fly. The bass

Lake Harney

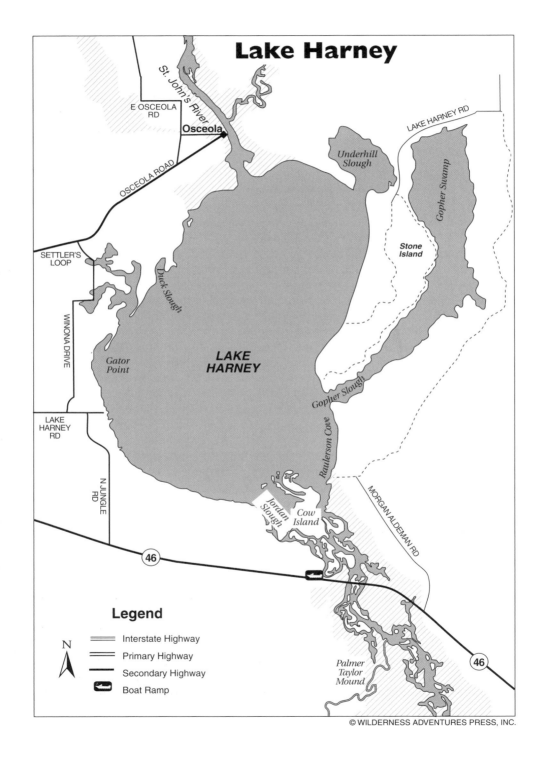

Legend

N

Interstate Highway
Primary Highway
Secondary Highway
Boat Ramp

© WILDERNESS ADVENTURES PRESS, INC.

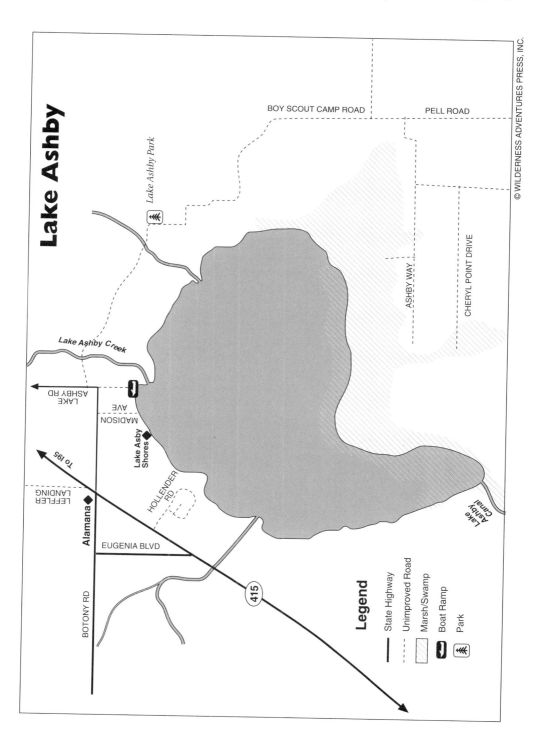

Lake Ashby

BOY SCOUT CAMP ROAD

PELL ROAD

Lake Ashby Park

ASHBY WAY

CHERYL POINT DRIVE

Lake Ashby Creek

LAKE ASHBY RD

MADISON AVE

Lake Asby Shores

To I95

LEFFLER LANDING

HOLLENDER RD

Lake Ashby Canal

Alamana

EUGENIA BLVD

BOTONY RD

415

Legend

— State Highway
--- Unimproved Road
▨ Marsh/Swamp
🛥 Boat Ramp
⫷ Park

are most active from March through May, although they will take flies during low-light conditions throughout the summer and into the fall.

Flyfishers using small poppers and terrestrials take bream along the shorelines. Their season is a little longer than that of the largemouth. Bream will feed well from May through mid-October. Late in the day, especially in the summer, they can also be taken in open water on the same small poppers. Look for crappie to be out in the pads and next to cypress trees along the shoreline in early spring.

To your left about half a mile, there is a wooden boardwalk that crosses a pocket in the eastern side of Lake Ashby. The boardwalk has hundreds of pilings and blocks access to the back portion of the bay (except to kayaks and canoes). The boardwalk and closely spaced pilings offer structure and shade all day long to fish seeking refuge.

To get to Lake Ashby, get off I-95 at Exit 84B and go west on State Road 44 for 4.8 miles. Turn left at State Road 415 and go 5.4 miles south to Lake Ashby Road. Turn left onto Lake Ashby Road and go 0.5 mile, bearing right on the dirt road to the single-lane ramp. There is limited room to maneuver your trailer and tow vehicle, and the parking is limited to about six vehicles.

A long, wooden boardwalk offers early spring structure for Lake Ashby's bass and crappie.

The Middle (Central) Basin

Before Europeans settled in North America, the Timucuan Indians lived in east-central Florida and called the St. Johns River *Welaka*, or "river of lakes." In its midsection, the river repeatedly widens and narrows to form a series of large lakes. Many of these lakes, or wide spots in the river, have noteworthy fisheries that have contributed significantly to the fishing lore of Florida.

In the area that I refer to as the Middle Basin, the St. Johns River begins to move out of the flat, low-lying marshes found in the headwaters and through slightly higher ground that once served as an island separating the Atlantic Ocean from this ancient saltwater arm of the sea. Today, what is now the St. Johns River drains central Florida and most of the tributaries flowing into the river come from the west. With a clearly defined channel averaging about 15 feet deep, the twists and turns of the St. Johns River offer an opportunity to get out of winds that cause flyfishers problems in the more open areas such as those encountered in the headwaters.

The major tributaries in this central portion of the river are Wekiva Springs and Alexander Springs. The run between these two springs and where they enter the St. Johns River is only a few miles long, but both have their own unique and interesting ecosystem. These and other springs in the midsection of the river add millions of gallons of crystal clear water every day to the St. Johns River. Where springs and creeks empty into the river, look for striped bass and sunshine bass. This area of the river has the saline barrier left from eons ago, and while great for stripers and sunshine bass, as well as migratory American shad, it does preclude the upriver movement of largemouth bass.

Be mindful of the protected manatees from West India that make their winter home in these numerous springs with constant 72-degree water. They use the river as a highway to get to the springs and spend most of the non-winter months in the river. Boaters must be certain to obey the posted signs regulating boat speeds on the river so that propellers do not inadvertently strike slow-moving manatees.

The middle portion of the St. Johns River has massive live oak trees lining the banks that are many hundreds of years old. Looking beyond the banks, you will see wooded preserves that gradually rise in elevation. Through these gently rolling preserves flow well-defined creeks and streams that frequently have their source in underground springs that have formed their own network of subsurface rivers.

A vast assortment of animals lives in the wooded corridor along the St. Johns. Look for black bear, deer, gray fox, and bobcat to come to the water's edge to drink. Also along the edge, you will continue to see numerous alligators keeping a watchful eye on potential prey. There also will be an assortment of waterfowl including egrets, osprey, and an occasional bald eagle.

The Middle Basin is an area of big black bass. In addition, the striped bass and sunshine bass will test your fly fishing tackle. Use a larger fly rod than you did in the Upper Basin, one capable of handling these bigger, stronger fish. An 8-weight rod is probably as much as you'll ever need, though. If you have a good drag on your reel, a

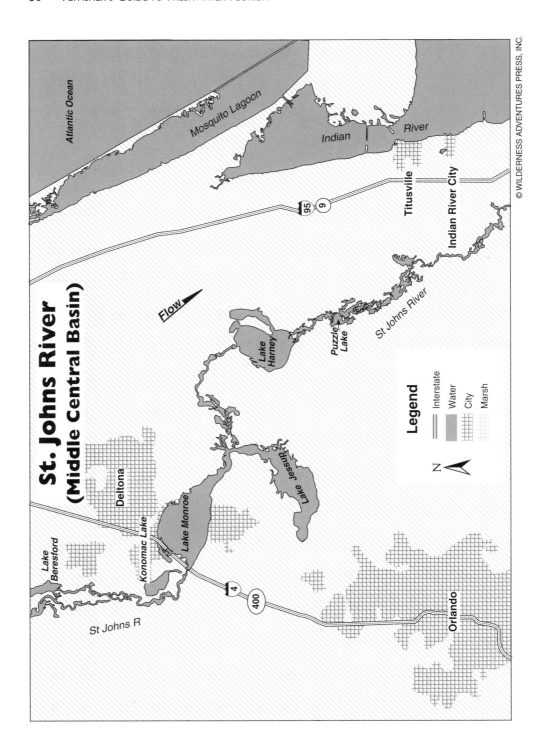

St. Johns River
(Middle Central Basin)

Legend

Interstate
Water
City
Marsh

N

Atlantic Ocean

Mosquito Lagoon

Indian River

Titusville

Indian River City

Flow

Lake Harney

Puzzle Lake

St Johns River

Lake Jessup

Deltona

Lake Monroe

Konomac Lake

Lake Beresford

St Johns R

4

400

Orlando

95
9

6-weight rod is a nice all-around choice. There are plenty of bream and crappie in this portion of the river that provide steady action, and the American shad provide seasonal excitement in winter and early spring.

From the town of Astor to the south end of Lake George, there is excellent bass fishing. While much of the river throughout the entire 300-mile course offers abundant cover and structure, this area is perhaps the least saline, and large numbers of big bass are taken here. As with the stripers and sunshine bass, the mouths of feeder creeks are an excellent place to look for schooling bass. Try casting a fly into the eddy alongside the water where it enters the river. Select a pattern that imitates baitfish, such as a streamer or a Clouser with a size 2 hook. Recall that these are schooling bass in the 1-3 pound range. Either black or white with a hint of olive, blue, or gray on the back would be an excellent color combination.

Much of the river will have vegetation extending out from the shoreline. In spring and early summer, look for bass, crappie, and bream in the lily pads, especially if grass is also present. Bass are prone to spawn in eelgrass that is often associated with the flats. There is shade beneath the vegetation in which these fish can hide and ambush minnows and insects. A Clouser is again an excellent choice for both bass and crappie, and a terrestrial pattern should be used if bream are being targeted.

I will give directions to the various lake and river ramps on the southern portion of the Middle Basin from Interstate 4, which crosses the St. Johns River just downstream (north) of Lake Monroe near Sanford and provides easy access to much of the Middle Basin. The northern portion of the Middle Basin is best accessed from State Road 40, which runs east/west from Daytona Beach and I-95, passing through the midsection of Florida and crossing I-75 in Ocala.

MULLET LAKE, MUD LAKE, AND THORNHILL LAKE

These three small lakes, each about 500 acres, are closely related and offer good bream fishing. Access to each lake is gained from a different ramp.

The ramp to Mullet Lake is at Mullet Lake Park. From I-4, take Exit 51 and go east on State Road 46, through Sanford and onto the intersection with State Road 415A (9.4 miles). Continue another 1.5 miles on SR 46, and upon reaching Mullet Lake Park Road, turn left and go 2.2 miles to the park and single-lane ramp on the left side of the road. There is paved parking for 12 vehicles, and bathroom and picnic facilities are available at the park.

Mud Lake is nearby. Again from I-4, take Exit 51 and go 9.4 miles east on SR 46. After leaving Sanford, turn left onto State Road 415 and go 2.8 miles north. Turn right onto Lemon Bluff Road and go another 3.7 miles. There is a single-lane ramp and unimproved parking for four vehicles. The area available to maneuver a vehicle and trailer is also limited.

Thornhill Lake is the easiest of these three closely related lakes to reach. Take Exit 51 from I-4, and go 9.4 miles east through Sanford on SR 46. Again, turn left onto SR 415 and within a mile, there is a ramp and marina at Cameron Wight Park on the left where SR 415 crosses the St. Johns River. Thornhill Lake is to your left as you enter the river, 0.5 mile downstream (north). Upon reaching Thornhill Lake, the river appears to split. If you go left, you will stay in the river channel and go on to Lake Monroe. By going right, you are immediately at Thornhill Lake.

The thick vegetation on Mud Lake provides good cover for bass, bream, and crappie.

LAKE JESSUP

Lake Jessup (10,000 acres) is not on the mainstream of the St. Johns River, and as such, is not a wide spot along its course. Instead, Jessup is a large, very shallow lake off to the side of the river that is known to have some of the best bream fishing in the St. Johns River system. Bass fishing, however, is poor. Use extreme caution when navigating the lake, as there are islands that are sometimes barely submerged. Boaters should used caution in the summer months when late afternoon storms moving off both the east and west coasts converge on central Florida. Wave action in large, shallow lakes can become quite fierce and pelting rain adds to the difficulty of navigating a boat. Lightning strikes will motivate you to get off the water, and the best course of action is to leave when the summer sky starts to darken in the afternoon.

Typically, the depth varies between two and four feet on Lake Jessup, although in the northeast corner near the mouth of the St. Johns River, it can be as much as eight feet. In this area, striped bass and sunshine bass can often be taken in good numbers, especially in the spring.

To get to Jessup, take Exit 51A off I-4 and go east 10.4 mile on State Road 46A, through Sanford (SR 46A merges with SR 46 in Sanford), to where SR 46 crosses the St. Johns River. Cameron Wright Park has two one-lane ramps with paved parking for 20 vehicles. Lake Jessup will be to your right (south) as you launch.

There is another ramp at Lake Jessup Park that will give you access to the west side of the lake. From I-4, take Exit 50 east onto Lake Mary Blvd. and go east for 6.5 miles. At South Sanford Avenue (one block beyond Sanford Ave./CR 427), turn right and go south for 2.3 miles. Lake Jessup Park has a two-lane ramp with paved parking for about 40 vehicles.

LAKE MONROE

Lake Monroe (9,500 acres) is an excellent crappie lake, with the best season being winter and early spring (December thru March). Look in open water during the winter and move toward shoreline cover as spring progresses.

This large, saucer-shaped lake averages about seven feet deep and is another lake vulnerable to wind. The deeper water bulrush patches along the southeast portion of the lake (south side of Mothers Arms) are a good location in early summer when low water makes access to eelgrass beds and other bulrush patches nearly impossible. In addition to crappie, look for sunshine bass (in all months except summer) near the east and west ends of the lake where the St. Johns River enters and leaves.

Lake Monroe is easily accessible from I-4. Take Exit 52 and go left 0.2 mile north on US 17-92. Before crossing the St. Johns River, turn right into Lake Monroe Wayside Park. Lake Monroe is to your right as you launch from one of the two single-lane ramps. There is semi-improved parking for about 30 vehicles. You are at the western end of Lake Monroe where it narrows back to a channel of the St. Johns River.

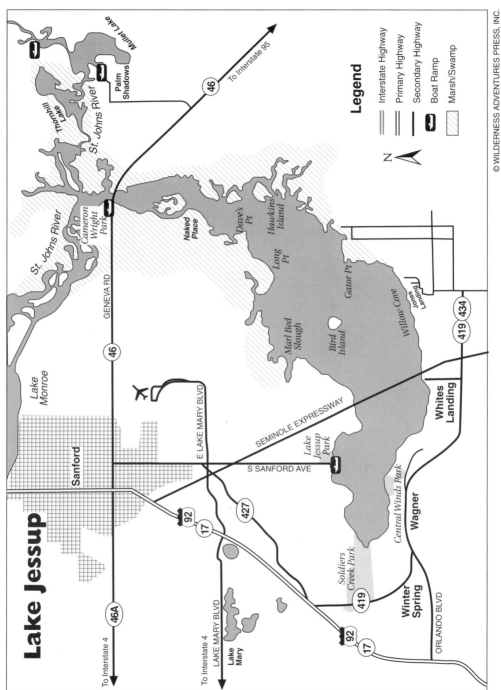

Lake Jessup

Legend

Interstate Highway
Primary Highway
Secondary Highway
Boat Ramp
Marsh/Swamp

N

© WILDERNESS ADVENTURES PRESS, INC.

To access Lake Monroe from the south side, again exit I-4 at Exit 52 and turn right (south) on US 17/ 92 for 3.5 miles, staying alongside the lake. As US 17/92 makes a sweeping right turn to go into Sanford, continue straight onto East Seminole Blvd. for 0.4 mile. There is a large municipal ramp (two double-lane ramps and two single-lane ramps) with paved parking for 50 vehicles. Lodging is also available at the ramp.

There is also a ramp on the northern side of Lake Monroe. Take Exit 53 off I-4 onto Enterprise Road and go east for 1 mile to the community of Enterprise. Turn right onto Main Street and go one block to Lakeshore Drive. Turn left onto Lakeshore Drive and go 1.1 miles to the single-lane ramp on the right. The unimproved parking is limited to eight vehicles.

At Wayside Park, you can access the western side of Lake Monroe near US 17/SR 92 (pictured) and the I-4 overpass.

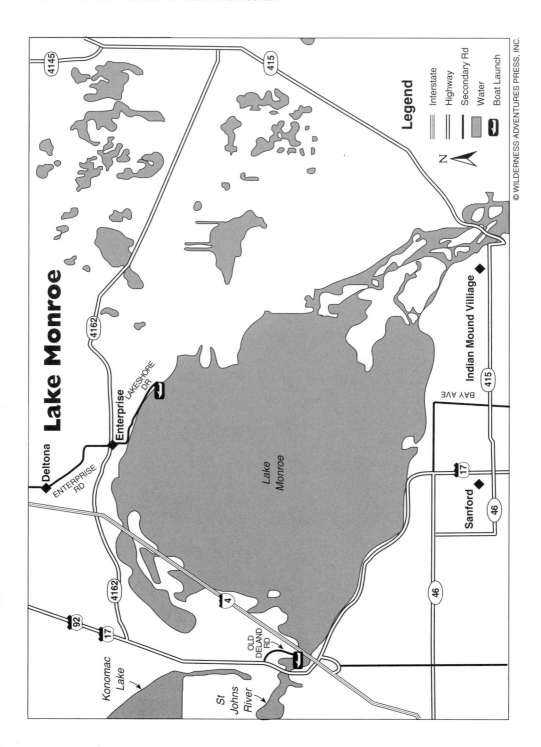

Lake Monroe

Legend

- Interstate
- Highway
- Secondary Rd
- Water
- Boat Launch

N

© WILDERNESS ADVENTURES PRESS, INC.

4145

415

Deltona

Enterprise

ENTERPRISE RD

LAKESHORE DR

4162

92

17

4162

4

OLD DELAND RD

Konomac Lake

St Johns River

Lake Monroe

Indian Mound Villiage

BAY AVE

415

Sanford

17

46

46

Konomac Lake

Barely a mile downstream from Lake Monroe is Konomac Lake (about 800 acres). While there is no ramp directly on this lake, you can reach it through a canal off the St. Johns River about half a mile west of the ramp described below. Konomac offers good shelter on a windy day, but it does not have a significant fishery. Fly fishermen using brightly colored Clousers can catch crappie in early spring near shoreline cover. A healthy population of smaller largemouth bass and bream is also present, and these can be taken on a size-2 popper.

To get to Konomac Lake, take Exit 52 off I-4 and turn left (north) for 0.7 mile, crossing the US 17-92 Bridge. The ramp at Lake Monroe Park is on the right just after crossing the St. Johns River.

Flyfishers can get to Lake Monroe and Konomac Lake from the ramp at Lake Monroe Park.

The Wekiva River

The Wekiva River drains a 130-square-mile area east of Orlando in Orange, Seminole, and Lake Counties. ("Wekiva" is a Creek Indian word meaning "flowing water.") From the headwaters at Wekiwa Springs, spewing forth 42 million gallons of water a day in what is now Wekiwa Springs State Park, the river runs for 16 miles to the St. Johns River. (Note the slight difference in spelling between the springs and river. "Wekiwa" is a Creek Indian word meaning "spring of water" or "bubbling

Lake Monroe is a large lake famous for its early spring crappie fishery. The municipal ramp at Sanford can accommodate just about any boat.

water.") The upper portion of the river is shallow and heavily used for tubing and floating by residents of Orlando and central Florida, especially on weekends.

The last couple of miles of the Wekiva River are of most interest to flyfishers. The small river begins to widen and slow, and in the spring striped bass and sunshine bass can frequently be found in good numbers.

A small, motorized boat can be used to fish the lower portion of the river. It is not uncommon to see black bear and bald eagles along the shorelines of the Wekiva and St. Johns River in this area, as well as deer, gray fox, and bobcat.

To get to the Wekiva River, leave I-4 at Exit 51 and go west on State Road 46 for 4.8 miles. Just before crossing the bridge over the river, turn right on Wekiva Park Drive and go 1 mile to Katie's Landing, the last commercial site on this small tributary before coming to the St. Johns River.

As you move about a mile northward past where the Wekiva River enters the St. Johns River, there is another ramp at High Banks. Take Exit 53 off I-4 onto Dirksen Drive and go west for 2.5 miles. In DeBary, turn right onto US 17/92 and go 1.8 miles to High Banks Road. Turn left onto High Banks Road and go west for 2.9 miles to the single-lane ramp where the road dead-ends. The launch area has unimproved parking for 15 vehicles. A marina, gas, and food are available.

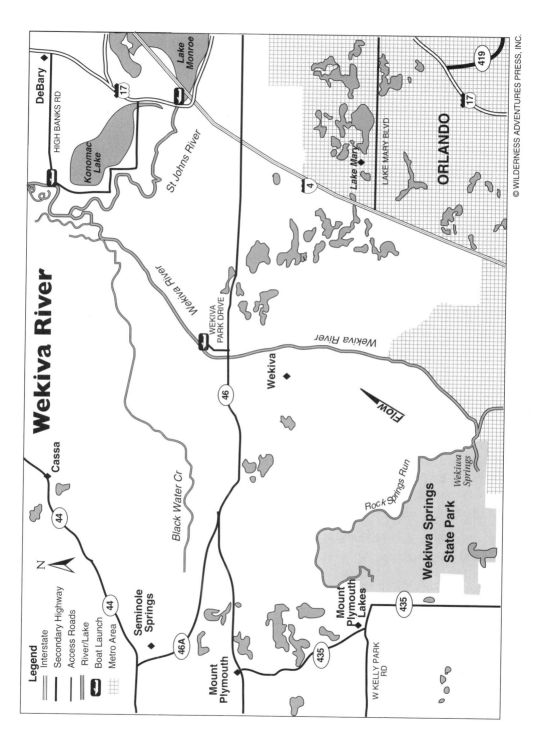

Wekiva River

Near DeBary, a single-lane ramp gives access to the St. Johns River.

BLUE SPRING STATE PARK

The next ramp on the St. Johns River is at Blue Spring State Park. The springs, the second largest single spring in the state and the largest on the St. Johns, are a noted wintering spot for manatee. The run from the spring to the river is about a mile and does not offer much of interest to the flyfisher. The point at which the spring run enters the river, however, often yields good catches of striped bass and sunshine bass.

From I-4, take Exit 54 and go west on State Road 472 and go 2.8 miles to Orange City. Turn left onto US 17-92 and go south for 1.5 miles. At West French Avenue, turn right and go 2.1 miles to Blue Spring State Park. Do not turn left into the park, but continue straight on what becomes a washboard gravel road for 1 mile. There is a poorly maintained paved ramp and improvised launching from the bank. There is limited parking and the area does not look very secure. Across the river from the ramp is a good pocket with lily pads and bonnets that offers sanctuary for bass, crappie, and bream.

LAKE BERESFORD

Lake Beresford, at 800 acres, averages about six feet deep in the open water portions. There is little grass and only a few bonnets growing along the lake's edge. Still, it is an outstanding lake for bream early and late in the day during the summer. Unfortunately, many homes rim the lake and it is a popular skiing lake. There is no public ramp.

To get to the private ramp, take Exit 56 from I-4 and go 6.6 miles west on State Road 44. You will go through Deland and turn left onto Old New York Avenue (County Road 4110). Go 1.5 miles, crossing railroad tracks twice and turn left onto Lakeview Drive. Go 1 mile to Tropical Resort and Marina at the end of the road. There is a single-lane paved ramp with unimproved parking for 10 vehicles.

A manatee feeds on lake vegetation.

North of Blue Springs, a favorite wintering home for manatee, is a launch maintained by the state park.

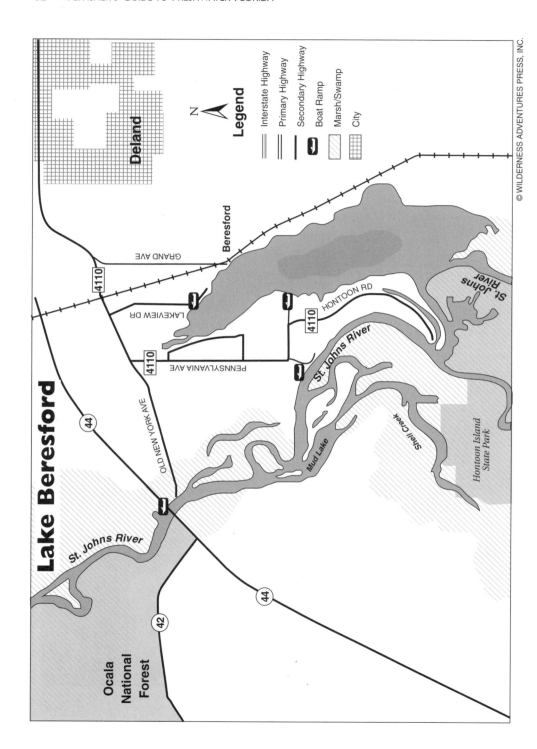

Legend

Interstate Highway
Primary Highway
Secondary Highway
Boat Ramp
Marsh/Swamp
City

Deland

Beresford

GRAND AVE

4110

LAKEVIEW DR

4110

PENNSYLVANIA AVE

4110

HONTOON RD

4110

St. Johns River

St. Johns River

Mud Lake

Shell Creek

Hontoon Island State Park

Lake Beresford

OLD NEW YORK AVE

44

St. Johns River

42

44

Ocala National Forest

© WILDERNESS ADVENTURES PRESS, INC.

Ed Stone Park

This launch site gives flyfishers access to Lake Beresford upstream and Lake Woodruff downstream. This portion of the river yields bragging-sized largemouth and many crappie in the two-pound range from the lily pads and shoreline vegetation in early spring. Bream fishing is consistent from spring through fall.

To get to the launch site, take Exit 56 from I-4 and go west on State Road 44 for 4.6 miles to Deland. From Deland, continue west on State Road 44 for 5.1 miles to Ed Stone Park. The entrance is on the right just before crossing the bridge. There is a six-lane ramp with semi-improved parking that is capable of accommodating 95 vehicles. Bathroom and picnic facilities are available and marinas with food and fuel are nearby.

Ed Stone Park, where SR 44 crosses the St. Johns River, offers access to a scenic portion of water.

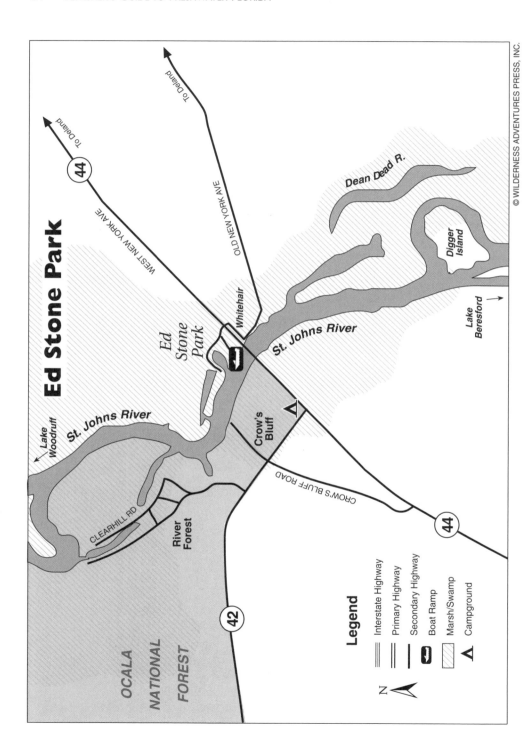

Ed Stone Park

Ed Stone Park

St. Johns River

St. Johns River

Dean Dead R.

Digger Island

Lake Beresford

Lake Woodruff

Whitehair

Crow's Bluff

River Forest

OLD NEW YORK AVE

WEST NEW YORK AVE

CROW'S BLUFF ROAD

CLEARHILL RD

To Deland

To Deland

44

44

42

OCALA NATIONAL FOREST

Legend

Interstate Highway	
Primary Highway	
Secondary Highway	
Boat Ramp	
Marsh/Swamp	
Campground	

N

Lake Woodruff and Spring Garden Lake

Lake Woodruff is a shallow 2,200-acre lake that averages just over four feet in depth. Woodruff is an excellent crappie lake in late winter and early spring. Many flyfishers have success by fishing open water with an intermediate sink-tip line, and others cast a Clouser close to cover along the shoreline and at the mouths of the lake using a floating line. Besides cold-weather crappie, Lake Woodruff also yields good catches of bass and bream.

There is no public launch site on Lake Woodruff. The nearest private launch is at Highland Park Fish Camp. Take Exit 56 off I-4 and go west on State Road 44, through Deland, for 7.2 miles. Shortly after you exit Deland, turn right onto Grand Avenue and go north for 2.3 miles. Turn left on Highland Park Road for 0.9 mile, crossing railroad tracks. Turn right onto Audubon and go 0.3 mile, then left to the fish camp. There are two paved single-lane ramps and unimproved parking for about 20 vehicles at the fish camp. Bait, limited tackle, and food is also available.

Connected to Lake Woodruff by a creek running through the marsh is Spring Garden Lake to the northeast. Spring Garden Lake sees a lot of recreational boating (kayaks, canoes, and paddle boats), and while there is a good population of largemouth bass and bream, you can expect to be annoyed by the presence of others during periods of warm weather. In the winter, recreational boaters are seldom on the water and a flyfisher can take a few small black bass and panfish using a popping bug. Ponce de Leon Springs supplies water for Spring Garden Lake, but the lake is only one or two feet deep in the middle, although the rim averages about three feet deep.

Spring Garden Lake (Ponce De Leon Recreation Area)
has activities for the entire family.

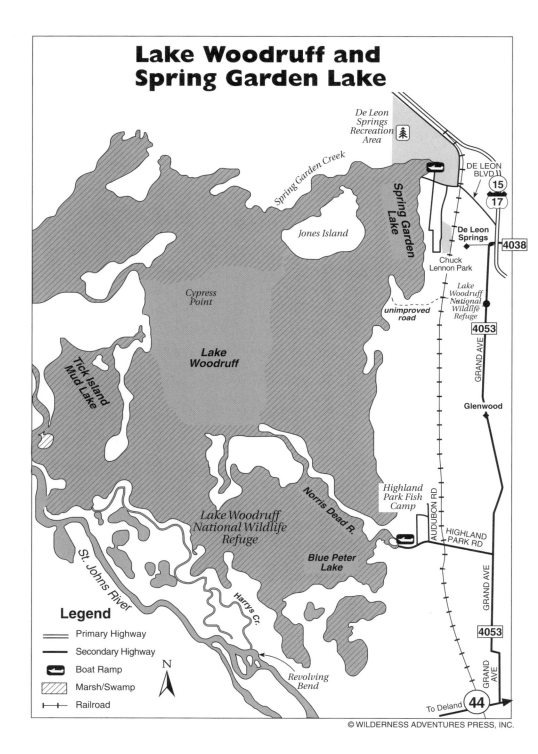

Lake Woodruff and Spring Garden Lake

De Leon Springs Recreation Area

Spring Garden Creek

DE LEON BLVD

15
17

Spring Garden Lake

Jones Island

De Leon Springs

4038

Chuck Lennon Park

Cypress Point

Lake Woodruff National Wildlife Refuge

unimproved road

4053

Lake Woodruff

Tick Island Mud Lake

GRAND AVE

Glenwood

Norris Dead R.

Highland Park Fish Camp

AUDUBON RD

HIGHLAND PARK RD

Lake Woodruff National Wildlife Refuge

Blue Peter Lake

St. Johns River

Harrys Cr.

GRAND AVE

4053

Legend

═══ Primary Highway

─── Secondary Highway

🛶 Boat Ramp

▨ Marsh/Swamp

┣━┿━┥ Railroad

N

Revolving Bend

GRAND AVE

To Deland 44

© WILDERNESS ADVENTURES PRESS, INC.

The area is interesting, however, in that there is an old gristmill at De Leon Springs State Recreation Area where breakfast is prepared on a tableside griddle. An angler could rent a canoe or a kayak at the recreation area and fish for a few hours while family members swim in the historic springs or picnic at the park.

To get to Spring Garden Lake (De Leon Springs Recreation Area) take Exit 56 off I-4 and go west on State Road 44 for 4.6 miles. Turn right on US 17 in Deland and go north for 8 miles. Turn left onto Ponce De Leon Blvd. and go 0.9 mile to the park entrance. The ramp is a single-lane, paved ramp and there is parking for about five vehicles. Elsewhere in the recreation area, there is ample paved parking for in excess of 50 vehicles.

ALEXANDER SPRINGS

While crystal clear and beautiful in the upper portions, the run from Alexander Springs to the St. Johns River offers little for the flyfisher except in the tannic waters of the lower portion. Here, stripers and sunshine bass like to gather in the cool, flowing water as it meets the St. Johns River. Like waters in the upper portion of the St. Johns, a small boat will be necessary and an occasional fallen tree means that it may be necessary to portage a kayak, canoe, or johnboat.

There is one ramp serving the lower portion of the Alexander Springs run. Take Exit 88 off Interstate 95 near Daytona Beach and go west on State Road 40 about 28 miles to where it crosses the St. Johns River in Astor. Cross the river and proceed through Astor for another 2.8 miles. At SR 445, turn left and go south for 4.7 miles. Turn left onto Forest Road 552 (a narrow dirt road) and go 4.5 miles to the steep, one-lane paved ramp. There is unimproved parking for about 10 vehicles.

An angler prepares to fish Alexander Springs, a tributary of the St. Johns River with a good population of sunshine bass.

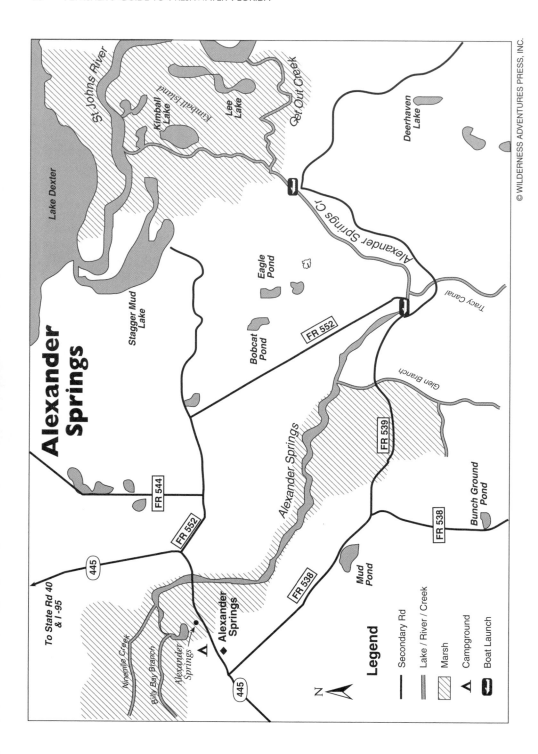

Alexander Springs

Legend

— Secondary Rd

— Lake / River / Creek

Marsh

△ Campground

🛥 Boat Launch

N

To State Rd 40 & I-95

© WILDERNESS ADVENTURES PRESS, INC.

Lake Dexter

Lake Dexter (1,902 acres) is east of the St. Johns River and connected to Lake Woodruff by Tick Island Creek. The creek is about eight feet deep and easily navigated. Lake Dexter averages about six feet deep in the middle, sloping upward toward its shoreline. This is another excellent crappie lake in the late winter and early spring. Lake Dexter is also a very good bass lake in the spring and fall. In the summer months, bass fishermen should fish during low-light periods. Bream fishing also rates as excellent from spring through fall. At the west end of Lake Dexter, along the river channel, look for stripers and sunshine bass in the spring and fall.

There are no ramps on Lake Dexter, but on the west side of the St. Johns River, directly across from Lake Dexter, there is a commercial ramp at Powell's Fish Camp. This area is best reached from the north, rather than from I-4. From I-95 in Daytona Beach, take Exit 88 onto State Road 40 and go west for about 28 miles. After crossing the St. Johns River at the town of Astor, turn left onto Alco Road and go south for 4.5 miles (only the first 2 miles are paved). The road ends at the river. The single-lane ramp is paved and there is unimproved parking for about eight vehicles.

Lake Diston

Lake Diston is a shallow lake of about 1,200 acres with good crappie and bream fishing. The largemouth bass run small, but an occasional over-sized fish is taken. Note the marsh at the north end and Little Haw Creek that flows into Dead Lake and onto Crescent Lake and the St. Johns River.

To get to Lake Diston, take Exit 88 off Interstate 95 near Daytona Beach and go west on State Road 40 for 13.5 miles. Turn right onto SR 11 and go north for 8.8 miles. At Cody's Corner, turn left onto SR 304 and go 2.6 miles. Turn left onto SR 305 and go another 2.6 miles. Lastly, make a left onto Lake Diston Drive (CR 2009) and go 1.3 miles to the lake. There is a one-lane ramp with unimproved parking for about four vehicles.

Lake George

Many anglers regard Florida's second largest lake, Lake George (46,000 acres), as the outstanding bass fishing lake in Central Florida. The Florida Fish and Wildlife Conservation Commission in likewise impressed by Lake George as evidenced by its recent selection as one of the top 10 bass lakes in the entire state. Averaging about 10 feet deep, the lake is unique in that the bottom is nearly uniform throughout its 12-mile length and 6-mile width.

Extensive vegetation provides excellent cover and habitat for bass, crappie, and bream, especially along the eastern shoreline. When the tide is outgoing (flowing to the north), try the grass beds at the northern end of the eastern side. When the tide is flooding (flowing to the south), look at the grass beds toward the southern end of

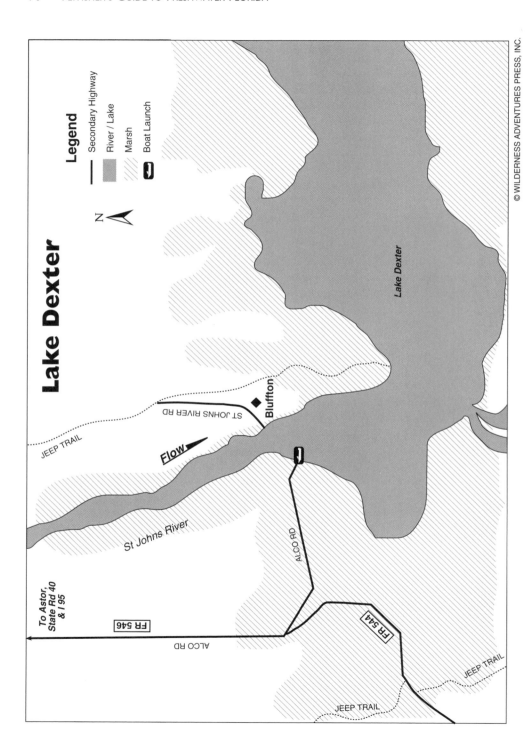

A noisy, deer-hair popper enticed this Lake George largemouth.

the eastern side. Here, bass will most often be in submerged grass just outside the emerging grass in 3-5 feet of water. Start at the outer edge of the submerged grass and work toward the shallower water where the grass begins to break the water. Bass in Lake George seem to prefer clean water over areas that have been subject to heavy wave action for several days, which makes the water dirty with stirred sediment. Choose a noisy, topwater popper or a larger Gurgler since you are fishing in water that barely covers submerged grass. The bigger it is and the more ruckus it makes, the better. A weedless fly will be helpful in navigating through vegetation that may be floating on top of the water.

At the south end of the lake where the St. Johns River enters Lake George, jetties are the favorite hangout for the lake's stripers and sunshine bass in both spring and fall. Old wooden bombing targets extend above the water line in the eastern half of the lake, and this structure seems to hold baitfish that are much to the stripers' liking. There can be some terrific topwater action from October through April as large schools move in to feed. Try a white foam Gurgler using a floating line on a reel with plenty of backing. When the topwater feed stops, quickly change to a streamer and be prepared for a jolting subsurface strike.

Three spring runs (Juniper, Salt, and Silver Glen) deposit a large volume of highly saline water into the western side of Lake George. In addition, if there are northerly winds for a long, sustained period, the incoming tide can reach all the way down to Lake George. As a result of the increased salinity, especially in the area where the feeder salt springs enter from the west, grass shrimp can be found. These small shrimp are excellent forage for largemouth bass, bream, striped bass, and sunshine bass. Fly patterns in size 6-8 that imitate grass shrimp, such as a Muddler Minnow or any of the saltwater shrimp patterns on a similarly sized hook, are favorites on Lake George. These should be fished around eelgrass and other vegetation that is near the spring discharge. Do not hesitate to go up these feeder salt springs, especially if stripers and sunshine bass are your targeted species.

When lake temperatures cool in the winter, these three saline feeder creeks originating from underground springs provide a constant supply of 72-degree water, the warmest water in the area. This definitely attracts more than a few fish to the western side of the lake during the winter months and into early spring.

Drifting the open water and casting Clousers on a sink-tip line can produce excellent catches of crappie in the summer once the fish are located. There is a lot of water to cover, however, and a depthfinder showing concentrations of fish is helpful. When the waters start to cool, look for the crappie to move toward shoreline cover as they prepare to spawn.

There are a number of ramps that can be used to access Lake George. Most of these, however, are from the many fish camps that rim the lake. From the south along State Road 40, one can launch in the river north of the town of Volusia and motor north a mile or two (depending upon the launch selected) to Lake George. Take Exit 88 off I-95 and go about 26 miles west to Volusia. Here, there are several signs directing you to any of half a dozen fish camps with fee ramps. These also offer gas, lodging, snacks for the boat, but almost no fly fishing tackle.

To access the east side of Lake George, use US 17/SR 15, which intersects SR 40 about 19 miles west of I-95. About 10 miles north of the SR 40 and US 17/SR 15 intersection is the community of Seville. Go west on CR 305 (there is a quick right then left turn as you begin) for 4 miles to a fish camp at Willow Point. There, for a fee, you can launch from the one-lane cement slab with unimproved parking for four vehicles. This puts you close to productive fishing along the east shoreline.

From the west side of Lake George, exit SR 40 onto SR 19 and go north for 5.9 miles. On your right will be Silver Glen Spring and a ramp that provides access to the run. There is a $3 fee for access into the Ocala National Park and the launch is suitable for kayaks and canoes only.

About 10 miles north is another Ocala National Park area ($3 fee to enter). Salt Springs Recreation Area has very nice facilities for camping, and canoe rentals are available. The marina will accommodate small boats and there are two additional launches available for registered guests.

There are two ramps at the north end of Lake George where it narrows to form the St. Johns River again. These are best reached from US 17/SR 15. Exit west onto CR 308 in Crescent City and go 8.1 miles. Turn left onto CR 309 and go south 3.7 miles to Georgetown Landing Road and the one-lane ramp. There is a fee to launch and the parking for about 10 vehicles is unimproved.

Continue south on CR 309 for about 0.3 mile to reach another ramp. Turn right onto Drayton Island Ferry Road and go down the potholed dirt lane for 0.2 mile. There is a small concrete slab with unimproved parking along the side of the road for about four vehicles.

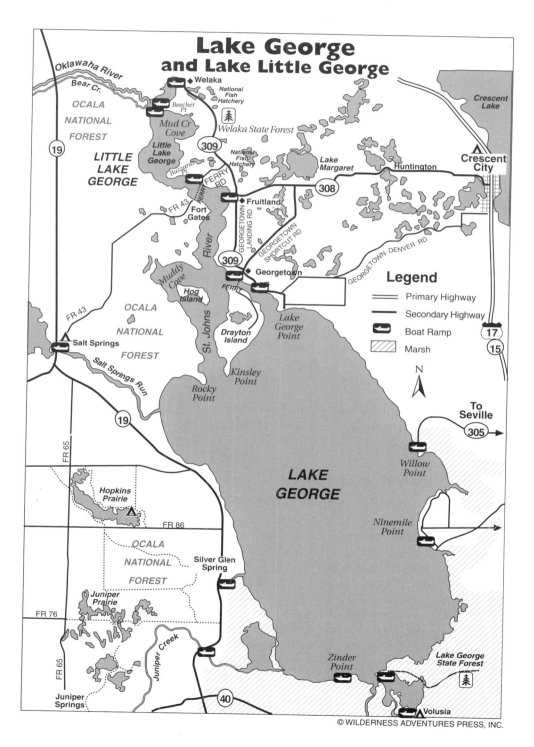

Lake George
and Lake Little George

© WILDERNESS ADVENTURES PRESS, INC.

LITTLE LAKE GEORGE

Little Lake George is not just another named wide spot in the St. Johns River system. It's a wide spot with five boat ramps because the fishing is so good! Beginning about five miles below (north of) Lake George, this five-mile stretch of the St. Johns offers perhaps the best striped bass fishing on the river. A subsurface spring called the Croaker Hole holds stripers from May through September and the fishing can be fast and furious. (Note: The striped bass move into the eastern portion of Lake George in an area known as the bombing range from October through April.)

On the east side of Little Lake George, Mud Creek Cove offers shallow water and extensive vegetation for largemouth bass, bream, and crappie. Many of the big bass for which the St. Johns River is noted have come from this area.

Access to Little Lake George is from the east, as the Oklawaha River enters from the marsh coming out of Ocala National Forest on the west side of the St. Johns River at this point. From US 17/SR 15 in Crescent City, take CR 308 west for 8.7 miles to the community of Fruitland. Turn right at the intersection of CR 308 and CR 309 and go north on CR 309 for 1.1 miles to Fort Gates Ferry Road. Turn left and the cement slab ramp is 1.2 miles to the west down the washboard dirt road. Parking is unimproved for barely two vehicles. There are better and more secure choices to the north.

By continuing north on CR 309, there is a much better ramp that gives easy access to Little Lake George. the town of Welaka is located 3.2 miles after the CR 308/309 intersection. At the only traffic light, turn left onto Elm Street (CR 308B) and go two blocks to the site with tow one-lane ramps. There is unimproved parking for eight vehicles.

In addition to the public ramps, there are about 15 fish camps in the area with boats and motors to rent, tackle, food and lodging, guides to hire, and other amenities. The fishing is that good in the area of Little Lake George.

LAKE KERR AND LITTLE LAKE KERR

Lake Kerr and adjoining Little Lake Kerr (2,830 acres) are unusual in that there are places where depths exceed 20 feet at normal water level. Most bass in these lakes are less than 14 inches, although an occasional trophy-sized fish is produced here. Bass fishing is best in the spring and fall. Shellcracker and bluegill are good from spring through fall. Warmouth are best during late spring and early summer near banks with vegetation. Fly patterns that imitate grass shrimp are a good bet for these bream.

To get to Lake Kerr and Little Lake Kerr, exit State Road 40 and go north onto SR 19 for 16.8 miles. Just after Salt Springs, turn left onto CR 316 and go 6.2 miles to Forest Road 88. Turn left on FR 88 and go south 0.8 mile. Turn left on NE 140th Street and go 0.4 mile to the single-lane ramp. There is paved parking for nine vehicles.

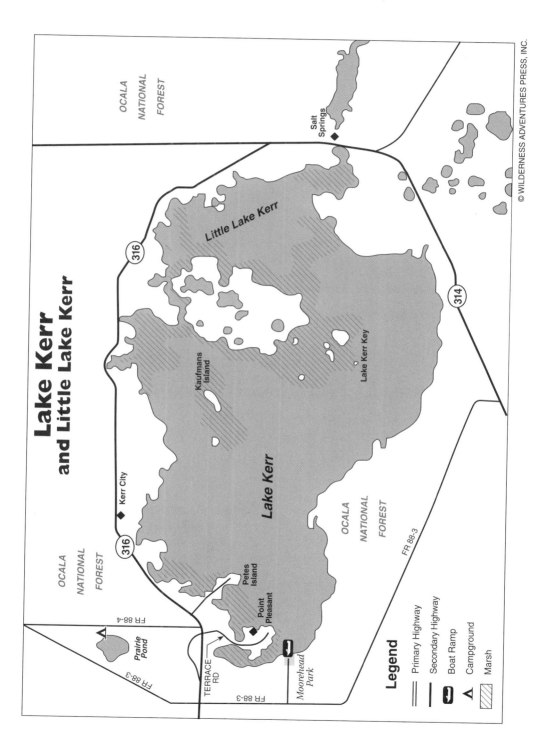

Lake Kerr and Little Lake Kerr

OCALA NATIONAL FOREST

Little Lake Kerr

Lake Kerr

Lake Kerr Key

Kaufmans Island

Kerr City

Petes Island

Point Pleasant

Moorehead Park

TERRACE RD

Prairie Pond

OCALA NATIONAL FOREST

OCALA NATIONAL FOREST

Salt Springs

316

314

316

FR 88-4

FR 88-3

FR 88-3

Legend

Primary Highway

Secondary Highway

Boat Ramp

Campground

Marsh

The Welaka National Fish Hatchery has several ponds where a variety of fish are raised.

WELAKA NATIONAL FISH HATCHERY

While in the area, be sure to stop at the museum and observation tower at the U.S. Fish & Wildlife Service's hatchery south of Welaka on CR 309. There are several ponds where a variety of species of fish are maintained through differing stages of development. This is a great place to spend an afternoon when it becomes windy, rainy, or too hot to continue fishing. The hatchery and museum are spread out over a couple of sites about two miles apart.

From Crescent City and US 17/SR 15, go west on CR 308 for 8.7 miles, turning right onto CR 309 at Fruitland. The national hatchery will be on your right, with a second location three miles ahead.

LAKE STELLA

Lake Stella, about 250 acres, is a municipal lake with homes along the eastern shoreline. The docks offer shade and cover to largemouth. In addition, crappie can be found around the pilings in early spring. The southwest corner has good cover for bream year-round and bass in the spring.

To get to Lake Stella, turn west onto Central Avenue from US 17 in Crescent City and go two blocks to the single-lane ramp. There is unimproved parking for 12 vehicles.

DEAD LAKE

Dead Lake is a small lake (about 200 acres) connected to Crescent Lake by Haws Creek. Dead Lake is eight feet deep in the middle and has good fishing for bream in the spring. A few good-sized largemouth are occasionally taken from the shoreline vegetation, along with crappie in the spring.

From Interstate 95, take Exit 91 and go west on State Road 100, through Bunnell, for 12.5 miles. Turn left on CR 305 and go south for 4.1 miles, then right onto CR 2006 for 3.9 miles to the one-lane paved ramp at St. Johns Park. There is unimproved parking for about five vehicles.

CRESCENT LAKE

Crescent Lake (15,960 acres) averages about 12 feet deep in its midsection. Crescent is an offshoot about five miles to the east of the St. Johns River, connected by Dunns Creek. Dunns Creek varies greatly in depth, averaging about 15 feet, but there are a few holes that go up to 40 feet deep.

Crescent Lake is an excellent bass lake with very good catches made in shallow water near eelgrass beds in the spring and around docks and structure in the fall. In addition, crappie are abundant in the winter and early spring in open water, some of them in excess of two pounds. In summer, a few crappie are taken from lily pads, and bass are most frequently found holding on the deeper docks and pilings.

To access the east side of the southern portion of Crescent Lake, take Exit 91 off Interstate 95 onto SR 100 and go west for 19.9 miles, through Bunnell, to Shell Bluff in Andalusia. Turn left onto Shell Bluff Road and go south for 0.5 mile down the narrow, dirt road to the ramp. There is an unpaved ramp and limited parking along the side of the road for about four vehicles.

To get to the west side of the southern portion of Crescent Lake, exit US 17 in Crescent City (the self-proclaimed "Bass Capital of the World") and turn east onto Central Avenue. The single-lane ramp is three blocks straight ahead. There is unimproved parking for six vehicles.

Farther north, there is another ramp on the west side of Crescent Lake. About 6.9 miles north of Crescent City near Pamona Park, exit US 17 and go east on East Main Street for 1.1 miles. Turn right onto Pomona Landing Road and go 1.3 miles to the poor dirt ramp at the end of the road. There is parking along the side of the road for two vehicles.

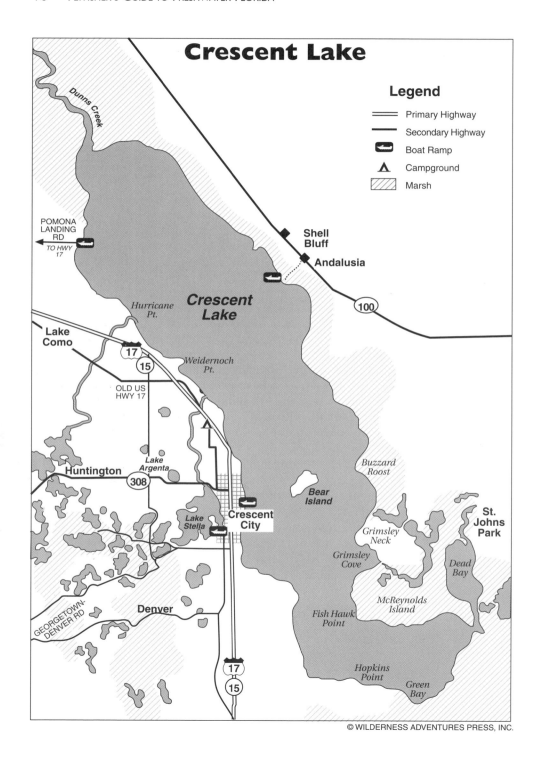

Crescent Lake

Legend

═══ Primary Highway

─── Secondary Highway

Boat Ramp

▲ Campground

Marsh

POMONA LANDING RD
TO HWY 17

Shell Bluff

Andalusia

100

Crescent Lake

Hurricane Pt.

Lake Como

17

15

OLD US HWY 17

Weidernoch Pt.

Lake Argenta

Huntington

308

Lake Stella

Crescent City

Bear Island

Buzzard Roost

St. Johns Park

Grimsley Neck

Grimsley Cove

Dead Bay

McReynolds Island

Denver

GEORGETOWN-DENVER RD

Fish Hawk Point

Hopkins Point

Green Bay

17

15

© WILDERNESS ADVENTURES PRESS, INC.

*An osprey is perched in a spruce tree
along the Oklawaha River.*

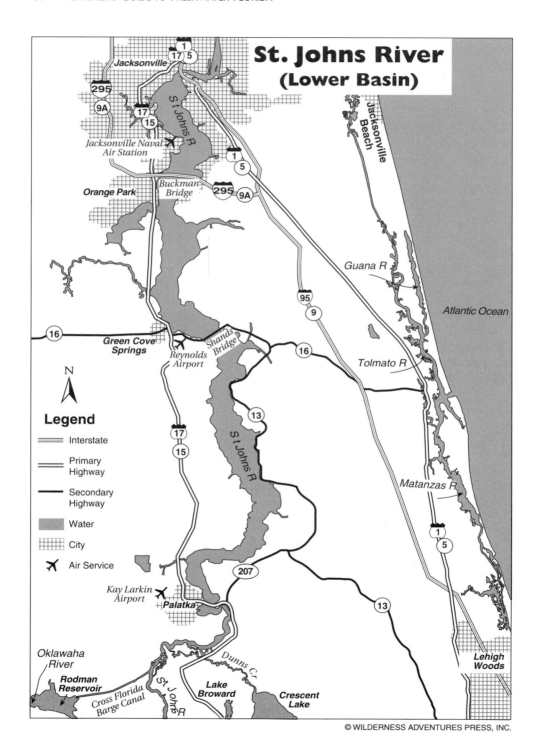

St. Johns River
(Lower Basin)

Jacksonville

Jacksonville Beach

St Johns R

295

9A

17

15

Jacksonville Naval
Air Station

Orange Park

Buckman
Bridge

295 9A

Guana R

Atlantic Ocean

95
9

16

Green Cove
Springs

Reynolds
Airport

Shands
Bridge

16

Tolmato R

13

N

Legend

≡≡≡ Interstate

══ Primary
Highway

▬ Secondary
Highway

▓ Water

▦ City

✈ Air Service

17
15

St Johns R

Matanzas R

1
5

207

13

Kay Larkin
Airport

Palatka

Oklawaha
River

Rodman
Reservoir

Cross Florida
Barge Canal

St Johns R

Dunns Cr

Lake
Broward

Crescent
Lake

Lehigh
Woods

© WILDERNESS ADVENTURES PRESS, INC.

The Lower (Northern) Basin

I have defined the Lower Basin as the northernmost part of the river from the confluence with the Oklawaha River, through Palatka, and on to the Mayport Inlet at Jacksonville. I have also included the Oklawaha River system, the major tributary along the entire 300-mile course of the St. Johns River system within this section.

The Oklawaha River has its headwaters in central Florida near Orlando and drains the central part of the state to the northeast. Check with local bait and tackle stores before attempting to fish these headwaters, as they have been low for several years. As you move northward along the Oklawaha, you leave the crowded and often overdeveloped urban lakes and move into the Ocala National Forest. Here, the gin-clear river flows through some of the most unspoiled lands in Region 1. The river bass will not be as large as their lake cousins, but they are numerous and feisty in the flowing water. Other species of bream are abundant and reward flyfishers who cast small poppers toward the shoreline. Along its 125-mile course, there are many large lakes, several of which are renowned fisheries. Rodman Reservoir is one that quickly comes to mind. Numerous dams along the Oklawaha River regulate both water flow and lake levels and these dams have locks that permit the passage of boats.

With the addition of the waters from the Oklawaha River, entering about 10 river miles before Palatka, and Dunns Creek, flowing into the river from Lake Crescent about five river miles before Palatka, the salinity of the St. Johns River is substantially diluted, becoming wider and more estuarine. In the portion of the river between Palatka and Jacksonville, it averages about 2 miles in width, increasing to almost 4 miles in and around the Jacksonville area.

In the Lower Basin, the largemouth and crappie fishery remains quite good, but with the increased salinity brought by the incoming tides, it does begin to taper off slightly from the world-class quality of the lakes and river in the Middle Basin. Still, dozens of national and local bass tournaments utilize Palatka as their headquarters for launching, weigh-in, and other tournament activities. This portion of the river continues to yield excellent catches of bream, especially in the springtime.

Because tides have a stronger influence than current in the Lower Basin, largemouth bass do not use the same holding and feeding locations on an incoming tide that they used on an outgoing tide. Look for them to be in an eddy behind structure or an obstacle that allows them to hold their position while using less effort. When tides are the same, look for them to be in similar positions relative to the direction of the tide. When tides are reversed, they will have moved on to eddies caused by the new tidal direction.

The addition of saltwater species following the incoming salt water on high tides adds many new opportunities for flyfishers. (Note: You will need a saltwater fishing license to take any of the saltwater species.) American shad pass through in winter on their run to spawn hundreds of miles upstream in the Upper Basin. Striped bass and sunshine bass, often found schooling in open water near the mouth of tributary waters and in underwater springs in the Middle Basin, now gather in large numbers around Memorial Bridge in Palatka, Shands Bridge in Green Cove Springs, and Buckman Bridge (Interstate 295) in Jacksonville. Snook can be found on most any dock in the Jacksonville area and immediately south, spotted seatrout readily take Clousers presented around grassy areas in the lower portion of the river south of Jacksonville, and on occasion, redfish make it all the way up (south) through the entire Lower Basin to the northern end of Lake George in the Middle Basin.

For the purpose of this freshwater guidebook, I'll stop the discussion of freshwater fishing opportunities in the St. Johns River at the Buckman Bridge (I-295) on the south side of Jacksonville. From this point north to Mayport Inlet, the St. Johns River is basically a saltwater fishery with water from the Atlantic Ocean moving into and out of the inlet.

THE OKLAWAHA RIVER

The Oklawaha River ("Great River" to the Seminole Indians) is a complex system with a rich history. Like the St. Johns River, it flows northward for about 125 miles along the western edge of the Ocala National Forest. Much of the river is unspoiled, and black bear, deer, and panther can be seen drinking along its shoreline. More than 300 different mammals live along the corridor, as do more than 200 types of birds. In addition, 110 identified species of fish give it one of the most diversified fish populations anywhere in the United States. About one-third of the way along its course, Silver Springs, the largest spring in Florida, daily pours 500 million gallons of crystal clear water into the Oklawaha River.

Steamboats traveled up the river from Palatka in the 1800s. This form of travel and shipping soon gave way to the railroad, and the Oklawaha has retained its unspoiled character and natural beauty. This was severely threatened in the mid-20th century when plans for a Cross-Florida Barge Canal included the Oklawaha River. Work on the barge canal was stopped in 1971, but about 7 miles of the straight canal still connect the lower portions of the Oklawaha River from Rodman Reservoir to the St. Johns River.

The Oklawaha Chain of Lakes has a portion of its headwaters in Lake Apopka about 10 miles west of Orlando. Water from Lake Apopka flows through the Beauclair Canal (where a dam controls the water level in Lake Apopka) on to Lake Beauclair. Another dam in Haines Creek between Lake Eustis and Lake Griffin controls the water level in Lake Ola, Lake Carlton, Lake Beauclair, Lake Dora, Lake Eustis, Little Lake Harris, and Lake Harris. A third dam (C-231 Canal) at Moss Bluff about 11 miles downstream (north) controls water levels in Lake Griffin and Lake Yale.

The remaining headwaters of the Oklawaha River are found in the Clermont Chain of Lakes flowing into Lake Harris through the Palatlakaha River. These lakes are very shallow with limited public access and are of little interest to flyfishers.

Through its midsection, the Oklawaha River flows along the western edge of the Ocala National Forest. This portion, after the addition of waters from Silver Springs just south of SR 40, is quite scenic, and the water flows at a rate of about 3 miles per hour. In addition to Silver Springs, several smaller springs also contribute gin-clear water along the way. Camping is allowed on the banks of the river in government owned land, and you have a very good chance of seeing eagle, turkey, otter, deer, bear, and panther as they move out of the forest to visit the river.

The middle portions of the Oklawaha provide excellent fishing for stringers of spotted sunfish and redbreast. In addition, bass fishing is quite good in the spring-time around fallen trees in the river, and becomes excellent in the impoundments in the lower portion of the river. Most noted among these is Rodman Reservoir, where many double-digit bass have been caught.

The remains of the Oklawaha River flow from Rodman Reservoir to the St. Johns River through the marsh in the eastern portion of the Ocala National Forest. There is no lock through the dam so anglers desiring to get to the St. Johns must utilize the aforementioned Cross Florida Barge Canal, a straight 7-mile ditch. There is a ramp just below the dam and anglers can launch at this site and fish downstream through the marsh to the St. Johns River, a distance of approximately 8 miles.

From Rodman Reservoir, the Cross Florida Barge Canal cuts a straight path for about 7 miles to the St. Johns River.

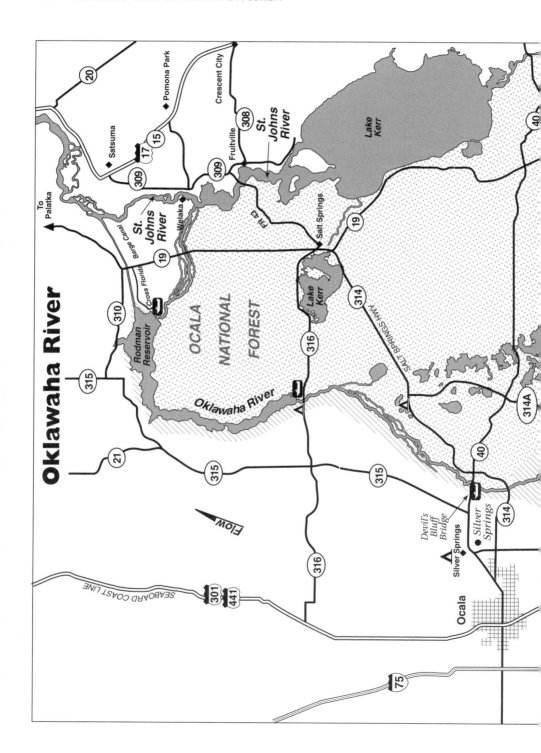

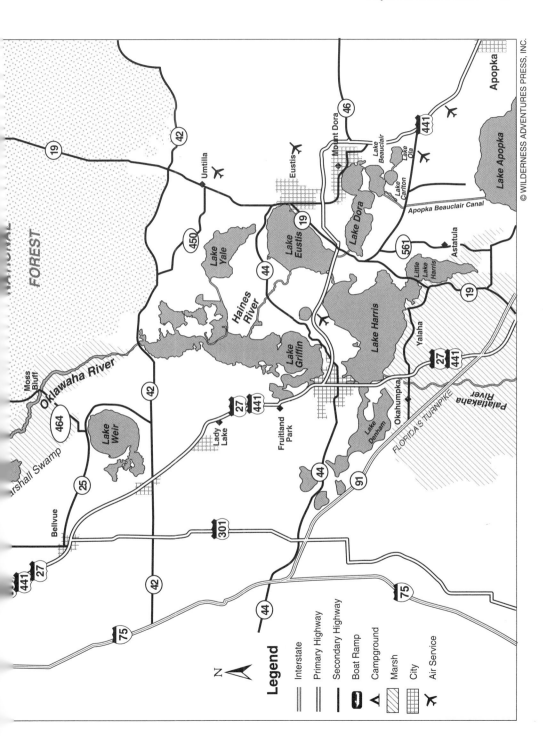

Legend

- Interstate
- Primary Highway
- Secondary Highway
- Boat Ramp
- Campground
- Marsh
- City
- Air Service

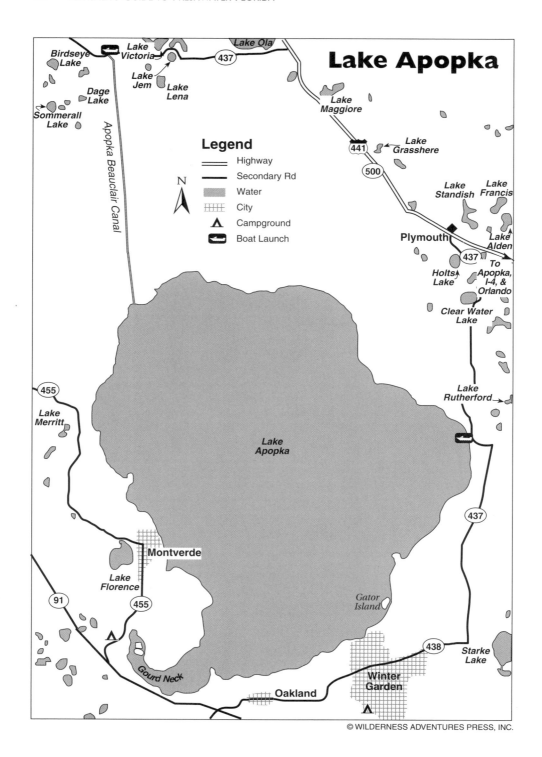

Lake Apopka

Birdseye Lake
Lake Victoria
Lake Ola
437
Lake Jem
Lake Lena
Dage Lake
Lake Maggiore
Sommerall Lake

Legend

─── Highway
─── Secondary Rd
▨ Water
▦ City
▲ Campground
⛵ Boat Launch

N

441
Lake Grasshere
500
Lake Standish
Lake Francis
Plymouth
Lake Alden
437
To Apopka, I-4, & Orlando
Holts Lake
Clear Water Lake

Apopka Beauclair Canal

455
Lake Merritt

Lake Apopka

Lake Rutherford

437

Montverde

Lake Florence

91
455

Gator Island

438
Starke Lake

Gourd Neck

Oakland

Winter Garden

Lake Apopka

Lake Apopka, 30,671 acres and averaging about six feet deep, is the uppermost lake in a series of lakes connected by canals that contribute to the headwaters of the Oklawaha River. Once noted as a famous bass fishery, Lake Apopka is now quite polluted and has poor quality fish habitat. Nonetheless, sunshine bass have been regularly stocked and grow quite well feeding on the abundant shad population. These fish reach four pounds by their third year, and it is common to take sunshine bass up to six pounds on flies. Both saltwater and freshwater shrimp patterns fished on a sink-tip line near the Gourd Neck Springs area work well for these great fighters.

Gourd Neck Springs is in the southwest corner of Lake Apopka and offers the best fishing opportunity on the lake. There is also a decent fishery for crappie in the same area. A Clouser fished on a sink-tip line will work well near the area of the boil.

To reach the east side of Lake Apopka from I-4 in Orlando, take Exit 33B and go north on US 441 for about 15 miles, passing through Apopka and on to the community of Plymouth. In Plymouth, turn left onto State Road 437 and go 5.2 miles to Magnolia Park. Turn right into the park and follow the road to the double-lane ramp. There is paved parking for 22 vehicles.

The Apopka-Beauclair Canal is about 7 miles long and connects Lake Apopka to Lake Beauclair. The dam to this locked canal controls the water level in Lake Apopka. To reach the one ramp in the canal from Orlando, take Exit 33 B off I-4 and go north for about 19 miles on US 441. Turn left onto SR 448 and go 3.6 miles to the entrance to Lake Jem Park. Turn right into the park and follow the road to the single-lane ramp. There is unimproved parking for 20 vehicles. From the ramp, it is about five miles south (left) to Lake Apopka and 2 miles north (right) to Lake Beauclair.

Lake Beauclair, Lake Carlton, and Lake Ola

Lake Beauclair is the largest of these three central Florida lakes at 1,111 acres, while Lake Carlton and Lake Ola to the south are each about 500 acres. Water quality is better than Lake Apopka, but still not as good as other lakes downstream (north) that are more removed from the extensive development associated with central Florida. Bass fishing is poor. In cooler months, crappie can be good some years. Lake Beauclair averages about 8 feet deep, and a canal at the northeast corner connects it to Lake Dora.

Of these three lakes, only Beauclair has a ramp. From I-4 take Exit 51 onto State Road 46 and go 18.5 miles to Mount Dora. Turn left onto SR 441 and go south 1.9 miles to Tangerine. Turn right onto Dudley Avenue and go 1.1 miles, turn left onto Dora Drive and go 0.5 mile, then right onto Earlwood for 0.6 mile. There is a paved single-lane ramp at Trimble Park with paved parking for up to 30 vehicles.

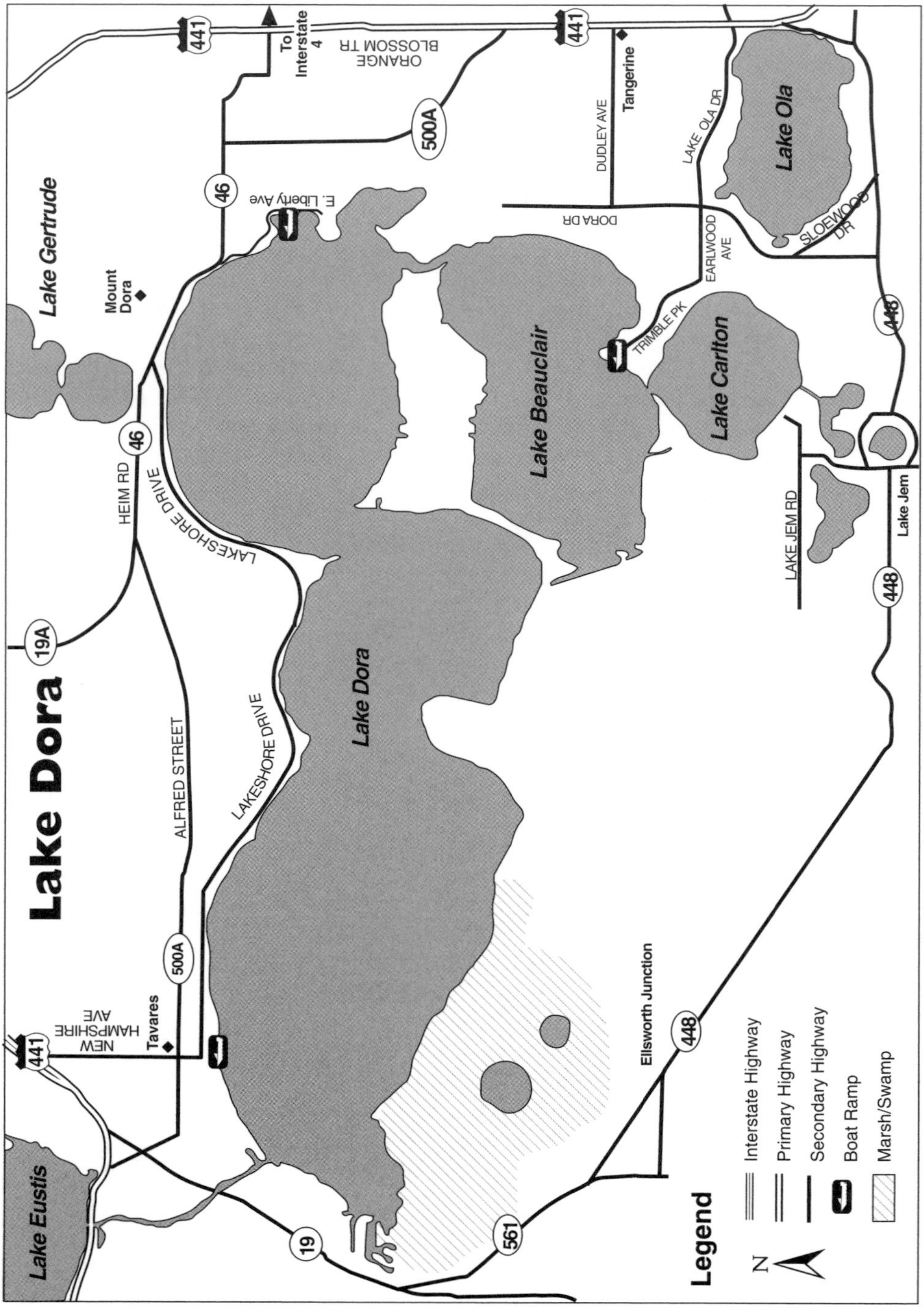

Lake Dora

Lake Gertrude

Lake Eustis

Lake Beauclair

Lake Carlton

Lake Dora

Lake Ola

Lake Jem

441

441

500A

46

46

500A

19A

19

561

448

448

448

To Interstate 4

ORANGE BLOSSOM TR

E. Liberty Ave

DUDLEY AVE

Tangerine

LAKE OLA DR

DORA DR

EARLWOOD AVE

SLOEWOOD DR

TRIMBLE PK

LAKE JEM RD

Lake Jem

Ellsworth Junction

HEIM RD

LAKESHORE DRIVE

ALFRED STREET

LAKESHORE DRIVE

NEW HAMPSHIRE AVE

Tavares

Mount Dora

Legend

N

▦	Interstate Highway
	Primary Highway
	Secondary Highway
🛥	Boat Ramp
▨	Marsh/Swamp

Lake Dora

Lake Dora (4,475 acres) averages about 10 feet deep. Bass fishing, along with crappie and bream fishing, improves as you move down the southern edge of Lake Dora away from development, especially in the spring. There are some very nice bed and breakfasts in the town of Mount Dora along the eastern edge of the lake.

To get to the eastern portion of Lake Dora, take Exit 51 from I-4 and go 18.9 miles west on State Road 46 to Mount Dora. Turn left onto US 441 and go 0.2 mile to E. Liberty Avenue. Turn right onto E. Liberty and go 0.4 mile to Gilbert Park. Turn right into the park and follow signs to the three-lane ramp with both paved and unpaved parking accommodating about 25 vehicles.

The western half of Lake Dora can be accessed from the community of Tavares. From SR 46 in Mount Dora, go right (west) on US 500A for 4.5 miles to Tavares. Turn left on New Hampshire Avenue to Wooten Park and the two single-lane ramps with paved parking for 11 vehicles.

The town of Mount Dora, with wonderful shops and eateries, is located along the eastern edge of Lake Dora.

LAKE EUSTIS AND TROUT LAKE

Lake Eustis is a little deeper than the previous lakes in this portion of the Oklawaha River's headwaters (sometimes called the Harris Chain of Lakes). At 7,806 acres, Lake Eustis averages between 10 to 12 feet deep, although there are a couple of depressions that go 20 feet. Trout Lake, in the northeast corner of Lake Eustis, has only 102 acres.

The deeper depressions hold sunshine bass and a sink-tip line will get a shrimp pattern down to them. You may also pick up crappie using this technique when they are in open water during summer, fall, and early winter months. Bass and bream are best caught in the spring from the grass and bonnets that rim the lake.

To get to the southern portion of Lake Eustis, take Exit 51 off I-4 and go 18.5 miles to Mount Dora. As you enter town, turn right onto US 441 and go north around Mount Dora for about 8 miles until the town of Tavares. At the intersection where US 441 and State Road 19 split, go right on US 441 for 1.2 miles and the double-lane ramp will be on your right. There is paved parking for up to 96 vehicles.

There is another paved ramp in the northeast corner of Lake Eustis. As above, take US 441 north and go 5.1 miles to the intersection with State Road 19. Turn right on SR 19 and go 1.9 miles into the town of Eustis. Turn left onto Citrus Avenue and go 0.4 mile (it becomes Lakeshore Drive) to the launch site. It has three one-lane ramps with paved parking for 8 vehicles and unpaved parking for an additional 16 vehicles.

Lake Eustis is a deep lake in the Harris Chain of Lakes.

Lake Eustis and Trout Lake

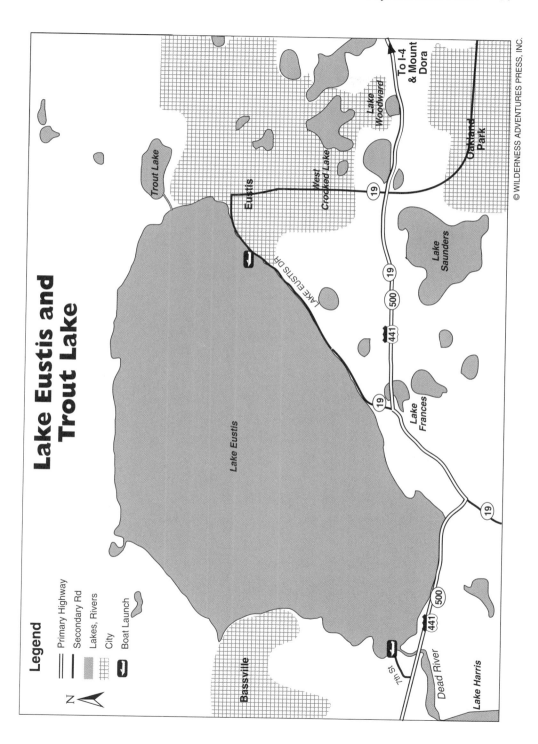

Legend

N

Primary Highway
Secondary Rd
Lakes, Rivers
City
Boat Launch

Trout Lake

Eustis

West
Crooked Lake

Lake
Woodward

To I-4
& Mount
Dora

Oakland
Park

19

LAKE EUSTIS DR

Lake
Saunders

19

500

441

Lake Eustis

19

Lake
Frances

Bassville

7th St

441

500

19

Dead River

Lake Harris

Lake Harris
and Little
Lake Harris

Legend

	Interstate Highway
	Primary Highway
	Secondary Highway
	Boat Ramp
	Marsh/Swamp

N

Lake Harris and Little Lake Harris

Lake Harris (13,788 acres) was once regarded as the best bass fishing lake in the Oklawaha Chain of Lakes. In the early 1990s, disease caused the fishery to decline, but it has since rebounded and is now on the upswing. Lake Harris also has a very good population of crappie. They spawn in the shoreline grass from December through April, and later in the year they move out to open water where water depths average around 14 feet. There is a 3-mile trough of unusually deep water along the southern edge of the lake where depths plummet to as much as 30 feet. Look for sunshine bass, which have been extensively stocked in Lake Harris, to be feeding in this area.

Bream are best taken in the vicinity of the State Road 19 bridge at the south end of the lake and on down into Little Lake Harris (2,739 acres). Depths here average about 10 feet, and there is some excellent shallow water at the south end of Little Lake Harris where largemouth bass, crappie and bream congregate in the spring.

To get to the western portion of Lake Harris, go 2.9 miles south on US 27 after the split where it separates from US 441 in Leesburg. The double-lane ramp is on your left, and there is paved parking for 52 vehicles.

The southern end of Lake Harris can be accessed from a very nice park at the northern end of the Howey Bridge, SR 19. Hickory Point Recreational Facility has been built by the Lake County Water Authority and it has 12 paved ramps giving quick access to both Lake Harris and Little Lake Harris. This modern facility has paved parking for about 75 vehicles and several other amenities for the family. No overnight camping is allowed, however.

Little Lake Harris has a ramp along the eastern side. From CR 561 in Astatula, turn onto Florida Avenue at the intersection with SR 48 and go west 0.8 mile to the single-lane paved ramp with semi-improved parking for six vehicles.

Hickory Point Recreational Facility at the north end of the SR 19 Bridge offers amenities for the entire family, as well as access to both Lake Harris and Little Lake Harris.

CLERMONT CHAIN OF LAKES

Lake Louisa, Lake Susan, Crescent Lake, Lake Minnehaha, Lake Minneola, Cherry Lake, Palatlakaha River, Lake Lucy, and Lake Emma

The lakes that make up the Clermont Chain of Lakes form the second major source of the Oklawaha River. These interconnected lakes drain through the Palatlakaha River into Lake Harris and then into the Oklawaha River, eventually ending up in the St. Johns River. As such, they are part of the St. Johns River system, although it is more than a hundred miles by fishing boat from these headwaters to the St. Johns.

With the exception of Lake Minneola and Cherry Lake, these lakes have tea-colored water. Cypress, live oaks, and palms line the shores, and lilies, bonnets, and emerging grass grow near the banks. These lakes are very attractive, but the fishing is difficult. They are all Fish Management Areas and special rules apply (see the section on freshwater fishing regulations for rules pertaining to Fish Management Areas).

Lake Louisa (3,634 acres) is the largest and southernmost lake in this chain and the only one with a ramp. There are several fish attractors marked by buoy in Lake Louisa. Bream and crappie are the dominant species. Try fishing the west side early in the spring.

To get to the ramp at the north end of Lake Louisa from State Road 50 in Clermont, go south on US 27 for 0.2 mile. Turn right onto Hook Street for 0.3 mile, then left onto Lakeshore Drive for 3.5 miles. Turn left onto Hull Road and go 1.1 miles to the one-lane paved ramp with semi-improved parking for 15 vehicles.

Lake Susan (81 acres) is the next lake to the north. It is a shallow lake that opens into Lake Minnehaha (2,261 acres). South of Lake Minnehaha, but not connected to Lake Susan, is Crescent Lake (143 acres). Crescent Lake is small but always worth a look in the spring when crappie and bream spawn along the shoreline cover. Lake Minnehaha borders the south side of Clermont. Fishing on Lake Minnehaha is best around shoreline vegetation at the southern end where water from Lake Susan and Crescent Lake enter and in the northwest corner in Cypress Cove.

Bordering the north side of Clermont is Lake Minneola. This lake is clearer than the others and fly patterns imitating threadfin shad work well here for largemouth bass. This lake also has a good population of bream and crappie. There is a launch site in Clermont that can be reached from SR 50. Go north on 12th Street for 0.2 mile, then right (east) on West Minneola Drive for 0.3 mile to the two one-lane ramps with paved parking for 10 vehicles.

Moving through the marsh to the northwest will put you on Cherry Lake (396 acres). This lake is very difficult to access by boat. There is a ramp about three miles away, but a shallow marsh makes the trip difficult.

The ramp mentioned above is on the Palatlakaha River. Like the St. Johns River in its most southern headwaters region, the channel of the Palatlakaha River is hardly

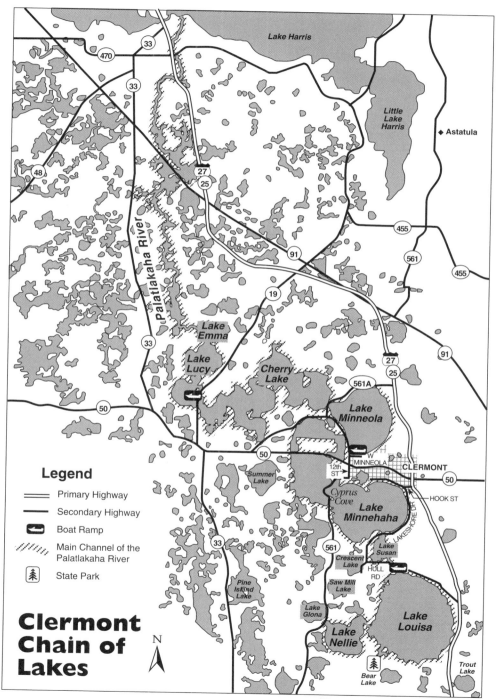

Clermont Chain of Lakes

Legend

- ═══ Primary Highway
- ─── Secondary Highway
- Boat Ramp
- ///// Main Channel of the Palatlakaha River
- State Park

N

Lake Harris

Little Lake Harris

◆ Astatula

Palatlakaha River

Lake Emma

Lake Lucy

Cherry Lake

Lake Minneola

Summer Lake

MINNEOLA

CLERMONT

W 12th ST

Cyprus Cove

Lake Minnehaha

LAKESHORE DR

HOOK ST

Lake Susan

Crescent Lake

HULL RD

Saw Mill Lake

Lake Glona

Pine Island Lake

Lake Nellie

Bear Lake

Lake Louisa

Trout Lake

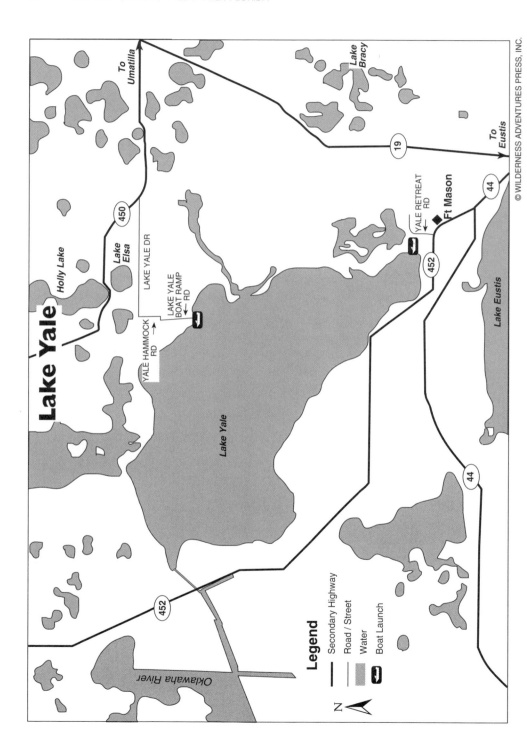

Lake Yale

Legend

Secondary Highway
Road / Street
Water
Boat Launch

discernable at this point. To get to this ramp, go west from Clermont on SR 50 for 5.1 miles. Turn right and go north on SR 19 for 1.4 miles, and the ramp (J. Ray, R. L., and J. B. Arnold Brothers Park) is on your left after crossing the creek. There are two one-lane ramps with paved parking for about eight vehicles. This area requires a small, shallow-draft boat to navigate the waters.

By going through the marsh to your right, you move along the course of the Palatlakaha River and next come to Lake Lucy (335 acres) and Lake Emma (175 acres). Like those in the Middle Basin of the St. Johns River, these two lakes are no more than wide spots along the river's course. The Palatlakaha River meanders through the marsh for another 10 miles before flowing into Lake Harris to the north. There are several more named lakes in the marsh, but they are not accessible by boat, nor connected with the Palatlakaha River.

LAKE YALE

Lake Yale (4,042 acres) currently has a better bass fishery than other lakes in the Oklawaha Chain of Lakes because there is not nearly as much development along its shoreline. In the spring, look for largemouth, crappie, and bream in the southeastern portion of the lake. During the warmer months, crappie and sunshine bass will be in open water near the canal in the northwest corner that connects Lake Yale to Lake Griffin and the Oklawaha River.

There is a single-lane ramp yielding good access to the northeast portion of Lake Yale. From Eustis, go north on SR 19 for 6.1 miles and just after leaving Umatilla, turn left on SR 450. Go west on SR 450 for 1.8 miles, turn left on Lake Yale Road and go 1.4 miles. At the "Y" in the road, bear left for another 0.3 mile and follow Lake Yale Boat Ramp Road to the ramp. There is unimproved parking for 10 vehicles.

In the southeast corner of Lake Yale there is a double-lane ramp with unim-proved parking for 20 vehicles. At the intersection of SR 19 and SR 44 as you are leav-ing the north side of Eustis, turn left on SR 44 and go west for 1.5 miles. Turn right onto SR 452 and go 0.5 mile to Yale Retreat Road. The ramp is about 0.2 mile on the left.

LAKE GRIFFIN

Lake Griffin (16,505 acres), like Lake Harris, has suffered from water quality and habi-tat problems due to extensive development in the area. Once an outstanding lake for largemouth bass, the lily pads and other vegetation were cleared, and bass fishing is no longer what it once was. Mid-lake depths average about nine feet.

Crappie fishing is quite good, however, beginning in the winter months and peaking in spring when they move to shoreline cover to spawn. Fish the northern portion of the lake from Treasure Island down the lake past Bird Island and continu-ing northward. This same area of Lake Griffin also has good bream fishing in April and May. Look for the sunshine bass to be in the deeper water located just south of Picciola Island in the southwest corner of Lake Griffin.

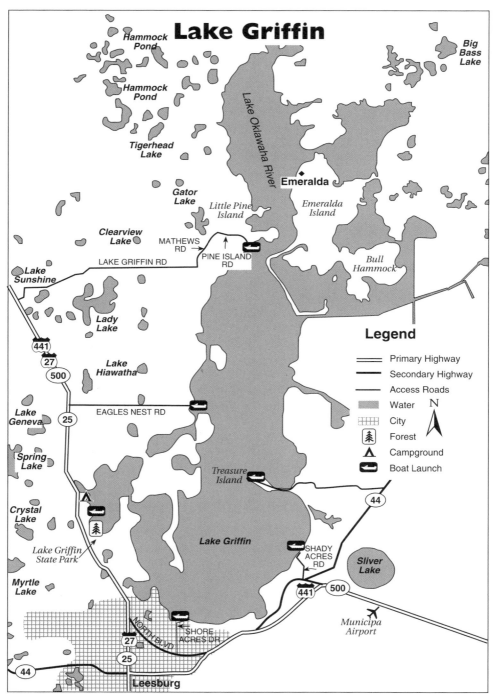

Lake Griffin

Hammock Pond

Big Bass Lake

Hammock Pond

Tigerhead Lake

Lake Oklawaha River

Gator Lake

Clearview Lake

MATHEWS RD

LAKE GRIFFIN RD

PINE ISLAND RD

Little Pine Island

Emeralda

Emeralda Island

Bull Hammock

Lake Sunshine

Lady Lake

Lake Hiawatha

EAGLES NEST RD

Lake Geneva

Spring Lake

Crystal Lake

Lake Griffin State Park

Myrtle Lake

Treasure Island

Lake Griffin

SHADY ACRES RD

Sliver Lake

Municipal Airport

SHORE ACRES DR

NORTH BLVD

Leesburg

Legend

═══	Primary Highway
▬▬▬	Secondary Highway
───	Access Roads
	Water
	City
⚘	Forest
▲	Campground
▬	Boat Launch

N

There are several public access points for Lake Griffin. From the intersection of US 27 and SR 44 in Leesburg, go north on US 27 for 3 miles to Lake Griffin State Park. Enter to your right and the road goes straight to the one-lane ramp. There is paved parking for about 50 vehicles, and camping/picnic facilities are available.

By continuing north on US 27 for another 1.4 miles, you can access another ramp on the west side of Lake Griffin. Turn right on Eagles Nest Road and go east 2.9 miles to Eagles Nest. There is a one-lane paved ramp with unimproved parking for about four vehicles.

By going another 1.7 miles north on US 27, you can get to productive waters at the north end of Lake Griffin from the west side. Turn right onto Lake Griffin Road and go 5.1 miles east, following the signs to the paved one-lane ramp that puts you in the canal of a trailer park community.

Perhaps the best ramp in the area is in Leesburg itself. Hurlong Park provides access to the southern portion of the Lake Griffin. It is accessed directly off US 27 and the single lane ramp has paved parking for 15 vehicles.

About 2 miles east of Leesburg, at the intersection of US 441 and CR 44, cross the intersection and go 0.6 mile on Shady Acres Road to another ramp. This ramp is overgrown and has unimproved parking for only three vehicles. I do not recommend using this ramp.

Knight Boat Ramp at Hurlong Park in Leesburg offers good access to the southern end of Lake Griffin.

Rodman Reservoir

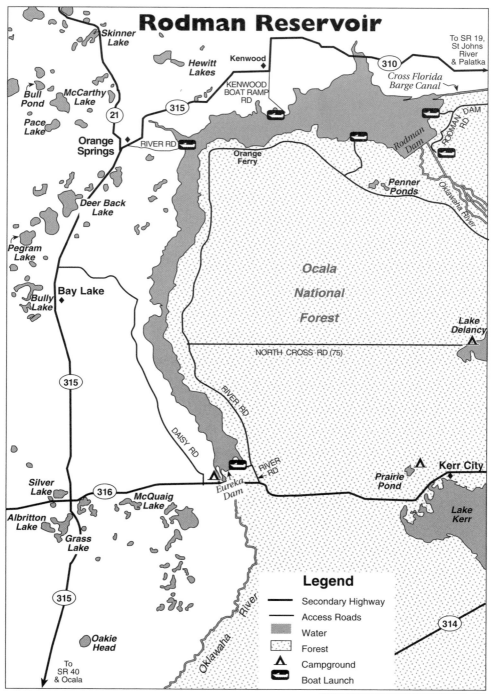

To SR 19,
St Johns
River
& Palatka

Cross Florida
Barge Canal

Skinner Lake

Hewitt Lakes

Kenwood

KENWOOD BOAT RAMP RD

Bull Pond

McCarthy Lake

Pace Lake

Orange Springs

RIVER RD

Orange Ferry

Rodman Dam

RODMAN RD

Penner Ponds

Oklawaha River

Deer Back Lake

Pegram Lake

Bay Lake

Bully Lake

Ocala

National

Forest

Lake Delancy

NORTH CROSS RD (75)

RIVER RD

DAISY RD

Silver Lake

McQuaig Lake

Eureka Dam

RIVER RD

Prairie Pond

Kerr City

Albritton Lake

Grass Lake

Lake Kerr

315

Oklawaha River

Oakie Head

To SR 40 & Ocala

314

Legend

——	Secondary Highway
—	Access Roads
▓	Water
∴	Forest
⛺	Campground
🚤	Boat Launch

© WILDERNESS ADVENTURES PRESS, INC.

Oklawaha River
(Lake Griffin to Rodman Reservoir)

The Oklawaha River winds northward for about 25 miles from Lake Griffin through the western edge of Ocala National Forest and on to Rodman Reservoir. The river has a definite channel as it moves out of the marsh in central Florida, and although there are many named lakes east of the river, these natural lakes are independent of the Oklawaha River system.

This portion of the Oklawaha is very scenic, with a canopy of trees overhead. Silver Springs, the largest spring in the state, is about 4 miles to the west and there is a ramp where SR 40 (Delk's Bluff Bridge) crosses the Oklawaha River just below (north) where Silver River deposits the spring's crystal clear waters into the river.From Ocala, go west on SR 40 for about 8 miles. The ramp is on the south side of the road at the west end of the bridge.

Bass fishing is good throughout this portion of the river, especially in the spring. Bream, redbreast, and spotted sunfish are usually found out of the river's channels in slow moving or still water. The water is very clear, and fish that you can see will likely see you, as well. A fluorocarbon leader testing no more than 6 pounds will help; make it a longer one, perhaps 10 or 11 feet.

This portion of the river ends at Eureka Dam and the river widens and pools to form Rodman Reservoir (Lake Oklawaha).

Rodman Reservoir (Lake Oklawaha)

Rodman Reservoir (9,200 acres) begins with the Eureka Dam crossing the Oklawaha River. For several years after being impounded in 1968, Rodman Reservoir was noted as one of the outstanding bass fisheries in the country. As it aged, the bass fishing declined, but some really large bass (several over 10 pounds) are caught every year. Recent drawdowns (drawdowns are presently conducted every 3-4 years to control aquatic weed growth, as well as for fish enhancement) have returned this great lake to prominence. In 2000, Florida's two largest bass (17 and 15 pounds) came from Rodman Reservoir, and the Florida Fish and Wildlife Conservation Commission recently selected it as one of the top 10 bass lakes in the state.

Rodman Reservoir is long and narrow by large lake standards. Most Florida lakes are shallow, round, saucer-shaped lakes, but the "dog-leg right" appearance of Rodman reminds you that you are fishing a river channel that has been flooded. The upper (southern) portion is still riverine as it continues to meander northward after the dam for about 8 miles. The channel averages 10-14 feet deep, and on both sides shallow water filled with stumps, logs, and beds of thick hydrilla make navigation difficult and fishing excellent. This upper area is also noted for redbreast and stump-knockers, and the reservoir's shorelines are the spawning ground for bream in the spring. The stump fields also give up good stringers of big crappie.

The middle portion of Rodman Reservoir turns from a south-to-north course to a west-to-east course as it runs along the northern boundary of the Ocala National Forest for 3 or 4 miles. The 90-degree change in the channel's direction ensures that a flyfisher can find places to get out of the wind. The lake begins to widen after the direction change, with several points and coves filled with cover.

The lower portion of the reservoir is substantially wider with a less erratic shoreline. The shoreline in the main pool, however, is noted for its crappie in the spring, as well as bluegill and shellcrackers. The average depth of the channel has increased to 15-20 feet as it moves toward Rodman Dam in the southeast corner. Rodman Dam precludes boaters from access to the remainder of the Oklawaha River as it moves on to the St. Johns River. In the northeast corner, though, the Cross Florida Barge Canal gives boaters access to the St. Johns River.

You are not going to be able to run your boat wide-open safely on Rodman unless you are very familiar with the stump fields. There are too many submerged trees, both fallen and cut to stumps, to risk prop damage. But doesn't it all look so fishable? As you attempt to pattern your targeted species, look for other variables in addition to the woody cover. It might be a certain depth at which the fish are holding, submerged grass leading to a flat, or the river's old channel edge. In the spring, it is pretty straightforward. Toss your weedless, deer-hair popper into the thickest cover you can find in shallow water and make a lot of commotion for a shot at a memorable bass. During the rest of the year, bass will spend their days in the deeper water of the nearby channel, moving onto the stump flats during low-light conditions to feed. The popper will work early and late in the day, but you will need to probe your way toward deeper water with a Clouser or similar pattern during the middle of the day.

For crappie, the Clouser is also the fly of choice, but not too heavy in the shallow stump fields. Try either a size 2 or 4. You might want to go to a bend-back hook or a fly with a weedguard to prevent getting hung up on underwater wood. For bream, it's a small popper in size 8 or10.

Consider using a heavier leader while fishing Rodman. Your line is likely to cut a zigzag through the stumps with a fish of any size, and you will appreciate the abrasion resistance as you and Mr. Big saw back and forth against a couple of trees. Fluorocarbon works well for leader material under these conditions.

Below Rodman Dam, fly fishing for striped bass can be excellent in the tailrace in spring and early summer. Fly patterns in white (often with an olive back) that imitate threadfin shad work well. Look to general streamers and Lefty's Deceivers when the water is moving, and when combined with cloud cover or low-light conditions, the stage is set for some exciting fishing. If you are in a school of feeding stripers, also give a white foam Gurgler a few minutes of your time.

There is a ramp providing access to the upper (southern) portion of the lake. From Ocala, take SR 40 east for 5.5 miles to CR 315. Turn left and go north on CR 315 for about 10 miles to CR 316. Turn right and go east for 3.5 miles to River Road. Turn left and go 0.5 mile north on River Road, and then turn left to the ramp (0.5 mile) near the Eureka Dam.

Ramps to the middle portion of Rodman Reservoir are approached from the

Rodman Reservoir's shallow water is filled with stumps, logs, and vegetation. Navigation is difficult, but some behemoth bass make this area their home.

Striped bass fishing can be excellent below the Rodman Dam
tailrace in spring and early summer.

north side. Take SR 19 south out of Palatka for 9.1 miles. At the intersection with CR 310, turn right and go west for 7.9 miles to the intersection with SR 315. Turn left and go south 0.8 mile on CR 315. As CR 315 makes a sweeping right turn, continue straight onto Kenwood Boat Ramp Road to the lakeside launch site. There are two one-lane ramps with unimproved parking for about 60 vehicles.

By continuing on SR 315 through the sweeping right turn and going another 5.1 miles, you will come to the community of Orange Springs. Turn left onto N.E. 245th Street and go 1.6 miles to a one-lane ramp with paved parking for about 20 vehicles.

To access the lower portion of Rodman Reservoir, take SR 19 south out of Palatka for 9.4 miles, and just after crossing the Cross Florida Barge Canal, turn right onto Rodman Road and go 3 miles east to the Rodman Recreatonal Area. There are two ramps here. The first (Rodman Area) goes to the reservoir. Bear right 0.75 miles and follow the signs to reach it. There are campsites and two one-lane ramps with unimproved parking for about 20 vehicles. The second ramp is just below Rodman Dam and returns you to the Oklawaha River. There are two one-lane ramps with paved parking for about 40 vehicles.

LOWER OKLAWAHA RIVER (RODMAN DAM TO ST. JOHNS RIVER)

As SR 19 crosses the Oklawaha River, there is a one-lane ramp on the south side of the bridge with unimproved parking for about five vehicles. This would put you about midway between Rodman Dam and the St. Johns River. Here, the Oklawaha River is wide and easily navigated, with shoreline structure offering the best opportunity for flyfishers to take bass and bream. Downstream, sunshine bass and striped bass will move out of the St. Johns River and move toward the dam. Look for feeding fish in early morning and during periods of limited visibility. To get to the bridge, take SR 19 south out of Palatka for about 13 miles. Cross the SR 19 Bridge, and the ramp is on your left.

ST. JOHNS RIVER (PALATKA TO JACKSONVILLE)

In the area where the Oklawaha River enters from the west, the influx of such a large volume of pure, fresh water lowers the salinity of the St. Johns River. Directly across the river and entering from the east, Dunns Creek adds even more fresh water. Fish this area! The place where most small feeder creeks enter the St. Johns River could be considered hotspots, but this one sizzles. Recall that Dunns Creek (see Crescent Lake in the Middle Basin) has several deep holes. These attract largemouth and stripers in the midday heat of summer. Near the mouth of Dunns Creek, there is the Seven Sisters Island area. There are many experienced flyfishers who regard this as the premier fishing spot along the entire St. Johns River system. The islands cause the water to be channeled as it flows around them and the current increases. This makes fly fishing viable when the river is otherwise sluggish. There will be eddies on the backside of these islands that hold largemouth and stripers in the summer and fall. The topwater action can be fantastic for flyfishers using poppers and large Gurglers.

There is a small ramp at the south end of the bridge where US 17 crosses Dunns Creek. This ramp is about 7.5 miles south of Palatka and the unpaved launch site will only accommodate small boats. There is unimproved parking under the bridge for about 5 vehicles.

As we move up the St. Johns River, there is a ramp on the east side at Shell Harbour. This area is across the river from the marsh between the Oklawaha River and the Cross Florida Barge Canal, about 3 miles north of Welaka. To get to this ramp, take US 17 south out of Palatka, crossing the St. Johns. Go about 10.2 mile and turn right on CR 309 near Satsuma. Go 2.6 miles to Shell Harbour Road and turn right. The single-lane ramp is 0.3 mile ahead at the end of Shell Harbour Road. There is unimproved parking for 10 vehicles.

Before Palatka, there is another ramp on the west side of the river across from where Dunns Creek and Murphy Creek enter the St. Johns River. The creeks in the area across from the ramp frequently have sunshine and striped bass around their mouths. To get to this ramp, go south on Moseley Avenue in Palatka. At the end by the golf course, bear right toward Ravine State Gardens and then make a left onto Lundy Road. Continue on Lundy Road about 2 miles to the ramp at the end.

Moving on toward Palatka, the river has steep, well-defined banks. It is still narrow and with the additional water being carried, the depths reach as much as 35 feet in the main channel. This is an area where surface action from schooling stripers can break out in early morning and late evening. Watch for diving gulls to give this away. You will want to race over in your boat and use both the wind and current to move you into good casting position. Try a Lefty's Deceiver or a light colored popper.

In Palatka, there are ramps at each end of the Memorial Bridge where US 17 and SRs 15, 20, and 100 cross the St. Johns. On the west end of the bridge is the Palatka Ramp. Turn south onto 3rd Street (River Street) and go three blocks to the park entrance on the left. There is a double-lane ramp with paved parking for 28 vehicles.

On the east end of Memorial Bridge is the East Palatka ramp. Go 1.9 miles east on

*Riverdale Park gives access to some good crappie
and bream fishing in the St. Johns River.*

US 17 to Pico Road. Turn right and go 0.2 mile to the single-lane ramp at the end of the road. There is unimproved parking for 20 vehicles.

The next ramp downriver is about 3 river miles north at Elgin Grove. From East Palatka, exit US 17 and go north on CR 207 for 4.1 miles. Turn left onto CR 207A and go west for 4.3 miles to East River Road. Turn left on East River Road and go one block to Magnolia Avenue. Turn right on Magnolia Avenue and go 0.4 mile to the single-lane ramp at the end of the road. There is unimproved parking for 10 vehicles.

The St. Johns River widens substantially after Palatka and ceases to meander as it moves northward to the Atlantic. The depth drops off from the pre-Palatka numbers to around 20 feet and all the way to Jacksonville, the river is somewhat like a lagoon. Fishing for bass and crappie remains good, although not at the same high level as the Middle Basin. The bass do not seem to move around as much in this area as they did in the defined lakes of the Middle Basin. Instead, school-sized bass lie in grass beds beside shallow flats and wait for baitfish to pass by. The topwater feeding is furious, but often short-lived. When it stops, put on a Clouser and fish deeper, especially around any nearby structure.

Fishing for sunshine bass and striped bass can be excellent, especially at the mouths of creeks in the fall and around the larger bridges during the rest of the year. Flyfishers using Deceiver patterns frequently catch striped bass up to 25 pounds.

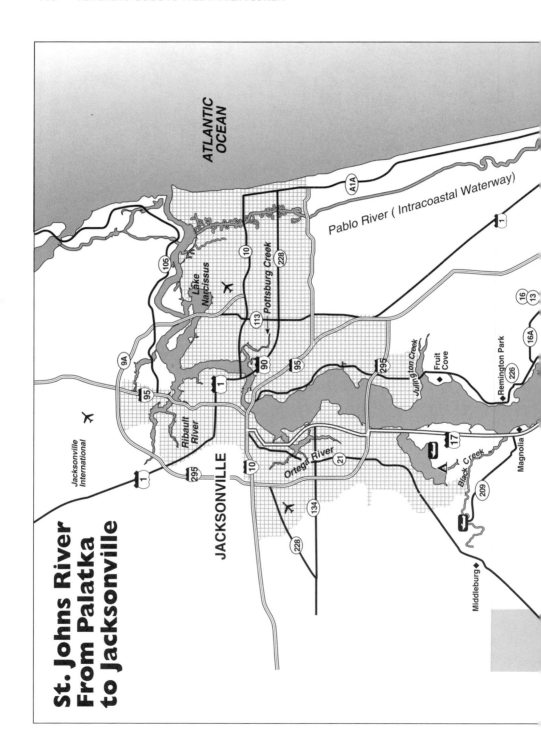

St. Johns River From Palatka to Jacksonville

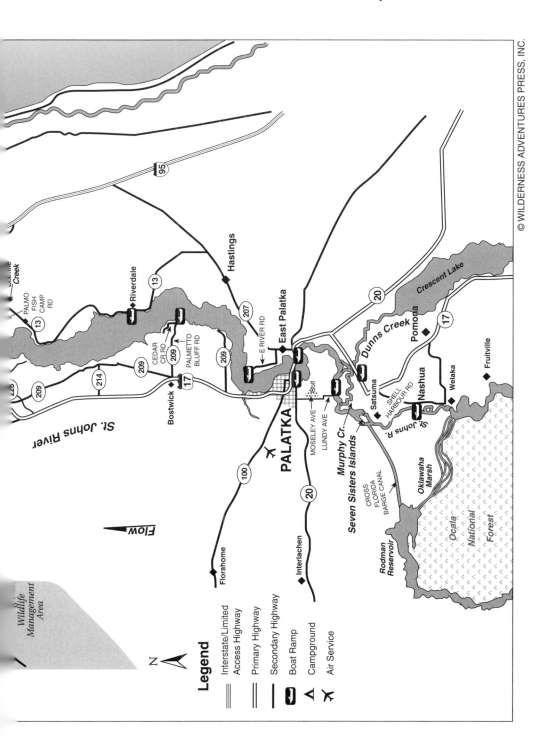

© WILDERNESS ADVENTURES PRESS, INC.

Legend

Interstate/Limited
Access Highway

Primary Highway

Secondary Highway

Boat Ramp

Campground

Air Service

An excellent launch site for the lower St. Johns River is at the end of Shands Bridge near Green Cove Springs.

Look for schooling activity early and late in the day, especially if it is overcast.

These same creek mouths have very good populations of bream. Look for red-breast, stumpknockers, bluegill, and sunfish around any standing trees and stumps in the water. Also, the shoreline just above and below creek mouths often has grass, lily pads, and weed growth that holds largemouth and crappie. In the springtime, bream fishing can be excellent along shoreline vegetation and cover.

What this section of the river lacks in scenery beauty (and that is only relative to waters in the Upper and Middle Basins, as the St. Johns still retains a charm that is all its own), it more than makes up for it in diversity of fish. The addition of several saltwater species moving with the incoming tide offers flyfishers a unique opportunity to catch both freshwater and saltwater fish on successive casts. (A saltwater license is required to take any saltwater species.)

Continuing downriver about 5 more miles, there are two ramps across from one another. On the west side of the St. Johns is a single-lane ramp at Palmetto Bluff. From Palatka, go north on US 17 about 7 miles to SR 209 (do not take the first CR 209 about 3.5 miles north of town). Turn right onto CR 209 and go 4.5 miles to Cedar

Creek Road. Turn left onto Cedar Creek Road and go one block, then left onto the boat ramp road. The ramp is one block on your right. There is unimproved parking for 10 vehicles.

Farther north on the east side is the ramp at Riverdale. From East Palatka, turn north on SR 207 and go 13.2 miles through Hastings. About 3.2 miles after leaving town bear left onto CR 13. Go north on CR 13 for 8.8 miles and the one-lane ramp (Riverdale Park) will be on the left at the community of Riverdale. There is unimproved parking for about 10 vehicles.

There are several ramps another 10 miles downstream near the town of Green Cove Springs. The first four are on the east side of the river. For each of these, directions will be from the east end of the Shands Bridge (which crosses the St. Johns River east of Green Cove Springs) where SR 13 and 16 come together.

At Palmo Cove there is a single-lane ramp with unimproved parking for 5 vehicles. From the SR 13/16 intersection at the east end of the Shands Bridge, go south about 5 miles (1.2 miles after SR 13 and 16 split), staying on SR 13. Turn right onto Palmo Fish Camp Road and go 1.9 miles to the ramp at the end of the road.

There is another ramp at Sixmile Creek, about 1 mile south on SR 13 after SR 13 and 16 split. This gravel ramp is now an afterthought of a bar/restaurant establishment that also conducts eco tours. They will permit launches during the week when the parking lot is not being used, but not on busy weekends.

At Trout Creek Park, there is a double-lane ramp and unimproved parking for 25 vehicles. From the intersection of SR 13 and 16 at the east end of Shands Bridge, go south on SR 16 for 2.7 miles to Trout Creek Park. Turn left onto Collier Creek Road and make an immediate left into the park.

The next ramp is also south of the intersection of SR 13 and 16 at the east end of Shands Bridge. Go south for 1.1 miles and turn right on Moody Canal Road. Go right at the fork in the road to the one-lane gravel ramp with very limited parking.

On the west side of the St. Johns River, there are two ramps near Green Cove Springs. About two miles east of Green Cove Springs, there is paved ramp on SR 16 at the west end of Shands Bridge. Turn onto Shands Pier Road and go to the one-lane ramp. There is unimproved parking for about eight vehicles. The other ramp is located where you leave Green Cove Springs and head north on US 17. The ramp is on the right side of the road about 0.5 mile after leaving town (as you cross Governor's Creek Bridge), with paved parking for 25 vehicles.

Georges Lake

Georges Lake (650 acres), like most lakes in central Florida, is a relatively shallow lake lying in marshy wetlands. The surrounding shoreline is more developed than most lakes, but the southeastern part of the lake is shallower and less developed. Falling Branch Creek flows from the southeast corner for about 12 miles to the St. Johns River.

The bass in Georges Lake run small, but there is a good population of bream and crappie. Try the docks in the spring for crappie by allowing a sink-tip line to fall a couple of feet before beginning to strip. The crappie will not want to rise very far to take a fly. The bream can be found from spring through fall along the southeastern shoreline and the vegetation that extends out from it.

To get to Georges Lake, go north from Palatka on US 17 for 11 miles and turn left (west) onto State Road 214 (Georges Lake Road). Go 8 miles and then left onto South Bellamy Road. Continue for 3.8 miles and Georges Lake is on your left.

BLACK CREEK

Black Creek offers excellent bass fishing in the dark, tea-colored water that gives the creek its name. The dark color comes from the tannic acid in the roots of the cypress trees that line the banks. Black Creek offers a picturesque 13-mile run to the St. Johns River with lily pads, stumps, and shoreline trees providing sanctuary for largemouth bass, crappie, and several species of bream. In addition, there are some deep holes—believed to be the result of collapsed limestone deposits or caverns—that go as deep as 80 feet. This is most unusual for Florida freshwater fishing.

Largemouth bass fishing is excellent during the spawning months of March, April, and May. Crappie are not as good in Black Creek as they are in Lake Asbury to the south of the fork just after Middleburg. Fishing for redbreast, bluegill, and sunfish is excellent around shoreline cover throughout the summer. Look for striped bass to move up the creek in winter.

Where Black Creek meets the St. Johns River, there is a launch site with 3 one-lane ramps and paved parking for 50 vehicles. This ramp is about 2.5 miles north of Green Cove Springs. From US 17/SR 15, make a right onto Knight Road to the ramps.

The ramp at Rideout Ferry will get you to about the middle point of Black Creek. Take Exit 4 off I-295 and go south on SR 21 for 5.1 miles. Turn left onto SR 224 (not the SR 224 that you crossed after going 2.4 miles on SR 21) and go 2.6 miles to the intersection with SR 220. Turn right on SR 220 and go 2.5 miles to SR 209. Turn left on SR 209 and go 1.8 miles to Old Ferry Road. Turn left and go 0.5 mile to the single-lane ramp at Rideout Ferry. There is paved parking for 13 vehicles.

There is another ramp farther upstream in the town of Middleburg. Take Exit 4 off I-295 as above and continue south on SR 21 for 12.3 miles to Middleburg. Turn left onto SR 220E (Main Street) and go 1 mile to the single-lane ramp. There is paved parking for 20 vehicles and unimproved overflow parking for another 20 vehicles.

DOCTORS LAKE

Doctors Lake (3,397 acres) lies on the west side of the St. Johns River about 3 miles south of the Buckman (I-295) Bridge. The US 17 Bridge marks the beginning of the lake near the St. Johns River. The water is tea-colored, and the lake floor drops to about 12 feet in the middle. There are numerous coves and creeks that break the wind. Grass is the primary vegetation in the southern portion of the lake and Duck

Creek, Swimming Run Creek, and Mainard Brook offer good habitat for largemouth and bream in these southern reaches.

Along the northwest side, there are numerous docks in the area of Orange Park. These offer fabulous structure for fish to forage around and a mixed bag of large-mouth, crappie, and snook can usually be found in this area. Other saltwater species come and go with the tides.

To get to Doctors Lake, take Exit 3 off I-295 near Jacksonville and go south through Orange Park for 5.7 miles. Turn right onto SR 220 and go 1.7 miles. Turn right again onto Lakeshore Drive and the double-lane ramp (Lakeshore Boat Docking Facilities) is 1.4 miles ahead on your right at Hog Point as the road makes a sweeping left turn to run along the side of the lake. There is unimproved parking for about 40 vehicles.

Suzie Reihl's redfish moved into Doctors Lake with an incoming tide.

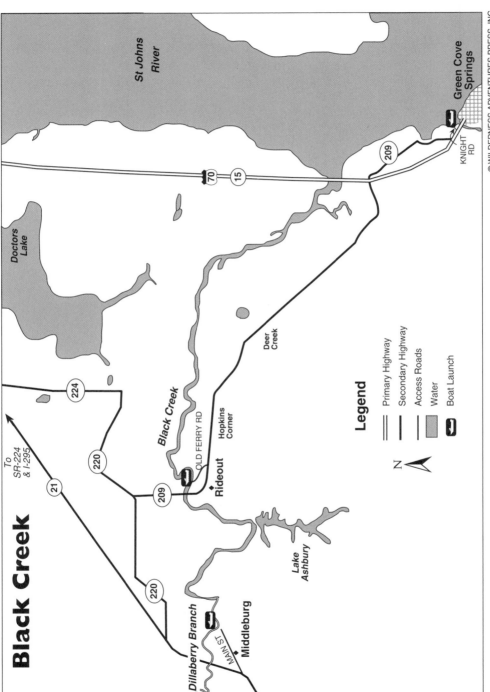

Black Creek

St Johns River

Doctors Lake

Green Cove Springs

KNIGHT RD

209

70
15

Deer Creek

224

To SR-224 & I-295

21

220

209

Black Creek

OLD FERRY RD

Hopkins Corner

Rideout

220

Lake Ashbury

Dillaberry Branch

MAIN ST

Middleburg

Legend

≡ Primary Highway
| Secondary Highway
| Access Roads
▨ Water
🛥 Boat Launch

N

© WILDERNESS ADVENTURES PRESS, INC.

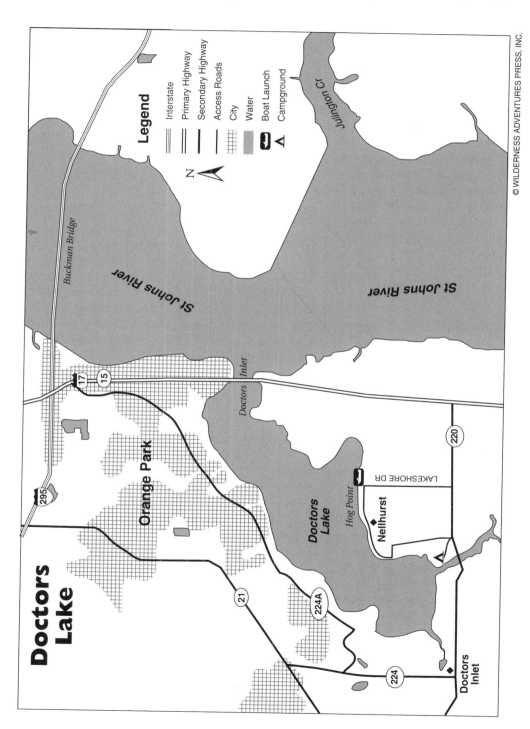

Doctors
Lake

© WILDERNESS ADVENTURES PRESS, INC.

Region 1 Waters Not Associated with the St. Johns River System

There are several lakes within Region 1, both manmade and natural, that have significant fisheries but do not permit boaters to gain access to the St. Johns River. Many of these are quite small and they are usually part of a system of lakes in an area. Those in the Ocala National Forest tend to be deep (by Florida standards) and filled with dark, tea-colored water. They are not particularly fertile, usually supporting smaller bass. These lakes, however, do have a few really large bass that have become experienced as they age. These lakes also have good bream populations around their shorelines.

In the headwaters region of the St. Johns River, the marsh has suffered from drainage modifications and farming (agricultural and livestock) runoff in the past three decades. Large amounts of soil and runoff that would have been filtered as they slowly moved through the marsh have been deposited directly into the headwaters of the river. Clear, sandy bottoms have become shallow, muck and slime-filled areas that often become impassable during periods of low water. Recognizing the problem, agencies from local, state, and federal governments are working together to try and correct the problem. Part of the solution has been to create a series of large "retention reservoirs" into which the drainage and runoff waters are pumped. Here, the highly fertile sediment will be given an opportunity to settle to the bottom and be absorbed by the reservoir's vegetation. During times of drought, these waters can be made available for irrigation of farmland.

There are five retention reservoirs in the St. Johns River restoration project: the St. Johns Water Management Area (Farm 13/Stick Marsh Reservoir); the Blue Cypress Water Management Area (Ansin-Garcia Reservoir); the Knight Property (as yet unnamed); the 3-Forks Reservoir; and the Fort Drum Marsh Conservation Area. These large, manmade reservoirs tend to be very shallow and choked with weeds. They also offer incredible waterfowl hunting areas, and one of these, Farm 13/Stick Marsh, has already gained national recognition for the fishing opportunities available in its fertile waters, which will be discussed in detail in the pages that follow.

The Fort Drum Marsh Conservation Area (7,000 acres) is quite shallow and has not been stocked with fish. The existing fish population was not significant and the area is not recommended at this time.

The Knight Property is located west of the Farm 13/Stick Marsh Reservoir and has an excellent population of bass and bream. There is no boat access, however, except by carrying a boat over a levee. This is an area to watch, as there are plans to breach a levee in the future, which could make this a hot lake in a few years.

The 3-Forks Marsh Conservation Area (10,000 acres) was flooded in 1999 and the fishery is not fully developed. However, expectations are that this will be the premier recreational fishing gem of the entire project.

Ansin-Garcia Reservoir

Ansin-Garcia Reservoir (10,750 acres) is a manmade reservoir that averages between 1.5 and 6 feet deep. Annual water level fluctuations often make it too shallow to navigate during periods of low water. There is a variety of vegetation on Ansin-Garcia, including cattails, hydrilla, peppergrass, and several species of floating water lilies.

There is a good fishery for smaller largemouth bass, and an occasional trophy is produced. Crappie and bream are also present. Topwater flies made of deer hair and popping bugs are favorites here.

To get to Ansin-Garcia Reservoir, take Exit 68 from I-95 near Vero Beach and go west on SR 60 for 7.1 miles to SR 512. Turn right and go north 1.5 miles to the reservoir. There is a double-lane ramp and paved parking.

Fellsmere Reservoir (Farm 13/Stick Marsh)

The "Stick Marsh" (6,500 acres) was created in 1987 and opened to fishing in 1989. It quickly became one of the best bass fishing lakes in the country, if not in the entire world. Averaging about 4 to 8 feet deep, the flooded timber has yielded numerous bass of 10 pounds or more from around trees and hydrilla. Catches of 50 to 100 bass a day during the first five years were common.

Although catch rates have declined the past five years, Jim Porter, who has fished Farm 13/Stick Marsh 100 to 150 days a year since it opened in 1989, says, "I will be the first to admit that the catch rates are down from the heyday years of 1990 to 1995. But that decline has nothing to do with a decline in the numbers of fish. It has to do strictly with the anglers' abilities to adapt and adjust to the changing habitat." His log books support his conclusions. From 1990 through 1995, he caught over 4,000 bass each year. In 1995, he averaged 38 bass per trip, with trips seldom lasting more than 4 hours. Since 1996, he has averaged about 2,500 bass per year, and his catch rate is now about 24 fish per trip. The average size is now between 2 and 3 pounds, although he still catches 250 bass a year over 5 pounds. About a dozen 10-pounders come over the side of his boat each year, with the largest to date a whopping 15.2 pounds.

As it has begun to age just a little, Farm 13/Stick Marsh has remained an outstanding fishery through the turn of the century and the Florida Fish and Wildlife Conservation Commission had an easy pick when they selected the Stick Marsh as one of the top 10 bass lakes in Florida. To maintain the world-class fishery, lake regulations require that all bass must be returned to the water unharmed.

Upon launching at Farm 13/Stick Marsh, you enter a rim canal with a high levee to the left. To your right, beyond a very low dike, are flooded trees and brush remaining in their original state as far as the eye can see. (Hence the name Stick Marsh.) This old boggy swamp is now at a depth of about eight feet.

There is a 90-degree turn about two miles down the canal. Here, the Stick Marsh remains on the right with several openings through the dike to permit access. On the left, beyond another small dike, is Farm 13. Clumps of flooded trees remaining from

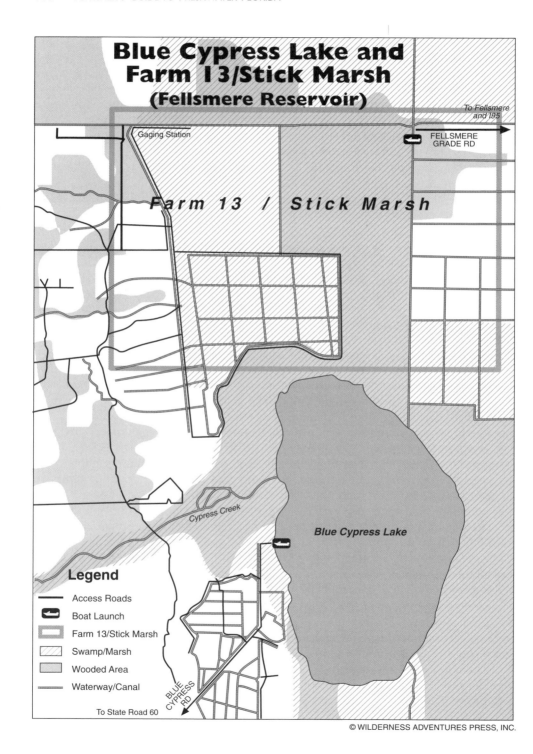

Blue Cypress Lake and Farm 13/Stick Marsh
(Fellsmere Reservoir)

To Fellsmere
and I95

Gaging Station

FELLSMERE
GRADE RD

Farm 13 / Stick Marsh

Cypress Creek

Blue Cypress Lake

Legend

— Access Roads
Boat Launch
Farm 13/Stick Marsh
Swamp/Marsh
Wooded Area
— Waterway/Canal

BLUE CYPRESS RD

To State Road 60

© WILDERNESS ADVENTURES PRESS, INC.

an orchard are neatly arranged in an area that is mostly open. A line of straight brush marks an old levee that parallels a manmade irrigation canal that was necessary for the old farm of about 8-10 acres. With the entire farm diked and flooded, the canal now has 20 feet of water in it. There are also numerous other smaller canals and ditches, along with submerged roads, culverts, and potholes. Shallow grass beds closely border the main canal.

The dike separating the main canal and Farm 13 has been breached in several places to permit boat access. These openings allow for a slight movement of water, and this current is a key to successful fishing along the dike. Moving surface water can also be produced by wind, as the Farm 13/Stick Marsh area is subject to coastal winds. Look for islands of vegetation and water that may be moving between them with eddies behind. Bass on this reservoir love to hang on the break line between the eddy and the wind-blown water. Frequently, moving water can also be found near the active water level control gates that feed into Farm 13, as well as the control gate near the launch area. Flyfishers should fish early and late in the day, if possible. In summer, heavy rains cause frequent discharges from the water control structures located on the reservoir and the area around these can produce some outstanding catches in moving water.

Fellsmere Reservoir (Farm 13/Stick Marsh)
is behind the rim canal and row of palms.

You'll need a fly rod with some backbone for this area. An 8-weight rod is not too big. For the most part, you will be fishing near the surface and a weight-forward floating line is a good choice. A deer-haired frog pattern with a size 1 or 1/0 hook, protected by a monofilament weedguard, that makes a commotion and pushes a lot of water works well.

Crappie fishing is excellent around the fallen and standing timber, as well as in the hydrilla in the central portion of the reservoir. Some of the best crappie fishing, however, is found in the rim canal around the Stick Marsh where the water depth averages a little more than in the flooded timber. Look for the crappie to be in deeper areas during the summer and fall. They'll begin to move into flooded timber late in the winter. By spring, they seem to be everywhere, especially near cover in shallower water. During one four-month period (December through March), 250,000 crappie were estimated to have been taken from Farm 13/Stick Marsh. Try casting a chartreuse Clouser or similar brightly colored flies. These can be fished on a floating line in the spring, but the rest of the year will require an intermediate sink-tip line to get the fly down to the "speckled perch." The crappie average about one pound, with heavier fish very common.

In the rim canal around the Stick Marsh, fishing for bream holds it own with the excellent bass and crappie fishing. The bream also run big, averaging about a pound and easily covering the palm of a man's hand. These are scrappy fish on light rods. Cast a terrestrial pattern toward the canal's edge in the spring and early summer and success is almost certain.

From late fall to late spring, the Stick Marsh is heavily fished (note the 150 parking spaces with an overflow area). Plan accordingly.

To get to the Stick Marsh, take Exit 69 off I-95 and go west on State Road 512 for 3.2 miles to Fellsmere. Turn right on SR 507 and go north for 3.4 miles to Fellsmere Grade Road. Turn left on Fellsmere Grade Road and go west for 6.2 miles to the double-lane ramp at Barney Green. There is unimproved gravel parking for 150 vehicles (with additional parking along the roadway).

BLUE CYPRESS LAKE

This is one of Florida's most scenic lakes. Blue Cypress Lake is 4½ miles wide, 7 miles long, covers 6,555 acres, and has numerous creeks entering along the marsh and cypress swamp shoreline. The lake has good fishing for largemouth bass year-round near fallen trees and standing cypress. In addition, the FWC has placed fish attractors in the lake that provide habitat for largemouth bass, crappie, and bream. Since 1997, sunshine bass have also been stocked in the lake by the FWC. The sunshine bass, along with crappie, are best caught during cooler months. In the spring, bream fishing heats up with bluegill fanning their crater-like beds along the shoreline. Other members of the bream family that will grab a fly in the waters of Blue Cypress Lake include the shellcracker, warmouth, and spotted sunfish. Try the canal on the north side and along edges of lily pads.

To access the lake, take State Road 60 west from the Vero Beach exit (Exit 68) off I-95 for 17.5 miles. At Blue Cypress Road, turn right and go 4.5 miles north to the single-lane ramp. The unimproved parking lot will accommodate 15 vehicles. There is a marina and fish camp nearby where food and fuel can be obtained.

South Lake and Fox Lake

Just west of Titusville in the marshes of the St. Johns National Wildlife Refuge are two lakes that are easily accessed by flyfishers, although they offer no access to the St. Johns River system. Fox Lake (about 250 acres) has a ramp and is connected to South Lake (about 1,000 acres) by a canal.

These two lakes receive quite a bit of fishing pressure from local anglers. Flyfishers not already in the area should probably ignore the small bass and panfish in these shallow, over-fished waters.

To get to Fox Lake, get off I-95 at Exit 79. Go east on State Road 50 for 0.5 mile and turn left onto State Road 405 (South Street). Go north 2.2 miles and turn left at Fox Lake Road and continue west 1.5 miles to the single-lane ramp at Fox Lake Park. There is an unimproved parking lot that will accommodate 20 vehicles and bathroom/picnic facilities are available.

Lake Butler Chain

Lying northeast of Lake Monroe in the community of Deltona are numerous lakes between 75 and 150 acres. There is no public access to these lakes, and while of interest to local residents for bream and crappie, they do not have largemouth bass of significant size and do not serve as a destination for visiting flyfishers. These lakes are not the more-famed Butler Chain of Lakes lying in central Florida near the Disney World complex (see Region 3).

Lakes Dias, Dan George, Skull, Winona, Clifton, Odom, Tedder, and Johnson

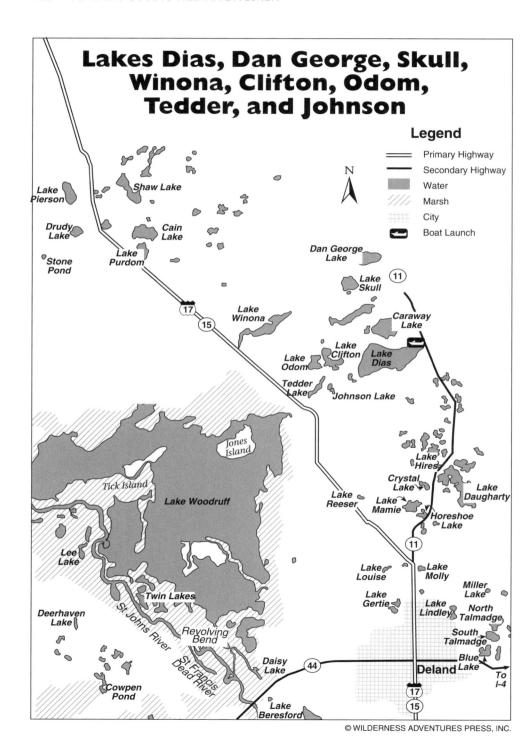

Legend

═══	Primary Highway
────	Secondary Highway
▨	Water
▨	Marsh
▦	City
🚤	Boat Launch

N

Lake Pierson

Shaw Lake

Drudy Lake

Cain Lake

Stone Pond

Lake Purdom

Dan George Lake

Lake Skull (11)

Lake Winona

Caraway Lake

Lake Clifton

Lake Dias

Lake Odom

Tedder Lake

Johnson Lake

Jones Island

Tick Island

Lake Woodruff

Lake Hires

Crystal Lake

Lake Daugharty

Lake Reeser

Lake Mamie

Horeshoe Lake

Lee Lake

(11)

Twin Lakes

St. Johns River

Lake Louise

Lake Molly

Miller Lake

Deerhaven Lake

Revolving Bend

Lake Gertie

Lake Lindley

North Talmadge

South Talmadge

St. Francis Dead River

Daisy Lake (44)

Blue Lake

Deland

To I-4

Cowpen Pond

Lake Beresford

(17)
(15)

© WILDERNESS ADVENTURES PRESS, INC.

LAKE DIAS, DAN GEORGE LAKE, LAKE SKULL, LAKE WINONA, LAKE CLIFTON, LAKE ODOM, TEDDER LAKE, AND JOHNSON LAKE

These lakes are north of Deland and offer good black bass and bream fishing. The black crappie catch is consistently very good, with an occasional large fish being caught. In 1988, a former state record crappie of 3 lbs., 8 oz. was taken from Lake Dias (711 acres). Largemouth bass are limited in number and usually small.

Of these lakes, only Lake Dias has a public ramp. Take Exit 56 off I-4 and go 4.6 miles to Deland. Turn right onto US 17 and go north 3 miles. Bear right onto State Road 11 and go 7.3 miles. The double-lane ramp at lake Dias Park is on your left. The paved parking lot will accommodate 15 vehicles and bathroom/picnic facilities are available.

Lake Dias yielded a former state record 3-pound, 8-ounce crappie in 1988.

LAKE DORR

Lake Dorr (1,765 acres) is one of the Ocala National Forest's larger lakes. Black crappie fishing is good in late winter and early spring and bream fishing can be very good in the summer. The largemouth bass are small, on average, but an occasional trophy-sized fish will be caught.

To reach this dark, tannin-stained lake from State Road 40, turn south on State Road 19 and go 11.7 miles. After passing the Ocala National Forest Recreation Site/Lake Dorr entrance off SR 19, go another 0.3 mile and turn left onto the narrow dirt road. The single-lane ramp is 0.2 mile down the dirt road and the primitive parking will accommodate 15 vehicles. The Ocala National Forest Recreation Site is a user fee area. There is a $2 parking fee for the semi-improved parking and access to the one-lane paved ramp. Campsites ($7) are available.

Lake Dorr offers good bream fishing along its shoreline in summer.

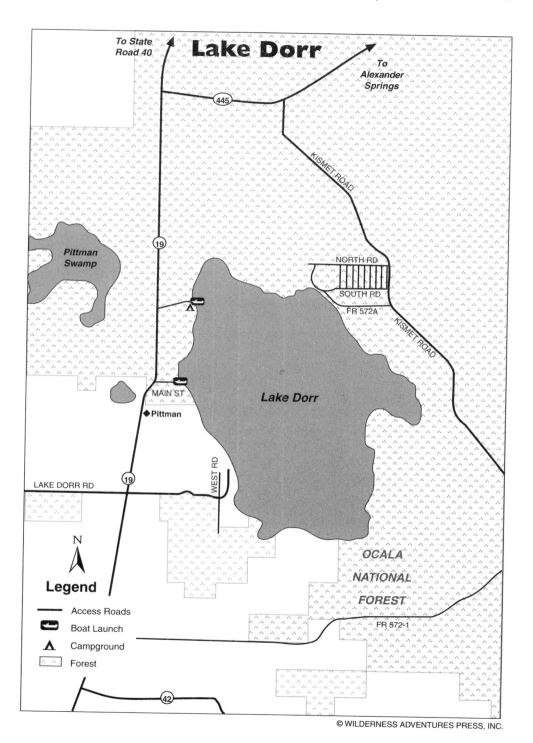

Lake Dorr

Legend
— Access Roads
Boat Launch
Campground
Forest

© WILDERNESS ADVENTURES PRESS, INC.

Farles Lake, Prairie Lake, Chain-O-Lakes, Sellers Lake, Beakman Lake, Wildcat Lake, North Grasshopper Lake, South Grasshopper Lake, Schimmerhorn Lake, Gobbler Lake, and Buck Lake

These lakes are in the Ocala National Forest between 4 and 8 miles west of the St. Johns River and just south of State Road 40. They offer good crappie fishing in the early spring and very good bream fishing from spring through fall. The largemouth bass average only about 10 inches, although an occasional wallhanger in excess of 10 pounds can be caught.

To reach these lakes, get on State Road 40. From the east, take Exit 88 off I-95 and go west about 33 miles on SR 40, crossing the St. Johns River, to State Road 19. The access to unusually clear and deep Wildcat Lake (258 acres) is directly off SR 40. It is on the south side of SR 40, one mile east of the intersection of SR 40 and SR 19. There is a one-lane paved ramp and parking for about 10 vehicles. Wildcat Lake has a park and swimming beach and this is a favorite spot for water skiing in the area. If possible, fish this lake early and late in the day during the middle of the week or during the winter when it gets less recreational use. Largemouth bass average 10 to 14 inches, although bass over 14 pounds have been caught from Wildcat Lake. Black crappie are good in late winter and early spring. Bluegill and shellcrackers are available from spring through fall.

Continuing west on SR 40 for another 1.5 miles, turn south onto SR 19 and go south about 3.3 miles. Access to South Grasshopper Lake is on your left from an unmarked dirt road across from Forest Road 599. You can get to Chain-O-Lakes by turning right on FR 599 and going 1.8 miles. Then turn left on the dirt road and go 0.8 mile to Chain-O-Lakes. By going east on the lake, you can access Sellers Lake and then Beakman Lake. These can also be accessed from SR 19 3.5 miles south of the SR 19/40 intersection. There is a one-lane paved ramp with parking for three vehicles off the right side of SR 19

Continue south on SR 19 another 1.7 miles, turn right on SR 445A and go 1 miles, and then turn right onto FR 595. Go 1.3 miles and turn left, and the dirt road leads to Buck Lake 0.5 mile ahead. From FR 595 above, by going another 1 mile (2.3 miles after turning right onto FR 595 from SR 445A) you can access Farles Lake on your right.

Lake Margaret

Lying between Crescent Lake and the St. Johns River (Little Lake George), Lake Margaret has good bream fishing in the spring and throughout the summer along the shoreline, especially in the southwest corner of the lake.

To get to Lake Margaret, go west on CR 308 for about 5 miles from Crescent City. Turn right and go 1.1 miles to the single-lane ramp with unimproved parking for about eight vehicles.

Other Area Lakes

Holly Lake	Lake Bracey	Lake Saunders
Lake Elso	Clear Lake	Lake Frances
Ella Lake	Lake Lincoln	Lake Gerrude
Island Lake	Lake Eldorado	Lake Leven
North Twin Lake	Lake Delhousie	Sand Lake
Lake Owen	Lake Murphy	Lake Amos
Lake Gibson	Lake Norris	Kitty Lake
East Lake	Lake Swatara	Neighborhood Lakes
Lake Umatilla	Lake Joanna	Lake Lucie
Lake Blanchester	East Crooked Lake	Mt. Plymouth Lake
Lake Murphy	West Crooked Lake	
Lake Senaca	Lake Woodward	

These lakes on either side of Umatilla are loosely connected through the marsh and lowlands to the Oklawaha River by way of the Harris Chain of Lakes. This is not a significant destination for traveling flyfishers, although bream and crappie can be caught, along with smaller bass in the springtime. Only Holly Lake has a boat ramp.

To get to Umatilla, take Exit 51 off I-4 and go west for 18.5 miles to Mount Dora. Turn right onto US 441 and go about 5 miles. Turn right onto SR 19 and go north for about 7 miles to Umatilla. To get to Holly Lake, turn left in Umatilla on SR 450 and go west 3.2 miles to the ramp on your right.

OTHER AREA LAKES, CONTINUED

Doe Lake	Tomahawk Lake	Waldena Lake
Trout Lake	Sunrise Lake	Cemetary Lake
Lake Catherine	Lake Bessiola	Redwater Lake
Lake Mary	Little Lake Bryant	King Lake
Long Lake	Lake Bryant	Deer Lake
West Clearwater Lake	Halfmoon Lake	Lake Jumper
Lake Pendarvis	Mill Dam Lake	Lake Lou
Blue Sink	Clear Lake	Lake Charles
Lake Fay	North Lake	Lake Eaton
Mud Prairie Lake	Owens Lake	Mud Lake
Shoesole Lake	Church Lake	

These lakes and ponds lie along the western edge of the Ocala National Forest, immediately to the east of the Oklawaha River. They vary greatly in depth and most are surrounded by grass with scattered bonnets and lily pads. Bass fishing can be good, although the size of most bass tends to be small. A few really large bass are taken from these waters each year, though. Fishing for bream and crappie is usually good.

Lake Bryant (767 acres) is one of the larger lakes in the Ocala National Forest, but it is not managed by the Forest Service. As such, there is no public ramp, but a fish camp off SR 40 on 183rd Ave. has a fee ramp.

Halfmoon Lake (340 cares) and Mill Dam Lake (210 acres) are easily accessed from SR 40. From Silver Springs, go east on SR 40 for 7 miles. Mill Dam Lake is to your north (left) and the Forest Service has an unimproved ramp about 0.2 mile on Forest Road 79. Halfmoon Lake is to your south (right). Take FR 79 south for 0.8 mile, then turn right on FR 79C and go 0.6 mile to the unimproved ramp.

Region 1 Hub Cities –
The St. Johns River System

The listings that follow are only a small sampling of the facilities available in the major hub cities.

THE UPPER (SOUTHERN) BASIN
Melbourne

ACCOMMODATIONS
Crane Creek Inn, 907 E. Melbourne Avenue, Melbourne, FL 32901; 321-768-6416
Colonial Motel, 1310 S. Harbor City Blvd., Melbourne, FL 32901; 321-723-5141
Guesthouse International Inn, 2900 N. A1A Hwy, Indialantic, FL 32903; 321-779-9994

CAMPING
Sebastian Inlet State Park, 9700 South A1A, Melbourne Beach, FL 32951; offers canoe, kayak, and powerboat rentals, and boat slip rentals are available; the park has 51 campsites overlooking the inlet; 321-984-4852

RESTAURANTS
Applebee's Restaurant, 3001 W. Eua Gallie Blvd., Melbourne, FL 32904; 321-242-8488
Carrabba's Italian Grill, 1571 Palm Bay Road, N.E., Palm Bay; 321-956-1900
Chart House, 2250 Front Street, Melbourne, FL 32904; Riverfront, fine dining, steaks, seafood, opens at 5 p.m.; 321-729-6558
Islands Fish Grill, 111 Fifth Avenue, Indialantic; 321-956-0559

FLY SHOPS AND SPORTING GOODS
Florida Sportsmen, 2771 W. New Haven Ave. Melbourne, FL 32904; 321-956-3474; Harry Goodes Outdoor Shop Inc., 1231 E. New Haven Ave., Melbourne, FL 32901; 321-723-4751
The Back Country, Unit C2046 Treasure Coast, Vero Beach, FL 32960; 561-567-6665
The Sports Authority, 1750 Evans Road., Melbourne, FL 32904; 321-722-0150
West Marine, 1509 N. Harbor City Blvd., Melbourne, FL 32935; 321-253-0980
West Marine, 1024 S. Harbor City Blvd., Melbourne, FL 32901; 321-676-9824

HOSPITALS
Health First Inc., Holmes Regional Center, 1350 S. Hickory St., Melbourne; 321-434-7000

AIRPORTS
Melbourne International Airport, One Air Terminal Parkway, Melbourne, FL 32902; 321-723-6227

AUTO SERVICE
Foreign Car Clinic, 2101 Aurora Road, Melbourne, FL 32935; 800-940-3661

FOR MORE INFORMATION
Melbourne/Palm Bay Area Chamber of Commerce, 1005 E. Strawbridge Ave., Melbourne, FL 32901; 321-724-5400

Titusville

ACCOMMODATIONS
Best Western - Space Shuttle Inn, 3455 Cheney Highway (SR 50), Titusville, FL 32780; 321 269-9100

Day's Inn - Kennedy Space Center, 3755 Cheney Highway (SR 50), Titusville, FL 32780; 321-269-4480

Ramada Inn & Suites, 3500 Cheney Highway (SR 50), Titusville, FL 32780; 321-269-5510

CAMPING
Cape Kennedy KOA, 4513 W. Main Street, Mims, FL 32754; 321-269-7361

RESTAURANTS
Dixie Crossroads Restaurant, 1475 Garden Street, Titusville, FL 32796; outstanding rock shrimp and other seafood items; 321-268-5000

Plantation on the Green, 137 Plantation Dr., Titusville, FL 32780; 321-385-9100

Roadhouse Grill, 3353 Columbia Boulevard, Titusville, FL 32780; 321-267-2408

FLY SHOPS AND SPORTING GOODS
The Fly Fisherman, 1114 S. Washington Ave., Titusville, FL 32780; 321-267-0348

Skeeter Lagoons Bait & Tackle, 3910 S. Washington Ave., Suite 106, Titusville, FL 32780; 321-383-2001

HOSPITALS
Parish Medical Center, 951 N. Washington Ave., Titusville, FL 32796; 321-268-6102

AIRPORTS
Titusville-Cocoa Airport Authority, 355 Golden Knights Boulevard, Titusville, FL 32780; 321-267-8780

AUTO SERVICE
The Auto Shop, 520 N. Washington Ave., Titusville, FL 32796; 321-383-0693

FOR MORE INFORMATION
Titusville Area Chamber of Commerce, 200 S. Washington, Ave., Titusville, FL 32780; 321-267-3036

The Middle (Central) Basin
Daytona Beach

Accommodations

Days Inn, 1608 North US 1, Ormond Beach, FL 32174; intersection of I-95 and US 1; 386-672-7341

Ramada Inn Surfside, 3125 S. Atlantic Ave., Daytona Beach Shores; on the beach;386-788-1000

Super 8 Speedway, 2992 W. International Speedway Blvd., Daytona Beach; near the Daytona 500 racetrack; 386-253-0643

Camping

Tomoka State Park, 2009 North Beach Street, Ormond Beach, FL 32174; sitting at the confluence of the Tomoka River and the Halifax River, the site was long ago used by Native Americans because of the fish-filled waters in the lagoon; a boat ramp and canoe rentals are also available; 386-676-4050

Restaurants

Barnacle's Restaurant & Lounge, 869 S. Atlantic Ave. (A1A), Ormond Beach; 386-673-1070

Billy's Tap Room & Grill, 58 E. Granada Blvd., Ormond Beach, FL 32174; 386-672-1910

Chart House, 1100 Marina Point Dr., Daytona Beach; fine dining; 386-255-9022

Inlet Harbor Marina & Restaurant, 133 Inlet Harbor Road, Ponce Inlet, FL 32127; 386-767-5590

Fly Shops and Sporting Goods

East Coast Outdoors, 385 S. Yonge St., US 1, Ormond Beach, FL 32174; 386-672-5003

The Fishin' Hole, 450 N. Beach Street, Daytona Beach, FL 32114; 386-252-9804

West Marine, 125 Basin St., Daytona Beach, FL 32114; 386-226-9966

West Marine, 2400 S. Ridgewood Ave., So. Daytona Beach, FL 32119; 386-760-0660

Hospitals

Halifax Medical Center, 303 N. Clyde Morris Blvd., Daytona Beach; 386-254-4000

Airports

Daytona Beach International Airport, 700 Catalina Dr., Suite 300, Daytona Beach; 386-248-8069

Auto Service

Robbins Service Center, 113 Taylor Ave., Daytona Beach; 386-252-4181

Silver Star World Wide Auto Repair, 74 N. US Hwy 1, Ormond Beach, FL 32174; 386-672-5455

For More Information

Daytona Beach/Halifax Area Chamber of Commerce, P.O. Box 2475, Daytona Beach, FL 32115; 386-255-0981

Deland

ACCOMMODATIONS
Best Inn University, 644 Woodland Blvd., Deland; 386-734-5711
Deland Country Inn, 228 W. Howry Ave., Deland; 386-736-4244
Orange Tree Inn, 1010 N. Woodland Blvd., Deland; 386-734-0670

CAMPING
Blue Spring State Park, 2100 West French Ave., Orange City, FL 32763; manatee winter in the run between the spring and the St. Johns River; in addition to campsites, there are 6 cabins available; 386-775-3663
Hontoon Island State Park, 2309 River Ridge Road, Deland, FL 32720; on the St. Johns River, the park is accessible by ferry and has campsites w/o electricity and rustic cabins; 386-736-5309
KOA Deland/Orange City Kampgrounds, 1440 E. Minnesota Ave., Orange City; 386-775-3996

RESTAURANTS
Belly Buster's Restaurant, 930 N. Woodland Blvd., Deland; a small, local sandwichshop with a great steak and cheese sub; 386-734-1611
Fish Tales Seafood Restaurant, 142 N. Woodland Blvd., Deland; 386-785-1237
Three Palms Casual Dining, 1330 N. Woodland Blvd., Deland; 386-734-6001

FLY SHOPS AND SPORTING GOODS
Family Bait & Tackle, 2827 W. SR 44, Deland; 386-740-1505
Highland Park Fish Camp, 2640 Highland Park Road, Deland; 386-734-2334

HOSPITALS
Florida Hospital, 701 W. Plymouth Ave., Deland; 386-943-4522

AIRPORTS
Deland Municipal Airport, 1120 FLightline Blvd., Deland, FL 32724; 386-734-9755

AUTO SERVICE
Kollinger's BP Service, 340 N. Woodland Blvd., Deland; 386-734-6636

FOR MORE INFORMATION
DeLand Area Chamber of Commerce, 336 N. Woodland Blvd., DeLand, FL 32720; 386-734-4331/800-749-4350

Sanford

ACCOMMODATIONS

Best Western Marina Hotel, 530 N. Palmetto Ave., Sanford, FL 32771; great location on the St. Johns River next to large municipal ramp; 407-323-1910

Holiday Inn Express, 3401 S. Orlando Drive, Sanford, FL 32771; 407-320-0845

Springhill Suites by Marriott, 201 N. Towne Blvd., Sanford, FL 32771; 407-995-1000

CAMPING

Wekiwa Springs State Park, 1800 Wekiwa Circle, Apopka, FL 32712; extensive equestrian trails; canoe rentals are available; 407-884-2009

RESTAURANTS

Cattle Ranch Restaurant, 2700 S. Sanford Ave., Sanford, FL 32773; 407-321-5761

Otter's Riverside Restaurant, 4380 Carraway Place, Sanford, FL 32771; 407-323-3991

Wolfy's On the River, 530 N. Palmetto Ave., Sanford, FL 32771; 407-322-2150

FLY SHOPS AND SPORTING GOODS

O-Fishy-Al's Hand Crafted Lures, 309 Idylwilde Dr., Sandford; 407-330-4040

The Sports Authority, 100 N. Entrance Road, Sanford, FL 32771; 407-302-3704

HOSPITALS

Orlando Regional - South Seminole Hospital, 555 W. SR 434, Longwood; 407-767-1200

AIRPORTS

Orlando Sanford International Airport, Three Red Cleveland Blvd., Sanford, FL 32773; 407-324-9681

AUTO SERVICE

Clouse Car Care Center, 555 W. First Street, Sanford, FL 32771; 407-322-2821

FOR MORE INFORMATION

Greater Sanford Chamber of Commerce, 400 E. First St., Sanford, FL 32771; 407-322-2212

THE LOWER (NORTHERN) BASIN
Jacksonville

ACCOMMODATIONS
Comfort Suites, 1180 Airport Road, Jacksonville, FL 32218; 904-741-0505
Fairfield Inn by Marriott, 8050 Baymeadows Circle West, Jacksonville, FL 32256;
904-739-0739
Holiday Inn Express Hotel & Suites, 4675 Salisbury Road, Jacksonville, FL 32256;
904-332-9500

CAMPING
Little Talbot Island State Park, 12157 Hecksher Dr., Jacksonville, FL 32226;
904-251-2320

RESTAURANTS
Beef 'O' Bradys, 12630 Beach Blvd., Jacksonville, FL 32246; 904-565-0050
China King Super Buffet, 14333 Beach Blvd., Jacksonville, FL 32250; 904-223-8889
G & C Seafood, 10391 Old St. Augustine Road, Jacksonville, FL 32257;
904-288-6804

FLY SHOPS AND SPORTING GOODS
B & M Bait and Tackle, 2789 SR A1A, Mayport, FL 32233; 904-249-3933
Fishin Buddy Bait & Tackle, 13642 Atlantic Blvd., Jacksonville, FL 32224;
904-221-0865
Salty Feather Shop and Guide Service, 3733 Southside Blvd., Jacksonville, FL
32216;
888-847-2589
Steve's Tackle Box, 5506 Seaboard Ave., Jacksonville; 904-777-4823
The Sports Authority, 6000 Lake Grey Blvd (Westland Park Center), Jacksonville,
FL 32244; 904-771-9001
The Sports Authority, 9292 Arlington Expressway, Jacksonville, FL 32225;
904-725-9181
Tidewater Outfitters Inc., Bldg 10 Amelia Village, Amelia Island, FL 32034;
904-261-2202
West Marin
5951 University Blvd., Jacksonville, FL 32216; 904-733-6128
4415 Roosevelt Blvd., Jacksonville, FL 32210; 904-388-7510
14180 Beach Blvd., Jacksonville Beach, FL 32250; 904-821-5033
311 Blanding Blvd., Orange Park, FL 32703; 904-276-4343

HOSPITALS
Memorial Hospital Jacksonville, 3625 University Blvd. So., Jacksonville, FL 32216;
904-399-6111

Airports
Jacksonville Airport, PO Box 18018, Jacksonville, FL 32229; 904-741-2000

Auto Service
Mobicare of Jax, 9395 Phillips Hwy., Jacksonville, FL 32256; 904-464-0355

For More Information
Jacksonville Chamber of Commerce, 3 Independent Drive, Jacksonville, FL 32202; 904-366-6600

Palatka

Accommodations
Holiday Inn Riverfront, 201 N. 1st Street, Palatka, FL 32177; 386-328-3481

The Moorings at Crystal Cove, 247 Crystal Cove Dr., Palatka, FL 32177; 386-325-1055

St. Johns Motel, 329 US Highway 17 So., East Palatka; 386-325-2278

Camping
Kenwood Recreation Area, 300 Kenwood Boat Ramp Road, Palatka, FL 32177; 386-312-2273

Restaurants
Golden Corral, 501 Hwy 19 No., Palatka, FL 32177; 386-328-4040

San Mateo Seafood Restaurant, Inc., 480 S. Highway 17, San Mateo, FL 32187; 386-325-1871

Sonny's Real Pit Bar-B-Que, 425 State Road 19 No., Palatka, FL 32177; 386-328-4655

Fly Shops and Sporting Goods
Messers Eastside Bait & Tackle, 145 Highway 17 So., East Palatka, FL 32131; 386-328-4895

The Tackle Box Pro Shop, 619 Highway 19 So., Palatka, FL 32177; 386-328-9311

Hospitals
Putnam Community Medical Center, 611 Zeagler Drive Palatka, FL 32177; 386-328-5711

Airports
Kay Larkin Municipal Airport, 4015 Reid Street, Palatka, FL 32177; 386-329-0148

Auto Service
B-M Tire & Auto Service Center, 4102 Crill Avenue, Palatka, FL 32177; 386-328-5307

For More Information
Putnam County Chamber of Commerce, P.O. Box 550, Palatka, FL 32178; 386-328-1503

St. Augustine

ACCOMMODATIONS

Casablanca Inn Bed & Breakfast on the Bay, 24 Avenida Menendez, St. Augustine, FL 32080; 904-829-0928

Hilton Garden Inn, 401 A1A Beach Blvd., St. Augustine, FL 32084; 904-471-5559

Marion Motor Lodge, 120 Avenida Menendez, St. Augustine, FL 32084; 800-258-2261

CAMPING

Indian Forest Campground, 1505 SR 207, St. Augustine, FL 32086; 904-824-3574

RESTAURANTS

Creekside Dinery, 160 Nix Boatyard Road, St. Augustine, FL 32086; 904-829-6113

O. C. White's Seafood & Spirits, 118 Avenida Menendez, St. Augustine, FL 32084; 904-824-0808

Sunset Grille, 421 A1A Beach Blvd., St. Augustine, FL 32080; 904-471-5555

FLY SHOPS AND SPORTING GOODS

Hook, Line, and Sinker, 107 Yacht Club Drive, St. Augustine, FL 32084; 904-829-6073

West Marine, 1030 S. Ponce de Leon Blvd., St. Augustine, FL 32086; 904-810-5353

HOSPITALS

Flagler Hospital, Inc., 400 Health Park Blvd., St. Augustine, FL 32086; 904-819-5155

AIRPORTS

St. Augustine/St. John County Airport Authority, 4796 US 1 No., St. Augustine, FL 32095; 904-825-6860

AUTO SERVICE

Hi-Tech Auto Repair, 1416 Old Moultrie Road, St. Augustine, FL 32084; 904-829-1974

FOR MORE INFORMATION

St. Augustine & St. Johns County Chamber of Commerce, 1 Riberia St., St. Augustine, FL 32084; 904-829-5681

Highland Park Fish Camp near Deland gives anglers access
to some outstanding bass, bream, and crappie fishing.

Region 2 North-Central Florida

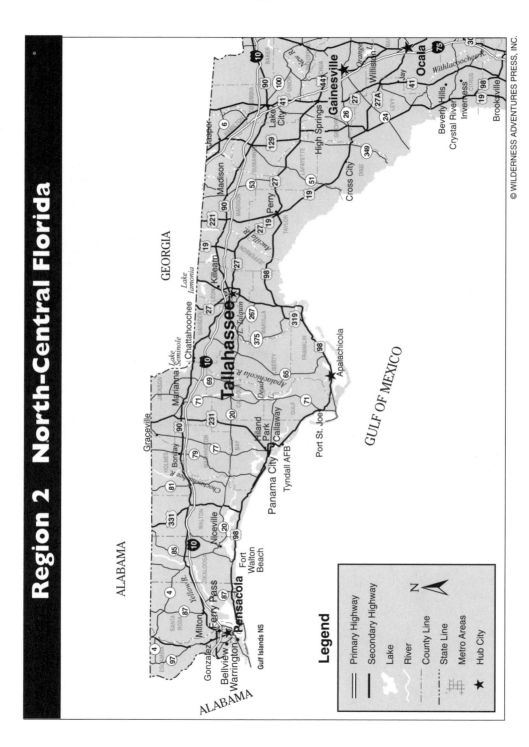

Legend

Primary Highway
Secondary Highway
Lake
River
County Line
State Line
Metro Areas
★ Hub City

N

GULF OF MEXICO

ALABAMA

GEORGIA

ALABAMA

Tallahassee

Pensacola

Gainesville

Ocala

North-Central Florida

Region 2

Get away from the stress of city life. Paddle softly, listen to the sounds of the breeze gently rustling through the trees, marvel at a deer high up on a bank watching you, see an occasional raccoon or otter, or an alligator sunning himself. Then when the sun sets, listen to the call of the owl, supper over a campfire and sleep out under the stars. This is wonderful medicine with miracle healing powers for one's psyche. If there's such a thing as a southern "God's Country," this has got to be close.

Bill Logan, *Canoeing and Camping the Beautiful Suwannee River*

The many rivers of north Florida need to be experienced for a flyfisher to understand how different these waters are from those in the rest of the state. Fly fishing can be very good for a variety of species throughout the year and outstanding for select fish at certain times. Dark, tea-stained water flows at a leisurely pace between banks lined with cypress and palms. Wildlife abounds in the water, on land, and overhead in the typically clear blue sky. It is certainly a different kind of beauty from the majestic, snow-capped mountains of the Rockies, but for a flyfisher who wants to get close to nature, I suggest getting into a canoe, kayak, or johnboat and spending a few hours (or days) on the rivers of North Florida sampling the elixir that is such "wonderful medicine with miracle healing powers for one's psyche."

Unlike Region 1, where a single river system gives life to numerous lakes, many of them quite large, the area in north-central Florida that I refer to as Region 2 has several river systems but very few lakes of any substantial size. Lake Seminole, lying on the Florida/Georgia border, may be the only lake in the entire region from which you cannot readily see from one end to the other. (Florida, however, only gets to claim a small portion of the southwest corner of Lake Seminole, as the state line bisects the Chattahoochee River.)

The east-west distance along the northern boundary of Region 2 is about 300 miles, about the same distance as the flat coastal area through which the St. Johns River flows in Region 1.

North Florida has gently rolling hills with ridges like a washboard that run from the Florida/Georgia border south to the Gulf of Mexico. Because northern Florida has the highest relief in the state, the valleys between these hills cradle numerous streams, some with fish indigenous only to that river system. For example, the

A 5-weight rod is an excellent match for the smaller black bass in Region 2.

Suwannee bass and the shoal bass are each separate and unique species of black bass having a very limited range in Florida. None of these streams flow north like the St. Johns River, and none flow east into that river. An area of high ground called the Trail Ridge separates the 300-mile-wide northern portion of Region 2 from the massive St. Johns River system.

The numerous meandering streams in Region 2 reach the Gulf of Mexico in areas referred to as the "Panhandle" and the "Big Bend." These names originate from the physical characteristics of the narrow landmass in northwestern Florida and the long, sweeping turn made by the coastline in this area. Like the rivers flowing into them, these coastal areas harbor fertile fishing grounds.

The streams in north Florida are on par with the best warmwater streams anywhere in the country, although they do not yield trophy black bass equaling the size of those in the St. Johns River and its lakes. Seldom does any river give up bass as big as those found in larger lakes and impoundments. Nonetheless, there are five species of black bass (largemouth bass, spotted bass, redeye bass, Suwannee bass, and shoal bass) that a flyfisher can catch in north Florida. Note the absence of smallmouth bass. Since some of these species of black bass can only be caught in this region, the state records all come from waters in Region 2. In addition, the area consistently produces big panfish, as evidenced by the fact that numerous state records have also been established for assorted panfish caught from this region. Striped bass, white bass, and sunshine bass have been stocked in many of the rivers with great success.

Stripers need long stretches of flowing water cooler than that found in Florida's rivers to have any chance to reproduce, but the annual stockings ensure that a good population of quality fish is maintained in the rivers and streams. State records for striped bass, white bass and sunshine bass also come from Region 2. Although the biggest largemouth bass in the state do not come from this region, most of the largest specimens of other species of interest to flyfishers do come from the fantastic waters found here.

As previously mentioned, the streams of north Florida flow only in one direction—toward the Gulf of Mexico. That can be helpful to an angler, as fish will take-up residence on certain structure and be prone to stay or return there. In Region 1, their position often changed depending upon the direction of the St. Johns River tidal flow. Not so in Region 2. That variable is taken out of the fish-finding equation.

Nowhere in the state of Florida will you find consistently more scenic and unspoiled water. The waters are clean and the fish will be well marked in the clear water. With the many twists and turns on these streams, you will surely be able to get out of any wind yet fly fish along a productive shoreline. In their upper reaches, many of these rivers and streams are shallow, narrow, and have a bit of a gradient. They are designated as canoe trails, and flyfishers using canoes and kayaks can get away from the beaten path and fish some breathtakingly beautiful water.

The lakes in Region 2 are small and deep by Florida standards. Likewise, the bass run smaller, and none of these lakes are ranked among the top 10 bass fishing lakes in the state, despite the fact that this region is the largest in terms of land area of the three freshwater regions. This does not mean that the fishing is bad in the lakes of Region 2. On the contrary, it is very good for both panfish and black bass. The potential for a lunker bass, however, is not as great as it is in Regions 1 and 3.

The Florida Game and Fresh Water Fish Commission (GFC) manages many of the lakes in the northern portion of the state. The GFC limes and fertilizes these lakes in an effort to improve fishing. Some of the lakes (called Fish Management Areas) have special bag and length limit regulations unique to those waters. Be sure to check posted signs at the ramp. (See also the information on Fish Management Areas in the "Florida Freshwater Fishing Regulations" section of this book.)

You can probably get away with a single fly rod for most of Region 2. My personal preference is a 5-weight, which I consider my basic river rod. It will handle all of the panfish, and the black bass on most waters will likely be around two pounds. All but the largest stripers can be whipped with a mid-weight rod. (Only for striped bass below the dams at Lake Seminole and Lake Talquin would I want to use an 8- or 9-weight rod.) The fly reel need not be anodized to prevent corrosion by salt unless you are going to fish the last 5 or 6 miles of a brackish coastal river. Select a weight-forward floating line that matches the rod and moves easily through the guides. The water will be clearer than in other parts of the state, so a small diameter leader or one made of fluorocarbon is a good choice.

Once you move inland from the coastline of the Panhandle and Big Bend, the waters will be less crowded. Vast areas of land have been dedicated to national and

The weather is cooler in northern Florida, and winter mornings may require protective clothing.

state forests and these remain largely undeveloped. Because of the large areas set aside for forestlands, the road system is not as well developed and rapid movement from one locale to another is not always possible. Interstate 10 is the primary artery for east/west movement across the northern portion of the region, while Interstate 75 runs north/south along the axis on which the state is tilted. I have selected State Road 40 as the southern boundary of Region 2. SR 40 bisects the state near its mid-section, and as we will see in Region 3, the waters south of this area drain south toward Lake Okeechobee, rather than toward the Gulf of Mexico like those in Region 2. Within the region, the distance between bridges can sometimes be several miles. If you are in a motorized boat, that is not a problem. However, if you choose to float a canoe or kayak in the upper reaches of rivers, make sure that you have put-in and take-out sites on the same side of the river or you may end up doing may more traveling by car than by boat.

The weather in northern Florida is cooler than in other parts of the state, and seldom are the days oppressively hot. You can fish all day if you have the stamina to wave a graphite wand that long. Water temperatures in lakes may remain high well into the fall, but the spring-fed streams will stay cool. In winter, northern Florida will get frost and an occasional dusting of snow. Monitor any tropical storms that may be in the Gulf of Mexico, as these will almost certainly move north and east, crossing the Panhandle all too frequently.

Let's begin at the western edge of the Panhandle and move east across northern Florida...

ESCAMBIA RIVER

The Escambia River flows out of the southern portion of Alabama and through the Panhandle of Florida to Escambia Bay. Except for the first 10 miles as it flows into the state, the area around the river is a wetland swamp. These upper waters give up good catches of bream to flyfishers using small poppers, especially in the spring.

All along its course, numerous feeder creeks and streams flow into the Escambia River from both the east and west. These offer good spring bream fishing, and in summer, look for bass to lie in eddies below where streams enter the river. As you move downstream, look for sunshine bass hanging around the mouths of these feeder creeks. Cast a size 1 Baby Bunker to each of these creeks along the lower half of the river.

The best fishing occurs in the lower reaches of the river in the "delta" region. These last five miles before reaching Escambia Bay offer flyfishers one of the best opportunities for variety in the state. In late summer, fly fishing for sunshine bass can be outstanding. Try a light colored Deceiver on a size 1 hook early and late in the day where you see schooling activity or birds diving into the water. In early spring, crappie move toward shoreline cover and can be taken from fallen treetops and sloughs in January and February by anglers using Clouser Minnows. As spring progresses, look for bass and bream in the delta area to spawn near shoreline structure in shallow water. As with the upper portion of the river, a small size 4 popper or terrestrial pattern will take lots of bream. Increase your popper to about size 1 for the bass. Don't overlook shrimp patterns, as these tasty treats move out of the bay and into the river in this area. The belly of many a bass has been found stuffed with shrimp when they are running in the river. As the season progresses into early fall, look for the bass to school in open water. Try a light colored streamer stripped slowly or a Clouser Minnow (size 1) fished more quickly to trigger a strike from these competitive fish.

There are only two bridges crossing the Escambia River in Florida. The northernmost bridge is near the Alabama/Florida line where State Road 4 crosses the river. The only other crossing is about 20 miles south where SR 184 crosses just above the delta region about 15 miles north of Pensacola.

To get to ramps along the Escambia River, take US 29/State Road 95 north from Pensacola. US 29/SR 95 runs on the west side of the Escambia River about one to three miles from the river channel all along its course. In the delta region, there is a good ramp about 10 miles north of Interstate 10 in Pensacola. Turn right onto Becks Lake Road and go east three miles to the single-lane ramp. This gives you good access to the delta in the area of Brosnaham Island.

About six miles farther north, there is a popular put-in at Molino. Turn right from US 29/SR 95 onto SR 182 and go two miles to the small town of Molino. The single-lane ramp is on the east side of town at the road's end.

The next ramp that is accessible from US 29/SR 95 is about 10 miles north. Turn right near the community of McDavid onto Mystic Springs Road and go about 0.8 mile to McDavid Ramp at the end of the road. This single-lane ramp has unimproved parking that will accommodate 12 vehicles.

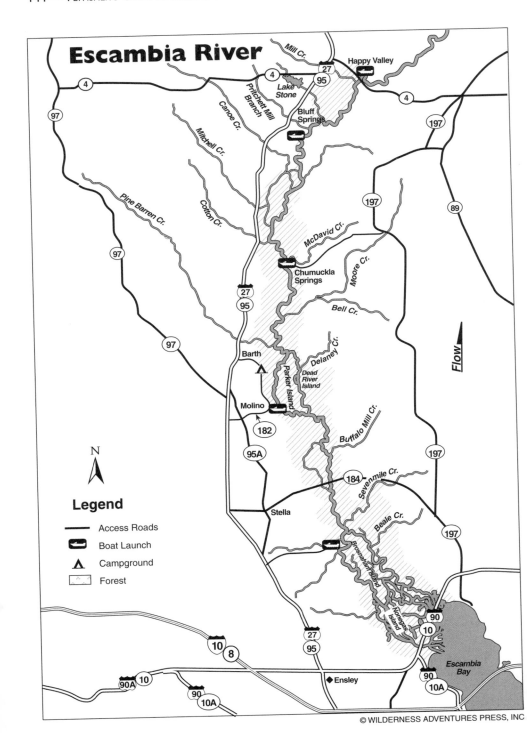

Escambia River

© WILDERNESS ADVENTURES PRESS, INC

There is another single-lane ramp about 5 miles north near the community of Bluff Springs, but the fishing in this area is not all that reliable. Continuing another five miles, turn right onto SR 4 at Century and go 1.6 miles east to the bridge where SR 4 crosses the Escambia River. Turn left just before crossing the bridge and there is a single-lane ramp about 0.2 mile upriver in the community of Happy Valley.

The only access to the Escambia River from the east side is midriver at Chumuckla Springs. It is not worth the effort and risk to your tow vehicle when you can go north or south 10 miles, cross the river at one of the two bridges, and get access off US 29/SR 95, which affords more secure parking.

LAKE STONE

Lake Stone is a 130-acre lake managed by the Florida Game and Fresh Water Fish Commission (GFC) located west of US 29/State Road 95 near Century, two miles south of the Alabama/Florida line. Water discharged from Lake Stone flows east for 2.5 miles in what is known as Wiggins Branch before emptying into the Escambia River.

The GFC limes and fertilizes Lake Stone each year to increase fish production. Bream fishing is good in the spring on small poppers (size 4). Flyfishers in the area prefer light colors during the day and darker colors at sunrise and early in the evening. Bass are on the small side and the same small poppers will catch them, too. The crappie fishery is not significant.

To get to the Lake Stone ramp, go south from Century for 0.5 mile on US 29/SR 95. Turn right onto SR 4 and go west for 1.5 miles. Turn left onto the paved drive leading to the single-lane ramp. There is paved parking for 30 vehicles.

BEAR LAKE

Bear Lake (107 acres) is also managed by the Florida Game and Fresh Water Fish Commission. Historically, Bear Lake has had a very good fishery for bluegill, and flyfishers will do well in late afternoon and early evening with a small popper (size 8) with rubber legs. Fishing for bass and bream is often very good in the spring. A cricket pattern (Dave's Cricket, size 10) would be a good choice for bream, and a size 4 deer-hair popper would make a good choice for the smaller-sized bass in Bear Lake.

Bear Lake is located in Blackwater River State Forest and there are excellent camping facilities available near the launch site. To get to the ramp, leave Interstate 10 at the Crestview exit (Exit 12) and go north on State Road 85 for 3 miles. In Crestview, turn left onto SR 4 and go west for about 20 miles. Turn right onto Bear Lake Road and go 0.5 mile to the single-lane ramp on the right. There is paved parking for 30 vehicles.

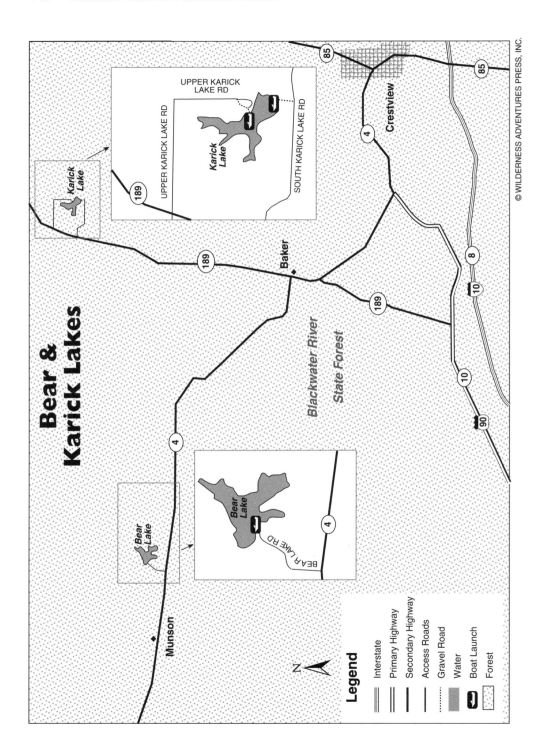

Bear &
Karick Lakes

UPPER KARICK LAKE RD

UPPER KARICK LAKE RD

SOUTH KARICK LAKE RD

Karick
Lake

Karick
Lake

Crestview

Baker

Blackwater River

State Forest

Bear
Lake

BEAR LAKE RD

Bear
Lake

Munson

Legend

Interstate
Primary Highway
Secondary Highway
Access Roads
Gravel Road
Water
Boat Launch
Forest

N

© WILDERNESS ADVENTURES PRESS, INC.

KARICK LAKE

Karick Lake (65 acres) is a small lake maintained by the GFC, and it is also limed and fertilized to increase fish production. While bream fishing is only fair, the bluegill fishery is regarded as outstanding in the spring and early summer. A small (size 8), rubber-legged popper fished toward shore will be the only fly you need. Cast it and let it lay. Do not strip it, but twitch it ever so slightly if there is no "slurp" after about a minute. Bass fishing can be good in the spring on larger popping bugs.

There are two ramps on this small lake. To get to the south side of Karick from Interstate 10, take Exit 12 and go north on SR 85 for 3 miles. In Crestview, turn left onto SR 4 and go 7 miles to Baker. In Baker, continue north on SR 189 (SR 4 will turn to the west) for 6.8 miles. At Karick Lake Road South, turn right onto the dirt road and go 1 mile to the single-lane ramp. There is unimproved parking for 25 vehicles and paid camping is allowed.

To get to the north side of the lake from I-10, proceed to Baker as above. In Baker, continue north on SR 189 for 7.5 miles. At Karick Lake Road North, turn right onto the dirt road and go 1 mile, then right at the intersection 0.6 mile to the single-lane ramp with unimproved parking for 25 vehicles. Paid camping is also allowed.

BLACKWATER RIVER

The headwaters of Blackwater River can be accessed at Blackwater River State Park, 15 miles northeast of Milton, off State Road 90. The primary activity in the upper reaches is canoeing and the river is considered one of the purest sand bottom rivers in the world. Fly fishing in the area requires a very small tippet (5x) and long leaders. Bream are the primary target.

The river is often too shallow for motorized boats and once a canoe or kayak is launched, it is 15 miles to Milton. There are no bridges or paved roads that dead-end at the river's edge. In the area of Milton, however, it is a different story. The river widens and becomes very fishable as it leads on to Blackwater Bay. The freshwater above Milton is very interesting as it gets channeled around islands. Bass fishing is not really that good, but in the spring small poppers will keep you interested. The primary fishery here, as it was in the headwaters, is for bream. Small terrestrials and poppers will tempt the bluegill and redbreast sunfish along shorelines in spring and early summer.

To get to the ramp at Milton, get off Interstate 10 at Exit 10 and go north on SR 87 for 5 miles. As you enter Milton, you can access the river at the bridge where SR 87 crosses.

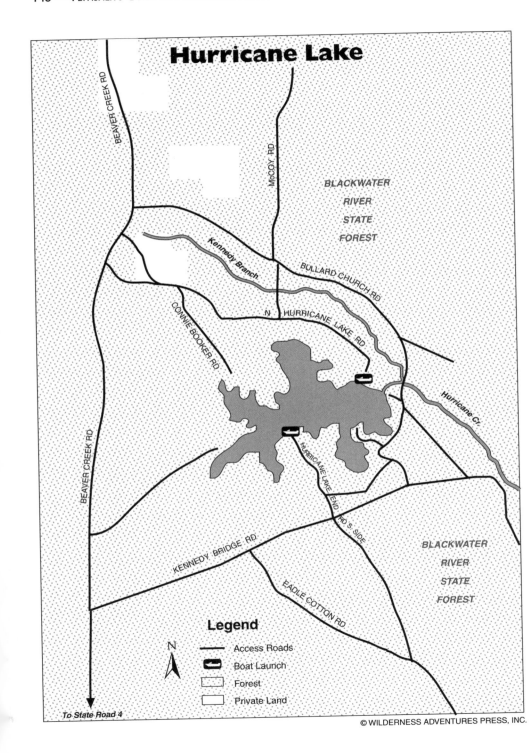

Hurricane Lake

BEAVER CREEK RD

McCOY RD

BLACKWATER
RIVER
STATE
FOREST

Kennedy Branch

BULLARD CHURCH RD

N HURRICANE LAKE RD

CONNIE BOOKER RD

Hurricane Cr.

BEAVER CREEK RD

HURRICANE LAKE END RD S SIDE

KENNEDY BRIDGE RD

EADLE COTTON RD

BLACKWATER
RIVER
STATE
FOREST

Legend

N

Access Roads

Boat Launch

Forest

Private Land

To State Road 4

HURRICANE LAKE

Hurricane Lake (318 acres) is yet another lake that is limed and fertilized by the Florida Game and Fresh Water Fish Commission to increase fish production. This lake, unlike most in the area, has a reputation for larger bass. It also differs from most Florida lakes in that it is not shaped like a shallow round bowl. Instead, it has numerous fingers and deep-water coves reminiscent of many Tennessee Valley Authority (TVA) lakes. Bass fishing is best in the spring and early summer around shoreline structure. A larger deer-haired popper (size 1 or 1/0) fished during low-light conditions is an excellent choice for the bass here. Bream fishing can only be described as fair.

There are two ramps providing access. The ramp on the south side of Hurricane Lake can be reached by getting off Interstate 10 at the Crestview exit (Exit 12) and going north on State Road 85 for 3 miles. In Crestview, turn left onto SR 4 and go west for about 13 miles. Turn right onto Beaver Creek Road and go 5 miles. Turn right on Hurricane Lake South and go 2.5 miles. The single-lane ramp is to your left at the intersection. There is unimproved parking for 25 vehicles and paid camping is allowed.

To reach the north side of the lake, proceed as above from I-10 to Beaver Creek Road. After turning right onto Beaver Creek Road, go 7.5 miles and then right again onto Hurricane Lake Road North. Go 1 mile and at the intersection, turn left onto the dirt road and go another mile to the single-lane ramp with unimproved parking for 20 vehicles. Paid camping is allowed.

KINGS LAKE, HOLLY LAKE, AND JUNIPER LAKE

These three lakes are north of the community called DeFuniak Springs. Juniper Lake (670 acres) is maintained by the Florida Game and Fresh Water Fish Commission and has two public ramps. Neither Kings Lake or Holly Lake (each approximately 350 acres) has a public ramp. A number of trophy bass are taken from the extensive flooded timber in Lake Juniper each year. Deer-haired poppers and swimming frog patterns (size 1) with monofilament weedguards work best for the bass that take up residence in the extensive underwater trees and snags. In spring and early summer, small poppers and cricket patterns fished along the shoreline account for numerous bluegills and other bream.

To get to the north side of Juniper Lake, leave Interstate 10 at the DeFuniak Springs exit (Exit 14) and go north on US 331/State Road 83 for 2 miles into Defuniak Springs. In town, make a right turn and then a left, staying on SR 83. Continue north for another 3.8 miles to Catts Island Road. Turn left and go 1.3 miles to the single-lane ramp at Catts Island. There is unimproved parking for 16 vehicles.

You can get to the south side of Juniper Lake by exiting I-10 and continuing through DeFuniak Springs as above. This time, however, go only 2.5 miles on SR 83 after leaving town. Turn left onto Juniper Lake Road and go 0.8 mile to the single-lane ramp at Juniper Lake Dam. There is unimproved parking for 20 vehicles.

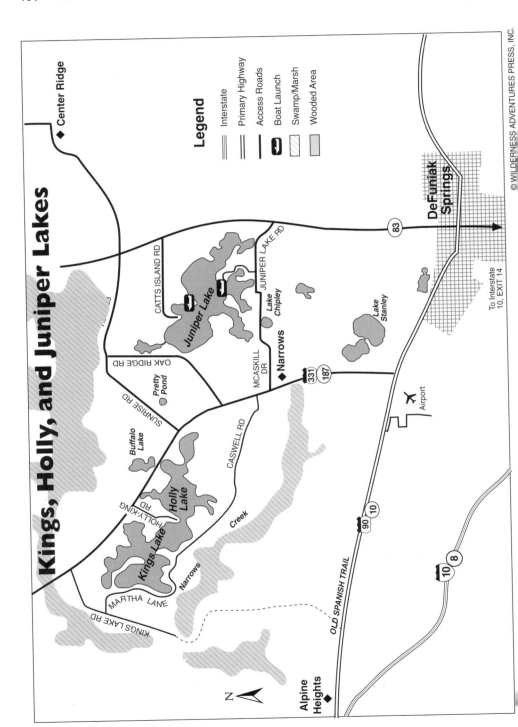

Kings, Holly, and Juniper Lakes

Legend

Interstate
Primary Highway
Access Roads
Boat Launch
Swamp/Marsh
Wooded Area

Center Ridge

DeFuniak Springs

To Interstate 10, EXIT 14

83

CATTS ISLAND RD

JUNIPER LAKE RD

Juniper Lake

Lake Chipley

Lake Stanley

OAK RIDGE RD

MCASKILL DR

Narrows

331

187

Pretty Pond

SUNRISE RD

Airport

CASWELL RD

Buffalo Lake

Holly Lake

HOLLY-KING RD

Creek

90

10

Kings Lake

Narrows

MARTHA LANE

KINGS LAKE RD

10

8

OLD SPANISH TRAIL

Alpine Heights

N

Brian Penrose begins to strip line while anticipating a strike on the Choctawhatchee River.

CHOCTAWHATCHEE RIVER

The Choctawhatchee River flows south past the Alabama/Florida line through wilderness and lush lowland marshes for 96 miles to the Gulf of Mexico at Choctawhatchee Bay. In its upper reaches, it is one of Florida's outstanding canoe trails. In the lower, wider, and slower portion far downstream, however, fishing is much better. Along the way, the state's largest population of beaver can be found.

Bluegill and shellcrackers are the primary target of flyfishers, with spring and summer the best times. In spring, especially around the full moon, look for fish to be bedding in sloughs and areas where the water has slowed. A small topwater popper will provide plenty of action. In the summer, try fishing early and late in the day. The black bass are found around treetops and stick-ups in the river, with spring and summer again the best time. These river bass seldom go more than a couple of pounds. Patterns that imitate crickets, grasshoppers, and other terrestrials work well, as do deer-haired poppers. In the lower portion of the Choctawhatchee River, there is a good population of sunshine bass, especially in the spring and fall. Look for them on the downstream (southern) end of sandbars in the eddy facing out toward the current. A Baby Bunker or other small, light colored baitfish pattern is the fly of choice.

The northern portion of the Choctawhatchee River is reached by exiting I-10 at Exit 16 and going north on County Road 279 for 1 mile. You can access the river from

Choctawhatchee River

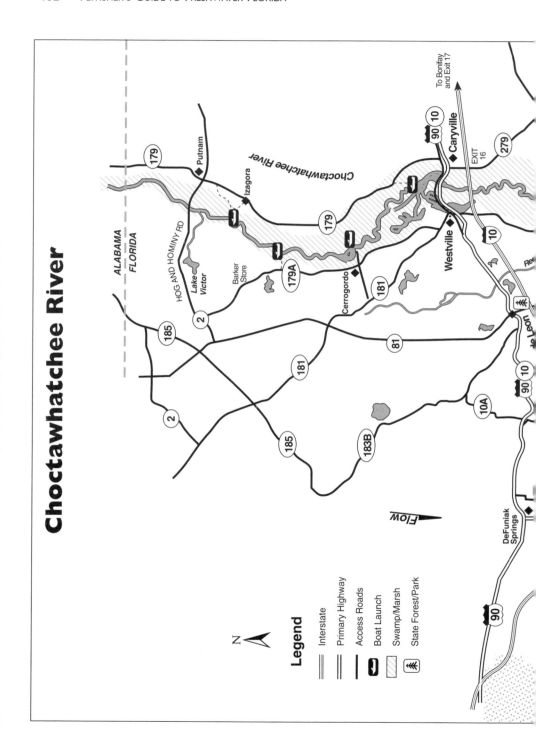

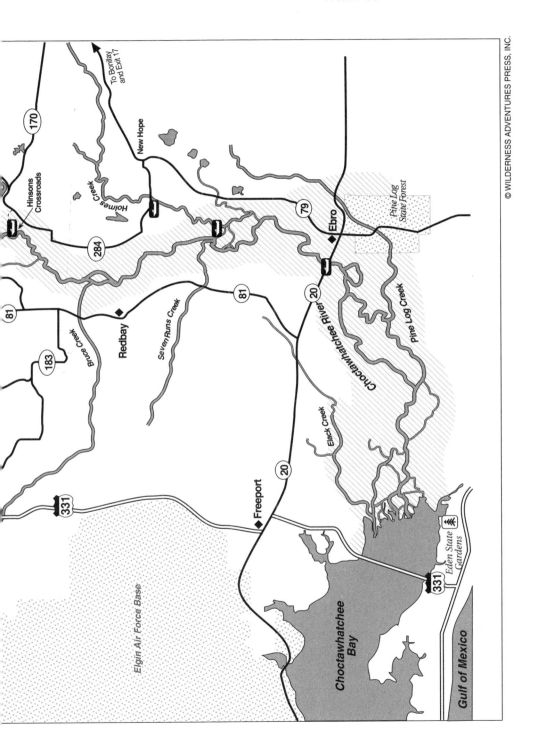

the west side by turning left onto US 90/State Road 10 and going west for 2.3 miles. Then turn right onto CR 179A at Westville and go north for 4.7 miles. Turn right at Cerrogordo onto the unpaved road (it is paved if you go to the left) and go east 0.8 mile to the single-lane ramp at the river.

There is another ramp on the west side that can be reached by continuing north on CR 179A for another 4.3 miles. Turn right on the unnamed dirt road and go 1.4 miles to the single-lane ramp at the Old Warehouse Landing. There is unimproved parking for 10 vehicles.

To access the river from the east side, turn right onto US 90/SR 10 after getting off I-10 and go 0.6 mile to CR 179. Turn left; going north on CR 179 you'll see several additional launch sites. The first ramp is about 2.6 miles north on CR 179. Turn left on Spring Park Road (a dirt road) and go 0.8 mile. Turn right on the unnamed dirt road and go 0.2 mile to the single-lane ramp in the marshy area. There is unimproved parking for six vehicles.

About 6 miles farther north on CR 179, there is a small, single-lane ramp off the dirt road to your left. Lastly, by continuing north on CR 179 for another 2 miles, you come to Izagora. Turn left and go 0.8 mile on the dirt road to the single-lane ramp at Curry Ferry. Here, there is unimproved parking for 10 vehicles.

The middle portion of the Choctawhatchee River can be reached by again taking Exit 16 off I-10, but this time go south on CR 279 for 4 miles. Turn right and go west on CR 284 for about 4.5 miles. Cross the intersection with CR 284 and continue on the dirt road to the single-lane ramp at Hinson's Crossroads. There is unimproved parking for 15 vehicles.

To reach the middle portion of the river from the west, take Exit 15 off I-10 and go south on SR 81 for about 3 miles. Turn left onto CR 181 and go north again for 3 miles. Just after crossing the bridge over Reedy Creek, turn right onto the dirt road (Cedar Log Road) and go 1.3 miles to the single-lane ramp at the river's edge. There is unimproved parking for three vehicles.

About 15 river miles downstream, Holmes Creek (described in the following pages) enters from a marsh to the east. I will refer to all of the Choctawhatchee River below Holmes Creek as the lower portion, and fly fishing improves as you move downstream toward the bay. Striped bass move downstream in the fall and congregate in the lower portion of the river to feed on the abundant forage fish. Flyfishers should try a bunker pattern or a 3- to 5-inch light colored Deceiver. Early morning and when skies are overcast offer the best opportunities for stripers. Largemouth bass like the slower moving water in the lower portion and will hang around shoreline structure and snags that extend out into the water. Both poppers and subsurface baitfish patterns will take the black bass.

To get to the lower portion of the river, exit I-10 at the Bonifay exit (Exit 17) and go south on State Road 79 for about 25 miles to State Road 20. Turn right onto SR 20 and go west for 1.8 miles to the single-lane ramp at the bridge where SR 20 crosses the river. The area between the SR 20 Bridge and Choctawhatchee Bay, about 12 river miles, is slow moving and very much like a marshy delta.

Lake Victor is primarily known as a bass lake. Brian Maloney admires the one he just caught on a deer-hair popper.

LAKE VICTOR

Lake Victor (130 acres) is primarily known as a bass lake. A few trophy bass are taken from its waters each year, especially in the spring and early summer months. Live-bait fishermen using wild shiners take most trophy bass, but flyfishers can try fishing a large fly like a Dahlberg Diver around floating vegetation. The bigger bass will feed early and late in the day. Bream fishing can be good from mid-May to July, especially around the time of the full moon. Terrestrials cast near visible beds are quickly taken.

The runoff from Lake Victor flows through Limestone Branch for about 2.5 miles as it makes its way to Choctawhatchee River. A flyfisher can wade some portions of this small stream for bream that readily take small poppers.

To get to the west portion of Lake Victor, you will need to get to State Road 2, which parallels the Alabama/Florida state line about three miles into Florida. From the intersection of SR 2 and SR 81, go east on SR 2 for about 5 miles. Turn right onto the unnamed dirt road and go 0.8 mile. Make another left on the next dirt road and go 0.2 mile to the single-lane ramp. There is unimproved parking for only three vehicles and because of the shallow water in front of the ramp, only small boats can be launched here. Given the lack of security, I do not recommend using this site.

To get to the east portion of Lake Victor, go east on SR 2 for about 6 miles from the intersection of SR 2 and SR 81. Turn right onto the unnamed dirt road and go 0.4 mile to the single-lane ramp. There is unimproved parking for five vehicles.

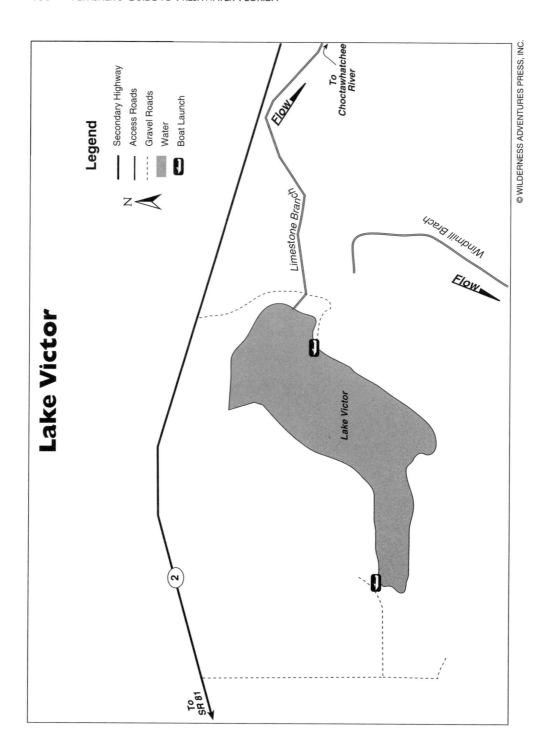

Lake Victor

HOLMES CREEK

Holmes Creek is a slow-moving tributary of the Choctawhatchee River that runs east to west through a swamp, which at times is hard to distinguish from the creek itself. In the upper portions, there are some high banks that define the channel and only a canoe, kayak, or johnboat can be used to fish. The fishing in Holmes Creek is consistently solid, and in the spring, it can often be quite good for bream and small bass. Cast a small popper toward shoreline cover and don't begin stripping too quickly.

To reach Holmes Creek, take State Road 79 south off Interstate 10 at the Bonifay exit (Exit 17) and go south for about 12 miles. The dirt road (Hightower Springs Road) to your right leads to the creek. There is a single-lane, unpaved ramp at the road's end. There is unimproved parking for six vehicles.

Continuing another 3 miles south on SR 79, you come to County Road 284. Turn right and go west for 2 miles. There is a single-lane ramp where CR 284 crosses the creek. Halfway between SR 79 and CR 284, the dirt road to your right leads to another small, unpaved ramp about a mile to the north.

By continuing south on SR 79 another 3 miles, you can reach Holmes Creek by turning right onto CR 284A and going west for about 1.5 miles. At the bridge crossing the creek, there is a single-lane ramp.

There is another small ramp providing access to the creek just before it joins the Choctawhatchee River. Cross the CR 284A Bridge and continue west for 0.2 mile, turn left on the dirt road, go 0.6 mile, turn left again, and go 0.6 mile to the single-lane ramp at the end of the road.

PATE LAKE

This 300-acre lake is very shallow and suffers during droughts and dry conditions, especially along the eastern edge. There is a reliable bream population, but bass fishing is spotty. Pate Lake is not a great destination for flyfishers, except locals with only a few hours to fish.

To get to Pate Lake, take Exit 16 off Interstate 10 and go south on State Road 279 for about 5 miles. The lake will be on your left, about a mile after crossing the intersection of SR 280. There is a single-lane ramp with parking for two vehicles.

CHARLES BAY

Charles Bay is a 100-acre lake that is deeper than nearby Pate Lake. It, too, is not a serious destination for out-of-state flyfishers traveling to Florida, but a single-lane ramp on the eastern edge does provide access for those in the area. Like so many Florida lakes, the water looks very "fishy," and a small popper will provide plenty of bream action. The bass, however, are small and the same size 8 popper will be fine for them, as well.

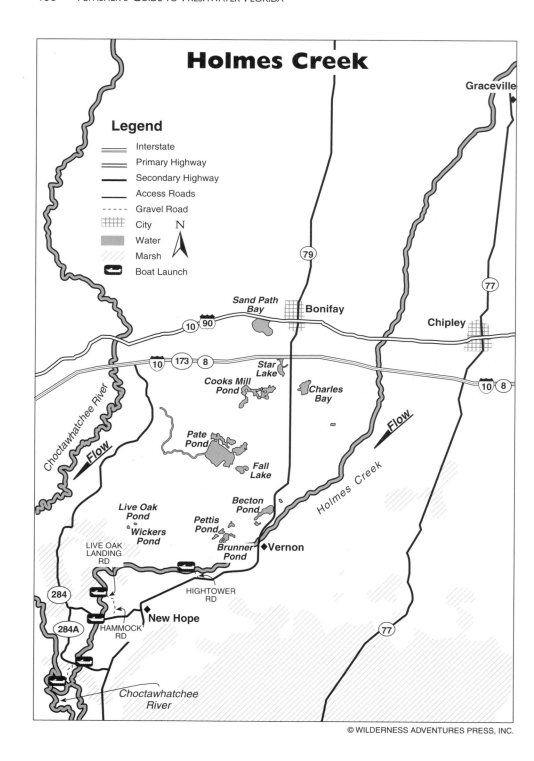

Holmes Creek

Graceville

Legend

Interstate	
Primary Highway	
Secondary Highway	
Access Roads	
Gravel Road	
City	N
Water	
Marsh	
Boat Launch	

Sand Path Bay

Bonifay

Chipley

79

77

10 90

10 173 8

10 8

Star Lake

Cooks Mill Pond

Charles Bay

Choctawhatchee River

Pate Pond

Flow

Fall Lake

Becton Pond

Flow

Holmes Creek

Live Oak Pond

Wickers Pond

Pettis Pond

LIVE OAK LANDING RD

Brunner Pond

Vernon

284

HIGHTOWER RD

284A

HAMMOCK RD

New Hope

77

Choctawhatchee River

© WILDERNESS ADVENTURES PRESS, INC.

To get to Charles Bay, take Exit 17 off Interstate 10 at the Bonifay exit and go south on State Road 79 for 2 miles. Turn left onto SR 280 and go 1.2 miles, and turn left again onto Chance Road. The single-lane ramp is a mile ahead on your left.

BLUE LAKE

At about 40 acres, Blue Lake is another "non-destination" lake unless you just happen to be in the immediate area. Flyfishers will again be fishing small poppers for bream and small bass.

To reach Blue Lake, take Exit 18 off of Interstate 10 and go south on State Road 77. The single-lane ramp is 0.3 mile on your left. There is parking for about six vehicles.

SANDHILL PONDS

Gin Lake	Payne Lake	North Spring Lake
Gap Lake	Dunford Lake	Bird Lake
Porter Lake	Hicks Lake	Long Lake
Hammond Lake	Lucas Lake	Sand Lake
Deadening Lake	Long Lake	Piney Lake
Watering Lake	Stewart Lake	Hammock Lake
Little River Lake	Green Lake	Rattlesnake Lake
Boat Lake	Dry Lake	Little Praire Lake
Golf Lake	Joiner Lake	Little Blue Lake
Gully Lake	Dog Lake	Big Island Lake
Grassy Lake	Negro Lake	Little Island Lake
Roach Lake	Deep Edge Lake	River Lake
Blue Homestead Lake	Major Lake	Court Martial Lake
Perch Lake	Open Lake	White Western Lake
Boggy Lake	Big Blue Lake	Britt Lake
Sweetwater Lake	Compass Lake	Merial Lake
Pine Log Lake	Crystal Lake	

These naturally occurring lakes are collectively referred to as the Sandhill Ponds. They average between 200 and 300 acres in size and are spread out over several counties. They are unusually clear and deep by Florida standards and some of the largest bluegill in the state are caught from them. Flyfishers will want to use a fluorocarbon leader because it is nearly invisible. It should be a couple of feet longer than usual to get the fly farther away from the fly line. A small, rubber-legged popper (size 8 Peeper Popper or size 10 Bluegill Bug) or a terrestrial (size 8 Dave's Hopper or Dave's Cricket) will take the big bluegill that move to the shorelines in spring and early summer to spawn. The bass fishing on these lakes is spotty and the fish are usually small.

Sandhill Lakes and Ponds

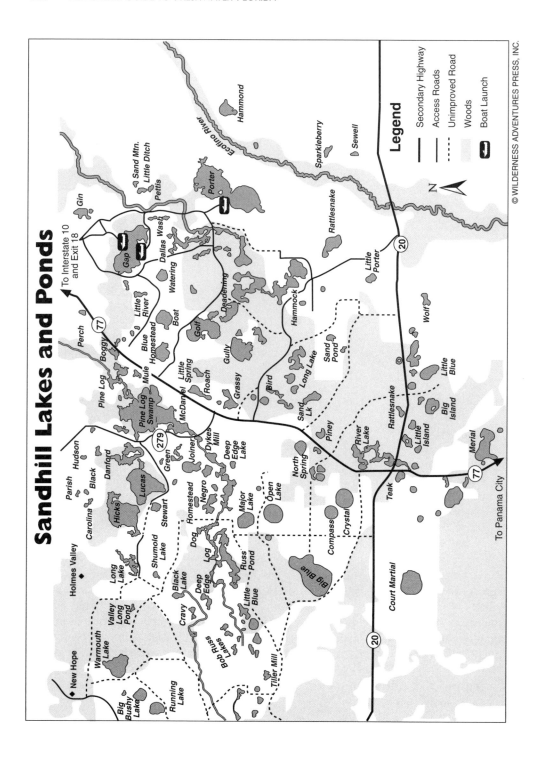

Legend

— Secondary Highway

| Access Roads

┊ Unimproved Road

Woods

🚤 Boat Launch

© WILDERNESS ADVENTURES PRESS, INC.

N

To Interstate 10 and Exit 18

To Panama City

Ecofina River

Hammond

Sand Mtn.
Little Ditch
Pettis

Porter

Sparkleberry

Sewell

Gin

Gap

Dallas Wash

Watering

Little River

Blue

Boat

Homestead

Golf

Deadening

Hammock

Rattlesnake

Little Porter

Wolf

Perch

Pine Log

Mule

Pine Log Swamp

McDaniel

Little Spring

Roach

Grassy

Bird

Gully

Long Lake

Sand Pond

Little Blue

Boggy

279

Green

Joiner

Dykes Mill

Deep Edge Lake

Sand Lk.

Piney

River Lake

Rattlesnake

Big Island

Little Island

Merial

Parish
Hudson
Black

Danford

Lucas

Stewart

Homestead

Dog

Negro

Log

Major Lake

North Spring

Open Lake

Compass

Crystal

Teak

Carolina

Hicks

Shumold Lake

Black Lake

Russ Pond

Court Martial

Holmes Valley

Long Lake

Cravy

Deep Edge

Little Blue

Big Blue

Valley Long Pond

Bob Russ Lakes

Tiller Mill

New Hope

Warmouth Lake

Running Lake

Big Bushy Lake

77

77

20

20

Only a few of these lakes have improved ramps, but most are accessible by canoe or johnboat carried in on a car top or in the back of a pickup truck. To get to the area, get off Interstate 10 at Exit 18 and go south on State Road 77 for about 13 miles. From here, you can go east or west on any of the ungraded and unmarked sand roads. Be careful not to get stuck. The faster you spin your tires, the deeper you seem to dig yourself into the sand. You might want to take a cell phone with you, just in case, and fish with a buddy who has a strong back capable of pushing you out of the sand.

This palm-sized panfish from the Sandhill Ponds took a popper.

ECONFINA RIVER

The Econfina River (a creek in the upper regions) is a legend among north Florida canoeists, as it is considered the most challenging of the state's many canoe trails. Limestone walls line the creek, forming chutes that leave little or no room to maneuver when a fallen tree causes an obstruction. The superb scenery might be worth a hike, but there is no reason to try and fish this area. Only the extreme lower portion of the Econfina River, where it turns from fresh to brackish as it empties into Deer Point Lake and then on to North Bay and the Gulf of Mexico, warrants any attention by the flyfisher.

This lower portion of the Econfina is known for its shellcracker fishing, especially from April to June. Flyfishers take them using small poppers and terrestrials. Early in the morning and late afternoons on into the evening are best. Other members of the bream family are available from spring through summer on small poppers. Bass take larger deer-haired poppers near shoreline cover. While not noted for its bass fishery, black bass in the lower portion of the Econfina River can become quite active in late spring and early summer as the river's water begins to warm.

To get to the lower portion of the Econfina River, go north from the coastline community of Panama City on US 231/State Road 75 for about 8 miles. After crossing the bridge at Bayou George, turn left onto County Road 167 and go north for about 5.5 miles to the bridge at McAllaster Landing. There is a single-lane ramp at the north end of the bridge. Go to your right (north) after launching and the large bay narrows over the course of the next 1.5 miles as you approach the river's mouth.

COMPASS LAKE

Compass Lake is a 350-acre, saucer-shaped lake in its southern portion. The northern portion (believed to be a different lake a century ago when the two were separated by a dirt road) is much more interesting, with coves and pockets along an irregular shoreline on the eastern edge. The lake has a good population of bream, but bass fishing is not noteworthy. Small poppers fished early and late in the day during spring yield decent catches of shellcrackers. Lake Compass is not a recommended destination because of its remote location and a fishery that is hardly remarkable.

If you choose to fish Compass Lake, get off Interstate 10 at Exit 19 and go south on US 231/State Road 75 for about nine miles. Turn left onto Lake Road and go one block to the single-lane ramp. There is parking for only two vehicles.

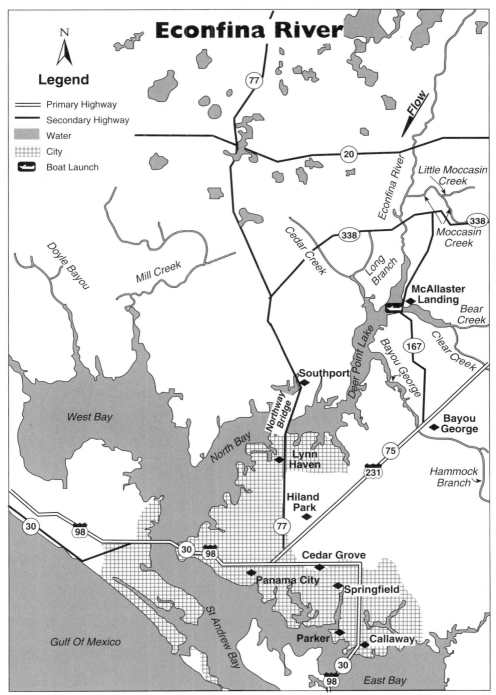

Econfina River

N

Legend

═══ Primary Highway
─── Secondary Highway
░░░ Water
▦▦▦ City
🛥 Boat Launch

77

Flow

20

Econfina River

Little Moccasin Creek

338

Moccasin Creek

338

Cedar Creek

Long Branch

Doyle Bayou

Mill Creek

McAllaster Landing

Bear Creek

Southport

Deer Point Lake

Bayou George

167

Clear Creek

West Bay

Northway Bridge

Bayou George

North Bay

Lynn Haven

75

Hammock Branch

231

Hiland Park

30   98

77

30   98

Cedar Grove

Panama City

Springfield

Gulf Of Mexico

St Andrew Bay

Parker

Callaway

30

98

East Bay

© WILDERNESS ADVENTURES PRESS, INC.

Numerous state record bream have come from Merritt's Mill Pond.
Water for the pond comes from Blue Springs. It later becomes
Spring Creek, a tributary of the Chipola River.

CHIPOLA RIVER, MERRITT'S MILL POND, AND DEAD LAKES

A fabulous fishery begins at Blue Springs in Merritt's Mill Pond and continues southward with the Chipola River until its confluence with the Apalachicola River 95 miles downriver. The Chipola widens in its lower reaches to form Dead Lakes.

The Chipola is home to the shoal bass, endemic to southwest Georgia and southeast Alabama. Their range in Florida is mostly limited to about 15 miles of the Chipola River (between Magnolia Landing and John Boy Landing) and upper portions of the Apalachicola River. As its name implies, the shoal bass feeds around shoals in the river, where it captures crawfish, minnows, and surface insects. The shoal bass is noteworthy in that it grows rapidly and to a substantial size (approaching eight pounds). It is a perfect target for flyfishers using a canoe to fish and wade.

The upper portion of the river above Florida Caverns State Park is scenic canoeing water that is of little interest to flyfishers because of its small size. At the state park, the Chipola disappears underground and reemerges a short distance later. There are caverns in the park that contain limestone stalactites and stalagmites, a rare sight in Florida.

Shortly after the state park, the first access point to the middle Chipola River can be found just north of Marianna. To get to this site, get off Interstate 10 at Exit 21 and go north on State Road 71 for about 7 miles to the town of Marianna. Turn right onto County Road 166 and go north for a mile. The single-lane ramp at Yancey Bridge has unimproved parking for six vehicles. At this point, the river is still very shallow and accessible only by canoes, kayaks, and johnboats.

About three river miles south of Marianna and about a mile above where I-10 crosses the Chipola River, Spring Creek enters from the east. The creek's crystal clear waters originate in Blue Springs. Immediately below the spring is Merritt's Mill Pond, a 202-acre impoundment. This pond is the premier shellcracker fishery in the entire state. From these waters came the state record shellcracker (4.86 pounds), caught in 1986, as well as other national and state line-class and tippet-class record fish.

The waters average about 6 feet in depth, with the deepest holes dropping to 20 feet or so. Spring is the best time to catch the super-sized shellcrackers, along with bluegill and other members of the bream family. Flyfishers should use a small popper with rubber legs (Peeper Popper, size 8) or larger terrestrials like Dave's Hopper or Dave's Cricket (both in size 8). The best time to fish is on overcast days when there is a slight ripple on the water's surface from wind or light rain. Because of the ultra-clear water, long leaders and light tippets are required.

Bass fishing is good, but the same clear water considerations regarding tippets apply. Just upgrade your hook size when bass are the targeted species.

To get to Merritt's Mill Pond, get off Interstate 10 at Exit 21 and go north on State Road 71 for 5.5 miles. Turn right onto County Road 164 and go east for 1.5 miles. Turn right onto Hunter Fish Camp Road and go 0.8 mile to the single-lane ramp. There is unimproved parking for 10 vehicles.

The next access to the Chipola River is about two river miles below where Spring Creek flows into the river. Again, get off I-10 at Exit 21 but this time go south on SR 71 for 0.8 mile. Turn right onto CR 280 and go west for a mile to the bridge crossing the Chipola River. The single-lane ramp is on the left, where there is parking for eight vehicles at what is locally known as Magnolia Landing.

There is another access point 6 miles south off SR 71. Turn right onto CR 278 and go west for 0.6 mile. At Peacock Bridge, turn left onto the dirt road and go 0.1 mile to the narrow, single-lane ramp. There is parking for only two vehicles. Be careful upon launching, as the river is quite swift at this point.

Continuing south on SR 71 for another 4 miles will bring you to the town of Altha. Turn right onto CR 274 and go west to access two more ramps in the midsection of the Chipola. The first is reached by going 2.7 miles west on CR 274 after leaving Altha. Turn right and go north on John Boy Road a mile to the single-lane ramp at John Boy Landing. There is unimproved parking for six vehicles.

The second ramp west of Altha is reached by going another 2.1 miles on CR 274 past John Boy Road. Cross the river and turn left onto the unnamed dirt road, heading south for 2 miles. Turn left again onto ramp road and go 0.5 mile to the single-lane ramp at Chipola Estates Landing where there is unimproved parking for two vehicles.

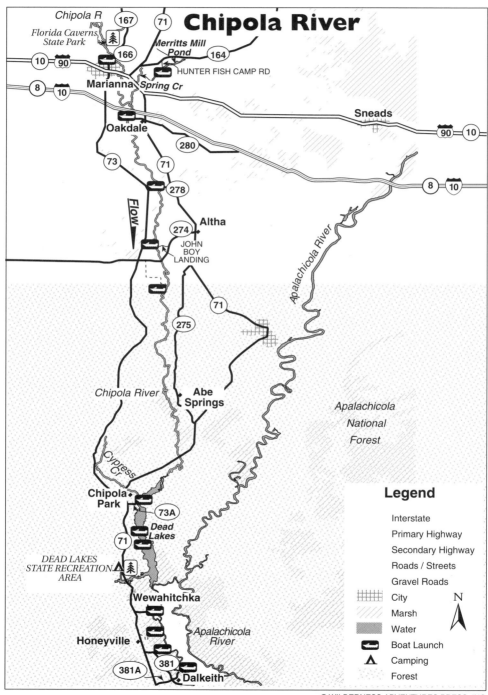

© WILDERNESS ADVENTURES PRESS, INC.

Just below this launch site is "Look and Tremble Rapid." The rapids are nowhere as bad as the name implies, and you can safely pass by going down the left side. Above and below the rapid, several small feeder creeks flow into the river from the east and west sides. The mouth of these should be fished with a crawfish imitation. I have had good success using saltwater flies that imitate shrimp (Whitlock's Shrimp, size 8) for this purpose.

The next ramp downstream can be reached by continuing south on SR 71 from Altha for 3 miles and then turning right onto CR 275. Go south on CR 275 for 7 miles to SR 20. Turn right onto SR 20 and go 1.5 miles to the bridge. Cross the bridge and make a right on the unnamed paved road. Go 0.3 mile to the single-lane ramp.

There is one more ramp on the east side of the river before SR 71 crosses the Chipola River. From the intersection of CR 275 and SR 20, continue south on CR 275 for 3.8 miles to the community of Abe Springs. Turn right on the ramp road and go 0.5 mile to the single-lane ramp. From here to the SR 71 bridge about 6 miles downstream, the river moves through a marshy area and begins to slow.

There are launch sites just above and below the bridge where SR 71 crosses the river. CR 275 rejoins SR 71 about 2.5 miles south of Abe Springs and another 3 miles south on SR 71 gets you to the bridge. The roads before and after the bridge take you to single-lane ramps.

You have now crossed the Chipola River on SR 71 and I will refer to this portion of the Chipola River as the lower section. The river immediately widens to an area known as Dead Lakes and then flows on through marsh to join with the Apalachicola River. Your remaining access points will be on the west side of the river.

Dead Lakes (6,700 acres), a naturally wide area in the river, is believed to have been formed when sand bars from the Apalachicola River (about a mile east of the southern tip of Dead Lakes) blocked the dark tannic waters of the Chipola and caused it to back up. When the water backed up, thousands of trees were killed (hence the name) and these subsequently provided habitat for fish. Be careful operating a motor here, as there are many submerged trees and snags just below the surface. The old river channel has depths that average about 15 feet for the length of the 8-mile-long, ½-mile-wide lake. At the lower end, Dead Lakes does have some areas with holes that reach 25 feet deep.

Flyfishers catch bluegill and shellcracker in the spring around flooded cypress trees using cricket and grasshopper patterns and small poppers. Bass fishing is good in both spring and fall in the same areas using larger deer-haired poppers.

There are numerous ramps along the western edge of Dead Lakes. Four miles after SR 71 crosses the river, the northern headwaters of the lake can be reached at Cypress Creek by turning left onto CR 73A. Go east on CR 73A for 0.5 mile and make a left onto Boat Ramp Road. There is a single-lane ramp at Cypress Creed with paved parking for 20 vehicles.

Continuing south on SR 71 for 7 miles, there are numerous ramps about ½ mile to your left (east) before coming to the community of Wewahitchka. One of the best of these is at Dead Lakes State Park. From Wewahitchka, go north on SR 71 for 1 mile and turn right onto State Park Road (there is a fee to enter the park) and go 0.5 mile to the single-lane ramp. There is secure, unimproved parking for 16 vehicles.

Dead Lakes ends at Wewahitchka, and the Chipola River flows another 10 miles toward the Apalachicola River. There is a wide marshy area leading to the confluence of these two great rivers with multiple river channels. Like the fishing in most marshy areas of Florida, it looks better than it is. In spring and early summer, black bass and panfish take up residence next to traditional shoreline structures and spawn in the shallows. These fish can be taken on poppers (size 4). Later in the year, these same areas yield an occasional fish but not as many as their "fishy appearance" would seem to indicate. Pay close attention to how you got to where you may be, as it is easy to get turned around in this area.

The first ramp in the short section of river below Wewahitchka is at Land's Landing. Go south on SR 71 for 1 mile and turn left onto the unnamed paved road leading directly to the single-lane ramp at its end. There is unimproved parking for 12 vehicles.

By continuing 1.5 miles south on SR 71 and turning left on the unnamed dirt road at Honeyville, an angler can reach another single-lane ramp. I do not recommend this one, however, as it does not give direct access to the river and requires local knowledge to navigate through the swamps.

The next ramp to the south is similarly remote. You can reach it, if you must, by going 1 mile south on SR 71 past Honeyville and turning left onto CR 381. Go south 0.5 mile and bear left to the single-lane ramp.

The final ramp before the Chipola River reaches the Apalachicola River can be reached by continuing south on CR 381 for 2 miles. At the intersection of CR 381A in Dalkeith, turn left and go 0.8 mile to the single-lane ramp. It is about 4 river miles to the Apalachicola. Look for sunshine bass and striped bass that have been stocked in the Apalachicola to make their way upriver into the Chipola at this point. During periods of low light, especially in the fall, look for them to be schooling. Try a Baby Bunker or large, light colored streamer.

CHATTAHOOCHEE RIVER

This river system flows south along the Alabama/Georgia line and on into Lake Seminole, serving as the boundary between Georgia and Florida for its last 15 miles. In these lower reaches, the river slows substantially and is dotted with numerous islands and oxbows. Striped bass and sunshine bass move into this area in the spring, and they can be caught with a Baby Bunker or a large, light colored streamer. When they are feeding on the surface, you may want to try a white foam Gurgler. The downcurrent side of islands, especially if there is an eddy, will be favorite feeding areas for the stripers. This portion of the river also yields good-sized bass in the spring, and large deer-haired poppers fished in the backs of oxbows and the many pockets off the river will turn up some fish. In late summer and the fall, look for largemouth and spotted bass to be in the current between the many islands. A much-overlooked

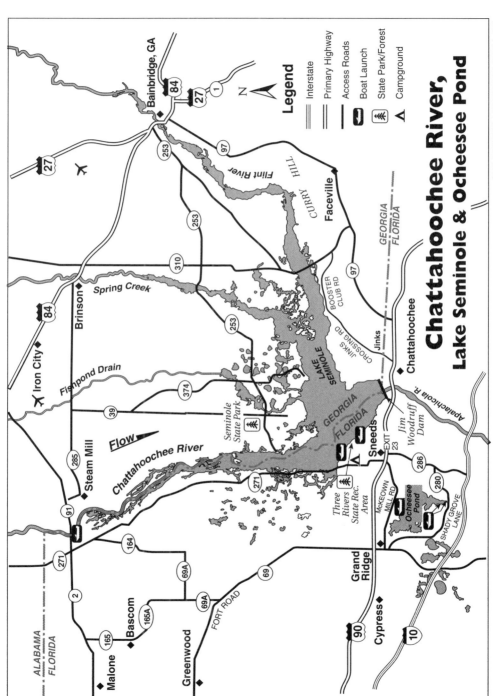

Chattahoochee River, Lake Seminole & Ocheesee Pond

Legend

Interstate
Primary Highway
Access Roads
Boat Launch
State Park/Forest
Campground

opportunity is the chance to take some bragging-sized crappie in early spring. The spawning crappie love to get next to flooded trees in about two feet of water. Try a small, brightly colored Clouser (size 2).

There is a single-lane ramp about a mile south of the intersection of the Alabama/Georgia/Florida state lines. Heading east on Florida State Road 2, turn right immediately before the bridge crossing the Chattahoochee River and go 0.2 mile to the launch site.

LAKE SEMINOLE

Lake Seminole is a 37,500-acre reservoir created by the Jim Woodruff Dam at the juncture of the Chattahoochee and the Flint Rivers near Chattahoochee, Florida. Most of lake is in Georgia, but about 8,000 acres in the southwest corner are in Florida. Anglers with a Florida license may fish in these state waters, but Georgia regulations pertaining to size and bag limits (generally more liberal than those of Florida) are in effect east of SR 271 (locally known as River Road), including the Florida waters, for all species. If you only have a Florida freshwater fishing license, it would be a good idea to check with a local bait and tackle shop to ensure that the area you propose to fish is entirely within the state of Florida. (By way of agreement, Florida anglers can fish south and west of an imaginary line from Chattahoochee Park on the east bank, through Navigation Mile Marker 3 on the Flint River, and south of Lake Seminole WMA to Navigation Mile Marker 6.4 on the Chattahoochee River.)

Much of Lake Seminole is standing timber that has been flooded, but most of the lake's waters are now covered with hydrilla. Water flowing from the dam gives birth to the Apalachicola River and the incredibly diverse fishery in that system. The three rivers in this area, the Chattahoochee, Flint, and Apalachicola, give rise to the name of the state recreation area (Three Rivers State Recreation Area) on the southwestern shore, two miles north of the town of Sneads.

Lake Seminole has an outstanding population of striped bass, hybrid bass, and sunshine bass stocked by Florida, Georgia, and the U.S. Fish and Wildlife Service. In the spring, these stripers move up the Chattahoochee River. During summer months, look for them near points in Lake Seminole near deep water, especially early and late in the day and during periods of low light, such as overcast and rainy days. In the fall, the stripers school just outside the old river channel near the dam and move up onto flats to feed on shad. Diving birds give away their location, especially late in the afternoon. Your fly needs to imitate a shad, a striper's primary forage. Consider trying a Baby Bunker or a large, light colored streamer. When stripers are feeding on the surface, you may want to go to a white foam Gurgler. The state record sunshine bass (a hybrid cross between a female white bass and a male striped bass) was caught from Lake Seminole in 1985 and weighed over 16 pounds. For many years, the record striped bass also came from these waters (38 pounds), but that record is now claimed by a 42-pounder caught in the discharge of Lake Seminole below Jim Woodruff Dam in the headwaters of the Apalachicola River.

Bass fishing can be good in the spring and summer on deer-haired poppers fished over the hydrilla. Bream fishing can often be excellent, especially when mayflies hatch. A Green Drake (size 10) would be a good choice—make color adjustments to better match those you see on the water.

To access the Florida portion of Lake Seminole, get off Interstate 10 at Exit 23 and go north on County Road 286 for 5 miles to Sneads. Turn left onto US 90/SR 10 and go west for 0.5 mile. Then turn right onto SR 271 and go north 2 miles to the Three Rivers SRA entrance on your right (there is a fee). The single-lane ramp is 0.8 mile inside the park, and there is parking for about 12 vehicles. In addition, there are excellent camping facilities available at Three Rivers SRA, and a separate ramp is available for use by campers. A stump field stretches for several hundred yards in front of the camping area and extends to the left as you look out over the lake. No matter where you choose to launch, be sure to check out this stump field for both largemouth and crappie in the early spring.

Closer to the dam, there is another ramp about a mile south of the Three Rivers SRA ramp. From Sneads, go right onto US 90/SR 10 for 1 mile and as you are about to leave town, turn left at Sneads Park onto Legion Road. The single-lane ramp is 1.5 miles ahead, with commercial marina facilities available.

Lake Seminole has an outstanding population of striped bass and sunshine bass.

The Jim Woodruff Dam creates Lake Seminole in north Florida. The discharge becomes the Apalachicola River, and striped bass fishing is excellent in the tailrace.

OCHEESEE POND

Ocheesee Pond (2,225 acres) is a mostly shallow reservoir with several thousand acres of bald cypress swamp rimming its shoreline. There are some deep holes of water (15 to 20 feet) that can be a reached by following boat trails.

Ocheesee Pond produces large bream and bass. Good areas are around stumps and snags in about 4 feet of water. The fish in Ocheesee Pond have a preference for grass shrimp, and a fly pattern like Joe's Grass Shrimp (size 6) will provide consistent action for quality-sized fish.

To get to the south side of Ocheesee Pond, get off Interstate 10 at Exit 23 and go north on County Road 286 for 2.5 miles. Turn left onto CR 280 and go west for 2.5 miles. Turn right onto Shady Grove Road and go 0.2 mile down the dirt road to single-lane ramp at Shady Grove. There is unimproved parking for 15 vehicles.

There is a ramp on the north side of Ocheesee Pond that can be reached from Sneads. Take Exit 23 and go north on CR 286 for 5 miles to Sneads. Turn left just before US 90/SR 10 onto McKeown Mill Road and go west for 2.5 miles. Turn left at Inwood and go 0.6 mile to the single-lane ramp.

APALACHICOLA RIVER

The Apalachicola River meanders 106 miles south from Lake Seminole at the Georgia/Florida line near the town of Chattahoochee across the Panhandle to the Gulf of Mexico at the town of Apalachicola. Measured by the volume of water being discharged into the Gulf, it is Florida's largest river. Fishing is best in the upper region (where it is influenced by the discharge of Lake Seminole) and in the lower region (where it is influenced by the bays and Gulf of Mexico). Perhaps the description should be "fabulous fishing" in these areas and merely "good fishing" in the middle region.

A review of where some of Florida's state record fish were caught causes the Apalachicola to stand out from so many other very good river systems in Region 2. Of interest to flyfishers, state records have been established for redeye bass, spotted bass, striped bass, and white bass on the Apalachicola River.

A great place to start for stripers (collectively referring to striped bass, white bass, and sunshine bass) is the Jim Woodruff Dam. The dam impounds the Chattahoochee River and Flint River, forming Lake Seminole. As the last reservoir in the two river systems, the lake is often weed-filled from fertile runoff. Not so in recent years, however, as long periods of infrequent rain have cleared the lake's waters. The amount of water being discharged now is only what is necessary to meet hydroelectric needs. As a result, the tailrace waters below the dam are only a trickle compared to what they used to be, and the old river channel has again been exposed. This concentrates the stripers as they move upriver toward the dam and presents an outstanding opportunity for flyfishers without a boat to get close to some terrific action. There is good access from the shore on the east side from Jim Woodruff Dam to Race Shoal (about 0.9 mile) and from the dam to State Road 90 (about 0.6 mile) on the west side. The property between the dam and SR 90 belongs to the Corps of Engineers. There is a catwalk below the dam, but flyfishers can walk down the steep bank to get to the water's edge.

Spring and fall offer tremendous opportunity below the dam for these stripers. Fish early in the day, as the best topwater action usually ends an hour after the sun rises. If the day is overcast, or if a heavy mist hangs above the water, the period of feeding may be extended a bit. Often, another period of feeding occurs just before sunset. Flyfishers should toss a white popper or a white foam Gurgler using a weight-forward floating line for added distance. A bunker pattern with either an olive or blue/gray back would make a good pattern for subsurface fish. These are very strong fish, and you should have a stainless steel hook (size 1 or 2). Also, be sure that your drag works properly and that you have a minimum of 100 yards of backing on your fly reel. Any fish in fast flowing water is a handful, but a striper could easily empty your spool. Better make that 200 yards of backing!

To get to Jim Woodruff Dam, get off Interstate 10 at Exit 24 and go north on County Road 270-A for 1.2 miles. Turn right onto CR 269 and go north for 6 miles to the town of Chattahoochee. There, turn left onto US 90/SR 10 and go 0.8 mile to the

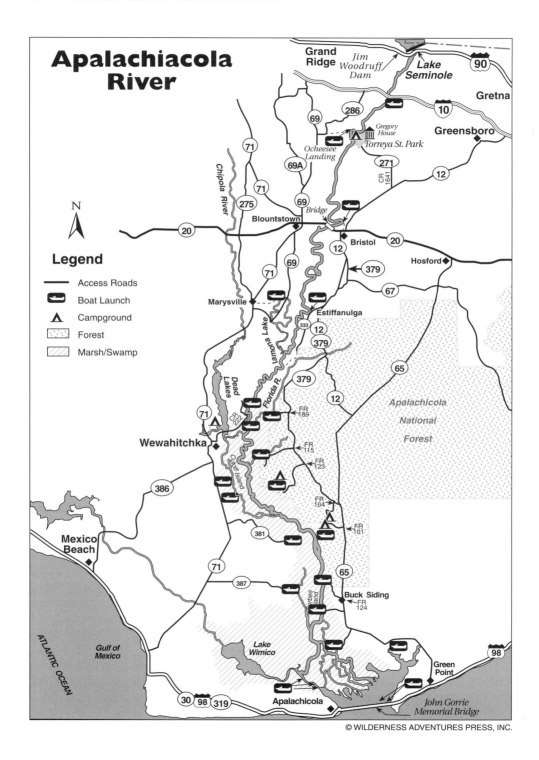

© WILDERNESS ADVENTURES PRESS, INC.

dam. There is a double-lane paved ramp with unimproved parking for 15 vehicles on the east side about 0.5 mile below where US 90/SR 10 crosses the Apalachicola River.

As you move south (downriver), there are no roads or bridges crossing the river until you get to Interstate 10 about 7 river miles downstream. The next bridge crossing the river is another 20 miles downstream at SR 20. Hence, if you want to get to a ramp on one side of the river or the other, you had better plan on a long drive.

There is a ramp on the east side of the river just south of where I-10 crosses the river, but you have to drive almost 20 miles from the nearest exit off I-10 to get to it. It is pretty remote and I would not feel secure leaving a vehicle there while trying to shuttle to the next take-out. The state record redeye bass was caught in the upper regions of the Apalachicola River near here, however.

Continuing another five miles downstream, there is a ramp that can be reached from the west side of the river. Get off I-10 at Exit 22 and go south on SR 69 for about 6 miles. Turn left onto CR 286 and go east for 3.6 miles. Turn left onto the unnamed dirt road and go 2.5 miles to the single-lane ramp (Ocheesee Landing) at the end of the road. There is unimproved parking for 10 vehicles.

Downstream about one mile is the Gregory House and Torreya State Park. This area has to be accessed by vehicle from the east side of the river. From the river town of Bristol, go north 13 miles on SR 12 to CR 1641. Turn left and follow signs to the park.

The Gregory House is a beautiful, fully restored plantation home built in 1849. The high bluffs along the river reach 150 feet, a rare sight in Florida, and the plants and hardwood trees are not common to other parts of the state. In fact, the Torreya tree grows nowhere else in the world except along the bluffs of the Apalachicola River. In addition, numerous other threatened or endangered plants can be found in the park.

The next ramp is about four river miles south of the Ocheesee Landing (3 miles south of Torreya State Park). Known locally as Red's Landing, the single-lane ramp has unimproved parking for 20 vehicles. From Exit 22, you will go south on SR 69 for about 9.2 miles. Turn left onto Red's Landing Road (dirt) and go 2.2 miles to the launch site. About half a mile north of the launch, Sweetwater Creek enters from the east and there is good panfishing up into the creek.

Unlike the Chipola River lying about 5 miles to the west, the middle portion of the Apalachicola has relatively few access points. This is a function of both the road system in the area and the quality of fishing. If there were better fishing, more ramps would be available. The next launch site is a one-lane ramp on the west side at the small town of Bristol. To get there, take Exit 25 off I-10 and go south on SR 12 for about 17 miles to the town of Bristol. Turn right onto SR 20 and go three blocks. Turn right go 0.5 mile to the ramp.

The midsection of the Apalachicola River does not have stripers to the extent that the upper and lower sections do. Nonetheless, it is a beautiful stretch of river with plenty of opportunities for black bass and panfish species. Bridges across the river remain far apart and getting to launch sites can be difficult. SR 20 does cross the river two miles west of Bristol and three miles east of Blountstown.

The next ramp downstream is south of Bristol on the east side of the river; continue about 8 miles south of town on SR 12. Turn right on CR 333 and go 1.8 miles to the community of Estiffanulga. Turn right on the unmarked dirt road and go 0.2 mile to the one-lane ramp.

On the west side of the Apalachicola River, there is a launch site in the headwaters of what is referred to as Iamonia Lake. From Blounstown, go south on SR 69 for 10 miles. SR 69 ends at a community known as Marysville and continue straight for 0.5 mile. Turn left onto the unnamed dirt road and go east for 0.5 mile to the single-lane ramp. Only canoes and similarly small craft can use this launch site. The access goes through the marsh for about a mile and becomes the river-like Iamonia Lake, entering the Apalachicola River about 2 miles later. Panfish and smaller bass can be found along the shoreline cover.

There are two launch sites about 12 river miles south that can also be reached from the west side of the river. The first is known as Wayside Park. From Blountstown, go south on SR 71 for about 25 miles to Wewahitchka (at the southern end of Dead Lakes on the Chipola River). From Wewahitchka, go east on CR 22A for 4 miles. Turn right onto Wayside Park Road and go 0.5 mile to the double-lane ramp at the end of the road. There is unimproved parking for 30 vehicles.

The next ramp south is known as Iola Landing. Go north on CR 22A for 3 miles, then turn right onto Iola Road and go 0.5 mile to the single-lane ramp with unimproved parking for 10 vehicles.

Over on the east side of the river, there are two ramps that give access to a number of creeks in the marsh. Local knowledge of the meandering creeks is necessary to have any hope of reaching the Apalachicola.

From Bristol, go south on SR 12 for about 13 miles. Turn left onto CR 379 and go south for about 7 miles. Turn right onto National Forest Road 189 and go west for 1 mile to the single-lane ramp that gives access to what is referred to as Florida River. There is unimproved parking for 20 vehicles.

By continuing another 3 miles south on CR 379, you can access the next ramp south. White Oak Landing, a single-lane ramp with unimproved parking for 16 vehicles, gives access to what is known as the River Styx. Turn right onto NFR 115 and go west 3 miles to the launch site.

There are also two ramps that can be reached by continuing another 2 miles south on CR 379. Turn right onto NFR 123 and go west 2.2 miles. Make a right onto NFR 123-B and go 1 mile to the two single-lane ramps. Like the other launch sites above, which are also in the Apalachicola Wildlife Management Area, these ramps are for small boats and give access to a winding system of creeks that move through the marsh toward the Apalachicola River several miles away. Local knowledge is required.

The last launch site in the middle section is also in the marsh and away from the river, although not so much as the previous ramps. Continue down CR 379 another 5 miles and turn right onto SR 65. Go south for 3 miles and turn right onto NFR 101. Go

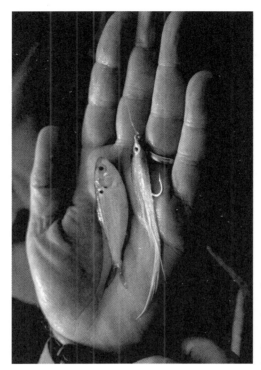

A Baby Bunker or large, light-colored streamer will do the trick for Apalachicola River stripers.

west for 1 mile and turn left onto NFR 101-B. Continue on the dirt road for 1 mile to the single-lane ramp. You can reach the Apalachicola River by going left for about a mile through low-lying marsh.

I will refer to the remaining portion of the Apalachicola River as the lower portion. Fishing rapidly improves as you move closer to the Gulf Coast and the river widens and slows. As it moves even closer to the Gulf, it takes on the characteristics of a delta and several fingers reach along the coastline.

Once again, stripers have been stocked by the hundreds of thousands and added to the fishery by both the U.S. Wildlife Service and the Florida Fish and Wildlife Conservation Commission. As mentioned elsewhere, fishing is best for stripers during low-light conditions, especially at first and last light of the day. White pencil poppers and foam Gurglers work well to entice topwater strikes. A Deceiver or a bunker pattern (Peterson's Baby Bunker, size 2/0) would be my choice for sub-surface fish. Largemouth bass hug the grasses along the shoreline and feed on shrimp moving up and down the rivers. There are also a number of sloughs off the rivers and topwater strikes by largemouth can be had in these areas on cork saltwater poppers like the Skipping Bug in a smaller size (size 2).

In addition, saltwater species such as tarpon and spotted seatrout will be present seasonally as you get closer to the coast. Look for tarpon to move up the river from East Bay in the summer months. Spotted seatrout take winter residence in the Apalachicola as it becomes a brackish coastal river.

I'll give directions for the remaining launch sites on the Apalachicola River from US 98/US 319/SR 30 as it moves along the coastline. About 4 miles east of the John Gorrie Memorial Bridge (5 miles wide) spanning Apalachicola Bay is the community of Green Point. SR 65 moves north out of this small town, and a flyfisher can gain access to the east side of the lower section of the Apalachicola from this road.

The first launch site in the lower portion of the widening Apalachicola River can be reached by going north from Green Point on SR 65 for about 15 miles. Turn left onto the National Forest Road at Buck Siding and go west for 1 mile. Turn right onto NFR 124 and continue for 3 miles to the single-lane ramp.

About 4 river miles south is another ramp that can be easily reached off SR 65. From Green Point, go north for about 13.5 miles and turn left onto the NFR and go 2.2 miles to the single-lane ramp at the river where the road ends.

The river splits into several fingers as it moves across a delta to empty into the Gulf. Lacking bridges across the low-lying wetlands, only the easternmost (East River) and westernmost (Apalachicola River) rivers have launch sites. All of these rivers (including St. Marks and Little St. Marks Rivers) have good striper fishing, as well as seasonal fishing for several saltwater species.

To get to the East River, go north on SR 65 from Green Point for about 10 miles. Turn left onto the NFR and go 2.5 miles to the single-lane ramp.

There is a launch site about 7 miles north of Green Point off SR 65. This single-lane ramp quickly leads to West Bayou and on to East Bay and then Apalachicola Bay. This would not be considered freshwater, however.

To get to the Apalachicola River in its lower reaches, cross the John Gorrie Memorial Bridge into the coastal town of Apalachicola on the west end of the bridge. This town was built at the mouth of the river where extensive oyster beds lay. In the early 1800s, Apalachicola was an important port for trade, commerce, and shipping. From Apalachicola, go north onto CR 384 for about 2.5 miles to the community of Bay City. There are two single-lane ramps in town, as well as one more about 1.5 miles north at the end of CR 384.

OCHLOCKONEE RIVER

The Ochlockonee River is a small, narrow river flowing into Florida from Georgia and is best suited for canoes, kayaks, and johnboats that draft little water. During periods of low water, the upper portion can be difficult for motorized boats, as snags and log-jams restrict travel. The river has a very good population of panfish, which make their home in the deeper water around root wads. Flyfishers should drift a terrestrial pattern by a piece of structure for bluegill and shellcrackers. Small topwater poppers also take redbreast along shorelines in portions of the river with still water. The Ochlockonee is the only river in northwest Florida to have Suwannee bass. Look for

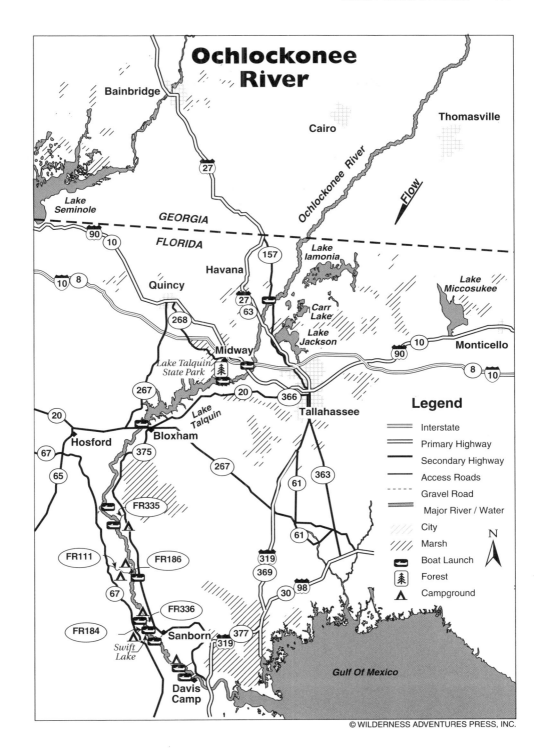

Ochlockonee River

Bainbridge

Cairo

Thomasville

27

Ochlockonee River

Flow

Lake
Seminole

GEORGIA

90
10

FLORIDA

157

Lake
Iamonia

Lake
Miccosukee

Havana

10
8

Quincy

27
63

Carr
Lake

Lake
Jackson

10

90

Monticello

268

Midway

Lake Talquin
State Park

8
10

267

20

366

20

Lake
Talquin

Tallahassee

Legend

Hosford

Bloxham

375

267

61

363

67

65

61

FR335

FR111

FR186

319
369

61

30
98

67

FR336

FR184

Sanborn

319

377

Swift
Lake

Davis
Camp

Gulf Of Mexico

≡	Interstate
═	Primary Highway
▬	Secondary Highway
—	Access Roads
- - -	Gravel Road
▬	Major River / Water
///	City
///	Marsh
⛴	Boat Launch
🌲	Forest
⛺	Campground

N

them around shoals, as well as wood structure, and try a crawfish or grass shrimp pattern.

Lake Talquin divides the river into upper and lower portions. In early spring, white bass move out of the lake and upstream into the river toward the crossing of US 90 west of Tallahassee. A glass minnow (size 1) would be an excellent choice for these smallest of stripers.

The first Florida access to the Ochlockonee River can be reached by taking Exit 29 off Interstate 10 at Tallahassee and going north on US 27/SR 63 for about 4 miles. Turn right onto CR 157 and go north for 3.5 miles. The single-lane ramp is on the right after crossing the river. There is unimproved parking for 12 vehicles.

The next downstream access is about 5 miles west of Tallahassee where US 90/SR 10 cross the river. There is a single-lane ramp with parking for 10 vehicles.

The last launch site for the upper portion of the river is at the Lake Talquin State Recreation Area. After crossing the Ochlockonee River on US 90/SR 10 about 5 miles west of Tallahassee, continue west another 1.2 miles and turn left onto CR 268. Go west on CR 268 for 3 miles to Midway. Turn left and follow the signs to the recreational area and launch site about 3 miles ahead.

When Jackson Bluff Dam was built across the river in 1927, Lake Talquin was formed. The river below the lake and dam are referred to as the lower portion of the Ochlockonee. Flowing all the way to the Gulf of Mexico, these waters remain shallow, narrow and scenic. In the fall and early spring, opportunities for striped bass can be very good below the dam. Redbreast sunfish, bluegill, shellcrackers, and black crappie offer excellent fishing in the spring and early summer all along the lower portion of the river. In addition, black bass can be found around treetops and snags located throughout this portion of the river. In the summer, low water concentrates the fish in the deep holes and these can offer some excellent opportunities.

The first ramp on the lower Ochlockonee is below the dam at Lake Talquin. Take SR 20 west out of Tallahassee and go about 20 miles. Turn right about 0.5 mile before crossing the Ochlockonee and follow the signs toward the dam. The single-lane ramp is 0.5 mile ahead.

Two roads parallel the river as it moves downstream. The road system in the area is not good, and few bridges cross the rivers in northwest Florida. On the east side of the Ochlockonee River is County Road 375 and on the west side of the river is State Road 67.

The next launch site downstream can be accessed from the west side of the river. After crossing the river on SR 20/CR 267, continue west about 14 miles to Hosford. Turn left onto SR 65 and go 3 miles south. Turn left onto SR 67 and go about 8.5 miles south. Turn left onto the dirt road and go 0.8 mile to the one-lane ramp.

Continuing down the west side of the river, there is a launch site that can be reached by going south another 5.5 miles on SR 67. Turn left onto National Forest Road 111 and go 2 miles. Cross the intersection and continue on what is now NFR 186. The single-lane ramp is 1.2 miles ahead.

Another launch site can be reached from the west side by continuing south on SR

67 another 3.5 miles and then turning left onto the dirt road. The single-lane ramp here is about 1 mile ahead.

The final ramp on the west side of the Ochlockonee River can be reached by going south another 3 miles to NFR 184. Turn left and go 0.7 mile to the single-lane ramp. This site is at the head of what is called Swift Lake it is wider and deeper than the river, which is 1 mile ahead. Upon reaching the river, you are about 10 river miles from Ochlockonee Bay and the Gulf of Mexico.

Going back up to Lake Talquin, you can access the river from the east side by turning off SR 20/CR 267 at Bloxham (about 19 miles west of Tallahassee) and going south on CR 375. To reach the first launch site, go about 10 miles south on CR 375 and then turn right onto National Forest Road 335. Go 1 mile to the single-lane launch site.

To get to the next launch site, go south another 10 miles on CR 375. Turn right onto NFR 336 and go 1 mile to the single-lane ramp. Once again, you are about ten river miles from Ochlockonee Bay and the Gulf, but you are directly on the river, which remains narrow and shallow at this point.

There is another launch site that can be reached by going south on CR 375 another 2 miles. Turn right at Sanborn (across from NFR 314) and go west on the dirt road for a mile to the single lane ramp.

Below this point, the river starts to straighten and widen, soon taking on delta-like characteristics. There are two more ramps on the east side before the river becomes brackish. Continue past Sanborn on CR 375 as it swings away from the river for about 6 miles. Turn right onto CR 299 and go south on CR 299 for 3 miles. Turn right onto NFR 338 and go 1.5 miles (bearing right to stay on NFR 338) to the single-lane ramp.

The last launch site on the east side can be reached by continuing south on CR 299 for another 1.3 miles. Turn right onto the dirt road leading to Davis Camp and go a mile to the single-lane ramp.

LAKE TALQUIN

Lake Talquin (8,850 acres), located about 20 miles west of Tallahassee, is one of the better all-around fishing lakes in the state and has a national reputation for its black crappie. Created in 1927 when the Ochlockonee River was impounded, the lake has flourished and continues to do so.

The state record black crappie (3.83 pounds) was caught here, as well as an uncertified state record chain pickerel. In addition, the lake has good populations of stripers (white bass and striped bass); bream (bluegill, shellcrackers, stumpknockers, and redbreasts); and largemouth bass.

The lake is about 10 miles long and a mile wide, with numerous fingers on both sides where creeks once joined the river. The old river channel runs down the east side of the lake, which averages about 15 feet deep. Picture a narrow, shallow stream that has been dammed, causing water to back up for 10 miles in the impoundment.

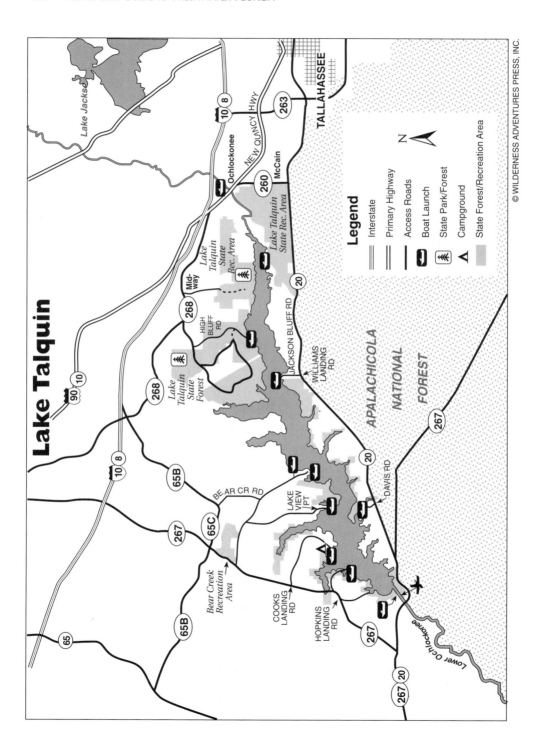

Lake Talquin

Legend

Interstate
Primary Highway
Access Roads
Boat Launch
State Park/Forest
Campground
State Forest/Recreation Area

N

© WILDERNESS ADVENTURES PRESS, INC.

Below the Jackson Bluff Dam on Lake Talquin,
the striped bass fishing can be excellent.

The upper end of the lake has depths that average much less than those of the lower portion. This is function of the gradient of the old stream. In this case, Lake Talquin has depths as much as 40 feet near the dam. The water tends to be clear, with little vegetation. There are plenty of tree stumps and logs near the shorelines and back in the fingers and coves.

The white bass are best caught in March above the lake as they move into the river to spawn. When they return, look for them around points extending out into the main lake during low-light conditions. Flyfishers should try a grass shrimp pattern or a glass minnow. These are very sporting fish on a 6-weight fly rod.

Striped bass are stocked annually in the lake and are best caught in the fall when they school. They can be located late in the afternoon when they push shad to the surface, and gulls gather over them to feed on the shad, as well. There will be a lot of topwater strikes and a white pencil popper or white Gurgler will take the 5- to 8-pound stripers. I would also consider a Baby Bunker or a small Deceiver for subsurface fish. Use an 8-weight outfit if you are specifically targeting striped bass. Don't forget about the good striper fishing below the dam in both spring and fall.

The bream fishing is best in the spring. Crappie fishing in Florida occurs earlier than it does in northern states. January and February offer the best opportunities for "specks" that have moved to the shorelines to spawn. Look for the fish to be next to wooden structure, both tree stumps and blowdowns. A brightly colored Clouser will do the trick. Crappie do not like to rise in the water column to feed, so you need to

The current state record crappie (3.83 pounds) came from Lake Talquin.

get your fly down to their strike zone. Since they have moved to shallow water, there is no need for a sinking line, however.

Other members of the bream family also move to shoreline cover to spawn, but they do so a little later in spring. Look for them to move into the backs of the fingers and coves around March and April, especially around the full moon. A terrestrial pattern or a small popper fished early and late in the day is best. This fishing can be excellent during the spring and into early summer.

Largemouth bass also prefer structure, and you will find them in the same areas as the crappie and other panfish. While not known as a trophy bass lake, there is a very good population of quality-sized largemouth in Lake Talquin. Flyfishers often get a pleasant surprise while fishing for bream in the spring when their line goes streaking to the side after the hook has been set. If targeting largemouth specifically, I would use a deer-haired popper and keep it close to shoreline structure.

There are several launch sites servicing Talquin, with most of the private, pay sites on the east (Tallahassee) side of the lake. To launch near the upper end, go west on SR 20 from Tallahassee for about 12 miles. Turn right onto Williams Landing Road and go 0.8 mile to the single-lane ramp. There are at least six commercial sites as you continue west on SR 20 with the lake about a mile to your right. There is a launch site near the dam about 20 miles west of Tallahassee off SR 20. Turn right onto Davis Road and go 0.5 mile to the one-lane ramp.

To access the other side, go west from Tallahassee on US 90/SR 10 for about 6 miles. Turn left onto CR 268 and go west 5 miles (through Midway) to High Bluff Road. Turn left and go 3.5 miles to the single-lane ramp at High Bluff Landing. There is unimproved parking for 31 vehicles.

The remaining ramps on the west side are reached from CR 267. The best way to proceed is to go west from Tallahassee on SR 20 for about 22 miles, crossing the Ochlockonee River just below the dam. Turn right onto CR 267 and go north for 3 miles. Turn right onto Hopkins Landing Road and go 0.8 mile to the single-lane ramp at Hopkins Landing. About 0.2 mile farther north on CR 267 is Cooks Landing Road. Turn right and there is another single-lane ramp about 2 miles ahead at Cooks Landing.

Continuing north another 3 miles on CR 267 is Bear Creek Recreation Area. Turn right onto CR 65C and go east for 1.5 miles. At the split in the road, you can go right to the launch site at Lake View Point (3 miles ahead) or go left 2.5 miles. There are two single-lane ramps providing ready access to the middle of the lake.

As you can see by the number of ramps on Lake Talquin, both public and commercial, the lake is highly regarded by anglers in the area—good fishing is the reason.

Lake Jackson's largemouth bass readily take foam and deer-hair poppers.

LAKE IAMONIA

Lake Iamonia (5,757 acres) is frequently covered with vegetation. The lake has a reputation for large panfish that can be caught in the spring and early summer, but largemouth bass fishing can only be described as fair. You will have to maneuver your boat through the vegetation and make short casts to small openings to fish Lake Iamonia. Try small, rubber-legged poppers and let them set still on the water early and late in the day.

To get to the south side of Lake Iamonia, go north from Tallahassee on US 319/SR 61 for about 5 miles. Turn left onto CR 154 and go west on CR 154 (Bannerman Road) for about 2.5 miles. Turn right onto Bull Heady Road and go 2 miles to the single-lane ramp.

There is a much better launch site on the north side of Lake Iamonia. Continue north on US 319 /SR 61 for another 7 miles. Turn left onto CR 12 and go west for 2.2 miles. Turn left onto Lake Iamonia Road and go 1.8 miles to the single-lane ramp. There is unimproved parking for 25 vehicles.

LAKE JACKSON, CARR LAKE, LAKE ELIZABETH, LAKE OVERSTREET, LAKE HALL AND LAKE MCBRIDE

This grouping of lakes lies immediately north of Tallahassee (all within 10 miles) and suffers from the effects of spreading urbanization and over-development. Lake Jackson (4,004 acres) is by far the largest and most interesting of these lakes. At times, it has had a national reputation for outstanding catches of trophy-sized largemouth bass. However, at other times, things haven't been so good...

On September 16, 1999, Lake Jackson was drained nearly dry. It was as if someone had pulled the stopper out of a bathtub and let all the water drain away. The lake is natural and does not have a stream or river feeding it. Consequently, it is dependent upon rainfall to maintain an adequate water level, typically about 8 to 10 feet deep. However, there are two sinkholes that become active during drought cycles and can drain most of the water out of Lake Jackson overnight. (Florida has a system of underground rivers that run through limestone caves and tunnels. The roof above one of these tunnels occasionally caves-in and what ever is above sinks into the abyss.) This happened eight times in the 20th century and who knows how many times before that.

Exposing the bottom of a Florida lake is often done to enhance fishing, and the natural draining of Lake Jackson is not all bad. Accumulated muck can be dredged and removed and new plant life will soon emerge. Baitfish flourish once again, and their predators quickly get fat feeding on them. Typically, there will be very strong year-classes of largemouth caught three to five years after such a drawdown or draining. Fly fishing for largemouth bass should be outstanding during the spring of 2003 and for a couple of years thereafter.

Again, topwater flies (deer-hair poppers, size 1 or 2) would be an excellent

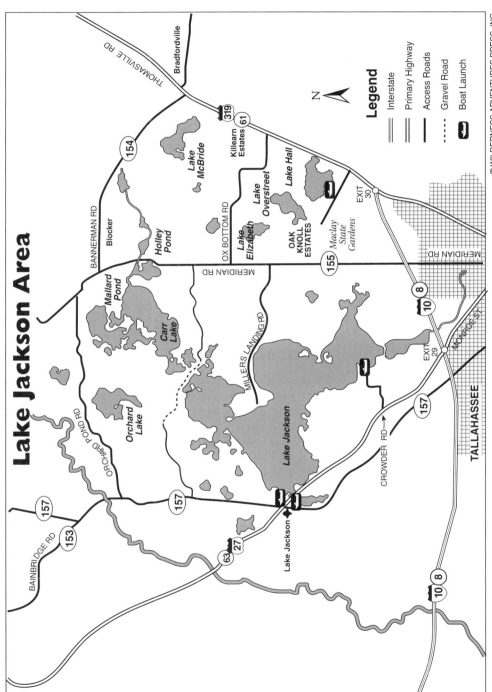

Lake Jackson Area

THOMASVILLE RD

Bradfordville

154

Lake McBride

319

61

Killearn Estates

BANNERMAN RD

Blocker

Holley Pond

OX BOTTOM RD

Lake Overstreet

Lake Hall

EXIT 30

Lake Elizabeth

OAK KNOLL ESTATES

Maclay State Gardens

155

MERIDIAN RD

MERIDIAN RD

Mallard Pond

Carr Lake

8

10

ORCHARD POND RD

Orchard Lake

MILLERS LANDING RD

Lake Jackson

EXIT 29

MONROE ST

157

157

CROWDER RD →

157

153

157

BAINBRIDGE RD

27

63

Lake Jackson

TALLAHASSEE

10 8

N

Legend

≡ Interstate

‖ Primary Highway

| Access Roads

┊ Gravel Road

▯ Boat Launch

choice. Fish around shoreline grasses in the early spring months. By summer, fishing will be best early and late in the day. There is also a good population of bluegill and shellcrackers, along with crappie. As in other lakes, crappie fishing is going to be at its peak during February for anglers casting Clouser Minnows toward shoreline cover. The other panfish will take a terrestrial pattern or a small popper, especially early and late in the day into the summer. On the full moon in May, try casting a terrestrial around the crater-shaped beds visible near the shoreline. A hookup is a sure bet.

To get to these lakes north of Tallahassee, get off Interstate 10 at Exit 29 and go north on US 27/SR 63 for about 2 miles. Turn right onto Crowder Road and go 1 mile to the single-lane ramp (Crowder Landing) at the southern end of Lake Jackson.

Continue another 2 miles on US 27/SR 63 and there are two single-lane ramps on your right just before and after the intersection with CR 157. These two ramps are visible from the road, as it runs alongside the lake.

The other lakes near Lake Jackson and immediately north of Tallahassee are much smaller. Lake Carr is about 500 acres, but Lakes Elizabeth, Overstreet, McBride, and Hall are only about 150 acres. These small lakes are surrounded by homes and offer little opportunity to experience quality fishing. Only Lake Hall has a ramp.

To get to the launch site at Lake Hall, get off I-10 at Exit 30 and go north on US 319/SR 61 for 0.5 mile. Turn left into the Maclay State Gardens park/lake complex and follow the signs to the single-lane ramp.

LAKE MICCOSUKEE

Lake Miccosukee (6,226 acres) is a shallow, hard-bottomed lake with good fishing for largemouth bass and bream. It is a private lake, and the shoreline is lined with trees instead of homes. The water is dark and tannic stained. Shoreline cover includes moss, lily pads, coontail, and cattail. Hence the Indian name "Lake of Grass."

Bluegill are abundant and flyfishers will do well with terrestrials and small poppers around the shoreline vegetation in the spring. Fish from Lake Miccosukee are brightly colored. Crappie can be caught close to wood structure in the water in early spring. Largemouth bass seldom get to be trophy-sized, but there are plenty of 2-pounders.

To get to Lake Miccosukee, get off Interstate 10 at Exit 33 and go north on US 19/SR 57 for 4.5 miles to Monticello. Turn right onto US 90 /SR 10 and go 6.5 miles to the single-lane ramp on your right (Lake Miccosukee South). There is unimproved parking for six vehicles.

There are a couple of ramps on the north end of the lake, but these launch sites are much more difficult to get to. From the intersection of US 19/SR 57 and US 90/SR 10 in Monticello, continue north on US 19/SR 57. As you are leaving town, turn left onto CR 259 and go 0.4 mile. Make another left and the two single-lane ramps are about 5 and 6 miles ahead on your left. These sites are not very secure, and I do not recommend them.

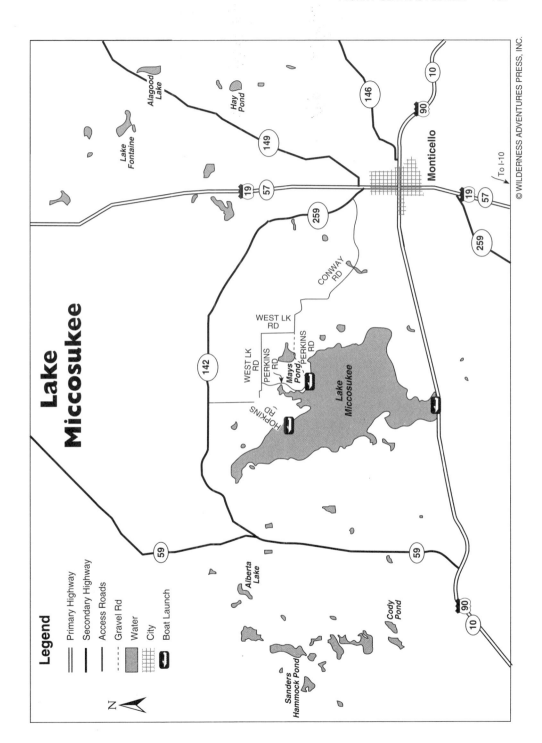

Lake Miccosukee

Legend

— Primary Highway
— Secondary Highway
— Access Roads
- - - Gravel Rd
Water
City
Boat Launch

N

Alagood Lake

Hay Pond

Lake Fontaine

10

146

90

Monticello

To I-10

19
57

149

19
57

259

259

CONWAY RD

WEST LK RD

WEST LK RD

PERKINS RD

PERKINS RD

Mays Pond

HOPKINS RD

142

Lake Miccosukee

59

59

Alberta Lake

Cody Pond

10

90

Sanders Hammock Pond

© WILDERNESS ADVENTURES PRESS, INC.

*The Suwannee River is as beautiful today as when
Stephen Foster wrote "Old Folks at Home."*

SUWANNEE RIVER

This is the river Stephen C. Foster memorialized in the lyrics of his 1851 song "Suwannee River" (a.k.a. "Old Folks at Home"), which became Florida's state song. Most of the headwaters are found in the Okefenokee Swamp in Georgia, but almost as soon as the undefined maze enters Florida, it starts to look like a river. The Suwannee winds its way through 8 counties in Florida for a distance of about 225 miles before reaching the Gulf of Mexico at the Big Bend town of Suwannee.

As it meanders about in northern Florida, the Withlacoochee and Santa Fe Rivers join the Suwannee's dark, tannic stained waters. The coloration, often referred to as being similar to tea, comes from a discharge from the roots of cypress trees found in the Okefenokee Swamp and lining the river's edge. While tannic stained waters often look very "fishy," I have found that such rivers seldom hold fish in good numbers. This is certainly the case with the upper portion of the Suwannee River. As you can see from looking at the map, the boat ramps are greater in number and closer together as you move downstream below the merger with the Santa Fe. Likewise, the fishing is better in these lower reaches.

The Suwannee River has a species of black bass known as the Suwannee bass. These seldom get to be more than 12 inches and a fish approaching 2 pounds is considered large. The state record came from the Suwannee, although they are also found in the Ochlockonee River. Most of these bass are caught downstream from the Santa Fe confluence, where the state record was taken.

As the Suwannee River enters Florida, it is no more than a small stream. The volume of the stream, however, depends upon the amount of rainfall that has been received in the southeastern part of the United States, and it is subject to some wild fluctuations. If the river is "up" because of heavy rains, these upper waters can offer some challenging times. With several small rapids, and one Class 2 rapid (Big Shoals), above White Springs near Interstate 75, these are not waters to be run by canoes or johnboats that have been fully loaded with valuable fly fishing tackle.

Many people regard the run from White Springs downstream for about 45 miles to the Suwannee River State Park, where the Withlacoochee River merges its clear waters with those of the Suwannee River, as the most scenic portion of the river. Numerous springs bubble-up from the ground in this stretch and begin to increase the size of the Suwannee and make it navigable by motorized boats. The springs, however, make hardly an impression on the river's size when compared to the addition of water from the Withlacoochee River. Although motors can be used at this point, watch carefully for boulders hidden just below the Suwannee's dark waters. Unlike submerged logs, a limestone rock is not very forgiving to the lower unit of an outboard motor.

I refer to the waters between the Georgia/Florida state line and the junction of the Withlacoochee River at the state park as the upper portion of the Suwannee River. Flyfishers can occasionally catch small black bass and a few panfish using terrestrial patterns. Fishing is generally not that good in the dark, tannic-stained waters of the upper portion, however. Try drifting flies through moving water below shoals, as well as next to fallen trees and root wads near the shoreline. The fish in the upper portion are not big, but they are made strong by the fast-moving water.

You can reach the northernmost launch site by getting off Interstate 75 at Exit 86 and going east on State Road 6, through Jasper, for a distance of about 24 miles. A mile before crossing the Suwannee River, turn left onto Woodpecker Road and go north for 4 miles. Turn right onto the dirt road and go 0.5 mile to the single-lane ramp. The river at this point is no more than a canoe trail and wildlife is abundant. People and boats are not.

There is a locally used launch under the bridge at SR 6. It is not paved, nor is the lane leading to it. Parking is not secure, but if you wanted to canoe or kayak these upper waters, you might want to consider it.

The next public ramp is at White Springs. This launch is below Big Shoals and a motorized johnboat could be safely used in all except the lowest water conditions from this point downstream. Get off I-75 at Exit 84 and go east on SR 136 to the intersection with US 41/SR 25/CR 100 in White Springs. Turn right at the intersection onto US 41/SR 25/CR 100 and go 0.5 mile. With the bridge crossing the Suwannee River in sight, make a right and go 0.3 mile to the single-lane ramp.

The next launch site is about 40 miles downstream. This is a beautiful stretch of

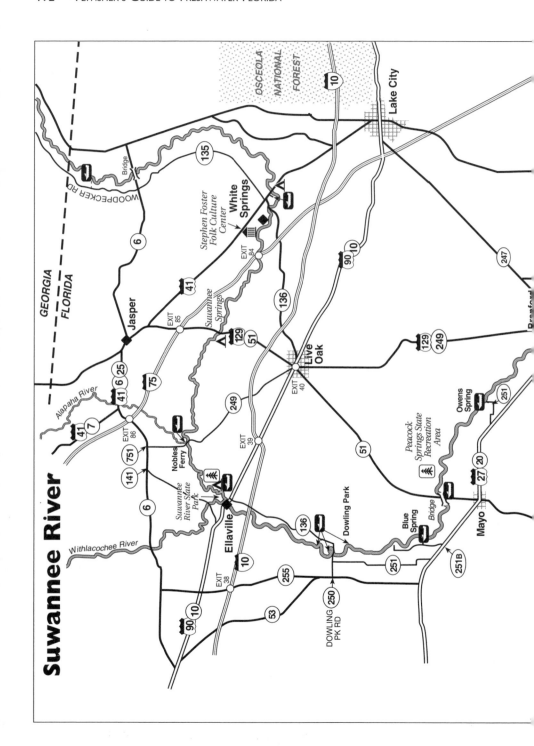

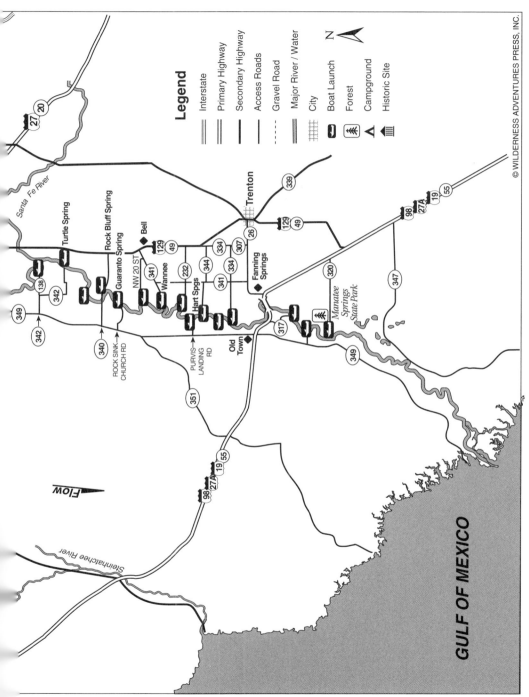

A steep paved ramp gives boaters access at Suwannee River State Park.

river showing few signs of development. The river moves at a leisurely pace and you can easily fish while floating in your small craft. Small black bass and panfish continue to be available, but in limited numbers. To get to this site, which is about 0.2 mile above the confluence of the Alapaha River, get off I-75 at Exit 86 and go west on SR 6 for 3.3 miles. Turn left onto CR 751 and go 3.5 miles to the single-lane ramp on the right side of the road just before River Bridge Park. The launch site, known as Nobles Ferry, has unimproved parking for 25 vehicles.

The Suwannee River State Park is about 4 miles downstream. There is a good ramp and improved campsites are available (no cabins). There are also several historic landmarks at this strategic Civil War site, and the area is home to great horned owls, turkeys, woodpeckers, otters, beavers, alligators, red-tailed hawks, and gopher tortoises. The banks are lined with limestone for the most part, but where there is sand or soft dirt, look for tracks from deer that have come down to the water's edge to drink. The state park is within a few miles of both I-10 and I-75. To get to the launch from I-10, get off at Exit 39 and go west on US 90/SR 10 for 5 miles to the park entrance on your right. From I-75, get off at Exit 86 and go west on SR 6 for 5 miles. Turn left onto CR 141 and go south for 5 miles. Turn left onto US 90/SR 10 and go east for 2 miles to the state park entrance on your left.

After the confluence of the Withlacoochee River at the state park, the Suwannee River begins to widen and the speed also seems to increase. There continues to be little development along the river's edge and it is easy for a flyfisher to lose track of time in this tranquil atmosphere. Fishing remains good, but because of the increase in size, there are only occasional shoals. Cast your fly to the numerous blowdowns and root wads that extend out from the shoreline. Stick with terrestrials like a Dave's Hopper (size 2). Fishing begins to get better and redbreast sunfish are particularly common in this part of the river.

The next take-out is about 14 miles downstream at a site known as Boundary Bend. From Interstate 10, go south at Exit 38 on CR 255 for about 8 miles. Now it gets a little tricky and, as you will see later, the next launch site provides much easier access. At the graded crossroads, turn left and go 2.5 miles east to a second graded crossroad. Turn right and go another 2.5 miles to the graded crossroads. Now turn left and take the left fork towards Mill Creek South, a Wildlife Management Area, and continue straight past the tower to the single-lane ramp. There is unimproved parking for five vehicles.

About 1.5 miles downstream is a very good launch/take-out at Dowling Park with parking for 25 vehicles. From Exit 40, go south on SR 51 through Live Oak for about 7 miles. Turn right onto CR 250 and go west for 12 miles to the Suwannee River Bridge and the park.

There is another good ramp about two miles downstream. Continue as above for the Dowling Park launch site, but cross the Suwannee River on CR 250 and go another 0.7 mile to CR 251. Turn left onto CR 251 and go south for 1.5 miles to Sand Pond Road. Turn left onto Sand Pond Road and go another 1.5 miles to the single-lane ramp. There is unimproved parking for 30 vehicles.

The next ramp is about 7 miles downstream at Blue Spring. From I-10, go south from Exit 38 onto CR 255 for about 15 miles. Turn left and go east on US 27/SR 20 for 4 miles. Turn left again on CR 251-B and go north for 2 miles. Turn right and the single-lane ramp is 0.8 mile ahead at the end of the road. This is not a very secure location.

The next launch site is about 4 miles downstream on the south side of the bridge where SR 51 crosses the river. Take Exit 40 through Live Oak and go south on SR 51 for about 18 miles to the single-lane ramp after crossing the bridge.

Numerous springs continue to add water from both sides of the river, and it gets imperceptibly larger with each addition. The Suwannee River is now wide and only the banks hold your interest. There continues to be redbreast and other panfish, as well as better numbers of small black bass.

At Ownes Spring, there is a single-lane ramp. From I-10, get off at Exit 38 and go south on CR 255 for about 15 miles. Turn left onto US 27/CR 20 and go east for about 13 miles, through Mayo, to CR 251. Turn left onto CR 251 (be careful, as CR 251 crosses US 27/CR 20 three times in a 2-mile stretch) the first opportunity that you get, go east for 1.8 miles. At the 4-way intersection, continue straight for about 0.5 mile, then left for 0.8 mile to the launch site. There is unimproved parking for 12 vehicles.

The next access point is about 6 miles downstream. Continue east on US 27/SR 20 for another 5 miles and turn left onto the dirt road. The single-lane ramp is 1.5 miles ahead.

About 2.5 miles downstream, US 27/SR 20 crosses the Suwannee River. The river has become so wide at this point that anything not motorized is really impracticable. This is certainly the case when, another 8 miles downstream, the Santa Fe River merges from the east. There is a marked improvement in the fishing, however, below the merger of these two rivers.

To get to the US 27/SR 20 Bridge, go south onto CR 251 from Exit 38 off I-10 for about 15 miles. Turn left onto US 27/SR 2 and go about 20 miles (thru Mayo) to the bridge. For the sake of simplicity, I'll first give directions to ramps on the west side of the river between the bridge where US 27/SR 20 crosses the Suwannee River and where US 98/US 19/SR 55 crosses the river (about 45 miles downstream), and then do so for the east side of the river.

The main route (CR 349) along the west side of the Suwannee River can be reached from the US 27/SR 20 Bridge by going west on US 27/SR 20 for 1.5 miles. The first launch site below the bridge is at Hatch Bend. From the intersection of US 27/SR 20 with CR 349, turn left and go south on CR 349 for 4.3 miles. Turn left onto CR 342 and go 2.1 miles. Turn left onto CR 138 and go 2.3 miles to the single-lane ramp. There is unimproved parking for 30 vehicles.

The next two sites are both reached by continuing south on CR 349 for 3 miles to where CR 342 again meets CR 349. Turn left onto CR 342 and go east for 2.5 miles. Turn right and go 1.5 miles to the river. The southernmost ramp is 0.1 mile down the lane on your right. To reach the northernmost site, continue on CR 342 for another 1 mile, and then turn right. The launch is 1 mile straight ahead. Between these two launches, the Santa Fe adds substantially more water to an already wide and fast-moving river.

Downstream about 6 miles, CR 340 crosses the river and there is a good launch site at what is called Rock Bluff Springs. To get to CR 340 from the west side of the river, go 10 miles south on CR 349 from the intersection with US 27/SR 20. Turn left onto CR 340 and go 2.5 miles to the bridge crossing the river. The single-lane ramp is on the east side (to your right). There is unimproved parking for 20 vehicles.

Both largemouth and Suwannee bass can be caught in this portion of the river. Crawfish are their primary forage and flyfishers should probe around bluffs and fallen rocks with patterns that imitate these crustaceans. Redbreast sunfish continue to be plentiful.

The next ramp downstream that can be reached from the west side of the river is at Guaranto Springs. Continue south on CR 349 for 1.3 miles after the CR 340 intersection and turn left onto Rock Sink Church Road and go 2.4 miles to the single-lane ramp. There is unimproved parking available for 20 vehicles.

Purvis Landing is the next launch site that can be accessed from the west side of the river. It is about 15 miles downstream, although there are several launches on the east side of the river in this stretch. To get to Purvis Landing, continue south on CR

Okefenokee Swamp.

349 about 9 miles after the intersection with CR 340. (You are 3.3 miles north of the community of Old Town at the intersection of CR 349 and US 98/US 19/SR 55.) Turn left onto Purvis Landing Road and go 1.5 miles to the single-lane ramp. There is unimproved parking for 20 vehicles.

Let's go back upstream to the US 27/SR 20 bridge at Branford and come down the east side of the Suwannee River in the same midsection. From the bridge, go east on US 27/SR 20 for 4 miles to SR 49. Turn right and go south for all of the ramps on the east side of the river.

The first ramp on this side (you will cross the Santa Fe River about 2.5 miles after turning onto SR 49) can be reached by going south 10 miles on SR 49. Turn right and go 1.5 miles west on CR 340. Turn right and go another 1.5 miles, bearing to your left as you approach the river and the single-lane ramp.

By continuing another mile on CR 340, you will come to the bridge over the Suwannee River and the good launch site at Rock Bluff Springs (discussed previously).

The next site is about 4 miles downstream at Wannee Landing. Continue south on SR 49 for 2.5 miles to the community of Bell. Turn right onto CR 341 and go 3 miles. At the 4-way intersection, continue straight onto what is now SW 10th Street to the single-lane ramp 4 miles ahead. There is unimproved parking for 20 vehicles.

Downstream from Wannee Landing, the Suwannee River makes a couple of long, sweeping turns. There is deep water on the outside bends and you may want to switch to a sink-tip line to see what lurks in these depths. Again, a fly that imitates a crawfish or a shrimp would be a very good choice. In the early evening, look for a little topwater action on the inside of these bends in the shallow water. A deer-hair popper or a foam Gurgler should reward a patient flyfisher.

The next ramp downstream is also on the east side at the end of the turns. From the intersection of SR 49 and CR 340, continue south on SR 49 for 6 miles to CR 232. Turn right onto CR 232 and go west for 4 miles where it will make a 90-degree turn to the left. Turn right onto SW 70th Avenue and go 0.5 mile north. Turn right onto SW 25th Street and go 0.8 mile to the single-lane ramp known as Eula Landing on your right. There is unimproved parking for 25 vehicles.

Another launch site about 3 miles downstream can also be reached for the east side. Continue south on SR 49 another 2.5 miles after the intersection with CR 232. Turn right onto CR 344 and go west for about 4 miles and make the "dog-legged" right-then-left turn on CR 344. Continue on CR 344 for another 2 miles, bearing right at the river on SW 90th Avenue to the single-lane ramp at Hart Springs Park. There is unimproved parking for 20 vehicles.

The last ramp on the east side above the US 98/US 19/SR 55 Bridge can be reached by proceeding as above toward Hart Springs Park. When you get to the "dog-legged" right-then-left turn on CR 344, turn left onto CR 232 and go south for 2 miles. At the intersection with CR 334, turn right and go 2.2 miles to the single-lane ramp.

Access to the next two launch sites on the Suwannee River below the US 98/US 19/SR 55 Bridge is from the west side of the river. From the intersection of CR 349 with US 98/US 19/SR 55 in the community of Old Town, go east on US 98/US 19/SR 55 for 1.7 miles. Turn right onto CR 317 and go south for 2.3 miles to the single-lane ramp at Hinton Landing. There is unimproved parking for 20 vehicles.

The next site, New Pine Landing, can be reached by crossing US 98/US 19/SR 55 at Old Town and continuing south on CR 349 for 5.1 miles. At New Pine Landing Blvd., turn left and go 1.2 miles to the single-lane ramp. There is unimproved parking for 12 vehicles.

At this point, the Gulf of Mexico is about 25 miles downstream. There are still springs gushing forth crystal clear water, but not as many as in the midsection of the river. The tannic content of the water has diminished greatly and the fishing continues to be good. It is a wide marsh from here to the Gulf and there are no more bridges crossing the river.

The last access point is back on the east side of the river. One mile east of the bridge on US 98/US 19/SR 55 is the community of Fanning Springs, where road bends sharply to the right and directs you farther south. From Fanning Springs, continue south for 6 miles to CR 320. Just as you enter the town of Chiefland, turn right and go 5.2 miles west. Turn right again and go 2.5 miles to the double-lane ramp at New Clay Landing near Manatee Springs State Park. There is unimproved parking for 20 vehicles.

WITHLACOOCHEE RIVER

This Withlacoochee River comes out of Georgia. (There is another Withlacoochee River that drains into the Gulf of Mexico from headwaters in Green Swamp that is described in Region 3.) This small stream is really of little interest to flyfishers. Its dark, tannic-stained waters and red clay bottom do not bode well for fish populations. The river suffers from wild fluctuations in water level. During periods of low water, even a canoe must be carried across some of the shoals.

There are a couple of worn paths that have been used for launch sites on private property on the lower portion of the Withlacoochee above Suwannee River State Park. While the fly fishing does not warrant the effort, there are a couple of interesting areas along the way. Blue Springs is on private land just south of the bridge where SR 6 crosses the river. Also, as you move downstream, there are some huge limestone monoliths rising from the water's edge that take on the appearance of whatever your imagination permits. Flyfishers can expect to find limited numbers of small largemouth and Suwannee bass, as well as redbreast sunfish. Cast a terrestrial or small popper around fallen trees and stumps.

To get to the bridge and downstream launch sites, take Exit 86 and go west on SR 6 for about 10 miles to the bridge. Continue another 0.7 mile west and then turn left to get to the two ramps. Go south 0.8 mile and turn left again. The first site is 1.8 miles ahead. To reach the next site, continue on this road along the river's edge for 1.2 miles. Neither site has a ramp or secure parking. The Suwannee River is about 9 miles downstream at this point.

The Withlacoochee River adds quite a bit of water to the Suwannee River, which improves the flyfishing.

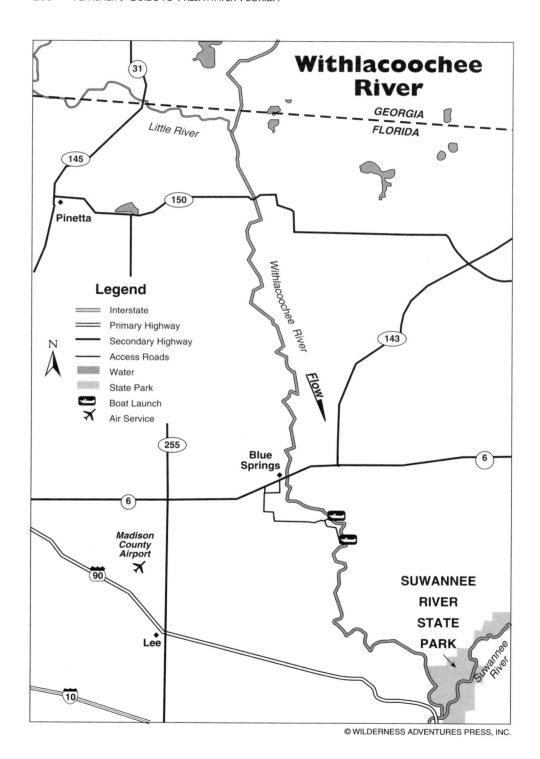

Withlacoochee River

GEORGIA
FLORIDA

Little River

Pinetta

Withlacoochee River

Flow

Legend

≡≡≡ Interstate
══ Primary Highway
━━ Secondary Highway
── Access Roads
▓▓▓ Water
░░░ State Park
⬳ Boat Launch
✈ Air Service

N

Blue
Springs

Madison
County
Airport ✈

SUWANNEE
RIVER
STATE
PARK

Suwannee River

Lee

© WILDERNESS ADVENTURES PRESS, INC.

The Withlacoochee River is quite scenic, but its dark tannic waters hold limited numbers of fish.

SANTA FE RIVER

The Santa Fe River begins its long journey to the Suwannee River in the marsh and lowlands east of Gainesville. Santa Fe Lake and Little Santa Fe Lake are on the eastern edge of the marsh and the river has its origins in water moving slowly out of these lakes. Along the way, numerous springs bubble forth their discharge, and soon the tiny stream becomes a river. It is subject to some wild water level fluctuations, though, depending upon the amount of rain that has fallen in north-central Florida. Anyone thinking about fishing the river should check to see that it is safe to do so. The Santa Fe River is not as tannic and tea-colored as the Suwannee River in its upper reaches and offers a better fishery along its entire course.

Santa Fe Lake (4,721 acres) is surrounded by cypress trees, as well as an excellent stand of maidencane and other grasses. These offer good habitat for largemouth bass and panfish. Early spring is the best time for bass fishing, and it falls off quickly after that. A deer-haired popper in brown or olive (size 1 or 2) would be my choice. Several 10-pound-plus largemouth have been taken from the lake, so be prepared for a thrill. Crappie fishing is best in February and March. Try a brightly colored Clouser Minnow around the standing cypress trees. Bream fishing is not a strong point of this lake, although a few can certainly be taken as incidental catches while fishing smaller flies in bass habitat. There is also a decent population of sunshine bass. Look for them to school early and late in the day around the bottleneck separating Santa Fe Lake from Little Santa Fe Lake, especially in the fall.

Little Santa Fe Lake (1,135 acres) is just to the north of Santa Fe Lake and many consider the two lakes to be one and the same. For the purpose of fishing, they are similar except that Little Santa Fe Lake has a large pocket of shallow water at the northern end leading into the marsh that soon becomes the Santa Fe River. Largemouth bass like to spawn over the hard bottom of these shallow waters in the spring. At other times of the year, this same area is always worth a look during low-light conditions. On the western shoreline, a canal enters from Lake Alto and the slight influx of water is often enough to hold a good population of game fish. The Little Santa Fe Lake has a good launch site on its eastern shoreline.

To reach the launch at Little Santa Fe Lake, go east from Tallahassee on SR 26 for about 14 miles. Turn left onto SR 21 and go north for 4 miles. Turn left onto SR 21-B and go 2.1 miles to the double-lane ramp on the right side of the road at the bottle-neck separating the lakes. There is unimproved parking for 20 vehicles.

There is another access point on the west side of Santa Fe Lake. Again, go east from Tallahassee on SR 26. About 9 miles out of town, turn left onto CR 1469 and go north for 2.2 miles. In the community of Earleton, turn right and go 0.2 mile to the single-lane ramp.

Connected by canal to Little Santa Fe Lake is Lake Alto (500 acres). Standing cypress trees rim the northern portion of this lake and both largemouth bass and crappie grow large in these waters. In the spring, fish the shallower northern end as fish move into this area to spawn. Look to open water by late summer and fall when the deeper water toward the southern end holds more fish.

To get to Lake Alto, go east from Tallahassee on SR 26 for 7 miles. At the intersection with US 301/SR 200, turn left and go north for 3 miles. As the road sweeps to the left at Shenks, turn right onto CR 325 and go 1.5 miles. Turn left and go 0.3 mile to the single-lane ramp at the end of the road. There is unimproved parking for five vehicles. If you are coming from the north, watch your speed around the town of Waldo (about 3 miles northwest of Shenks on US 301/200), as it has a reputation for issuing speeding tickets.

At times barely discernible, the river moves through the marsh and west towards the Suwannee River. About seven miles downstream, Lake Hampton (800 acres) adds water to the mix and the Santa Fe begins to have a discernible streambed as it leaves the marsh. Grasses also surround Lake Hampton, about 0.7 mile to your right up the run. Although not as large and well known as Lake Santa Fe or Little Lake Santa Fe, it yields its share of big bass. In addition, it has a more reliable population of bream. Small popping bugs with rubber legs (size 8) are good producers early and late in the day. Do not strip these too fast, as many strikes will occur while the fly sits dead still in the water.

To get to Lake Hampton, go northeast from Tallahassee on SR 24 for about 10 miles. At the intersection in Waldo, turn left onto US 301/SR 200 and go north for 5 miles. Turn left onto Navarre Avenue and go west for 0.5 mile. As the road swings to the right to go around the lake, the single-lane ramp will be on your left.

For the next 25 miles, the Santa Fe remains a small stream creeping its way west-

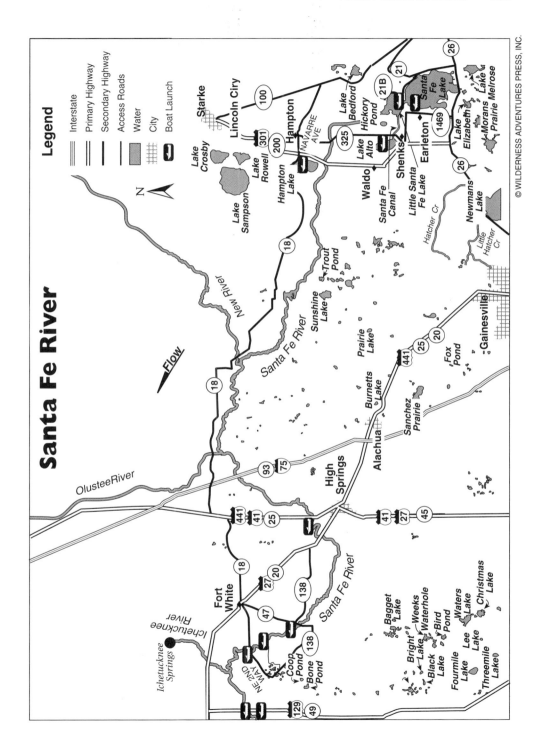

Santa Fe River

Legend

Interstate
Primary Highway
Secondary Highway
Access Roads
Water
City
Boat Launch

N

Flow

OlusteeRiver

New River

Santa Fe River

Lake Crosby

Lake Sampson

Lake Rowell

Hampton Lake

Starke

Lincoln Ciry

100

301

200

18

18

Hampton

NAVARRE AVE

Waldo

Santa Fe Canal

Trout Pond

Sunshine Lake

Prairie Lake

Burnetts Lake

Sanchez Prairie

Alachua

Lake Bedford

Hickory Pond

Lake Alto

325

Shenks

Little Santa Fe Lake

Earleton

Santa Fe Lake

Lake Elizabeth

Morans Lake

Lake Melrose

Prairie

Newmans Lake

Hatcher Cr

Little Hatcher Cr

21

21B

26

1469

26

20

25

441

Fox Pond

Gainesville

High Springs

93

75

441

41

25

41

27

45

Fort White

Ichetucknee River

Ichetucknee Springs

18

27

20

138

47

NE 2ND WAY

Coop Pond

Bone Pond

138

Santa Fe River

Bagget Lake

Bright Lake

Weeks Waterhole

Black Lake

Bird Pond

Waters Lake

Lee Lake

Christmas Lake

Fourmile Lake

Threemile Lake

129

49

ward. It is then joined by the New River, itself no more than a creek coming out of a marshy area to the northeast. The New River offers the flyfisher no access or opportunities to float and fish. The marsh is not a place to wade and the waters are too small to warrant the risk.

Continuing downstream, the Santa Fe meanders westward with only a little more size. During periods of low water, there are shoals over which not even a tube will float, much less a kayak, canoe, or johnboat. The frequent shallow shoals continue for another 25 miles, going under I-75. During periods of heavy rain, the river will get out of its banks and one can actually get lost, unable to tell where the river channel is located.

The first access point on the river is north of the community of High Springs. From Gainesville, go northwest on US 441/SR 25/SR 20 for about 18 miles to High Springs. As you enter town, go right onto US 441/US 41/SR 25. Go north for about 2 miles and as the road makes a long sweeping right turn to go over the river, turn left to the launch site. There is a set of rapids just below the launch site through which care should be taken with a loaded kayak, canoe, or johnboat. At this point, the Santa Fe is only a canoe trail and motorized boats cannot yet run the river. That will soon change, however, as numerous springs add their crystal clear water to the river and make it quite fishable.

Back to the town of High Springs, if you go left as you enter town, you will be on US 27/SR 20 going northwest. From this road, you can access the remainder of the Santa Fe, all the way to the intersection with the Suwannee River. Continuing on US 27/SR 20 about 10 miles after High Springs, you come to the small community of Fort White. Turn left and go south on SR 47 for 4 miles to CR 138 (Hollingsworth Bluff Road). Turn right and go 0.7 mile to the single-lane ramp at Hollingsworth Bluff. There is unimproved parking for 15 vehicles. This is really the first launch you should consider for putting in a kayak, canoe or johnboat loaded with fishing gear. Even from this site, you will likely have to drag it over a few shoals as you move downstream. There are no rapids of any consequence, however.

In this middle section of the river, excellent fishing begins for largemouth and Suwannee bass. These will be small fish, averaging about a pound. They are scrappy fighters in the swift water. Try a pattern that imitates a crawfish or shrimp below a set of shoals or in the eelgrass in the middle of the river. The clear water makes the fish skittish around shorelines, but these inhibitions are lost when there is abundant grass and lots of freshwater shrimp out in midstream. Redbreast sunfish will hold near fallen trees and root wads and a small terrestrial pattern will readily tempt these colorful panfish. Whenever a creek merges with the Santa Fe, look for assorted panfish to be around the mouth.

The next two launch sites are reached by continuing south on SR 47, crossing the Santa Fe River, and going 1.5 miles. At the intersection with CR 138, turn right and go west for 3 miles. After crossing a small marsh and as you approach a series of ponds, turn right and go 1.5 miles to the single-lane ramp.

The next site is about 1.5 miles downstream and a little more secure. Continue west on CR 138 for another mile. Turn right onto NE 2nd Way (Ira Bea Oasis Road) and go 2.4 miles to the single-lane ramp at Tudeen Park. There is unimproved parking for 5 vehicles.

To move west and farther downstream, let's go back to Fort White and the intersection of US 27/SR 20 with SR 47. By continuing west on US 27/SR 20 for 5 miles, you will cross the Ichetucknee River about midway between Ichetucknee Springs and the Santa Fe River (a run of about 6 miles). The Ichetucknee adds more water (233 million gallons a day) to what has become a very fine river. The springs are noteworthy as a tubing destination for folks from all over the state, especially students at the University of Florida in Gainesville. You won't want to fly fish on the upper portions of the Ichetucknee in summer, as scenic as it may be. There is a state park located here that rents canoes, and a single-lane ramp is available.

Below the confluence of the Ichetucknee and Santa Fe, it is only about 7 miles downstream to the Suwannee River. The fishing remains good for both largemouth and Suwannee bass, as well as for redbreast sunfish. The bass will be found in the midstream eelgrass. As the water gets deeper, you may want to go to a Clouser Minnow to get down to the tops of the grass. An intermediate sink-tip line and a shrimp pattern would be a better choice if you have a spare spool for your reel.

There are two launch sites remaining on the Santa Fe River. Continue going west on US 27/SR 20 across the bridge over the Ichetucknee River. Go 4.5 miles and turn left (south) onto US 129/SR 49. Go 2.5 miles and just before the bridge over the Santa Fe River, turn right onto River Road. Go 0.3 mile and turn left to the single-lane ramp at Sandy Point.

The last site is about a mile downstream, also off US 129/SR 49. Continue south on US 129/SR 49, cross the bridge, and go 1 mile. Turn right and go 0.5 mile to the single-lane ramp. The Suwannee River is downstream about one mile.

LAKE MUNSON

A couple of miles south of Tallahassee off SR 61, Lake Munson (300 acres) borders the eastern edge of the Apalachicola National Forest. This irregularly-shaped lake is rimmed by houses on the eastern edge, but is undeveloped along the western shoreline. Munson Slough enters in the northwest corner and flows out of the lake near the ramp on the east side.

The lake has good fishing for panfish, as well as decent largemouth bass. An occasional lunker is caught. Spring is the best time, and small rubber-legged poppers fished around shoreline vegetation works best for the panfish. The mouths of the sloughs should be fished with a deer-haired popper early and late in the day for largemouth bass that have moved in to feed. There is also a good population of crappie. Try a brightly colored Clouser Minnow around the dock pilings in early spring.

To get to Lake Munson, go south from Tallahassee on SR 61 for 2.5 miles after the intersection of SR 61 and CR 363. Turn right and the single-lane ramp is 0.1 mile ahead.

Suwannee Lake has standing cypress trees and once held numerous big bass. It is now past its prime.

SUWANNEE LAKE, WORKMAN LAKE, DEXTER LAKE, CAMPGROUND LAKE, LITTTE LAKE HULL, WHITE LAKE, TIGER LAKE, BACHELOR LAKE, AND PEACOCK LAKE

The town of Live Oak is about 15 miles west of the intersection of I-10 and I-75 and about 3 miles south of I-10 at Exit 40. There are several small lakes about 5 miles east of Live Oak that offer good opportunities for flyfishers near this major crossroads in northern Florida.

Most noted among these lakes is Suwannee Lake (63 acres). While small in size, it is big in stature. The lake is absolutely filled with cypress trees and big largemouth bass. Each year, several fish over 10 pounds are taken from these state-managed waters, although the numbers and average size has declined significantly in recent years. Suwannee Lake is manmade, with several earthen fishing fingers along the western edge that jut out into the lake to increase shoreline opportunities. The water depth is shallow along the edges, and there is thick vegetation. There are two old sinkholes at the northern end of the lake out in the trees that provide fish with about 20 feet of deep cover.

Suwannee Lake has special size limits for largemouth bass and crappie to ensure that fishing for these species remains exceptional. You will be fly fishing in heavy cover, so you may want to use a heavier leader to withstand rubbing against an abrasive tree trunk. Again, I would use an olive, deer-hair popper (size 1) early and late in the day. There are so many types of structure to choose from, and you will need to sample them to establish a pattern. The peak season is from January through May. Crappie suspend over deep water in the warm months, but move toward shoreline cover to spawn starting in January. A brightly colored Clouser Minnow will do the trick. There is also a good population of bluegill and redear. The peak fishing season for these panfish is midsummer, especially in the afternoon after rains wash insects out of the cypress trees and into the water. You might want to try a terrestrial pattern in the early evening when winds have calmed and the air temperatures have lowered. This small lake is a sleeper that is easily overlooked, but because of its convenient location it should be given a try. In addition, the state stocked sunshine bass here for a time, but they no longer do so.

To get to Suwannee Lake, take US 90/SR 10 east out of Live Oak for 1 mile. Turn left onto SR 49 and go north for 0.8 mile. Turn right onto 86th Street and go 1.2 miles. Turn left onto 91st Road (a dirt road) and go 0.3 mile to the entrance into the park on your right. The single-lane ramp is 0.3 mile ahead, and there is paved parking for 10 vehicles and unimproved overflow parking for another 25 vehicles.

Two of the other lakes east of Live Oak also have launch sites, but they are not managed for big fish like Suwannee. Smaller fish may be kept so fewer large fish are caught on a regular basis. You will be able to get away from the sometimes-crowded fishing on Suwannee Lake, however.

White Lake, at about 75 acres, offers good fishing for crappie, panfish, and largemouth bass, especially in the spring. Take US 90/SR 10 west from Live Oak for 4 miles. Turn right at the Suwannee Country Club and go 0.3 mile to the single-lane ramp with parking for 10 vehicles. There is a fee to launch and the ramp presently does not reach to the water because of drought.

ALLIGATOR LAKE AND WATERTOWN LAKE

On the outskirts of Lake City there are two very different lakes that offer fly fishing opportunities. Live Oak is about 8 miles southeast of the I-10/I-75 intersection and can be easily reached by going 2 or 3 miles from either interstate. While neither lake is a destination in its own right, if you should be staying in the area, they are worth looking into.

Alligator Lake (800 acres) is a shallow lake on the southeastern edge of town. Unfortunately, it has sinkhole problems. There are several sinkholes on both the northern and southern ends that drain directly to the aquifer. As a result of the dry conditions that Florida has experienced for the past several years, most of Alligator Lake is presently bone dry. The southern end has retained some water, but is very shallow. There is a dense algae bloom and the water clarity is very limited. Fish are reproducing only at a very limited rate, and overall, the conditions are quite poor. For any chance at a bass, use the largest Gurgler you can find, as you must "call" your fish to the lure since they cannot see it. Panfish are similarly tough in the pea-green-soup-colored water. At the present time, this lake should be skipped, but conditions may improve over the next few years if water levels rise. If this should be the case, Alligator Lake could become a very good lake again four or five years after it gets some water.

To get to Alligator Lake, get off I-10 at Exit 44 and go south on US 441/SR 47 for about 3 miles to the intersection with US 90/SR 10. (From I-75, take Exit 82 and go east on US 90/SR 10 for 3 miles to the intersection with US 441/SR 47.) From this intersection go south on US 441/SR 41 for 1.5 miles and immediately after passing the VA Hospital on your left, turn left on S.E. Clements and go two blocks to the single-lane ramp straight ahead. Again, there is presently no water in this lake's bed. There is unimproved parking for 20 vehicles.

Watertown Lake (46 acres) is on the northeastern edge of Lake City. It is a deeper lake (averaging about 10 feet) and offers excellent bass fishing, with several lunkers caught each year. Spring is the best time to fish this small lake for largemouth bass. There is also a good population of panfish, and the bluegill fishing can be excellent at times. Flyfishers should cast a terrestrial pattern or a small popping bugs with rubber legs (size 4) toward shoreline cover in the summer months, especially in early evening. Crappie fishing is only fair on Watertown Lake. Look to open water in the winter and then move toward shoreline cover in the spring when crappie move to the shallows to spawn.

Sinkholes have caused Alligator Lake to lose its water.

To get to Watertown Lake, from the US 441/SR 47 intersection with US 90/SR 10 in the middle of Lake City, go east on US 90/SR 10 for 1.7 miles. At the intersection with SR 100, cross the railroad tracks and bear left for 0.4 mile on N.E. Bassom Norris (locally known as Moose Lodge Road). Make a right onto N.E. Williams and go one block to the single-lane ramp. There is paved parking for 20 vehicles.

OCEAN POND

Ocean Pond (1,774 acres) is a round, dish-shaped lake about 12 miles east of Lake City. The lake lacks any remarkable terrain features, so three brush-type fish attractors have been added to offer some sanctuary. This is one of the few lakes (see also Lake Sampson) with a hard, sandy bottom that will support flyfishers who want to wade.

This is not a big bass lake, but flyfishers using poppers with rubber legs can make decent catches of small bass in the spring months. Crappie fishing is fair in the winter over the deeper water in the middle for those using a sink-tip line with a Clouser Minnow. The crappie have moved to the shorelines by February and a floating line may then be used. Panfish, bluegill, and redear fishing is regarded as poor. Ocean Pond has been stocked with sunshine bass, and fishing for these stripers is good in the winter months. Look for them over open water below diving birds. When they are feeding on the surface, a white Gurgler will readily take fish. When you see sunshine bass rising, know that many more fish are below them, and these can be taken with a Baby Bunker or a small Lefty's Deceiver. Many sunshine bass are also taken by crappie fishermen who are stripping their Clousers in deep water.

To get to Ocean Pond, go west for 8 miles on US 90/SR 10 after getting off Interstate 20 at Exit 45. Across from CR 231, turn right onto the Forest Road and go 0.8 mile to the single-lane ramp known as Hog Pen.

PALESTINE LAKE

Palestine Lake (972 acres) is a shallow lake that looks good to the eye but does not regularly yield quality fish. Flyfishers using small poppers (size 4) can catch a fair number of yearling-sized bass, but panfish (bluegill and redear) prospects are poor. Palestine Lake does offer a good fishery for crappie, though. In summer, anglers can try casting a Clouser Minnow in open water and letting it sink some before beginning to strip. By early spring, crappie will have moved toward the shorelines to spawn. There are some brush-type fish attractors present and these should be probed year-round for crappie. Sunshine bass have been stocked but do not offer a reliable fishery at present.

To get to Palestine Lake, get off I-10 at Exit 45 and go west on US 90/SR 10 for 8 miles. Turn right onto CR 231 and go south for 6 miles. Turn right and go 1.2 miles to the single-lane ramp.

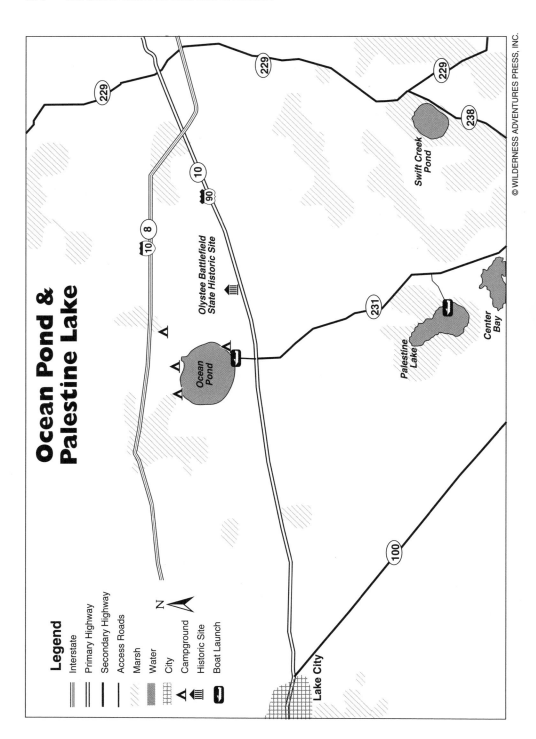

Ocean Pond & Palestine Lake

Legend

Interstate
Primary Highway
Secondary Highway
Access Roads
Marsh
Water
City
Campground
Historic Site
Boat Launch

N

Olystee Battlefield State Historic Site

Ocean Pond

Palestine Lake

Center Bay

Swift Creek Pond

Lake City

229
10
90
8
10
229
229
238
231
100

GOVERNOR HILL LAKE, BONNET LAKE, LORD LAKE, WILLIAMS LAKE, MATTHIS LAKE, UNION LAKE, COVE LAKE, WARD LAKE, CARELESS PRAIRIE, AND TOMLINSON PRAIRIE

To finish the discussion of fly fishing opportunities in north-central Florida, I will now move west across the state toward the Panhandle and drop a little to the south. We'll begin east of Steinhatchee, a coastal town better known to saltwater flyfishers for its redfish and seatrout opportunities. Moving inland about 20 miles across a marshy swamp, we come to several small ponds and lakes before getting to the Suwannee River, although only one of these has a ramp. The lakes are shallow and difficult to access. Security and safety will be an issue, as these lakes are a long distance from populated areas. This area is probably best left to locals. There is nothing remarkable enough about the fisheries at these lakes to warrant making them a serious fly fishing destination.

Governor Hill Lake has a small ramp that can be reached by going west on SR 26 from Gainesville for about 35 miles. Just before crossing the Suwannee River, go right onto US 98/US 19/SR 55 and over the bridge near Fanning Springs. Continue west for about 3 miles to the community of Old Town. Turn right and go north on CR 349 for about 11 miles. Turn left onto Rock Sink Church Road and go west for 2.8 miles. Turn left onto CR 353 and go 2.5 miles to the single-lane ramp. If you are tempted to fish any of the numerous ponds that you saw along the way, or want to continue and see others, watch out for rattlesnakes and cottonmouths, as the only way to access the water is to fish from the shoreline or possibly using a float tube. If you try the latter, you certainly do not have an appreciation for the area's reptiles.

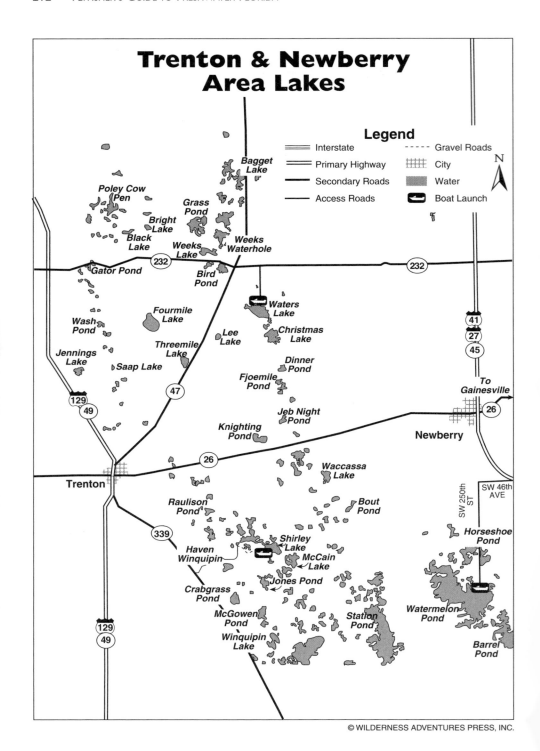

Trenton & Newberry Area Lakes

Legend

Interstate	Gravel Roads
Primary Highway	City
Secondary Roads	Water
Access Roads	Boat Launch

N

Bagget Lake

Poley Cow Pen

Grass Pond

Bright Lake

Weeks Waterhole

Black Lake

Weeks Lake

232

Gator Pond

Bird Pond

232

Waters Lake

Fourmile Lake

Wash Pond

Christmas Lake

Lee Lake

41

27

45

Jennings Lake

Threemile Lake

Saap Lake

Dinner Pond

Fjoemile Pond

To Gainesville

47

Jeb Night Pond

26

Knighting Pond

Newberry

26

Waccassa Lake

Trenton

Raulison Pond

Bout Pond

SW 46th AVE

SW 250th ST

339

Horseshoe Pond

Haven Winquipin

Shirley Lake

McCain Lake

Jones Pond

Crabgrass Pond

McGowen Pond

Station Pond

Watermelon Pond

129

49

Winquipin Lake

Barrel Pond

© WILDERNESS ADVENTURES PRESS, INC.

BAGGET LAKE, WEEKS LAKE, WATERS LAKE, BRIGHT LAKE, BLACK LAKE, FOURMILE LAKE, LEE LAKE, CHRISTMAS LAKE, THREEMILE LAKE, WACCASSA LAKE, SHIRLEY LAKE, McCAIN LAKE, BOWEN LAKE, WINQUIPIN LAKE AND WATERMELON POND

West of Gainesville, about 10 to 15 miles east of the Suwannee River, there is a five-mile-wide swamp that runs north-to-south for several miles, with a series of ponds and lakes that is more extensive than those previously described on the west side of the Suwannee River. Many are shallow and will be nearly dry during periods of drought. While not far from Gainesville in terms of road miles, this area is definitely desolate. Once again, extreme care should be taken by flyfishers choosing to fish these waters. While the risk of danger is not so much greater here than in other places, the ability to get help quickly is significantly reduced, and a cell phone is helpful.

The lakes have good populations of bass and bream. Because they get very little fishing pressure, there are some big fish in these waters. The reproduction rate is very low, however, so consider releasing your catch unharmed after a couple of pictures. Big topwater flies (size 1) are the way to go in these shallow waters. An olive Dahlberg Diver or Swimming Frog would be an excellent choice. The bream will take a small popper or a terrestrial pattern.

The northernmost lake with a ramp is Waters Lake. From Gainesville, go west on SR 26 for about 25 miles. In Trenton, turn right onto US 129/SR 49 and cross the railroad tracks. At the intersection, turn right onto SR 47 and go north for 8 miles. Turn right onto CR 232 and go 1 mile east. Turn right and go another mile to the single-lane ramp.

Shirley Lake is the next one with a ramp. Proceed west on SR 26 to Trenton. There, turn left onto US 129/SR 49 and go south for 0.8 mile. Turn left onto CR 339 and go 3.5 miles. Across from CR 346-A, turn left and then bear left for 1.8 miles. Turn right on the dirt road and go 1.2 miles to the single-lane ramp.

The last lake with a ramp is Watermelon Pond. This lake is the closest to Gainesville and also the largest—and it is the most heavily fished of these waters. To get to Watermelon Pond, again go west on SR 26 from Gainesville for 14 miles. At Newberry, turn left and go south on US 41/US 27/SR 45 for 2.5 miles. Turn right onto SW 46th Avenue and go 1.2 miles. Turn left onto SW 250th Street and go 3.6 miles to the single-lane ramp. There is unimproved parking for 25 vehicles.

LAKE KANAPAHA, LAKE ALICE, BIVANS ARM, PAYNES PRAIRIE, LEVY LAKES, WAUBERG LAKE, LEDWITH LAKE AND TUSCAWILLA LAKE

In the mixture of swamp, marsh, and prairie south of Gainesville, there are a number of large, shallow lakes. During periods of drought, these can become almost dry and unfishable. Only Wauberg Lake (254 acres) has water that is deep enough to have a ramp that remains serviceable. The lake is not open to boats with gasoline motors (electric trolling motors are permitted on canoes and johnboats) and it offers the small boat angler an opportunity to get away from boat wakes and crowds and fly fish in relative tranquility.

Wauberg's reputation is for crappie fishing more than any other species. The fertile green waters have a deep grass line that holds fish, except when they move to shorelines to spawn. Try a Clouser Minnow and let it sink to different levels until you find fish willing to feed. Crappie do not like to rise when they feed, so be persistent and try different depths. There are some big largemouth bass taken each spring near shoreline cover. Try a large (size-2/0) Dahlberg Diver in a frog color. Bream are easy targets for a rubber-legged popper during the summer months, especially late in the day.

Many of these lakes, including Wauberg, are located within Paynes Prairie State Preserve. This 21,000-acre preserve is one of the most significant natural and historic areas in all of Florida. There are 20 distinct biological communities located within this national landmark, including wet prairie, pine flatwoods, hammocks, swamp, and ponds. Hence, a vast array of wildlife (including eagles, hawks, waterfowl, wading birds, alligators, and otters) is present here. Nearby, a 50-foot observation tower gives a panoramic view of the preserve's prairie and marsh.

If you are traveling by car south on I-75, Gainesville is about an hour south of the Florida/Georgia state line. To get to Paynes Prairie State Preserve, take Exit 73 off I-75 about 12 miles south of Gainesville and go east on CR 234 for 2 miles. Turn left on US 441/SR 25 and go north for 1 mile. The preserve entrance is on your right, and you can follow the signs to the launch site.

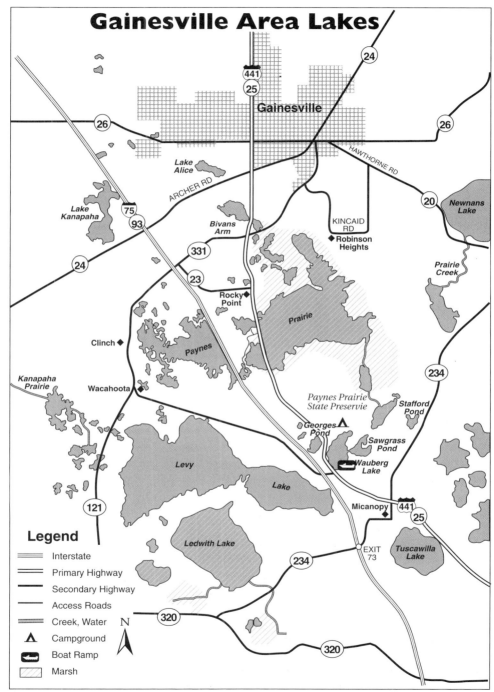

Gainesville Area Lakes

Gainesville

Lake Alice

Lake Kanapaha

Bivans Arm

KINCAID RD

♦ Robinson Heights

Newnans Lake

Prairie Creek

Rocky Point ♦

Prairie

Clinch ♦

Paynes

Kanapaha Prairie

Wacahoota ♦

Paynes Prairie State Preservie

Georges Pond ⛺

Stafford Pond

Sawgrass Pond

Wauberg Lake

Levy

Lake

Micanopy ♦

Ledwith Lake

EXIT 73

Tuscawilla Lake

HAWTHORNE RD

ARCHER RD

Legend

- Interstate
- Primary Highway
- Secondary Highway
- Access Roads
- Creek, Water
- ▲ Campground
- Boat Ramp
- Marsh

N

Newnans Lake is no longer the bass fishery that it used to be, but sunshine bass have been stocked in large numbers, and it is now perhaps the best lake in the state in which to catch these hard-fighting fish.

NEWNANS LAKE

Newnans Lake (5,800 acres) is about 2 miles east of Gainesville and offers outstanding fishing for both crappie and sunshine bass, as well as giving up more than a few lunker largemouth bass each year. Cypress trees surround the entire lake and when the water is up, bass and crappie love to get up in the flooded shorelines and feed in shallow water. Unfortunately, the lake has been at historic low levels the past few years and is not presently in good condition. When this changes and water levels again rise, look for some bodacious bass to be caught from Newnans Lake. In the meantime, there are sparse areas of emergent grasses, bulrush, and water lilies around the shoreline that hold smaller bass.

The state has annually stocked sunshine bass since 1979, and Newnans has been regarded as the best lake in the state to catch them for the past five years. In the spring, sunshine bass move to the north end of the lake where flowing water from creeks attracts them. Try a fly patterned after a grass shrimp such as Joe's Grass Shrimp (size 2). As waters warm, the fish move out over open water. There are brush-type fish attractors in the middle of the lake and flyfishers using sink-tip lines and a Clouser Minnow take plenty of fish in summer at deeper levels. In the fall, fishing begins to pick up as sunshine bass move up in the water column late in the afternoon, especially around the fish attractors near Palm Point in the southwest corner

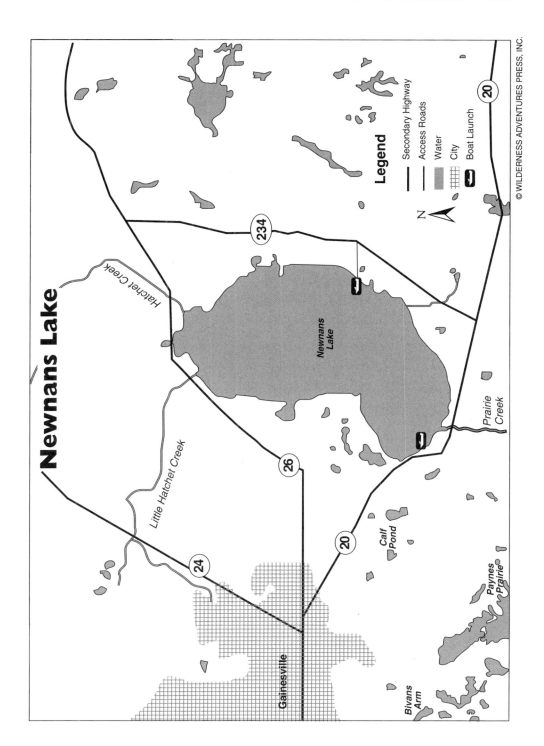

Newnans Lake

Newnans Lake

Hatchet Creek

Little Hatchet Creek

Prairie Creek

Calf Pond

Paynes Prairie

Bivans Arm

Gainesville

Legend

— Secondary Highway
— Access Roads
Water
City
Boat Launch

N

© WILDERNESS ADVENTURES PRESS, INC.

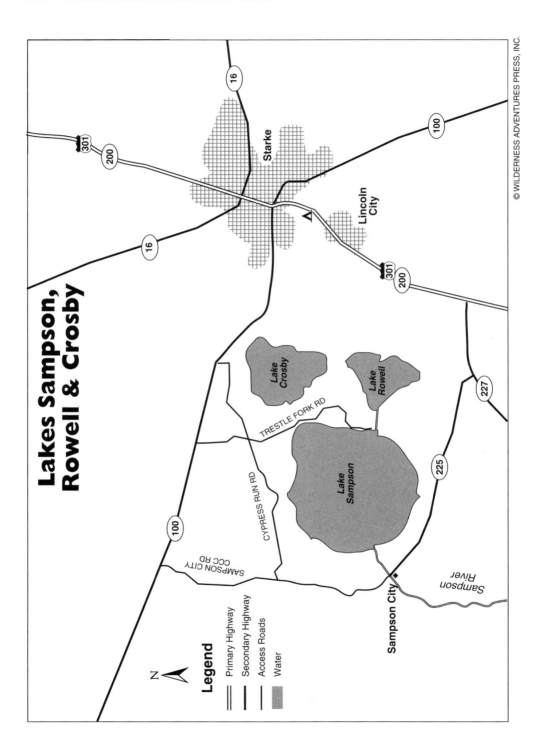

Lakes Sampson,
Rowell & Crosby

Starke

Lincoln City

Sampson River

Sampson City

Lake Crosby

Lake Rowell

Lake Sampson

TRESTLE FORK RD

CYPRESS RUN RD

SAMPSON CITY CCC RD

Legend

Primary Highway
Secondary Highway
Access Roads
Water

N

of the lake. Here, they can be taken on the surface by flyfishers using white Gurglers. There will be several fish below the surface for every one that you see busting shad on top. A small Deceiver or Baby Bunker (size 2) with an olive back would be an excellent choice.

Newnans Lake is renowned for its crappie fishery as well, and a two-pound fish is not at all uncommon. In early spring, crappie move to shoreline cover to spawn. Look for them around the base of cypress trees from February through April. They always like a brightly colored Clouser Minnow. When the waters warm, look for crappie to be suspended over the mid-lake fish attractors. Use an intermediate sink-tip line and be sure to "count" your line down as it sinks so that once you have had your first strike, you can get it back to that precise depth again. During the winter, crappie remain in open water, often suspended near the deepest holes.

Largemouth bass fishing is best around February and March when they move into the cypress trees to spawn. This is a good time for big deer-hair flies with a weedguard. If water tables remain low, make casts around the shoreline vegetation, especially early and late in the day. As the waters warm, bass fishing falls off pretty quickly.

To get to Newnan Lake, take SR 20 east from Gainesville for 2 miles. Earl P. Powers Park is on your left and it has two single-lane ramps that give you access to some shallow water in the southwestern part of the lake. There is paved parking for 20 vehicles in the park. Palm Point is about 2 miles up the lake on your left. If you continue another 2 miles on SR 20 and turn left on CR 234, there is another ramp on the east side of the lake. Go north on CR 234 for 2 miles and turn left again to the single-lane ramp 0.8 mile ahead. You are still about 2 miles from Palm Point, directly across the lake to your west.

LAKE SAMPSON, LAKE ROWELL, AND LAKE CROSBY

Although none of the lakes on this three-lake chain a couple of miles west of Starke has a boat ramp, they are included because one of the lakes (Lake Sampson) offers one of the best opportunities for flyfishers to wade in north-central Florida. Taken together, the lakes offer diverse habitat for both largemouth bass and panfish.

Lake Sampson (2,042 acres) has a hard sand bottom that permits wade fishing around a rim ringed by cattails, water lilies, and maidencane grass. The first few feet out into the lake where this vegetation grows tends to have a muck bottom, but once past the vegetation, the bottom is hard. Only the outer edge of the shoreline vegetation holds fish. The depth drops off slowly to about 12 feet, although there is a hole in the northeast corner where the dropoff is steeper. When lake levels are low, fish pull away from the shoreline and move out into the main lake where permanent plastic fish-attractors have been placed. Hydrilla and eelgrass are also present and some of the largemouth bass grow to very good size. Give the east side of the lake some attention in February, March, and April, especially around the mouth of the canal that connects Lake Sampson to Lake Rowell. Try a noisy popper to get their attention. Crappie fishing is fair from January through April as the "specks" move toward shoreline to spawn. The most reliable fishery on Lake Sampson is for bluegill and redear. These panfish are excellent from April through midsummer and readily take a small terrestrial or popper (size 6).

Lake Rowell (364 acres) has cypress trees surrounding the lake and a muck bottom seldom more than six feet deep that prevents wading. In addition, hydrilla can be dense at times and it makes fly fishing from the shoreline difficult and frustrating. There are some big bass taken each year from Lake Rowell, however, but seldom will flyfishers be able to get access to them. Crappie and bream grow large very quickly on this eutrophic lake and brush-type fish attractors have been put in place.

Lake Crosby (400 acres) has marsh on the west side with cypress trees that offer good sanctuary for largemouth bass. The bass fishing is good year-round, although the lake seldom yields anything more than yearling-sized fish. While crappie fishing is also good around the fish attractors in terms of numbers, size is lacking. Bream fishing is not very good. This lake stands alone, unconnected to either Lake Sampson or Lake Rowell a short distance away. Like Lake Rowell, it has a muck bottom that precludes wading, but there are a few spots along the northern shoreline where a flyfisher can make some casts.

To get to these three lakes, from the community of Starke (about 20 miles northeast of Gainesville) go west on SR 100 for 2 miles. Turn left onto Cypress Run Road. Lake Crosby is to your left. Continue on Cypress Run Road for 1.2 miles and turn left on Trestle Fork Road. Lake Sampson is a mile ahead on your right. Lake Crosby will be on your right at this point, and Trestle Fork Road ends at the canal connecting Lake Sampson and Lake Rowell another 0.5 mile ahead. Watch your speed in this area. Like Waldo 10 miles to the south, Starke has a bit of a reputation for issuing speeding tickets to motorists who exceed a posted limit by even a small amount.

Cypress trees surrounding Hampton Lake provide good spawning habitat for crappie and other panfish.

HAMPTON LAKE

Lying between Gainesville and Starke, Hampton Lake (800 acres) has cypress trees lining the edges that provide good cover for crappie and other panfish, along with largemouth bass. Like most north-central Florida lakes, Hampton Lake is best in the spring when spawning activity brings fish to shoreline cover. In winter, try fishing midday when waters warm and baitfish become more active. While largemouth bass tend to school, they do so more in the winter, and topwater strikes just beyond the standing cypress trees give away their location. These fish are yearling-sized, although an occasional lunker is taken. Try a glass minnow pattern (size 4), as the bass are feeding on some pretty small baitfish.

To get to Hampton Lake, go east on State Road 24 from Gainesville for about 10 miles. At Waldo, turn left onto US 301/SR 200 and go north for 5 miles. Turn right onto Navarre Avenue and go 0.5 mile to the single-lane ramp. There is unimproved parking for 10 vehicles.

LAKE LOWERY, MAGNOLIA LAKE, CRYSTAL LAKE, LAKE BEDFORD, BROOKLYN LAKE, LAKE GENEVA, LAKE HUTCHINSON, LAKE LILY, SWAN LAKE, AND HALFMOON LAKE

About 20 miles northeast of Gainesville is a community known as Keystone Heights that is located in the rolling sandhills of the central ridge of Florida. East of this ridge, rivers and streams flow toward the St. Johns River system. The ridge is not all that visibly prominent, but its presence serves as the eastern edge of Region 2 where rivers and streams flow southwest toward the Gulf of Mexico.

There are a number of lakes surrounding Keystone Heights. While none are particularly noteworthy in their own right, they offer local anglers good opportunities for largemouth bass, crappie, and other panfish, especially from early spring through early summer.

Brooklyn Lake (600 acres) is irregularly shaped and has a number of pockets and coves where fish like to go in early spring to spawn. These pockets and coves also provide flyfishers relief from the wind. In summer, fishing slows down quite a bit, but savvy flyfishers cast noisy topwater poppers around the many points early in the morning as fish move out of deeper water to feed.

To get to Brooklyn Lake, go west on SR 100 for 0.8 mile from the intersection of SR 100 and SR 21 in Keystone Heights. Turn right onto King Street and go 0.2 mile to the single-lane ramp on your right. There is unimproved parking for 10 vehicles.

Lake Lowery (250 acres) and Magnolia Lake (1200 acres), lying north of Keystone Heights, are connected to one another. These lakes are more typical of the saucer-shaped lakes commonly found in Florida. A good place to start fly fishing is near the mouth of the canal that connects them, as both largemouth bass and panfish like to hang around this area. A small popper with rubber legs or a terrestrial fly will take the panfish, as well as yearling bass. Crappie will not rise for a popper, so you will need to sink a Clouser or similar fly to the depth at which they are holding. An occasional lunker largemouth is taken from the north side of Lake Lowery where a creek drains a portion of the Camp Blanding Wildlife Management Area.

To get to Lake Lowery, go north on SR 21 for 1.9 miles from the intersection of SR 100 and SR 21 in Keystone Heights. Turn left at the entrance of the Camp Blanding WMA and go northwest 3.1 miles (passing the entrance to Magnolia Lake) on Treat Road. Turn right onto the dirt road and go 0.4 mile to the single-lane paved ramp.

To get to Magnolia Lake, go north on SR 21 for 1.9 miles from the intersection of SR 100 and SR 21 in Keystone Heights. Turn left at the entrance of the Camp Blanding WMA and go northwest 1.5 miles on Treat Road. Turn right onto the dirt road and go 0.1 mile to the single-lane paved ramp.

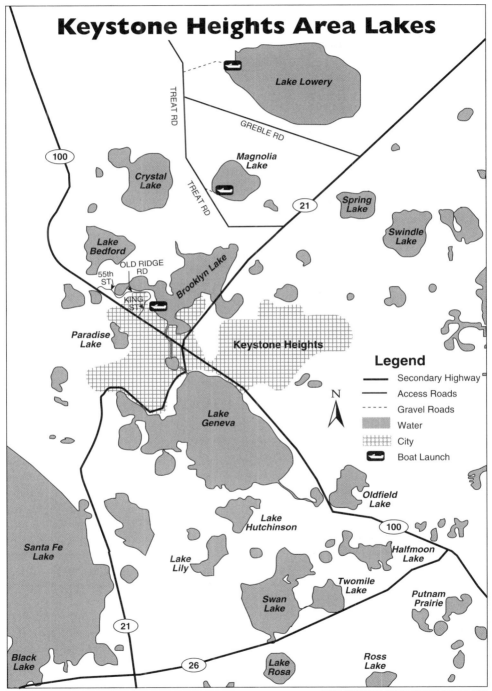

Keystone Heights Area Lakes

Lake Lowery

TREAT RD

GREBLE RD

100

Magnolia Lake

Crystal Lake

TREAT RD

21

Spring Lake

Swindle Lake

Lake Bedford

OLD RIDGE RD

55th ST

Brooklyn Lake

KING ST

Paradise Lake

Keystone Heights

Legend

Lake Geneva

N

— Secondary Highway
— Access Roads
- - - Gravel Roads
▨ Water
▦ City
🚤 Boat Launch

Oldfield Lake

Lake Hutchinson

100

Santa Fe Lake

Lake Lily

Halfmoon Lake

Twomile Lake

Putnam Prairie

21

Swan Lake

Black Lake

26

Lake Rosa

Ross Lake

© WILDERNESS ADVENTURES PRESS, INC.

This crappie fell for a brightly colored Clouser near one of the cypress tress that rim Lochloosa Lake.

LOCHLOOSA LAKE, LITTLE LOCHLOOSA LAKE, AND RIGHT ARM LOCHLOOSA LAKE

Lochloosa Lake and its two named branches (8,000 acres) are about 15 miles southeast of Gainesville (midway between Gainesville and Ocala) and are connected to Orange Lake by Cross Creek. Lochloosa Lake is best known for its crappie fishing, but it also offers very good bluegill, redear, and largemouth bass fishing. Water levels of lakes in this part of the state fluctuate, and for several years they have been low enough to leave many ramps and docks out of the water. Fishing, likewise, has its ups and downs, with periods of really good fishing occurring after water levels rise, flooding areas that were once muck bottom and now overgrown with vegetation. Cypress trees line much of the western shoreline of Lochloosa and most of the two branches, providing excellent shallow water habitat. This main lake averages about 8 feet deep, and the bottom tends to be hard and sandy. Grass beds and lily pads grow out from the shorelines.

Be sure to spend plenty of time in both Little Lochloosa Lake and Right Arm Lochloosa Lake, as well as around the Cross Creek canal leading to Orange Lake. These areas are in the southwest corner of Lochloosa Lake and offer tremendous cover, and this is where fish spawn in the spring. The canal can be fished from the bank by flyfishers and the Marjorie Kinnan Rawling State Historic Site makes a good

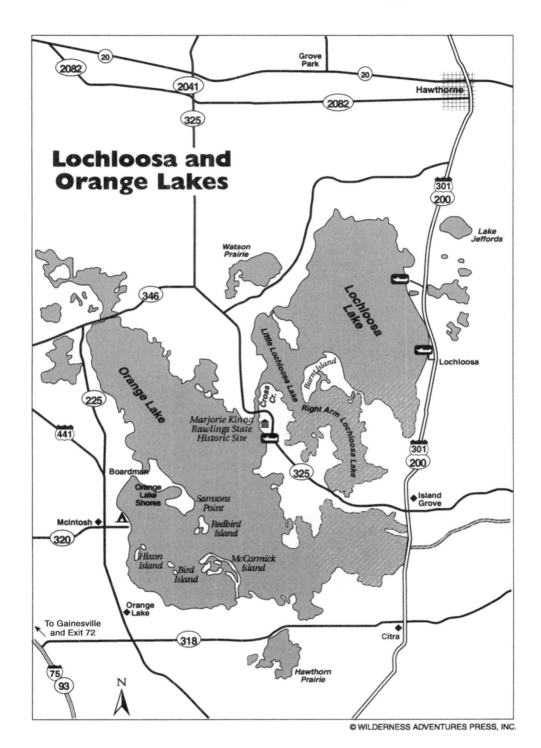

Lochloosa and Orange Lakes

20
2082
20
2041
Grove Park
2082
Hawthorne
325
301
200
Lake Jeffords
Watson Prairie
346
Lochloosa Lake
Lochloosa
225
441
Little Lochloosa Lake
Burnt Island
Orange Lake
Cross Cr.
Marjorie Kinnan Rawlings State Historic Site
Right Arm Lochloosa Lake
325
301
200
Boardman
Island Grove
Orange Lake Shores
Samsons Point
McIntosh
320
Redbird Island
Hixon Island
Bird Island
McCormick Island
Orange Lake
To Gainesville and Exit 72
318
Citra
75
93
N
Hawthorn Prairie

stopping place for a day trip. To get to the canal historic site, take Exit 72 between Gainesville and Ocala off Interstate 75 and go east on CR 318 for 8 miles. Turn left onto US 301/SR 200 and go north for 2.5 miles. Turn left onto CR 325 and go west 4 miles. The site is on your left.

Each year, several largemouth bass over 10 pounds are taken from this system. Flyfishers should fish large, deer-hair flies like a swimming frog or Dahlberg Diver (size 2) around the base of the cypress trees. The bream (shellcracker, bluegill, warmouth, and redear sunfish) in Lochloosa Lake have a preference for grass shrimp. In spring, the crappie will be against cypress trees and short casts using a Clouser Minnow will take slab-sized crappie. Look to open water where the fish will be suspended during the rest of the year. Let your Clouser sink to various depths until the fish are located. There are four brush-type fish attractors in the lake to congregate these fish in open water.

To get to Lochloosa Lake, take Exit 72 off I-75 and go east on CR 318 for 8 miles. Turn left onto US 301/SR 200 and go north for 5.5 miles. In the small community of Lochloosa, turn left and go one block to the single-lane ramp. The other ramp is 1.5 miles north. Again, turn left and go 0.5 mile to the single-lane ramp. Each has parking for about 20 vehicles.

ORANGE LAKE

Orange Lake (12,700 acres), like the Lochloosa system, is about 15 miles southeast of Gainesville, midway between Gainesville and Ocala. Standing cypress trees rim large portions of the lake, offering great habitat for spawning fish. There are also several islands in the southwest corner that provide additional shoreline and depth change in an already very good portion of the lake. Grasses and lily pads grow out from shoreline, and extensive marshes stretch to the south. The bottom of Orange Lake tends to be mucky. With such diverse shoreline, it's no surprise that there is a variety of wildlife in the area. Eagles sightings are quite common, and some of the islands are Audubon sanctuaries.

Water comes into Orange Lake from the Cross Creek Canal on the east and creeks leading from Newnans Lake near Gainesville in the northwest corner. The outflow is from the southeast corner of the lake. Orange Lake is also subject to fluctuations in water levels, and the northwest corner does not always bring water from Newnans Lake. When it does, however, be sure to fish the area thoroughly. This lake is known for yielding big bass (as well as good numbers of smaller, yearling-class bass), and this area is where they spawn in February and March. Crappie also use this area about the same time of year. In summer, bream fishing is the hot ticket, with bluegill, shellcrackers, and warmouth taking small poppers and terrestrial patterns late in the day.

To get to Orange Lake, use the ramp near the Marjorie Kinnan Rawling State Historic Site. Take Exit 72 between Gainesville and Ocala off Interstate 75 and go east on CR 318 for 8 miles. Turn left onto US 301/SR 200 and go north for 2.5 miles. Turn left onto CR 325 and go west for 4 miles to the single-lane ramp on your left.

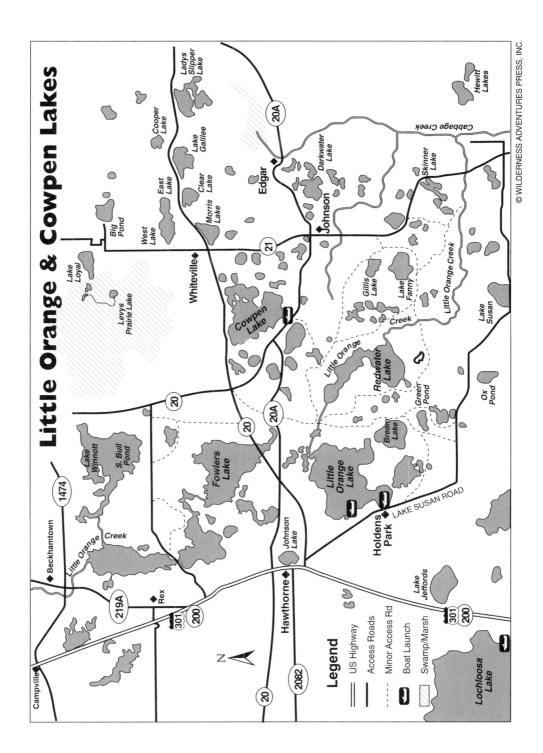

Little Orange & Cowpen Lakes

Ladys Slipper Lake

Hewitt Lakes

Cabbage Creek

Cooper Lake

Lake Galilee

20A

Darkwater Lake

Skinner Lake

East Lake

Clear Lake

Edgar

Johnson

Little Orange Creek

Morris Lake

West Lake

Big Pond

21

Whiteville

Gillis Lake

Lake Fanny

Lake Susan

Lake Loyal

Cowpen Lake

Creek

Levys Prairie Lake

Little Orange

Redwater Lake

Green Pond

Ox Pond

20

20

20A

Lake Wynnott

S. Bull Pond

Fowlers Lake

Bream Lake

Little Orange Lake

1474

Little Orange Creek

Johnson Lake

Holdens Park

LAKE SUSAN ROAD

Beckhamtown

Lake Jeffords

301

200

219A

Rex

301

200

Hawthorne

Campville

Lochloosa Lake

N

2082

20

Legend

═══ US Highway

─── Access Roads

- - - Minor Access Rd

▯ Boat Launch

▨ Swamp/Marsh

LITTLE ORANGE LAKE, COWPEN LAKE, AND LAKE JOHNSON

The area south of SR 20, midway between Gainesville and Palatka, has numerous small lakes. Most of these are private and do not have public access. The exception is Little Orange Lake, where there are two ramps, and Lakes Cowpen and Johnson. Like all lakes and ponds in the area, a long period of drought in central Florida has left them at historic lows. A johnboat or other shallow-water craft will have to be used to gain access to most of them.

Little Orange Lake has an interesting shoreline with some cypress trees standing in the northeast corner. There are several pockets that block the wind and a flyfisher should be able to find a good place to wave a wand. The lake has a good population of small bass, as well as panfish and crappie. The best opportunities come in the spring, and by summer, only the bream are willing to cooperate on a regular basis. Try a small, rubber-legged popper or terrestrial late in the day for bream and perhaps a few small bass.

To get to Little Orange Lake, go east from Gainesville on SR 20 for 14 miles. Turn right onto US 301/SR 200 and go south for 0.7 mile. After crossing the railroad tracks, turn left onto Holden Park Road and go 1.2 miles to the single-lane ramp on your left (the western side of the lake).

There is another single-lane ramp a half-mile ahead. Continue on Holden Park Road and at the intersection with S.E. 101st Avenue, there is a ramp at Holdens Park that gives access to the southern part of the lake.

Cowpen Lake is quite shallow and does not offer a reliable fishery, although a few panfish can be regularly caught by flyfishers using small poppers. The southern end of Cowpen Lake has a ramp that can be reached by going east from the SR 20 and SR 20A intersection about 2 miles east of Hawthorne. Go east for 4 miles on SR 20A, and the single-lane ramp will be on your left.

Because it is deeper, Johnson Lake, adjacent to Gold Head Branch State Park, has a reliable fishery for small bass and panfish, including crappie. This little lake is an enjoyable place to get away from crowded ramps and the wakes of other anglers' boats. Fishing will seldom be great, and the fish won't be particularly large, but you will catch enough bass and panfish by casting poppers to shoreline cover to keep you interested. To get to the state park and Johnson Lake, go east from Keystone Heights on SR 21 for 6 miles. The entrance to the park and ramp will be on your right. There are numerous cabins and camping and RV sites at the park.

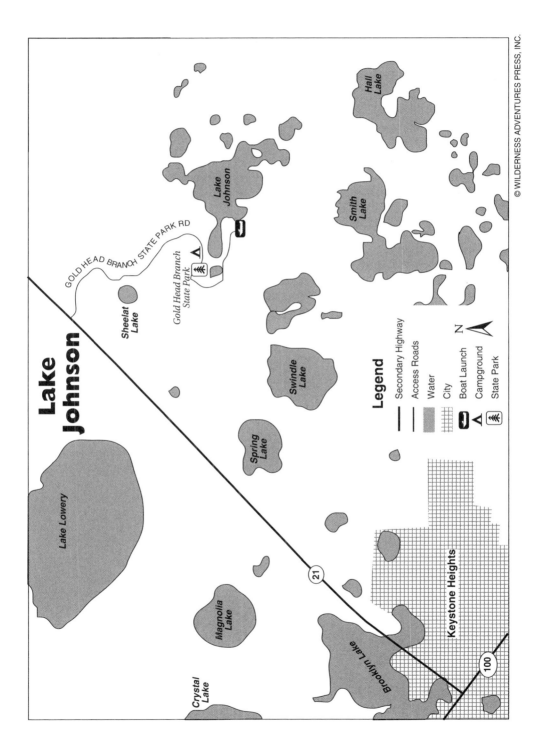

Lake Johnson

Hall Lake

Smith Lake

Lake Johnson

GOLD HEAD BRANCH STATE PARK RD

Gold Head Branch State Park

Sheelat Lake

Swindle Lake

Spring Lake

Lake Lowery

Magnolia Lake

Crystal Lake

Brooklyn Lake

Keystone Heights

21

100

Legend

— Secondary Highway

— Access Roads

Water

City

Boat Launch

Campground

State Park

N

Region 2 Hub Cities

The listings that follow are only a small sampling of the facilities available in the major hub cities.

Apalachicola Bay

ACCOMMODATIONS
Apalachicola River Inn, 123 Water Street, Apalachicola, FL 32320; 850-653-8139
Breakaway Marina & Motel, 200 Waddell Road, Apalachicola, FL 32320; 850-653-8897
Sportsman's Lodge, 99 North Bayshore Drive, Eastpoint, FL 32328; 850-670-8423

CAMPING
Ochockonee River State Park, P.O. Box 5, Sopchoppy, FL 32358; riverside campgrounds with canoe rentals; 850-962-2771
St. George Island State Park, 1900 E. Gulf Beach Drive, St. George Island, FL 32328;850-927-2111

RESTAURANTS
Apalachicola Seafood Grill & Steakhouse, 100 Market Street, Apalachicola, FL 32320; 850-653-8139
Caroline's Dining on the River, 123 Water Street, Apalachicola, FL 32320; 850-653-8139
Magnolia Grill, 99 11th St., Apalachicola, FL 32329; 850-653-8000

FLY SHOPS AND SPORTING GOODS
Forgotten Coast Outfitters, 94 Market St., Apalachicola, FL 32320; 850-653-9669
Survivors Island Bait & Tackle, 28 West Pine St., St. George Island, FL 32328; 850-927-3113
Wefing's Bait & Tackle, 56 Market Street, Apalachicola, FL 32329; 850-653-1333

HOSPITALS
Weems Memorial Hospital, 135 Avenue G, Apalachicola, FL 32329; 850-653-8853

AIRPORTS
(See Panama City.)

AUTO SERVICE
(See Panama City.)

FOR MORE INFORMATION
Apalachicola Bay Chamber of Commerce, 84 Market St., Apalachicola, FL 32320; 850-653-9419

Fort Walton Beach

ACCOMMODATIONS

Best Western Fort Walton Beachfront Hotel, 380 Santa Rosa Blvd., Fort. Walton Beach, FL 32548; 850-243-9444

Four Points Hotel by Sheraton, 1325 Miracle Strip Parkway - East, Fort Walton Beach, FL 32548; 850-243-8116

Holiday Inn Sunspree, 573 Santa Rosa Blvd., Fort Walton Beach, FL 32548; 850-244-8686

CAMPING

Rocky Bayou State Park, 4281 Hwy 20, Niceville, FL 32578; 850-833-9144

RESTAURANTS

Pranzo Italian Ristorante, 1225 Santa Rosa Blvd., Fort Walton Beach, FL 32548; 850-244-9955

Red Lobster, 326 Miracle Strip Pkwy., Fort Walton Beach, FL 32548; 850-664-2700

Two Trees Restaurant, 1955 Lewis Turner Blvd., Fort Walton Beach, FL 32547; 850-244-2388

FLY SHOPS AND SPORTING GOODS

Blue Bay Outfitters, 47 Hwy. 98 East, Destin, FL 32541; 850-650-6968/877-321-3474

Sockeye Beach & Sport, 20011 Emerald Coast Parkway, Destin, FL 32541; 850-654-8954

Sports Country, Inc., 434 Mary Esther Blvd., Fort Walton Beach, FL 32548; 850-664-0060

West Marine, 248 A Eglin Pkwy NE, Ft. Walton Beach, FL 32547; 850-863-8700

West Marine, 220 Eglin Pkwy NE, Ft. Walton Beach, FL 32548; 850-664-2254

HOSPITALS

Fort Walton Beach Medical Center, 1000 Mar Walt Drive, Fort Walton Beach, FL 32547; 850-863-7501

AIRPORTS

Okaloosa Regional Airport, 1701 SR 85N, Eglin AFB, FL 32542; 850-651-7160

AUTO SERVICE

Holmes Auto Repair, 15 Robinwood Dr. So., Fort Walton Beach, FL 32548; 850-243-1311

FOR MORE INFORMATION

Greater Fort Walton Beach Chamber of Commerce, 34 Miracle Strip Pkwy. S.E., P.O. Box 640, Fort Walton Beach, FL 32549; 850-244-8191

Panama City

ACCOMMODATIONS
Best Western Suites, 1035 E. 23rd St., Panama City, FL 32405; 850-784-7700
Country Inn & Suites, 2203 Harrison Ave., Panama City, FL 32405; 850-913-0074
La Quinta Inns & Suites, 1030 East 23rd St., Panama City, FL 32405; 850-914-0022

CAMPING
St. Andrews State Park, 4607 State Park Lane, Panama City, FL 32408; 850-233-5140

RESTAURANTS
Boar's Head Restaurant, 17290 Front Beach Road, Panama City, FL 32413; 850-234-6628
Loftin's Bar B-Q, 4900 Thomas Dr., Panama City, FL 32408; 850-249-2390
St. Andrew Bay Seafood Restaurant, 3001 West 10th Street, Panama City, FL 32401; 850-522-0722

FLY SHOPS AND SPORTING GOODS
C & G Sporting Goods, 137 Harrison Ave., Panama City, FL 32410; 850-769-2317
St. Andrews Light Tackle & Fly, 2303 W. 15th St., Panama City; 850-769-5873
West Marine, 1388 W. 15th St., Panama City, FL 32401; 850-763-1844

HOSPITALS
Gulf Coast Medical Center, 449 W. 23rd Street, Panama City, FL 32405; 850-769-8341

AIRPORTS
Panama City/Bay County International Airport, 3173 Airport Road, Panama City, FL 32405; 850-763-6751

AUTO SERVICE
St. Andrews Auto Care, 1014 Beck Ave., Panama City, FL 32401; 850-522-6525

FOR MORE INFORMATION
Panama City Beaches Chamber of Commerce, P.O. Box 9348, Panama City Beach, FL 32407; 850-235-1159

Pensacola

ACCOMMODATIONS
Courtyard by Marriott, 451 Creighton Road, Pensacola, FL 32504; 850-857-7744
Econo Lodge, 7194 Pensacola Blvd., Pensacola, FL 32505; 850-479-8600
Holiday Inn Express, 6501 N. Pensacola Blvd., Pensacola, FL 32505; 850-476-7200

CAMPING
850-623-6197

RESTAURANTS
Angus Seafood-Meats-Spirits, 1101 Scenic Hwy., Pensacola, FL 32503; 850-424-0539
Flounder's Chowder House, 800 Quietwater Beach Road, Pensacola, FL 32561; 850-932-2003
Norma's By-the-Bay, 500 Bay Front Pkwy., Pensacola, FL 32501; 850-438-9565

FLY SHOPS AND SPORTING GOODS
Gulf Breeze Bait & Tackle, 825 Gulf Breeze Pkwy., Gulf Breeze, FL 32561; 850-932-6789
The Sports Authority, 1220 Airport Blvd., Pensacola, FL 32504; 850-494-1611
West Marine, 3500 Barrancas Ave., Pensacola, FL 32507; 850-453-0010
West Marine, 7160 N. Davis Hwy., Pensacola, FL 32504; 850-476-2720

HOSPITALS
Gulf Breeze Hospital, 1110 Gulf Breeze Pkwy., Gulf Breeze, FL 32561; 850-934-2100

AIRPORTS
Pensacola Regional Airport, 2430 Airport Blvd., Pensacola, FL 32504; 850-436-5000

AUTO SERVICE
Knight's Automotive Service, 5135 W. Fairfield Dr., Pensacola, FL 32506; 850-453-0830

FOR MORE INFORMATION
Pensacola Area Chamber of Commerce, P.O. Box 550, Pensacola, FL 32593; 850-438-4081

Gainesville

ACCOMMODATIONS
Fairfield Inn by Marriott, 6901 NW 4th Blvd., Gainesville, FL 32607; 352-332-8292
Hampton Inn, 4225 SW 40th Blvd., Gainesville, FL 32608; 352-371-4171
Quality Inn - Gainesville, 3455 SW Williston Road, Gainesville, FL 32608;
352-378-2405

CAMPING
Paynes Prairie Preserve State Park, Route 2, Box 41, Micanopy, FL 32667; 50
campsites, lakes and ponds; 352-466-3397
Traveler's Campground, 17701 April Blvd., Alachua, FL 32615; 386-462-2505

RESTAURANTS
Outback Steakhouse, 3536 SW Archer Road, Gainesville, FL 32608; 352-373-9499
Stonewood Tavern & Grill, 3812 Newberry Road, Gainesville, FL 32607;
352-379-5982
Porter's Dining on the Avenue, 1 West University Ave., Gainesville, FL 32601;
352-372-0101

FLY SHOPS AND SPORTING GOODS
Brasingtons Adventure Outfitters, 2331 NW 13th Street, Gainesville, FL 32609;
352-372-0521
The Tackle Box, 1490 SE Hawthorne Road, Gainesville, FL 32641; 352-372-1791
The Sports Authority, 7400 W. Newberry Road, Gainesville, FL 32606; 352-331-
2235

HOSPITALS
North Florida Regional Medical Center, 6500 Newberry Road, Gainesville, FL
32614; 352-333-4000

AIRPORTS
Gainesville Regional Airport, 3880 NE 39th Ave., Gainesville, FL 32609;
352-373-0249

AUTO SERVICE
Alan's Superior Auto Repair, 3018 NE 19th Dr., Gainesville, FL 32609; 352-373-
5411

FOR MORE INFORMATION
Gainesville Area Chamber of Commerce, P.O. Box 1187, Gainesville, FL 32602;
352-334-7100

Ocala

ACCOMMODATIONS
Days Inn, 3811 NW Blitchton Road, Ocala, FL 34482; 352-629-7041
Hampton Inn, 3434 College Road, Ocala, FL 34474; 352-854-3200
Hilton Ocala, 3600 SW 36th Ave., Ocala, FL 34474; 352-854-1400

CAMPING
Ocala KOA, 3200 SW 38th St., Ocala, FL 34774; 352-237-2138

RESTAURANTS
Hops Grill & Bar, 2505 SW College Road, Ocala, FL 34474; 352-237-8182
Roadhouse Grill, 2105 SW 17th St., Ocala, FL 34774; 352-867-0082
Shell's Great Casual Seafood, 3415 SW College Road, Ocala, FL 34774; 352-873-9993

FLY SHOPS AND SPORTING GOODS
Leisure Time Fly Shop, 614 N. W. Highway 19, Crystal River, FL 34428; 352-795-3171
Scudder & Sons Outfitters, 2709 SW 27th Avenue, Ocala, FL 34474; 352-237-6685

HOSPITALS
Ocala Regional Medical Center, 1431 SW 1st Ave., Ocala, FL 34478; 352-401-1101

AIRPORTS
(See Gainesville.)

AUTO SERVICE
Fastlane Auto, 1894 NW 10th St., Ocala, FL 34475; 352-840-6911

FOR MORE INFORMATION
Ocala-Marion County Chamber of Commerce, 110 E. Silver Springs Blvd., Ocala, FL 34470; 352-629-8051

Tallahassee

ACCOMMODATIONS
Best Western Pride Inn, 2016 Apalachee Pkwy., Tallahassee, FL 32301; 850-827-7390

Holiday Inn Select, 316 W. Tennessee St., Tallahassee, FL 32301; 850-222-9555

Ramada Inn Tallahassee, 2900 N. Monroe St., Tallahassee, FL 32303; 850-386-1097

CAMPING
Edward Ball Wakulla Springs State Park, 550 Wakulla Park Drive, Wakulla Springs, FL 32305; 850-224-5950

RESTAURANTS
Barnaby's, 2331 Apalachee Pkwy., Tallahassee, FL 32301; 850-878-8700

Coosh's Bayou Rouge, 2910 Kerry Forest Pkwy., Tallahassee, FL 32308; 850-894-4110

Tommy D's Internationally Famous Belgian Fries and Kabobs, 685 W. Tennessee St., Tallahassee, FL 32301; 850-212-0551

FLY SHOPS AND SPORTING GOODS
Kevin's Fine Outdoor Gear, 3350 Capital Circle, NE, Tallahassee, FL 32308; 850-386-5544

West Marine, 4248 W. Tennessee St., Tallahassee, FL 32304; 850-574-3309

HOSPITALS
Tallahassee Community Hospital, 2626 Capitol Medical Blvd., Tallahassee, FL 32308; 850-656-5000

AIRPORTS
Tallahassee Regional Airport, 3300 Capitol Circle, S.W., Tallahassee, FL 32310; 850-891-7847

AUTO SERVICE
Eastern Automotive Services, 808 N. Monroe St., Tallahassee, FL 32803; 850-224-7364

FOR MORE INFORMATION
Tallahassee Area Chamber of Commerce, P.O. Box 1639, Tallahassee, FL 32302; 850-224-8116

Suwannee River Wildlife Refuge Canal.

Withlacoochee River.

Region 3- Central and South Florida

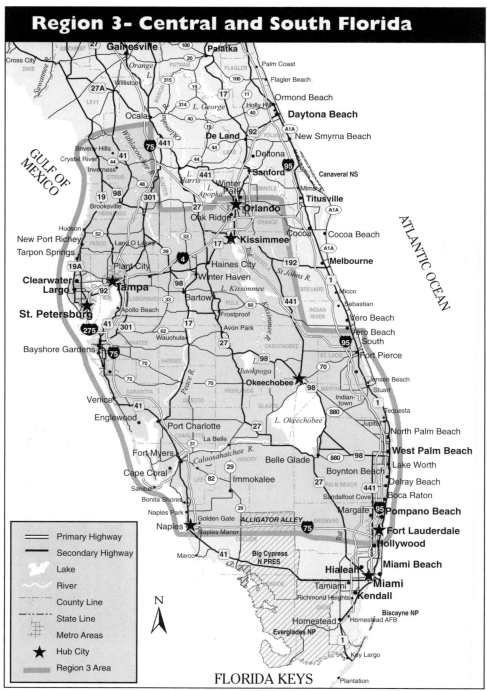

Legend:
- Primary Highway
- Secondary Highway
- Lake
- River
- County Line
- State Line
- Metro Areas
- ★ Hub City
- Region 3 Area

FLORIDA KEYS

© WILDERNESS ADVENTURES PRESS, INC.

Central and South Florida

Here are no lofty peaks seeking the sky, no mighty glaciers or rushing streams wearing away the uplifted land. Here is land, tranquil in its quiet beauty, serving not as the source of water, but as the last receiver of it. To its natural abundance we owe the spectacular plant and animal life that distinguishes this place from all others in our country.

—President Harry S. Truman, in his address at the Dedication of Everglades National Park, December 6, 1947

Region 3 is a large area that includes waters south of US 40 (as it bisects the state near Ocala) and extends south to the Everglades, omitting those streams that drain into the St. Johns River (see Region 1). This large, diverse area encompasses most of central and south Florida and offers more variety in fishing opportunities than either of the first two regions. The topography of the land is relatively flat, with an ever so slight tilt to the southwest. All of the rivers included in Region 3 drain toward the Gulf of Mexico, but there are fewer of them and they flow much more slowly than those in Region 2. Likewise, there are far fewer springs to nourish the rivers and streams and most freshwater fly fishing is done on the region's numerous lakes.

There are more lakes than you could probably visit in a lifetime, and certainly many more than you could ever hope to get to know well. Seven of the top 10 largemouth bass lakes in the state are in this region. Polk County alone has more than 500 lakes.

How about a lake (West Lake Tohopekaliga, a.k.a. Lake Toho, near Kissimmee) on which a bass tournament was held with a 5-fish weigh-in that yielded over 45 pounds of largemouth to an angler on a single day of fishing? This lake is included in our top 10, and it is scheduled for a drawdown in an effort to improve the fishery even more. This may be the best big-bass fishing lake in the country for the first part of the 21st century.

Also included in the list of top 10 lakes is Lake Kissimmee. After a significant drawdown in 1996, an additional 22 miles of shoreline were made accessible to the wade fisherman on this already outstanding lake. Catch rates have increased significantly, and you will be hearing remarkable things about the fishery in this lake for the next several years.

Kissimmee River.

Lake Okeechobee has over 700 square miles of water and has been a world-renowned fishery for many years. If you have watched fishing programs about large-mouth bass or crappie in Florida, you have surely seen one that featured this lake. Significant efforts have been made to return this lake to its prominent status (it still is a top 10, nonetheless). Both bass and crappie grow large and can go for long periods of time in the marshy waters of the "Big O" without being pressured by anglers. Surface schooling by bass also occurs in late spring and it is a sight to behold when hundreds of bass corral a school of shad and drive them to the surface. Once "penned" against the surface, the bass slash away at the forage fish. Be sure to have a baitfish pattern on a floating line for such an opportunity.

Finally, the northern portion of the Everglades offers a rich and diversified freshwater fishery before becoming brackish. Its marshy "sea of grass" yields to mangroves, mosquitoes, and perhaps the most awesome coastal fishing you will find anywhere (see the *Flyfisher's Guide to the Florida Keys,* by Capt. Ben Taylor). With its headwaters near Orlando in the Kissimmee Chain of Lakes, the Everglades slowly drain most of south and west-central Florida. It is a vast and unique ecosystem that is unrivaled anywhere in the world. We can only begin to touch upon its unique splendor in this guidebook.

In stark contrast to the unblemished beauty of the Everglades are the phosphate pits created by companies that once mined a large portion of the area between Tampa and Orlando. Ten million years ago, billions of phosphate particles (the remains of tiny sea organisms) were deposited on the shallow ocean floor then covering Florida, and along with sand and clay, settled into strata. As the ocean waters receded, phosphate beds were buried under sandy soil in the area of west-central Florida. About 40 years ago, huge pits were created as the phosphate was excavated. The mining companies have filled these pits with water and stocked them with a variety of game fish. The surrounding lands have been reclaimed and park-like settings created where the earth was only recently scarred by hundreds of phosphate pits. These reclaimed pits and surrounding land were then donated to state, county, and city governments for public use.

One of these reclaimed areas, Tenoroc Fish Management Area near Lakeland, has been named as one of the top 10 fishing sites in Florida for 1999, 2000, and 2001 (subsequent picks are not available as of this printing). This site is intensely managed by Florida's Fish and Game Commission to ensure that everyone who fishes one of Tenoroc's fourteen pits has a quality experience. Some pits have been set aside for children, while others are available for persons with physical limitations.

Region 3 has the warmest temperatures in the state, and this should be taken into account as you plan fishing trips. You should have sunscreen and sunglasses if you are going to be on the water for a long time. Be sure to bring plenty of water, as you are likely to perspire, especially if you wear dark-colored clothing. It is a good idea to take a break during the middle of the day. Many of the lakes have next to no shade in which to seek refuge from the sun. The area is flat, without relief, and the surrounding marshes do not support a root system except for cypress trees.

Two of the state's largest lakes (Okeechobee and Kissimmee) are in Region 3, and many other lakes in the region are also quite large. When these big bodies of water are also shallow, as with Okeechobee and Kissimmee, they can become quite rough when the wind picks up from the opposite shore. Some wind makes fly fishing difficult, but when an afternoon storm front approaches, it can get dangerous. Overturned boats are easily recovered in the shallow water, but that is not always the case with the angler. When the sky darkens and the wind starts to blow, seek shelter immediately.

Watch out for the afternoon rains that follow the wind. In summer, they will occur almost every day, as onshore breezes from the Atlantic and the Gulf collide mid-state. The two fronts compete for position with differing air temperatures and air pressures, each filled with moisture from waters warmed by a hot sun that has caused surface vaporization. The colliding fronts produce short periods of torrential rain and fierce lightning. You might want to have some rain gear tucked away, as these systems approach quite rapidly, and if they come from the direction you need to go to return to your launch site, count on getting wet.

Florida leads the nation in lightning strikes and nothing makes a better lightning rod than 9 feet of graphite held by a flyfisher standing on the deck of a boat in open water. This is pretty serious stuff that local anglers know about and treat with the highest respect. Often the lightning precedes the rain, as well as the wind, and it will be on the very leading edge of an approaching front, many miles ahead of threatening weather.

Central and south Florida have seen less than normal rainfall for the past several years. As a result, many lakes are at historic lows, with ramps out of the water and canals connecting lakes not navigable. Many boats are hanging in their slips with no water under them.

Seasonally, there is little rainfall from mid-December to mid-March and waters will be very clear. In the summer months, it can rain for an hour or so during late afternoon. Tropical storms are a possibility from midsummer through all of October. Keep posted on tropical storms well south of Florida and the direction any storm is expected to take, and heed all weather advisories. If you want to experience gridlock on a massive scale, be part of an evacuation order on Labor Day weekend, sitting still on an interstate with your back to a tropical storm system that is bearing down.

The road system in Region 3 is far better than Region 2's. Interstate 4 runs east-west across the center of the state, through Orlando and Tampa near the northern end of the region. Interstate 75 runs north-south near the west coast for the entire length of the region. In addition, a toll road (the Florida Turnpike) tracks the Kissimmee Chain of Lakes from Orlando almost to Lake Okeechobee. While state forests and vast areas of undeveloped land made up much of Region 2, in this region we have several areas of highly developed sprawl. Only Orlando and Tampa have a significant skyline, but their suburbs extend for many miles and offer lodging, restaurants, and roads that are sure to lead in the direction you want to go.

Disney World and other theme parks dominate the tourism industry in central Florida. It is a good place to bring your family to play while you wave your graphite wand. Have patience, though, as the road system was not designed to handle the amount of traffic that tries to move through Orlando at 5:00 p.m. in early June during the influx of tourists.

We'll start our tour of fly fishing opportunities in Region 3 at the northern end. It should not come as a surprise, then, that the first body of water is a river similar to many of those in Region 2. But you will quickly realize that this is a region with a character all its own.

During dry periods, the Withlacoochee's low water can be difficult to navigate in anything but an airboat.

WITHLACOOCHEE RIVER

The Withlacoochee River (from the Seminole Indian word meaning "Little Great Water") has its headwaters about 20 miles west of Walt Disney World in Green Swamp located in Hernando, Polk, Sumter, and Lake Counties. The river meanders slowly for some 150 miles to the north and west before reaching picturesque Yankeetown and the Gulf of Mexico. The first 10 to 15 miles of the river are difficult to distinguish from the swamp and there exists a symbiotic partnership between the two as they nourish each other. Cypress roots and decaying vegetation in the swamp give the headwaters of the Withlacoochee River a dark, tannic color that remains in the water throughout most of its journey toward the Gulf.

After flowing out of Green Swamp, the Withlacoochee River moves into the Withlacoochee State Forest. Covering nearly 150,000 acres, the area has been described by the World Wildlife Fund as one of the "Top 10 Coolest Places You've Never Seen in North America." There are trails throughout the forest for hikers, mountain bikers, and horseback riders, as well as rustic riverside picnic areas and campgrounds. Osprey and herons are common, and migratory waterfowl winter in the area. The forest is home to about every species of wildlife found in Florida, including deer, bear, bobcat, coyote, raccoon, otter, turkey, fox, wild hog, and squirrels aplenty. Many of these can be seen early in the morning drinking from the cool waters of the Withlacoochee. Turtles sun on fallen logs and alligators do the same along the shoreline.

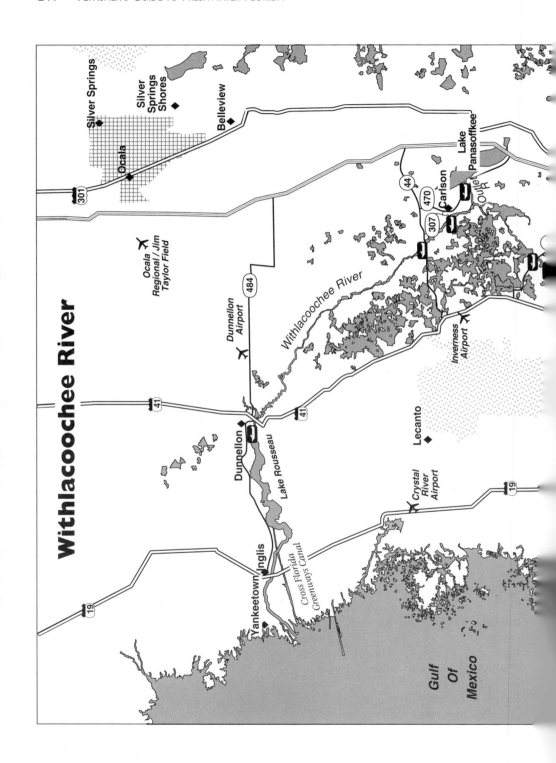

Withlacoochee River

Silver Springs

Ocala

Silver Springs Shores

Belleview

301

Lake Panasoffkee

Carlson

44

470

307

Outlet

Ocala Regional / Jim Taylor Field

Dunnellon Airport

484

Withlacoochee River

Inverness Airport

41

41

Dunnellon

Lake Rousseau

Lecanto

Crystal River Airport

19

19

Yankeetown

Inglis

Cross Florida Greenways Canal

19

Gulf Of Mexico

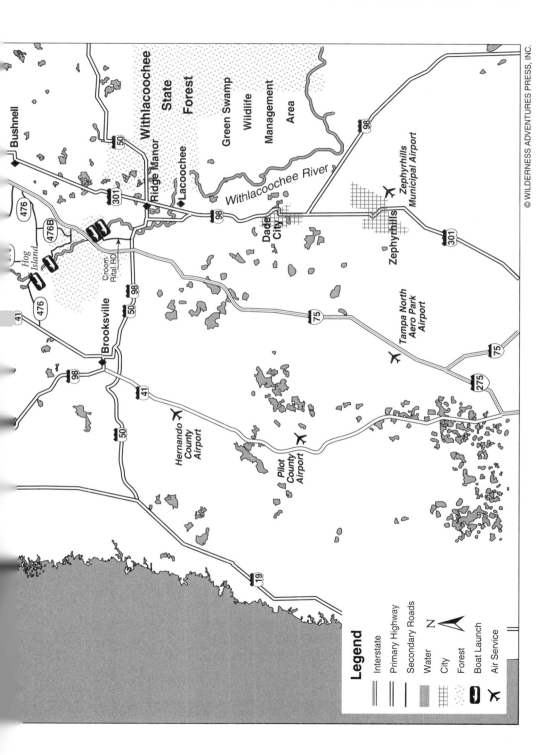

Bushnell

Withlacoochee State Forest

Green Swamp Wildlife Management Area

Ridge Manor

Lacoochee

Withlacoochee River

Zephyrhills Municipal Airport

Dade City

Zephyrhills

Hog Island

Croom Rital RD

Tampa North Aero Park Airport

Brooksville

Hernando County Airport

Pilot County Airport

Legend

Interstate

Primary Highway

Secondary Roads

Water

N

City

Forest

Boat Launch

Air Service

*The single-lane ramp at the SR 44 Bridge is a
popular access point for the Withlacoochee River.*

The river courses onward between lengthy portions of private land, giving rise to a sense of remoteness and inaccessibility. In 1903, the Inglis Dam was built for hydroelectric power about 10 miles upriver from the Gulf of Mexico, creating Lake Rousseau. The electric power plant has since been abandoned and the lake is now managed for fishing and recreation. Below the dam (toward the Gulf), the shoreline is more developed and the water changes from freshwater to brackish. Along with that change, the nature of the fishery changes, with snook, tarpon, seatrout, and red-fish, among other species.

The Withlacoochee is a tame river during most of its course, although it has been known to get out of its banks during extremely wet periods. On the other hand, during periods of exceptional drought, it may become necessary to portage over sand bars. The river is wide, shallow, and heavily vegetated in the slower portions, inter-spersed with narrow, deep, swift, and rocky stretches. Accordingly, quite a number of species of fish populate the variety of habitat this creates. Of greatest interest to fly-fishers are largemouth bass and assorted species of bream.

In the upper reaches of the Withlacoochee, bream provide the major fishery. When water levels are low, as they have been for several years, the river is narrow and fishing can be difficult. Redbreasts, bluegills, and warmouth are the most commonly encountered species. Flyfishers should try small poppers and terrestrial patterns near root wads and logjams. Access to these waters is very limited, typically off trails in the Withlacoochee State Forest. The river is not navigable at this point for anything except a canoe, kayak, or johnboat without a motor. Therefore, there are no public launch sites for a motorized boat, but you will find access for shallow draft boats off roads (US 301 and SR 50) crossing the Withlacoochee River.

Moving out of the state forest, the first public access is located at a wide spot in the river named Silver Lake where I-75 crosses. The north side of Silver Lake is shallow and marshy and should be explored for smaller bass and assorted bream. Small poppers (size 4) and river shrimp patterns are a good choice in this part of the river.

To get to the launch site at Silver Lake Recreational Area, get off I-75 at Exit 61 and go east on US 98/SR 50 for 1 mile. Turn left onto Croom Rital Road and go north about 3 miles to the lake and recreation area. There are two single-lane ramps.

The next public launch (Hog Island) is about five river miles downstream, but the access is too remote to highly recommend. To get there, take Exit 62 off I-75 and go west on CR 476-B for about 0.4 mile. As CR 476-B makes a sharp right, continue straight onto the forest road and follow it to the river and then parallel for about 4.5 miles.

There is a good launch site about 3 river miles downstream at Nobleton Wayside Park. From Brooksville (about 9 miles east of I-75 from Exit 61), go north on US 41 for 6.3 miles. Turn right onto CR 476 (Lake Lindsey Road) and go 4.5 miles to the single-lane ramp.

At this point in the river, bream (mostly stumpknockers and bluegills) will be found concentrated around obvious structure near any deeper water. The river is still narrow and shallow, and bass fishing is slow, especially during periods of low water.

About five river miles downstream, there are two more ramps about a mile apart. Both launch sites are best approached from the east side of the river by getting off I-75 at Exit 63 and gong west on SR 48. About 8 miles ahead, there is a single-lane ramp on the left side of the road where the bridge on SR 48 crosses the Withlacoochee River.

The other ramp is about one mile upriver. From the bridge crossing the river, go east on SR 48 for 0.6 mile and turn right onto CR 575. Go 0.4 mile and turn right again. Continue 0.3 mile to the river and launch site. The area surrounding both of these sites is low and marshy.

The next launch site is about 10 miles downriver on what is called Outlet River. This 3-mile body of water connects Lake Panasoffkee to the Withlacoochee River, and the launch site is where CR 470 crosses Outlet River. From here you can get to Lake Panasoffkee (1 mile to your east) or the Withlacoochee River (2 miles to your west). The double-lane ramp is at Marsh Bend Park. From I-75, get off at Exit 66 and go west on SR 44 for 6 miles. Turn left onto CR 470 and go south for 4.8 miles. At the park entrance, turn right and follow the road to the launch site. There is paved parking for 11 vehicles.

At this point in the river, Tsala Apopka Lake is about one mile to the west. This extensive lowland lake and several others also to the west are part of a marshy prairie bordering and supplying water to the Withlacoochee River.

There is a single-lane ramp about 2.5 miles downstream from where Outlet River joins the "With." The site is known as Carlson's Landing. Again from Exit 66 on I-75, go west on SR 44 for 6 miles. Turn left onto CR 470 and go 2.7 miles. Turn right onto CR 307 and go one block. Turn right again onto CR 300 and go 0.3 mile. Turn left onto NW 46th Road and this leads to the ramp just ahead. There is improved parking for 7 vehicles.

Three miles downstream is a popular access point at the SR 44 Bridge. From Exit 66, go west on SR 44 for 8.5 miles to the bridge crossing the river. The single-lane ramp is on the left side of the bridge. There is unimproved parking for 12 vehicles.

Although several bridges cross the river downstream, there are no public access points for more than 25 river miles. Note that several of these bridges have low clearance, too. The river remains narrow, but snakes through more steeply banked areas. As it does, it gains some speed while still remaining one of the more scenic waterways in the state.

Largemouth bass become more common and fishing for them improves from fair to good. The increased flow puts more oxygen into the water and washes more food into the mix, allowing the bass to occupy a variety of habitats. You may have to cast your fly around shoals, root wads, blow-downs, eddies, and assorted types of shoreline vegetation to find where the bass are feeding. A little effort, however, can locate a school of yearling bass that are willing to tug on your line. Try small terrestrial patterns, which will also take the panfish, or shrimp flies, minnow imitations, and the standard popping bugs.

The next access point is about a mile above Lake Rousseau near Dunnellon. From the intersection of US 41 and CR 484 in Dunnellon, go south on US 41 for 0.3 mile. The single-lane ramp will be on your right just before the bridge. There is unimproved parking for 18 vehicles.

About a mile downstream from the bridge, the river widens into Lake Rousseau. The stump- and vegetation-filled lake stretches for about 12 miles before moving its discharge westward for another 10 miles to the Gulf of Mexico. The 10-mile, straight-as-an-arrow Cross Florida Greenways Canal, a remnant of the failed Cross Florida Barge Canal project, is one of two waterways moving the waters of the Withlacoochee out of Lake Rousseau. The original river channel also moves westward to the Gulf.

Neither the canal or original river channel has striped bass (too warm), although sunshine bass have been stocked. They do not reach the size that they do in rivers in the northern part of the state, though. These waters offer a freshwater fishery as they leave Lake Rousseau and then turn brackish in their lower portion. Here, redfish, seatrout, and seasonal tarpon offer coastal fishing opportunities for flyfishers.

Lake Rousseau

Lake Rousseau (4,163 acres) is a narrow lake averaging about a mile wide (two miles at its widest point) running east to west for about 12 miles. Originally created as part of the Cross Florida Barge Canal, it is an old, stump-filled reservoir with quite a bit of residential development on both the north and south shorelines. Like Rodman Reservoir, a straight canal leads away from the lake, this time all the way to the Gulf of Mexico. There is a good population of redfish and seatrout in the canal, especially during the cooler months.

Vegetation (hydrilla, water hyacinths, water lettuce, and tussocks) causes navigation problems at times. The docks, stump fields, and vegetation create wonderful habitat for largemouth and bream, however. Flyfishers will need to find some open water and cast to the edges or probe near wooden structure. Deer-hair poppers in larger sizes work well for Lake Rousseau's lunker largemouth, but make sure that you have some with monofilament weedguards so that you can probe thicker cover. Several bass over 10 pounds are taken every year. Look to shoreline areas in the spring, and as waters warm, move out toward deeper water. Crappie follow the same seasonal pattern, as do the largemouth bass. Look toward the shoreline in the spring and move to deeper water the rest of the year. A brightly colored Clouser will be the fly of choice to imitate a minnow. If you are fishing for shellcracker and warmouth, try a fly that imitates a grass shrimp or cricket.

Goldendale Ramp gives good access to the east side of Lake Rousseau.

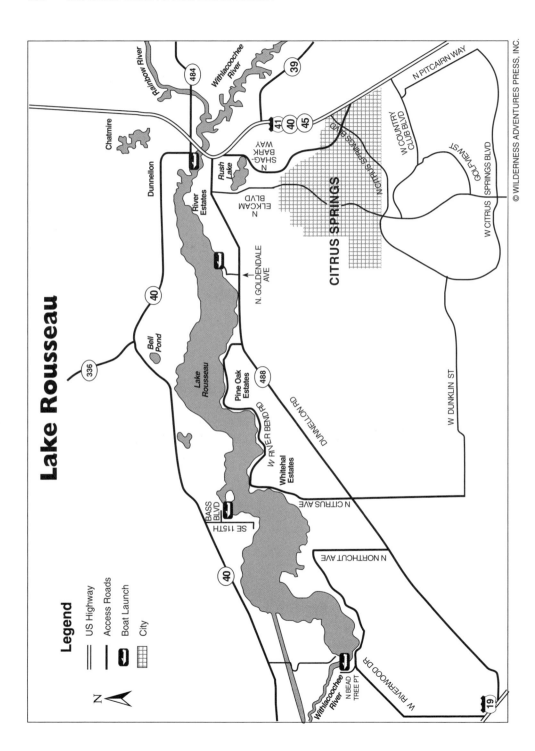

Lake Rousseau

There are numerous fish camps on both the north and south shores of Lake Rousseau in addition to the public launch sites mentioned below.

To get to the east end of the lake, go south from Dunnellon on US 41, and cross the Withlacoochee River. Go 0.2 mile and turn right onto County Road 488 (Dunnellon Road). Go west for about 2.3 miles to North Goldendale Avenue. Turn right and go 0.3 mile to the single-lane Goldendale Ramp.

To get to the Bass Avenue ramp about mid-lake on the north side, go east on State Road 40 from the intersection with US 19 in Inglis for 5.9 miles. Turn right onto S.E. 115th Avenue and go south for 0.8 mile. Turn left onto Bass Boulevard and go 0.1 mile to the single-lane ramp. There is unimproved parking for 20 vehicles.

There is a ramp at the dam at the extreme western end of the lake. From the intersection of SR 40 and US 19, go south on US 19 (crossing both the Withlacoochee River and then the canal) for 3 miles. Turn left onto West Riverwood Drive and go 2 miles to the single-lane ramp on your left.

Redfish and seatrout are found in the canal leading to the Gulf, especially in the cooler months.

LAKE PANASOFFKEE

Lake Panasoffkee (4,460 acres) is a shallow, spring-fed lake with water depths seldom exceeding four feet. This is an uncommon combination for a Florida lake, as lakes that are wide spots in a river tend to be on the shallow side, whereas spring-fed lakes usually are much deeper. A bass boat is not recommended even under normal conditions, but given the severe drought of the past several years, only a shallow draft johnboat with a trolling motor and weedguard should be used to fish Lake Panasoffkee.

Much of the lake's bottom is covered with dense eelgrass. This provides excellent habitat, especially for shellcrackers and bluegills. While some very good bass are occasionally caught, Lake Panasoffkee's reputation is mostly for bream.

Flyfishers should think shallow, and small poppers and slowly sinking terrestrials are the ticket to bluegill and shellcracker success. A 5- or 6-weight rod with a floating line is about right for these small, scrappy fighters. Look for white spots on the eelgrass and begin your fishing in these areas. The white spots are dead snail shells that are used by both bluegills and shellcrakers as spawning substrate. Those fishing for bass should cast larger poppers with weedguards around the edges of vegetation.

To get to Lake Panasoffkee, use a ramp on the Outlet River about a mile west of the lake (as detailed in the preceding coverage on the Withlacoochee River). As you enter the lake from the west side, there are several fish camps, as well as the town of Lake Panasoffkee to the south. Much of this western shoreline is developed with homes.

The ramp at Marsh Bend on the Outlet River gives access to Lake Panasoffkee, a shallow lake often fished by airboat.

Lake Panasoffkee

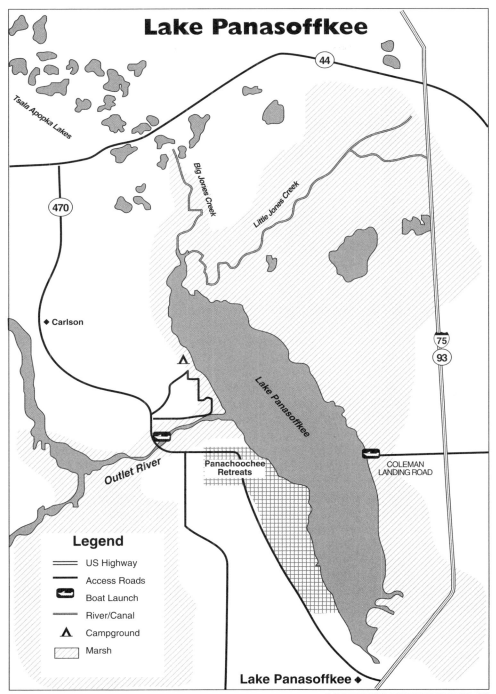

Tsala Apopka Lakes

470

44

Big Jones Creek

Little Jones Creek

♦ Carlson

Lake Panasoffkee

75

93

Outlet River

Panachoochee
Retreats

COLEMAN
LANDING ROAD

Legend

⚌ US Highway
━ Access Roads
🛥 Boat Launch
⚌ River/Canal
⛰ Campground
▨ Marsh

Lake Panasoffkee ♦

© WILDERNESS ADVENTURES PRESS, INC.

TSALA APOPKA LAKE

Tsala Apopka (19,111 acres) is a large, heavily vegetated marsh with numerous open areas of shallow water. Frequently, dense mats of floating vegetation cover large portions of these open areas. There are three pools of open water that are the result of both geography and water control devices. These three pools are frequently referred to by the names of the nearest towns (Floral City, Inverness, and Hernando). Water control devices connect the pools to one another, and access to the Withlacoochee River is by way of water control devices. Of the three pools, the Inverness Pool has historically yielded more and larger fish than has either the Floral City or Hernando Pools. When you see the lake for the first time, you will wonder whether there is more marsh than water. One good thing for flyfishers, however, is that it is always easy to get on the lee side of a clump of marsh and block at least a portion of any breeze.

The Withlacoochee River runs along the eastern side of Tsala Apopka Lake for a straight-line distance of about 20 miles, although if you were to navigate the river, it would be far more than twice that distance. The western edge of the lake is bordered by higher ground, US 41/SR 45, and several small towns. Access to the lake and the numerous fish camps is off the western side.

This is a difficult area to fish and I highly recommend using a guide, at least on the first trip into these waters. Those familiar with Tsala Apopka Lake catch good numbers of quality bass, crappie, and bluegill, as well as sunshine bass in the cooler months. But those new to the lake are going to have difficulty navigating and finding fish. Typically, springtime fishing means casting to the shorelines. However, there is so much shoreline here that you have little clue where to begin. Likewise, in the warmest and coolest months, fish typically go to deeper, open water. On Tsala Apopka, there is little open water and it is not necessarily any deeper than other places in the lake. If you are searching for deeper water, move toward the western shorelines and probe the water in areas near launch sites.

In winter, look for sunshine bass in areas of open water near the western shoreline. Often, diving gulls will help pinpoint their feeding activity, especially late in the afternoon. A Deceiver or Baby Bunker will have subsurface success, while a white foam Gurgler will take surface-feeding sunshine bass. Crappie hold in these same areas in summer and winter, but they move into the marsh to spawn early in the spring. A brightly colored Clouser is the fly of choice, as there will be no surface feeding. Small poppers and terrestrials will take bluegills around the edges of the marsh.

Bass are bass, and there are a lot of similar looking places for them to go. Pay close attention to the details of the place where you do catch one and look for similar conditions. It is difficult to pattern the bass in Tsala Apopka, as the differences between one place and another are very subtle. As mentioned, a guide will be invaluable in helping you get started. They may or may not be flyfishers, but they will know where the bass are located and how they'll react to current weather conditions.

Make sure that at least some of your bass bugs have their hooks covered with a weedguard.

Tsala Apopka Lake

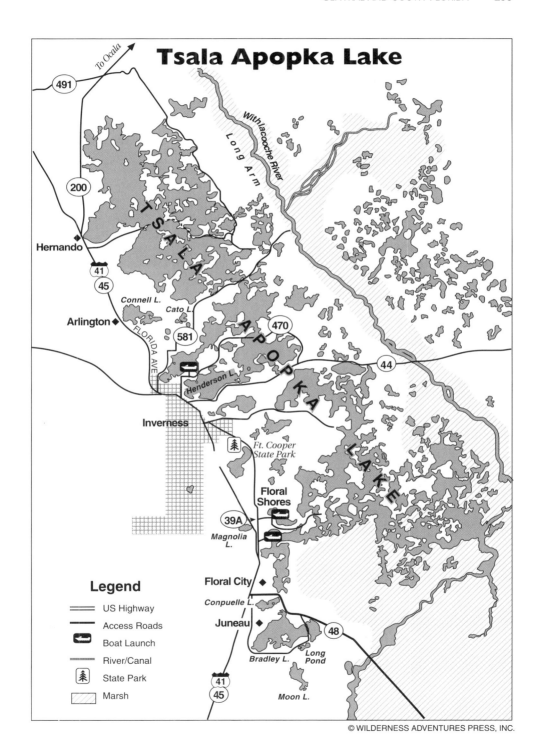

To Ocala

491

200

Withlacoche River

Long Arm

T S A L A

Hernando

41

45

Connell L.

Cato L.

Arlington

FLORIDA AVE.

581

A P O P K A

470

44

Henderson L.

Inverness

Ft. Cooper
State Park

L A K E

Floral
Shores

39A

Magnolia
L.

Floral City

Conpuelle L.

Juneau

48

Bradley L.

Long
Pond

41

45

Moon L.

Legend

═══	US Highway
───	Access Roads
🚤	Boat Launch
═══	River/Canal
🌲	State Park
▨	Marsh

© WILDERNESS ADVENTURES PRESS, INC.

The Hernando Pool is the northernmost pool on the lake. To get there, take Exit 68 off I-75 near Ocala and go about 20 miles west on SR 200. One-quarter mile before the intersection with US 41 in the town of Hernando, there is a single lane ramp on the left side of the road.

The Inverness Pool is in the central part of the lake. To reach it, exit I-75 as above and go west on SR 200. Turn left in Hernando onto US 41 and go south for 5 miles to Inverness. Turn left onto CR 470 and go east for 1 mile. Turn left onto Hickory Road and go 0.2 mile to the single-lane ramp.

To get to the southern pool from Floral City, continue south another 3 miles on SR 41 past the intersection with SR 44 in Inverness. There are two launch sites in the area. Turn left onto CR 39A and go east for 1.8 miles. Turn left onto E. Hampton Point Road and go 0.8 mile. Turn left again onto S. Point Drive and go 0.2 mile. Lastly, make a left onto E. Corvette Court and go one block to the small, single-lane ramp.

The second launch site can be reached by continuing south on SR 41 another 0.2 mile after the intersection with CR 39a. Turn left onto E. Hooker Point and go directly to the single-lane ramp 0.1 mile ahead.

*Low water and numerous grass islands make fishing the
Inverness Pool a difficult task.*

Glen McKinley found that bream hold close to the steep shoreline on Lake Weir.

LAKE WEIR AND LITTLE LAKE WEIR

Lake Weir (5,685 acres) lies just west of the Oklawaha River and the Ocala National Forest. It averages over 20 feet deep, but in many places water depths go 30 feet or more. Lake Weir is considered a deep lake by central Florida standards. There is only a narrow band of grass along the steeply sloping shoreline, and beds of pondweed to depths of about 10 feet. Fish attractors made of brush have been placed in water between 10 and 20 feet deep in about a dozen sites. Weir is highly developed, with numerous docks, and fishing pressure is heavy on weekends.

Because Lake Weir drops off to deeper water more quickly than other Florida lakes, bream and bass are caught closer to shore, holding in or on the edge of the pondweed. A floating line will take bass feeding early and late in the day on topwater flies, but a sink-tip line will be needed for periods when light is on the water and the bass are deeper. Flyfishers are going to find Lake Weir difficult for bass, as the fish tend to be deep much of the time. The shallow areas get heavy fishing pressure during periods of low light, but when the bass go deep, you are going to be blind casting to open water. While the lake might have a reputation as being a good bass lake, the fly fisherman is going to find it only fair.

You might also dredge up a crappie doing this with a fly that imitates a minnow or small baitfish in the summer and winter when they go deep. In spring, cast a Clouser close to dock pilings and let it sink a couple of feet before beginning to strip it back. Again, you could catch either a bass or a crappie with this technique. Bream

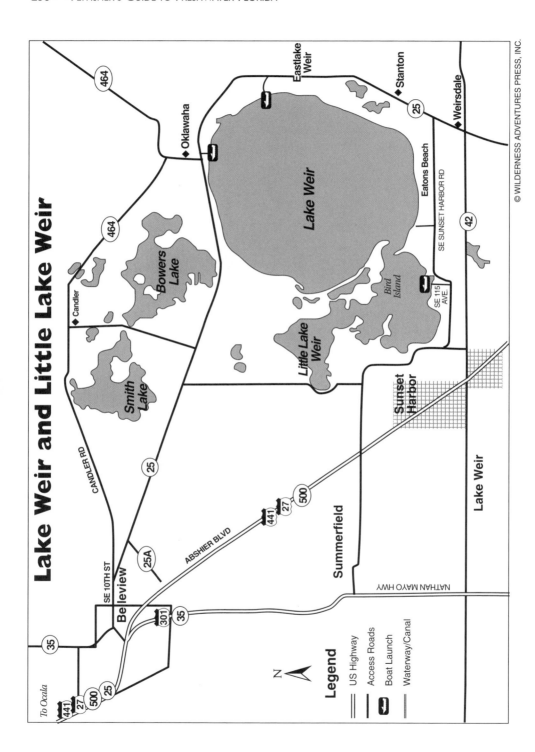

Lake Weir and Little Lake Weir

Legend

US Highway

Access Roads

Boat Launch

Waterway/Canal

N

Lake Weir

Eastlake Weir

◆ Stanton

◆ Weirsdale

25

◆ Oklawaha

464

42

Eatons Beach

SE SUNSET HARBOR RD

Bird Island

SE 115 AVE.

Bowers Lake

Candler ◆

464

Smith Lake

Little Lake Weir

CANDLER RD

25

Sunset Harbor

NATHAN MAYO HWY

Lake Weir

Summerfield

ABSHIER BLVD

441

27

500

SE 10TH ST

Beleview

25A

301

35

35

To Ocala

441

27

500

25

fishing can be excellent in the spring with 1-pound shellcrackers common in March and April. Small poppers and terrestrial patterns work best and should be cast close to shoreline cover.

At the southwest corner of the lake, a canal leads from the large cove to Little Lake Weir (320 acres). Still a deep body of water by Florida standards, it averages about 15 feet deep and also has steep shorelines. The same problems exist for fly-fishers on Little Lake Weir as they did on Lake Weir; namely, that the bass are in deep water. To compound the problem, Little Lake Weir has steep banks and little shallow water, making it only fair, at best, for fly fishing. The same techniques used on Lake Weir work at Little Lake Weir. Put on your spare spool with a sinking line and dredge the deepest water. Little Lake Weir has no launch site of its own.

To get to the northern end of Lake Weir, go south from Ocala on US 27/US 301/US 441 for 9 miles. Turn left onto State Road 25 in Belleview and go 8.1 miles to the community of Oklawaha. Turn right onto Central Avenue and go three blocks to the single-lane ramp.

There is another ramp on the east side of Lake Weir. Continue south on SR 25 through Oklawaha for another 2.7 miles. Turn right onto SE 134th Street Road and go 0.1 mile to the Hampton Beach Park entrance. There is a double-lane ramp with unimproved parking for 10 vehicles.

There is also a ramp on the south side of Lake Weir. Continue south on SR 25 for another 3.5 miles to the intersection with SR 42. Turn right and go 2.5 miles west to SE 115 Avenue. Turn right and go 0.5 mile, crossing Sunset Harbor Road, to the single-lane county ramp.

LAKE OKAHUMPKA AND LAKE DEATON

Both Lake Okahumpka (670 acres) and Lake Deaton (778 acres) are regarded as good bass lakes, and each year they give up more than an occasional big fish. Bream fishing can be good, too, especially in the spring. These two side-by-side lakes are difficult for flyfishers to fish, however, as they are thick with subsurface and surface vegetation. You will again want to turn to bass bugs and poppers that have a monofilament weedguard in order to avoid getting constantly fouled in the vegetation. Neither has much development along the shoreline, with Lake Okahumpka being surrounded mostly by farmland and pastures, while Lake Deaton has trees growing in close proximity.

There is not good access to either lake for a large, motorized boat, although small ramps capable of launching a johnboat do exist. While neither is a lake that you would select as a premier destination, if you happen to be in the Disney area and want a break from the crowds, try these lakes about half an hour to the northwest, just off the Florida Turnpike, between Leesburg and Wildwood.

To get to the lakes from I-75, take Exit 66 and go east on SR 44 for 1 mile. Turn left onto SR 44A and go east about 6 miles, passing through Wildwood. In the small community of Orange Home, turn right onto CR 167 and Lake Okahumpka is 0.2 mile ahead. Continuing about a quarter of a mile east on SR 44A, you can reach Lake Deaton by turning left onto CR 155 and going 0.1 mile. From the Orlando area, take the Florida Turnpike to the north and get off at the Wildwood exit (Mile Marker 304) and go north on US 301 to Wildwood. Take 44A east for 3 miles to Orange Home. Lake Okahumpka is to your right off CR 167 and Lake Deaton is to your left off CR 155, as described above.

LAKE LINDSEY

If you choose to fish Lake Lindsey (175 acres), do so only with a small johnboat or canoe. The lake is subject to fluctuations in water level that prevent getting a trailer into the water for launching at times. In addition, vegetation can be thick on Lindsey, making fly fishing very difficult for the bass and bream in these waters. The bass fishing is fair, but seldom are fish of any significant size caught. The bream are of average size and can be caught on poppers fished in open pockets. There are not many lakes in the surrounding area, and those nearby do not have much size to them. I recommend passing on Lake Lindsey unless you happen to be stuck nearby.

If you are determined to go, take Exit 61 off 1-75 and go west on US 98/SR 50 for 9 miles. In Brooksville, turn right onto US 41/SR 45 and go north for 5 miles to CR 476. Turn left onto CR 476 and go west for 1.8 miles. Turn right onto CR 581 and go one block north, then turn left onto Lake Street. The single-lane ramp is 0.1 mile straight ahead.

JOHNS LAKE, LAKE AVALON, BLACK LAKE, AND LAKE TILDEN

Johns Lake (2,424 acres) offers excellent habitat for bass, as well as bluegill, shellcracker, and crappie. The lake has an irregular shoreline with numerous coves and points. There are abundant opportunities for using wind to set up a drift in the direction you want to go, as well as finding a lee shoreline to get out of any wind. This is a good lake for flyfishers.

Unusual for Florida, the bottom of Johns Lake has a very irregular contour and the water level fluctuates naturally. With the ups and downs of these water levels, so goes the quality of the fishing. After long periods of low water levels, the fishing will improve dramatically with a rise. Scattered throughout the lake are areas of shallow water that permit emergent vegetation to grow and become islands with the changing water levels. These islands increase the amount of shoreline available and provide new areas for feeding and spawning. In essence, these islands become natural fish attractors. Be sure to visit them as you fish Johns Lake, as the bass and bream are sure to do so.

Lake Avalon, Black Lake, and Lake Tilden are each a couple of hundred acres and while nearby, the connecting waterways are too small to permit access by boat. Their features are more traditional in that they have rounded shorelines and a gently sloping bottom, presenting a saucer-like appearance.

My fly of choice for Johns Lake's largemouth bass is an olive-colored deer-hair popper (size 2) because there is so much shoreline and so many opportunities for a thunderous topwater strike. Bream fishing is good with a smaller popper or terrestrial, while crappie like the look of a Clouser Minnow.

To get to Johns Lake, from I-4 in downtown Orlando, take Exit 41 and go west on SR 50 for 18 miles. Turn left onto Lake Blvd. and go 0.1 mile to the single-lane ramp on your left. There is paved and unpaved parking for 20 vehicles.

*Lake Ivanhoe is a surprisingly good crappie lake
situated in downtown Orlando.*

THE LAKES OF GREATER ORLANDO

Lake Rose	Lake Lotus	Rock Lake
Lake Bennett	Lake of the Woods	Lake Mann
Starke Lake	Red Bug Lake	Clear Lake
Lake Olympia	Lake Howell	Lake Sherwood
Spring Lake	Lake Ann	Lake Herrick
Prairie Lake	Bear Gully Lake	Lake Steer
Lake Meadow	Lake Georgia	Turkey Lake
Trout Lake	Lake Irma	Lake Catherine
Lake Sims	Lake Minnehaha	Lake Holden
Lake Cora Lee	Lake Charity	Lake Jenny Jewel
Lake Rutherford	Lake Sybella	Lake Pinelock
Lake Fuller	Lake Maitland	Lake Underhill
Clearwater Lake	Lake Shadow	Lake Barton
Marshall Lake	Lake Lockhart	Lake Susannah
Holts Lake	Long Lake	Lake Corrine
Lake Standish	Lake Alpharetta	Lake Waunatta
Lake Francis	Crooked Lake	Lake Irma
Lake Alden	Lake Stanley	Lake Pearl
Lake McCoy	Lake Sherwood	Lake Fredrica
Prevatt Lake	Lawne Lake	Lake Barber
Lake Brantley	Lake Wekiva	Little Lake Conway
Fairy Lake	Lake Fairview	Lake Conway
Lake Kathryn	Lake Silver	Bay Lake
Lake Florida	Lake Kilarney	Lake Mary
Sand Lake	Lake Virginia	Lake Jessamine
Lake Pleasant	Lake Sue	and Lake Ellenore
Bear Lake	Lake Ivanhoe	

There are numerous lakes in the Orlando area, but many are closed to boating. Some allow lakeside residents to boat, with no public access by way of a launch site. Others allow the public to launch and use a lake for a fee. A few allow unlimited public access. The Orlando lakes vary greatly in size, shape, depth, water quality, and fish populations. There are some lakes that form a "chain," connected by narrow, deep canals. Roads and streets with bridges too low to permit bass boats to pass underneath often cross these canals.

There has been a severe drought for several years, and lake levels are currently at historic lows. It can only get better. You will note that many boats are hanging in their slips. If they were to be lowered, they would come to rest on dry land. The water levels have receded to the point that entire boat slips are above the water line. For the time being, the fish are concentrated, although not easily accessible. When the lakes

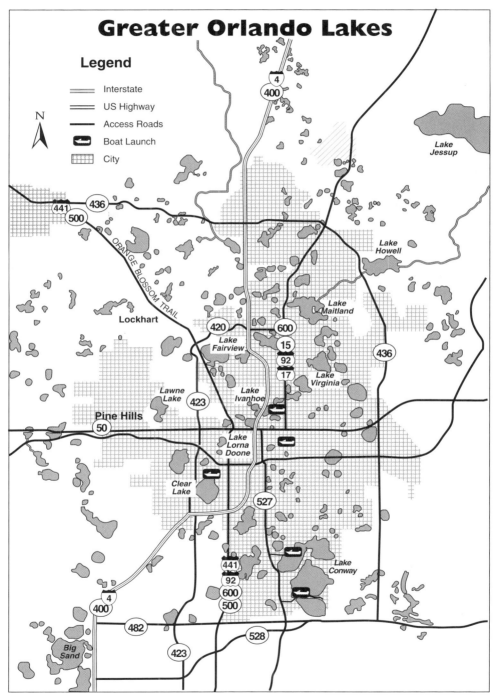

Greater Orlando Lakes

Legend

━━━ Interstate
━━━ US Highway
━━━ Access Roads
Boat Launch
City

N

Lake Jessup

441 / 436
500

Lake Howell

ORANGE BLOSSOM TRAIL

Lockhart

Lake Maitland

420 / Lake Fairview / 600
15
92
17 / Lake Virginia

Lawne Lake / 423 / Lake Ivanhoe

Pine Hills
50

Lake Lorna Doone

436

Clear Lake

527

441
92
600
500

Lake Conway

4 / 400

482

Big Sand

423

528

*Next to the Florida State Fairgrounds, Lawne Lake
is behind a park with every conceivable amenity.*

again reach full pool and vegetated shorelines are again submerged, there will be a bonanza of food and baitfish cover.

Another opportunity exists for flyfishers in the Orlando area that is often overlooked. The lakes and ponds managed by the Florida Fish and Wildlife Conservation Commission Urban Fishery Project offer opportunities for shoreline anglers to catch quality fish within the city limits. (For more information, see the section on Fish Management Areas later in this book.) If the family is busy at an Orlando tourist attraction and you would like to try a little fly fishing, there are several small ponds and lakes in the Orlando area from 5 to 125 acres that are specially managed for urban fishing. Lake Santiago in Demetree Park (5 acres), Lake Lorna Doone (14 acres), Lake Richmond (38 acres), and Lake Ivanhoe (125 acres) are located within parks to ensure public access. The banks and shorelines have been cleared and there should be little problem with backcasts. As the lakes are urban, you are much less likely to encounter snakes and alligators. Except for Lake Ivanhoe and Clear Lake, you will not likely encounter a boat, either.

The lakes of Greater Orlando have largemouth bass, bream, and crappie. Some of the larger lakes have been stocked and are managed for sunshine bass, too. Due to individual characteristics, fish populations vary from lake to lake. A deer-hair popper would be an excellent choice for largemouth bass on any of the lakes, especially early and late in the day. In addition, a streamer that imitates a minnow will likely get some attention. A brightly colored Clouser Minnow will take crappie and get down to fish when they are holding in deeper water, and a small popper will take panfish and smaller bass.

Lake Ivanhoe (125 acres) is a Fish Management Area bisected by Interstate 4 in the heart of Orlando. It has a good population of largemouth, with an occasional lunker being taken. Crappie are in good supply, as well, and they are known to hang around the ski jump during winter months. Yes, the lake is used for skiing during the summer, but you don't go to an urban lake next to an interstate highway to get away from people. Flyfishers walking around the perimeter can take bream along the shoreline. An outstanding fly shop (called The Fly Shop) is also located across the street on the eastern edge of the lake.

There is a single-lane ramp and paved parking for 5 vehicles with trailers and another 15 spots for single cars at the northeast corner of the lake. To get to Lake Ivanhoe, get off I-4 at Exit 41 (Colonial Avenue) and go east for about 4 blocks. Turn left onto Magnolia and go about 0.4 mile. Immediately after crossing the railroad tracks, turn right onto Orange Avenue, and with the lake on your left, go 0.3 mile to the launch site.

Lawne Lake (156 acres) is located in Gordon Barnett Park in the western portion of Orlando. The fishing is often quite good for largemouth bass, as well as for shell-cracker, bluegill, and crappie. Sunshine bass are stocked annually and often reach three or four pounds in just a couple of years. In addition to a fishing pier, the western shoreline has been cleared for bank fishing. The lake is situated just behind the Florida State Fairgrounds at the back of a very large park with every conceivable amenity.

To reach Lawne Lake, get off I-4 at Exit 41 and go west on SR 50 for 3.8 miles. There is a sign for the park just as you go past the fairgrounds on your right. Turn right and go along the edge of the fairgrounds 0.6 mile to the park entrance. Enter the park and follow signs to the double-lane ramp. There is paved parking for 27 vehicles.

Clear Lake (339 acres) is located in George Barker Park in the southwest portion of downtown Orlando, just south of the Citrus Bowl (Tinker Field). Largemouth bass, bluegill, shellcracker, crappie, and sunshine bass are plentiful. In addition, a restoration plan to improve the habitat for sportfish has just been completed and fishing should get even better. The park maintenance workers have cleared the shoreline adjacent to the ramp for bank fishing and flyfishers should find this much to their liking.

To get to Clear Lake, get off I-4 at Exit 37 and go west on Gore Avenue for 1.2 miles, crossing US 17/ US 92/US 441. As Gore Avenue ends at a sweeping right turn to become Orange Center Blvd., turn left onto Tampa Avenue. The park is two blocks ahead. The park and single-lane ramp are to your left. There is paved parking for 20 vehicles.

Lake Underhill (147 acres) is located in the eastern part of Orlando near the downtown (Herndon) airport. The East-West Expressway bisects the lake and the bridge's pilings provide excellent fishing structure. Underhill has a good population

*Like many lakes in Florida, you need to motor through a
short canal to get to Clear Lake.*

of small bass and crappie. Sunshine bass have also been stocked. There are parks on
both the northern and southern sides of the lake with bank fishing opportunities. Jet
skiers use the lake, and when they are present fishing is a lot less tranquil than it
would otherwise be—even in the middle of an urban area with an expressway passing overhead and an airport adjoining the shoreline. However, Underhill is easy to
reach if you are in Orlando, and watching the sunset while small planes land and
bream hit a popper is not a bad way to spend an evening away from home.

To get to Lake Underhill, get off I-4 at Exit 36 and go east on the East-West
Expressway (SR 408) for 2.5 miles. Get off the expressway at Exit 13 (South Conway
Road). Go one block to the traffic light and turn right onto Lake Underhill Road. Go
one block to the park entrance on your right. There is a single-lane ramp and paved
parking for 12 vehicles.

Lake Conway (1,075 acres) and Little Lake Conway (725 acres) are interconnected lakes in the southern portion of Orlando. They have a hard sand bottom and
depths that approach 30 feet at full pool. The bottom is irregular and there are high
spots in the open areas of the lake where peppergrass and eelgrass grow. Largemouth
bass often school around these mid-lake humps, especially in the fall, and topwater
fishing can be quite good. Choose a fly that mimics a shad or glass minnow and look
for concentrations of birds to indicate where the bass are feeding. In the spring, look
to shallow vegetated areas for bass, crappie, and bream. As is the case elsewhere, try
a brightly colored Clouser Minnow for the crappie and either a small popper or a ter-

restrial pattern for the bream. In the summer and winter, you will need a sink-tip line to dredge the deeper parts of these lakes for crappie.

To get to the southern side of Little Lake Conway, get off I-4 at Exit 41 and go east on US 50 for two blocks. Turn right onto SR 527 (Orange Avenue) and go south for 4.5 miles. Turn left onto Hoffner Avenue and go 0.3 mile to Randolph Place. Turn left onto Randolph Place and the lake is in sight straight ahead. The single-lane ramp (Randolph Boat Ramp) has paved parking for 15 vehicles.

There is another ramp (Fern Creek Boat Ramp) on the northern side of Little Lake Conway, but the approach is quite narrow, the turn around is difficult, and parking is along the narrow approach. To get to this single-lane ramp, go south on SR 527 (Orange Avenue) for 3.7 miles. Turn left onto Gatlin Road and go 0.8 mile. Turn right onto Fern Creek Avenue and go 0.3 mile to the launch site. I do not recommend using this narrow approach, though.

*Lake Underhill is bisected by an expressway and is
frequently used by jet-skiers.*

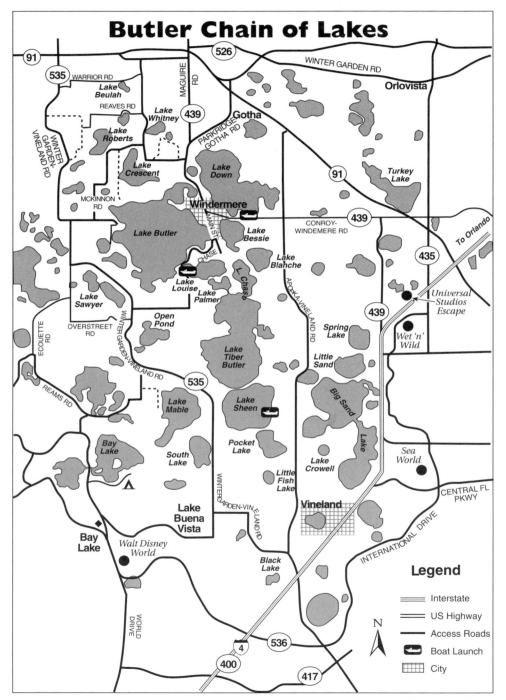

Butler Chain of Lakes

91
526
WINTER GARDEN RD
535 WARRIOR RD
Orlovista
Lake Beulah
REAVES RD
Lake Whitney
439
Gotha
MAGUIRE RD
PARKRIDGE-GOTHA RD
WINTER GARDEN-VINELAND RD
Lake Roberts
Lake Crescent
Lake Down
Turkey Lake
91
MCKINNON RD
Windermere
CONROY-WINDEMERE RD
439
435
Lake Butler
Lake Bessie
Lake Blanche
439
Universal Studios Escape
MAIN ST
CHASE
Lake Louise
Lake Palmer
L. Chase
APOPKA-VINELAND RD
Wet 'n' Wild
Lake Sawyer
OVERSTREET RD
Open Pond
Spring Lake
Little Sand
ECOUETTE RD
WINTER GARDEN-VINELAND RD
Lake Tiber Butler
REAMS RD
535
Lake Mable
Lake Sheen
Big Sand Lake
Bay Lake
South Lake
Pocket Lake
Lake Crowell
Sea World
Little Fish Lake
CENTRAL FL PKWY
Lake Buena Vista
WINTER GARDEN-VINELAND RD
Vineland
INTERNATIONAL DRIVE
Bay Lake
Walt Disney World
Black Lake
Legend

WORLD DRIVE
4
536
400
417
N

Interstate	
US Highway	
Access Roads	
Boat Launch	
City	

BUTLER CHAIN OF LAKES

Lake Roberts	Lake Palmer	Little Sand Lake
Lake Whitney	Lake Tibet Butler	Big Sand Lake
Lake Crescent	Lake Mable	Lake Willis
Lake Down	Pocket Lake	Lake Rubu
Lake Olivia	Bay Lake	Little Lake Bryan
Lake Butler	South Lake	Lake Bryan
Lake Bessie	Lake Cane	
Lake Chase	Spring Lake	

There are several lakes in this interconnected chain of lakes located about 5 miles southwest of Orlando, and there is not much reason to recommend them. Together, the lakes have almost 5,000 acres of water. They are clear with sand bottoms, and the channels that connect them are shallow, especially during extended periods of low rainfall. As a result, johnboats are your best bet to move between lakes when it is possible to do so.

The bass tend to be small and slow-growing, although an occasional lunker is caught. Flyfishers might want to use fluorocarbon leaders in the clear water. Crappie, bluegills, and shellcrackers are also available but not in impressive numbers.

The only launch site to the Butler Chain of Lakes is at Lake Down. To get there, take Exit 41 off I-4 and go west on SR 50 for 9.3 miles. Turn left onto CR 439 and go south through the town of Windermere for 4.5 miles to the single-lane ramp on your left at the south end of the lake. Parking is very limited.

LAKE LOUISE AND LAKE SHEEN

In close proximity to the Butler Chain of Lakes (and just northeast of the Walt Disney World complex) there are two other lakes with launch sites. Lake Louise (125 acres) is a shallow lake with an irregular bottom. The mid-lake islands offer a break from breezes and their shorelines should be explored, especially in the spring. To get to the launch site on Lake Louise from Windermere, continue south on Main Street (do not make the left turn to stay on CR 439) and at the edge of town, turn right onto West 12th Street (Chase Road). Go west (Lake Butler is off to your right) for 1.5 miles. The single-lane ramp is to your left.

Lake Sheen (300 acres) is near the southern end of this grouping of lakes. It is a typical saucer-shaped Florida lake with few remarkable features. There is a good population of small bass, along with crappie and bream. The eastern shoreline is heavily developed. To get to the launch site, from I-4 take Exit 29 and go west on SR 482 (Sand Lake Road) for 1.3 miles. Turn left onto Apopka Vineland Road and go south for 0.5 mile. Turn right onto Kilgore Road and go 0.7 mile. The single-lane ramp is to your right.

Two double-lane ramps on the east side of Lake Tarpon
attest to the improved fishing.

LAKE TARPON AND SALT LAKE

In the west-central part of the state, three miles inland from the Gulf of Mexico as the crow flies, north of Tampa Bay, past Safety Harbor, and through three miles of canal, there lies a freshwater lake less than 1.45 feet above mean sea level. And if you get the opportunity to do so, you should fly fish Lake Tarpon (2,534 acres). The Florida Fish and Wildlife Conservation Commission (FWC) regards it as one of the top 10 bass lakes in the state. The lake is of a manageable size for almost any boat, and although in close proximity to some larger cities, it gets relatively little fishing pressure.

Lake Tarpon is changing for the better. Around the middle of the 20th century it yielded bodacious bass, but then it declined due to low fertility and limited biological productivity. However, because of runoff from developed areas in the lake's watershed, the fertility has been enhanced to a degree that the lake is now very productive for both fish and plant populations. In the past 20 years, fish production has increased almost 100 percent. As fisheries managers recognize the potential for over-fertilization, the lake is closely monitored to preserve the historically good water quality and aquatic habitat. Anglers have been doing their share, too, releasing on average 85 percent of their catch. This percentage may not seem that high to a trout fisherman, but it does reflect quite favorably on anglers fishing for species found in warmer waters, especially big bass. You are encouraged to do your part to help raise the average even higher.

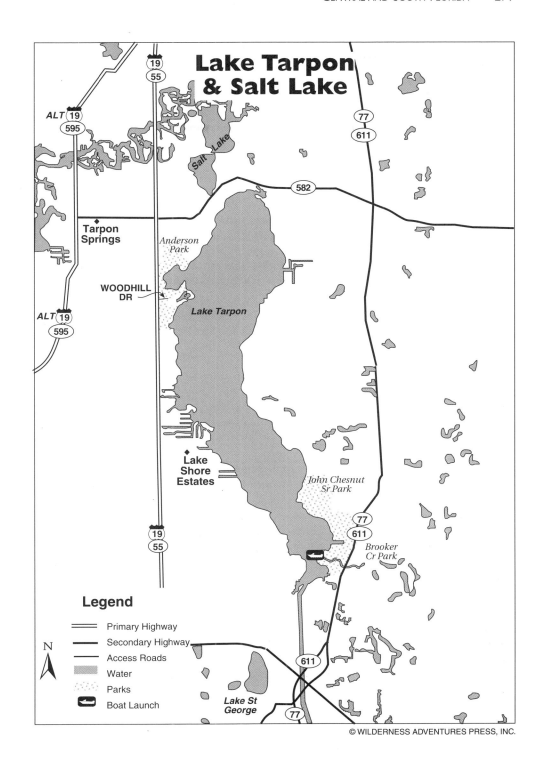

Lake Tarpon & Salt Lake

Legend

Primary Highway
Secondary Highway
Access Roads
Water
Parks
Boat Launch

N

© WILDERNESS ADVENTURES PRESS, INC.

This Fish Management Area is a about a mile wide and stretches four miles north to south. Lake Tarpon averages about 10 feet deep, although the eastern shoreline drops quickly into water 12 to 14 feet deep near Pasture Fence Point. Along the water's edge, bulrush, cattail, and tape grass beds offer cover for largemouth bass, crappie, and assorted members of the bream family. In summer months, bass school over mid-lake humps, especially those with submerged vegetation, and topwater action can be fantastic as they feed on shad.

The schooling bass typically weigh a couple of pounds, but each year several fish over 10 pounds are hooked in Lake Tarpon. In the 1940s, a 19-pound largemouth bass was caught from the lake, and it was regarded as the state record for many years until modern record keeping practices were established. The biggest bass are caught by anglers using live shiners, while worm fishermen catch their share of bragging-sized fish. A flyfisher can get in on the action, too. Schooling bass will readily take a light colored topwater popper or foam Gurgler in the summer. In addition, bass feeding subsurface will no doubt grab a Lefty's Deceiver that has been tossed into the action. Around the shoreline vegetation, try a larger deer-haired popper early and late in the day.

Crappie have been strong on Lake Tarpon the past couple of years. In early spring, look to shorelines and the dock pilings in the southwest corner of the lake. During summer and winter, you'll need a sink-tip line to probe some of the deeper water. No matter the season, a brightly colored Clouser will work for the "specks."

In the southwest corner, there are some residential canals. The docks in these areas offer shade and structure to bass and crappie. These should be visited on each trip, as the shelter they provide holds fish during every season. Line up your boat so that a fly can be retrieved along the shady side of several successive pilings. Try to get your cast as close as possible to these, as small baitfish hang around them until ambushed.

Bluegill and shellcracker fishing can be outstanding on Lake Tarpon, as well. The bluegill will be around the bulrush and cattails near the shoreline and a terrestrial pattern or small popper should prove successful. The shellcrackers will be over shell beds, and a pattern imitating a grass shrimp will do the trick.

To get to Lake Tarpon, go south for 1 mile on US 19 from the intersection of CR 582 and US 19 in the Gulf Coast community of Tarpon Springs. Turn left onto Woodhill Drive into Anderson Park. As you approach the lake, follow the signs and go left to the double-lane ramp. There is paved parking for about 15 vehicles.

To get to the lake from the east side, go east on CR 582 for 2 miles from the intersection of CR 582 and US 19 in Tarpon Springs. Turn right onto CR 611 (East Lake Road) and go south for 3 miles. Turn right into Brooker Creek Park immediately after crossing Brooker Creek and follow the signs to the two double-lane ramps. There is paved parking for about 25 vehicles.

North of Lake Tarpon, there is an estuary called Salt Lake. It is at the back of the winding Anclote River, once famous for its sponge trade, and it has a small freshwater fishery. There are no public ramps to the lake, although the coastal river does have limited access.

MOUNTAIN LAKE, NEFF LAKE, SPRING LAKE, ROBISON LAKE, NICKS LAKE, ST. CLAIRE LAKE, MUD LAKE, JESSAMINE LAKE, McCLENDON LAKE, ROBINSON LAKE, HANCOCK LAKE, MIDDLE LAKE, MOODY LAKE, AND LAKE IOLA

This group of lakes is located about 25 miles north of Tampa, just west of Interstate 75. West-central Florida is known for producing big bass, and these lakes yield more than their share of oversized fish each year. The lakes also have a very good population of bream and crappie, although local anglers are the only ones who usually fish for them. Only Mountan and Middle Lakes have decent launch ramps.

Mountain Lake (175 acres), like the others, has a good population of bass, bluegill, and crappie. On the south and west, where it connects to Neff Lake, the shoreline is very irregular and quite interesting. Although none of these lakes are deep, the bottom contour is more pronounced on this lake. Look for largemouth in vegetation growing from long points extending out into the water. Bluegill and crappie also use these same areas to spawn in the spring. Try a Clouser for the crappie and be sure to count it down to the level at which you get a strike so that you can return to this precise point again. For the bluegill, a small popper early and late in the day or dark terrestrial fly should do the trick. Bass want it big and noisy, and I prefer an olive deer-hair popper (size 1).

To get to Mountain Lake from I-75, get off at Exit 61 and go west on SR 50 for 4 miles. Turn left on CR 41 and go south for 2.9 miles. Turn right onto Mountain Lake Road and go 0.3 mile to the single-lane ramp. There is unimproved parking for 15 vehicles. Note: Because of low water levels on the lake, this ramp is frequently not usable.

Middle Lake (375 acres) is irregularly shaped and regarded as having good bass, bluegill, and crappie fishing. There are three extensive coves for spring spawning. The western cove connects to Hancock Lake, whereas the eastern cove drains to Moody Lake. Both of these areas warrant thorough investigation. The floating vegetation holds big bass underneath the shade and cover it offers, as well as providing a sanctuary for bluegill and crappie. A big deer-hair popper is my choice for a lunker largemouth on a fly.

To get to Middle Lake, get off I-75 at Exit 60 and go north on CR 41 for 1.9 miles. Turn left onto Dan Brown Road and go 0.7 mile to Townsend House Road. Turn left again and go 0.4 mile to the entrance to R. H. Pless Park. One more left into the park and follow the signs to the single-lane ramp where there is unimproved parking for 35 vehicles.

LAKE PASADENA

Lake Pasadena (500 acres) is definitely not a destination lake, but if you happen to be in the Tampa Bay area watching some spring training baseball games and have some time, you might want to add it to your list of lakes to check out. Lake Pasadena has several homes on the north shoreline near the launch site. The lake has a good population of largemouth bass, bream, and crappie. Bass like to spawn in the southeast corner in the spring. This is a good area to cast poppers and chuggers for bigger bass. The bream and crappie also use this area to spawn. In summer and winter, look to mid-lake depths for the crappie. Bass and bream will move onto shorelines to feed during periods of reduced light.

To get there from I-75 east of Tampa, get off the interstate at Exit 54 and go east on Fowler Avenue (SR 582) for 1.5 miles. Turn left onto US 301 and go north for about 18 miles through Zephyrhills. After leaving Zephyrhills, be sure to stay on US 301. About 5 miles after leaving town, turn left onto Clayton Avenue (CR 52A) and go 2 miles. Turn left onto Lake Pasadena Drive and go 0.3 mile to the single-lane ramp. There is limited parking.

LAKE THONOTOSASSA

Lake Thonotosassa (819 acres) is an extremely fertile lake about five miles west of Tampa. This is not a recommended destination. The water quality is poor, and it is a limited fishery. Flyfishers can catch a few largemouth bass in the spring, but they run small in size. Look to the southeast corner where Baker Creek feeds the lake. In an effort to improve the fishing, sunshine bass have been stocked regularly and these can be caught in the winter and spring. Sunshine bass congregate in the open water approaching 15 feet in depth close to the western shoreline. To add the lake's woes, it is difficult to launch a boat from the public ramp during periods of low water.

To get to Lake Thonotosassa from I-75 near Tampa, get off the interstate at Exit 54 and go east on Fowler Avenue (SR 582) for 1.5 miles. Cross US 301/SR 41 and continue east on CR 580, through the community of Thonotosassa, for 3.5 miles to the single-lane ramp. There is limited parking and the ramp may not extend into the water during periods of low water.

Lake Parker in Lakeland has good shoreline fishing and a double-lane ramp.

LAKE GIBSON, FISH LAKE, LAKE PARKER, LAKE BONNY, LAKE HOLLOWAY, CRYSTAL LAKE, SKYVIEW LAKE, LAKE BENTLEY, LAKE JOHN, LAKE HOLLINGSWORTH, LAKE HUNTER AND LAKE BONNET

Polk County in west-central Florida has 550 lakes, 80 with some form of public access. The lakes being discussed here are in and around the town of Lakeland, just south of I-4. Most of these lakes are quite small and are located within a park. Only two have launch sites. Lake Parker (2,272 acres) is on the northeastern edge of Lakeland near the Detroit Tigers spring training complex. If you are in the area early in the spring, a visit to Lake Parker in the morning and an afternoon game makes for a pleasant day. Lake Bonny (225 acres) is half a mile south of Lake Parker in the eastern part of town.

Both lakes have good bass, bluegill, and crappie populations. In addition, Lake Parker is regularly stocked with sunshine bass. These are readily available to flyfisher who fish near the power plant at the southeast corner of the lake. The power plant has built a long pier that provides excellent fishing opportunities. These lakes are shallow, averaging about 10 feet in depth. They are not so round and saucer-shaped as the smaller lakes in the parks, having an irregular shoreline that offers flyfishers a break from a light wind. Shallow water in the backs of coves serves as spring spawning areas and should also be checked early and late in the day during the summer months.

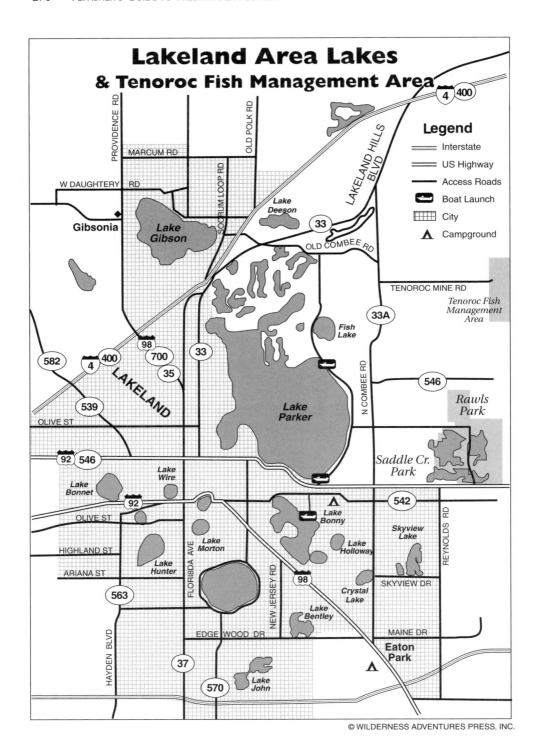

Lakeland Area Lakes
& Tenoroc Fish Management Area

Legend

═══ Interstate
── US Highway
── Access Roads
⊂⊃ Boat Launch
City
▲ Campground

© WILDERNESS ADVENTURES PRESS, INC.

Lake Parker yields several good-sized bass each year. Look to the northern end where the water is shallower and shoreline very irregular. Along the eastern and southern sides, the lake is surrounded by residential homes. The docks, however, offer shade and often hold smaller bass. In spring, crappie also like to move onto the docks in shallower water. Around the docks, a larger Clouser (size 2) allowed to sink will take bass. In the shallow water, try a deer-hair popper.

Many of the other lakes are in city parks that have good bank access for fly fishing. They are not likely to be crowded and the bluegill and bream are usually quite cooperative. While the bass tend to be small in these smaller waters, you can be sure that there is a resident "Mr. Big" who might decide that your fly is going to be his breakfast.

To get to the south end of Lake Parker, get off I-4 at Exit 16 and go east on US 92/CR 546 (Memorial Blvd.) for 5.6 miles (the last mile of which will have Lake Parker on the left side). Turn left into Sertoma Park and go one block to the double-lane ramp. There is paved parking for 30 vehicles. The park shoreline provides plenty of bank access for flyfishers without a boat.

Continuing on US 92/CR 546 another block past the park, you can turn left onto Lake Parker Drive and then move up and around the east side of the lake. Two miles ahead, there is a single-lane ramp in the northeastern part of the lake.

Lake Bonny has a single-lane ramp. Again, take Exit 16 and go east on US 92/CR 546 for 4 miles. At the intersection with SR 33, turn right and go south on SR 33 (Massachusetts Ave.) for 0.4 mile. Turn left onto Main Street and go 1.6 miles to the ramp, where there is paved parking for six vehicles.

Tenoroc Fish Management Area offers a variety of fly fishing opportunities.

TENOROC FISH MANAGEMENT AREA

You are about to discover what may be the best-kept fishing secret in all of Florida. We try to keep Tenoroc all to ourselves, but at the risk of being ostracized by the entire fishing fraternity, I feel compelled to let the word out. The Tenoroc Fish Management area is a 6,800-acre tract of land that was mined for phosphate from the 1950s to the mid-1970s. In 1982, the Borden Chemical Corporation donated the land to the state, presenting a challenge to develop recreational activities on the pillaged land site. In 1983, what was then known as the Florida Fish and Wildlife Conservation Commission (FWC) began to evaluate the potential of the pits, developed a fish management plan, and implemented extensive research studies (while creating a park-like setting in the areas surrounding the pits).

The research centered on ways to improve catch rates and the size of fish being caught. The FWC determined that the best way to achieve this goal was to limit the harvest of largemouth bass, bream, crappie, and sunshine bass. Assorted restrictive regulations were evaluated, including various length limits, reduced bag limits, total catch and release, the number of anglers who could be on a pit at a given time, the number of days a week that a pit could be fished, and which months that various pits could be fished. At present, Tenoroc utilizes a total catch-and-release strategy for largemouth bass, allowing all of them to grow to full maturity. Tenoroc Fish Management Area is regarded as one of the top 10 lakes for both largemouth bass and for crappie. It is that good.

Presently, there are 14 pits open to the public (with more planned) at Tenoroc, and fishing is permitted four days a week (Friday through Monday) from 6 a.m. to

5:30 p.m. A $3 daily use fee is charged. It is best to call ahead for reservations (863-499-2421) and these can be made up to 60 days in advance. You will need to check in at the main desk where regulations will be explained in detail and some good advice offered on what is biting in different pits.

There are both reclaimed pits and unreclaimed pits at Tenoroc. The reclaimed pits have shorelines that gradually slope into deeper water with shoreline vegetation such as cattail, bulrush, and other aquatic plants. The unreclaimed lakes have steep banks and brush-covered shorelines. The water tends to be green in color. The two different types of pits offer vastly different fishing opportunities. All in all, the various pits offer different shorelines, as well as different depths of open water, presenting a flyfisher with multiple fishing challenges.

There are seven boat ramps, four fishing platforms, abundant bank fishing access, and numerous picnic facilities with restrooms. Many of the pits have specific fishing regulations, and you must be aware of them before beginning to fish. For example, one pit may permit only the harvest of crappie, and these must be in excess of a certain length. Another pit may permit boats, but a child or a person with a disability must be on the boat and fishing.

The pits range in size from 7 to 227 acres. One, however, deserves special attention. Hydrilla Lake is the result of efforts to provide the most outstanding public fishery possible among the phosphate pit fisheries. This pit is presently open only on Friday and Sunday, and then to just one boat. It will be fished like this for a few months, and then completely closed to all fishing for a few months. There is a lottery to see who gets to fish Hydrilla Lake. A non-refundable $5 application will get your name in the hat, and if selected, there is a fee of $50 per angler. Numerous largemouth bass over 10 pounds are caught from Hydrilla Lake each year—a testament to the fact that a released fish lives to grow and be caught again.

Fishing techniques are no different here than elsewhere in Florida; it is just that the probability of catching big fish is much increased and there are likely to be fewer people on the water. Largemouth bass will be caught early and late near shoreline cover using big deer-hair poppers. Remember that in an unreclaimed pit the dropoff is quite rapid. You should have a spare spool with a full sink-tip line for use during the main part of the day. Try a bunker or other baitfish pattern and work it at a variety of depths. You will also want to use an 8-weight fly rod and reel, as you could very likely tangle with the bass of a lifetime. For crappie, stick with a Clouser Minnow. For bream, look to small poppers and terrestrials. The sunshine bass will take a baitfish pattern fished in open water. Look for fish breaking the surface early and late in the day during winter months.

Tenoroc Fish Management Area is located two miles northeast of Lakeland. To get there, get off Interstate 4 at Exit 20 and go south on SR 33 for 1.5 miles. Turn left onto CR 33A (Combee Road) and go south for 1.3 miles to Tenoroc Mine Road. Turn left onto Tenoroc Mine Road and go east for 1.7 miles to Tenoroc Fish Management Area and the check-in. You will be given a map to the pits that are open. There is ample parking at each pit. You will have to surrender your fishing license and you will be given a survey to complete. When finished fishing for the day, surveys and licenses will again be exchanged. The phone number is 863-499-2421.

There are 14 reclaimed and unreclaimed phosphate pits at Tenoroc.

BANANA LAKE AND LAKE HANCOCK

These two lakes are about 5 miles southeast of Lakeland. Banana Lake (200 acres) drains into Lake Hancock (3500 acres), which is located about two and a half miles away. Lake Hancock, in turn, is drained by Saddle Creek, the major contributor of the Peace River. The Peace is a popular stream for canoeists, flowing some 100 miles onward to the Gulf of Mexico.

Banana Lake has bass, bream, and crappie, but it is not a lake that one would select as a prime destination. This is another example of a small body of water mostly used by local anglers. Nonetheless, to get there, go east on US 98/SR 35/CR 700 from Lakeland for 3.5 miles. Turn right onto CR 540 (Clubhouse Road) and go west for 1.5 miles. Turn right onto Peterson Road and go north for 0.5 mile to the single-lane ramp. There is limited parking.

There are no public ramps on Lake Hancock, and access is extremely limited off the surrounding dirt lanes. The bottom of the lake has a lot of muck, and it is surrounded by marsh. Sunshine bass have been stocked in this lake.

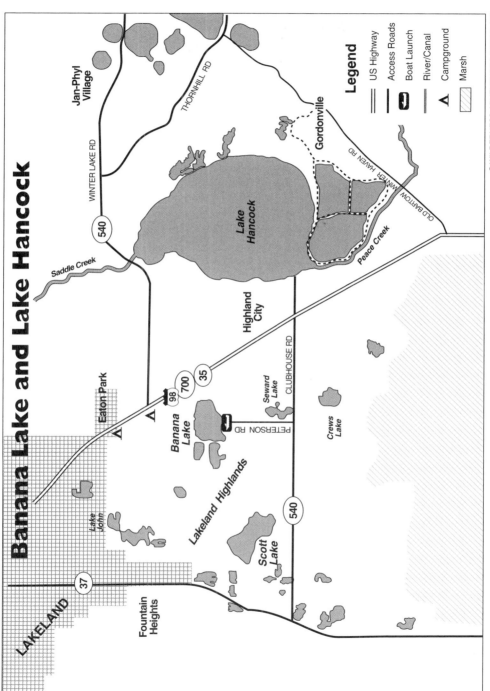

Banana Lake and Lake Hancock

Legend

US Highway
Access Roads
Boat Launch
River/Canal
Campground
Marsh

WINTER HAVEN CHAIN OF LAKES

Lake Agnes	Lake George	Eagle Lake
Lake Helene	Lake Mariana	Sears Lake
Clearwater Lake	Lake Jessie	Thomas Lake
Mud Lake	Lake Idylwild	Spirit Lake
Lake Tennessee	Lake Hartridge	Dinner Lake
Lake Juliana	Lake Connie	Grassy Lake
Lake Mattie	Lake Smart	Lake Hancock
Lake Arietta	Lake Fannie	Millsite Lake
Lake Whistler	Lake Henry	Lake McLeod
Lake Ariana	Middle Lake Hamilton	Lake Lulu
Lake Lena	Lake Hamilton	Lake Eloise
Lake Van	Lake Buckeye	Lake Summit
Lake Medora	Lake Maude	Lake Dexter
Lake Alfred	Lake Mirror	Lake Daisy
Lake Swoope	Lake Conner	Lake Fox
Gum Lake	Lake Deer	River Lake
Lake Lowery	Lake Howard	Lake Winterset
Bonnet Lake	Lake Silver	Lake Ruby
Hammock Lake	Lake Martha	Lake Bass
Lake Henry	Lake Elbert	Lake Myrtle
Lake Haines	Lake Ortis	Lake Hart
Lake Rochelle	Lake Mariam	Rattlesnake Lake
Lake Echo	Lake Florence	Crystal Lake
Lake Cummings	Lake Shipp	Lake Gywn

Midway between Orlando and Tampa in west-central Florida, dozens of lakes and ponds surround the town of Winter Haven. In a 10-mile by 10-mile square with Winter Haven in the center, there is easily as much water as there is land mass. The lakes tend to be shallow, bowl-shaped bodies of tannic-colored water, and many are rimmed by cypress tress standing along the water's edge. These lakes and the banks that surround them are often quite attractive, as evidenced by the beautiful grounds at Cypress Gardens on Lake Summit, where flowers of one type or another are in bloom year-round. Much of the surrounding area has been used for years as orange groves and orchards. A gently rolling landscape causes nutrients to runoff to a slight degree and the result is that some of the lakes are quite fertile.

I have seldom found tannic water to offer a really productive fishery, but the lakes in the Winter Haven area come close to being the exception. Many of these lakes yield outstanding catches of largemouth bass, crappie, and assorted members of the bream family. Sunshine bass have also been stocked.

Most lakes have bonnets growing around the perimeter, as well as grass that provides cover. Shoreline plants like cattail and maidencane also extend into the water, providing excellent habitat for largemouth and bream. Crappie use these areas to

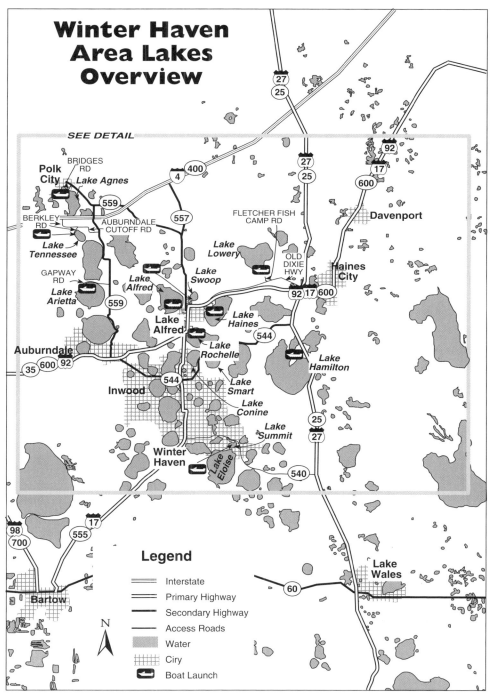

Winter Haven Area Lakes Overview

SEE DETAIL

27 25

92

BRIDGES RD
Polk City
Lake Agnes
400
4
27 25
17
600

559

BERKLEY RD
AUBURNDALE CUTOFF RD
557
Davenport

Lake Tennessee
Lake Lowery
FLETCHER FISH CAMP RD

GAPWAY RD
Lake Arietta
559
Lake Alfred
Lake Swoop
OLD DIXIE HWY
Haines City
92 17 600

Lake Alfred
Lake Haines
544

Auburndale
35 600 92
Lake Rochelle
544
Inwood
Lake Smart
Lake Hamilton

Lake Conine

Winter Haven
Lake Eloise
Lake Summit
25 27
540

98 700
17
555

Legend

≡≡≡ Interstate
══ Primary Highway
━━ Secondary Highway
── Access Roads
▨ Water
▦ Cirv
◼ Boat Launch

N

Bartow
60
Lake Wales

© WILDERNESS ADVENTURES PRESS, INC.

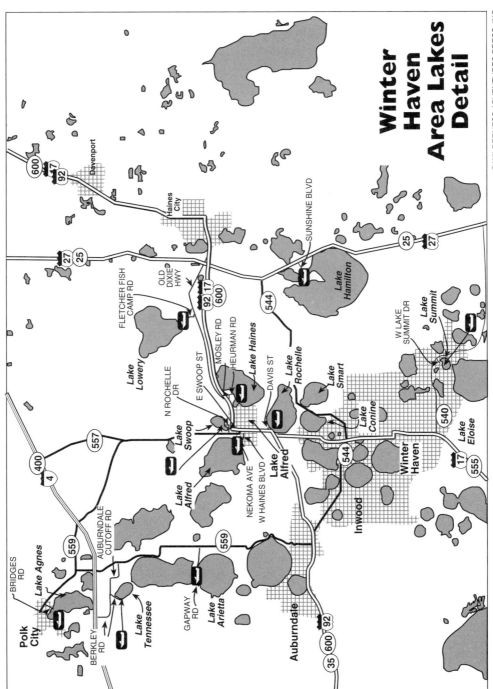

Winter Haven Area Lakes Detail

spawn in the early spring. Look to the open water for sunshine bass.

During periods of low water, as we have had for several years, navigation through the canals that connect the lakes is frequently not possible. Hence, those lakes with launch sites receive extensive fishing and recreational pressure while others go almost unutilized except by persons who reside on the lake and can get their boat into the water from their own dock. The fishing tends to be better when all of this use can be spread between the various lakes. You should inquire at local tackle shops whether the canals can be used to get between lakes so that you can find a relatively secluded area to fish.

The directions that follow are to public ramps, although there are fish camps on some of the lakes that have launch sites, as well. Note, also, that by using the canal system, you can get to many of the other lakes in the Winter Park area when the water is sufficiently high.

Lake Agnes (475 acres) is the only lake in this group north of I-4 with a launch site. The northern end of the lake has some residential development. To get to Lake Agnes, get off I-4 at Exit 21 and go north on SR 559 for 2.2 miles. In Polk City, turn left onto Bridges Road and go 3 blocks to the single-lane ramp.

Lake Tennessee (125 acres) is surrounded by orange groves and has a good population of panfish and small bass. To get to the launch site, go south on SR 559 from Exit 21 off I-4. Go south for 0.8 mile and turn right onto the unnamed road into the orchard and go 1.5 miles (making a right then left S-turn midway) to Berkley Road. Turn left and go 0.4 mile to the single-lane ramp on your left.

Lake Arietta (758 acres) is another bowl-shaped lake in the middle of an orange grove. A small feeder creek in the southwest corner provides a bit of interest. To get to Lake Arietta, go south on SR 559 from I-4 (Exit 21) for 3.2 miles. Turn right onto Gapway Road and go west for 1.6 miles. The single-lane ramp is on your left.

Lake Alfred (736 acres) transitions between orchards and residential properties in the community of Lake Alfred. The southwest corner of this lake is also the most interesting because of some irregular shoreline. To get to the lake, get off I-4 at Exit 22 and go south on SR 557 for 6 miles. As you come into town, cross the railroad tracks and turn right onto West Haines Blvd. then go west for two blocks. Turn right onto Nekoma Avenue and go north for one block, crossing the railroad tracks as you enter Lions Club Park to your left. Follow the signs to the single-lane ramp where there is unimproved parking for 20 vehicles.

Lake Swoope (88 acres) is a small lake near Lake Alfred. As above, exit I-4 at Exit 22 and go south on SR 557 for 5.8 miles. Just before crossing the railroad tracks and entering the town of Lake Alfred, turn left onto East Swoope Street and go east for two blocks. Turn left again onto North Rochelle Drive and go 0.3 mile to the single-lane ramp on your left.

Lake Lowery (903 acres) is a scenic lake surrounded by marsh. It is spring-fed, with a clear bottom. Bonnets and grass provide cover for some quality largemouth bass. There are some residential canals on the north end of the lake that hold crappie and bass. To access the lake, get off I-4 at Exit 23 and go south on US 27/SR 25 for 8 miles. Turn right onto US 17/SR 92 and go west for a block. Turn right again onto Old

Dixie Highway (Haines City Lake Alfred Road) and go west for 2 miles with the railroad tracks on your right. Turn right onto Fletcher Fish Camp Road and cross the railroad tracks, going 0.3 mile to the single-lane ramp.

Lake Haines (716 acres) is a good bass and crappie lake. There is substantial residential development on the west side, and the lake gets a lot of boat traffic. To get there, get off I-4 at Exit 22 and go south on SR 557 for 6 miles. Turn left onto US 17/SR 92 and go east for 1.2 miles. Turn right onto Huerman Road and go 0.1 mile. Turn left onto Mosley Road and go 0.3 mile to the single-lane ramp.

Lake Rochelle (578 acres) on the north side of Winter Haven has canals leading to Lake Conine (236 acres) and Lake Smart (275 acres). These are good bass and crappie lakes, although there is a lot of residential development. To get to Lake Rochelle, again take Exit 22 off I-4 and go south on SR 557 for 7 miles, through the community of Lake Alfred. As SR 557 begins to make a sweeping right turn, turn left onto East Davis Street and go one block to the single-lane ramp.

Lake Hamilton (2,162 acres) is the largest lake in this group and has some residential development at the north end. In addition to the bass and crappie that can be caught around docks, this lake has a good population of sunshine bass that school in open water. To get here, get off I-4 at Exit 23 and go south on US 27/SR 25 for 11 miles. Turn right onto Sunshine Drive and go 1 mile through the residential area to the single-lane ramp.

Lake Summit (68 acres) is a small lake on the southeast side of Winter Haven. This lake is connected by canal to Lake Eloise (1,160 acres) and on to others from here. These dark-water lakes are surrounded by scenic shorelines with cypress trees. They have a good population of bass, although they get a lot of boat traffic. To get to Lake Summit, get off I-4 at Exit 22 and go south on SR 557 for 12 miles. Turn left in Winter Haven onto SR 540 (Cypress Gardens Road) and go east for 2.5 miles. Turn right onto West Lake Summit Drive and go 0.4 mile to the single-lane ramp.

LAKE GARFIELD

Lake Garfield (655 acres) is the southernmost lake considered part of the Winter Haven Chain of Lakes. Like the others, it is quite scenic, with grass and bonnets extending out from the shoreline and into the lake's clear water. There is less residential development on Lake Garfield than on many others in the Winter Haven Chain.

There is good bass fishing, especially early in the spring. A feeder creek flows into Lake Garfield from the south (to the left of the boat ramp) and the creek that drains the lake to the north goes on to others in the chain of lakes. Be sure to check the southern end for spawning bass and bream.

To get to Lake Garfield, get off I-4 at Exit 23 and go south on US 27/SR 25 for 22 miles. At the intersection with SR 60 in the town of Lake Wales, turn right onto SR 60 and go west for 7.5 miles. Turn left onto CR 655A and go south for 1.3 miles to Lake Garfield Landing. Turn right and go 0.3 mile to the single-lane ramp.

The launch from a fish camp leads to Lake Marion.

LAKE MARION

Lake Marion (2,990 acres) has some very good bass fishing, and several wall-hanging lunkers come from these waters. Be sure to circle Bannon Island in front of the launch ramp, as yearling bass like to hang out here. At the northern end, a creek enters Lake Marion, and there is shallow water and aquatic vegetation to the west. This is a very good area for largemouth, crappie, and bream in the spring. This area bends around, offering good shelter from a light wind. Anglers should not overlook the extreme southern end, as it has emerging vegetation that holds baitfish, and in turn, predatory game fish. There is some residential development along the western shoreline. Lake Marion has been stocked with sunshine bass, and open water schooling is common.

To get to Marion, take Exit 23 off I-4 and go south on US 27/SR 25 for 9.5 miles. Turn left onto CR 544 and go east for 6.7 miles. Turn left onto Cowpen Road and go 0.2 mile north. Lastly, turn right onto Bannon Fish Camp Road and proceed to the single-lane ramp 0.3 mile ahead.

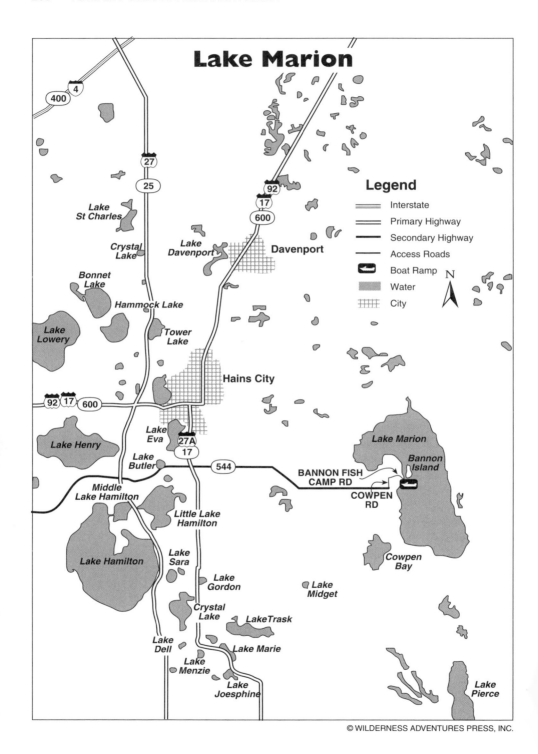

Lake Marion

Legend

Interstate
Primary Highway
Secondary Highway
Access Roads
Boat Ramp
Water
City

© WILDERNESS ADVENTURES PRESS, INC.

LAKE NANA, MUD LAKE, AND BUCK LAKE

This group of lakes lies southeast of the Orlando International Airport between the runways and CR 417 (Central Florida Greenway). The lakes are shallow and do not have launch ramps. There are no paved roads leading to them, although some well-worn trails do exist. This is not a place to take a rental car, even if you don't mind getting stuck. While these lakes offer flyfishers an opportunity to make some casts and catch small bass and assorted panfish on cork, foam, or deer-hair poppers, the urban lakes within the city limits of Orlando (covered earlier in Region 3) come with a much higher recommendation.

The Kissimmee Chain of Lakes

These lakes, starting less than 10 miles southeast of Orlando, serve as the headwaters for the Kissimmee River and numerous lakes that flow into Lake Okeechobee and contribute to what eventually becomes the Everglades. There are upwards of twenty public lakes ranging in size from 200 to 44,000 acres, offering more than 100,000 acres of outstanding aquatic habitat.

The lakes in the upper part of the system have dark, tannin-stained water that is relatively unproductive. The exception, East Lake Tohopekaliga, has clearer water and extensive vegetation that provides good fish habitat. Bass fishing can be very tough due to low productivity and a lack of proper sized forage. Crappie fishing is done most of the year in open water (deeper holes) and within shoreline vegetation during the spawn. Panfishing occurs primarily in open water, although flyfishers do take bluegill from the bulrush edges during summer.

The lakes in the lower part of the system have much more expansive vegetated areas. The contour is generally gently sloping, with shallow, relatively productive water. Most of the lakes in the lower chain have occasional problems with hydrilla. While the lakes in the upper chain tend to yield either small or large bass, the lower lakes have a good mix of sizes. West Lake Tohopekaliga's water level is presently being drawn down, and the exceptional fishery located there should become one of the very best in the nation by the time this guidebook is published. Because the lakes of the lower chain are so shallow, they are extremely sensitive to weather fronts. While the large bass get most of the attention, crappie fishing is the main activity for local anglers, especially in December and January. In addition to these two tremendous fisheries, the lower Kissimmee Chain also has some of the very best bream and shellcracker fishing in the country. The shellcrackers will be bedding in late March, while the bluegill will move into the backs of the same pockets in April and May.

UPPER KISSIMMEE CHAIN OF LAKES: LAKE HART, LAKE WHIPPOORWILL, AND LAKE MARY JANE

These lakes are located at the extreme northern headwaters of the system. The water looks good, but as I have previously noted, I do not find fishing to be all that productive in dark, tannin-stained, acidic waters. These three lakes do have interesting shorelines that offer points, coves, and a break from the wind. I recommend passing on these upper lakes for much more productive fishing in larger, nearby lakes. Their tranquility and scenic beauty may draw you back for a visit, however.

Lake Hart (1,850 acres) averages about 10 to 12 feet deep, with a couple of 20-foot holes near the southern end. To get to the launch site, also at the southern end of the lake, get off CR 417 (a bypass around Orlando known as the Central Florida Greenway) east of the airport and go south on CR 15 (Narcoossee Road) for 3 miles. Turn left onto Tindall Road and go east for 1.2 miles. Turn left and go 0.1 mile north to the single-lane ramp.

Lake Whippoorwill (250 acres) has no public access, although there is some residential development at the northern end.

Lake Mary Jane (1,158 acres) averages about 8 feet deep and has some residential development along the eastern shoreline. The extreme southern end has a creek that flows out into a marsh and on to more small lakes. Give this area a good look with topwater poppers early and late in the day. To get to Lake Mary Jane and the launch site in the northwest corner, get off CR 417 and go north on SR 15 (Narcoossee Road) for 1 mile. Turn right and go east and then south (the road bends) for 4.2 miles on Moss Park Road. The double-lane ramp is to the left of the office at Moss Park. There is unimproved parking for 30 vehicles.

EAST LAKE TOHOPEKALIGA AND LAKE RUNNYMEDE

East Lake Tohopekaliga (11,968 acres) is a large, bowl-shaped lake adjacent to and north of St. Cloud. There are few trees along the shoreline and the lake is very susceptible to wind. Other than St. Cloud, there is not much development on East Lake Toho. The bottom of the lake is sandy and the water is clearer than most lakes in the upper Kissimmee Chain. At times, the lake has had a problem with hydrilla. There are numerous islands of grass and reeds all around the rim of the lake. These provide good habitat for a better than average (for the Upper Chain) population of bass, bream, and crappie. The bass tend to school and concentrate on this lake, so you may have to move around until fish are found.

To get to East Lake Toho from the north, get on CR 417 (the Central Florida Greenway) to bypass Orlando. At the SR 15 (Narcoossee Road) exit, go south for 3 miles. Turn right onto SR 530 (Boggy Creek Road) and go west for 4 miles. Turn left onto Fish Camp Road and go south for 0.6 mile to the single-lane ramp.

To access the east side of the lake, continue south on SR 15 for another 3 miles. Turn right onto L Street and go west for 0.5 mile to the single-lane ramp at Chisholm Park.

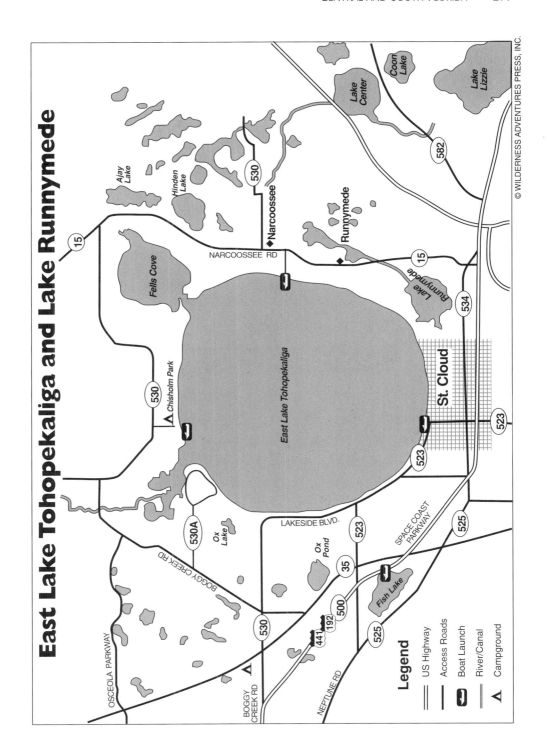

East Lake Tohopekaliga and Lake Runnymede

Legend
US Highway
Access Roads
Boat Launch
River/Canal
Campground

The southern launch site is in St. Cloud. To get there, continue south on SR 15 for another 3 miles to the intersection with US 441/US 192. Turn right and go west for 2.9 miles into St. Cloud. At CR 523 (Canoe Creek Road), turn right and go 1.2 miles to the launch site.

Lake Runnymede (200 acres) is an oval lake connected by canal to the southeast corner of East Lake Toho. There is no significant fishery in this small lake, but if the wind is rough on the bigger lake, you might find sanctuary here. When water is moving through the canal, action can pick up at each end. Try a shad pattern or a Baby Bunker and move it with the direction of water flow so that it gets below the surface. The only access to Lake Runnymede is from East Lake Toho through the canal.

The southern end of East Lake Tohopekaliga is easily reached from St. Cloud.

HIDDEN LAKE, LAKE MYRTLE, LAKE PRESTON, BULLOCK LAKE, LAKE JOEL, LAKE CENTER, COON LAKE, TROUT LAKE AND LAKE LIZZIE

About 5 miles east of St. Cloud are numerous lakes between 200 and 400 acres. Some have residential development, usually only on one side or at one end, but most do not. None of the lakes in this group has a public ramp, however. Those lakes with homes have paved roads, while those without development tend to just have trails.

The lakes are shallow and have some bass, bream, and crappie, but generally not of any substantial size. These lakes are best left to the locals and really can't be recommended as a destination worth much effort to fly fish.

ALLIGATOR LAKE, LIVE OAK LAKE, PEARL LAKE, BUCK LAKE, AND LAKE GENTRY

Alligator Lake (3,406 acres) is uncommonly deep for lakes in this area. In the northern half of the lake, there are two holes that drop quickly from the lake average of about 12 feet to depths of 30 feet. These holes are the summer home for the lake's crappie. You will need a sinking line and time on your hands to get a Clouser down to them, however. They run small in size, as do the bass and bream found around the shoreline vegetation.

To get to the launch site at the southern end of the lake, get off the CR 417 bypass around Orlando and go south on SR 15 for 9 miles to US 441/US 192. Turn right and go west for 0.8 mile to CR 534 (Hickory Tree Road). Turn left onto DR 534 and go south for about 5 miles (the road has a series of right and left bends) to Lakeshore Drive. Turn left and go 0.2 mile to the single-lane ramp at the end.

There is also access to both Alligator Lake and Lake Gentry by way of the canal (C-33) connecting them. As above, go south on SR 15 from the 417 bypass for 9 miles to the intersection with US 441/US 192. Turn right onto US 441/US 192 and go 0.8 mile to (CR 534) Hickory Tree Road. Turn left and go about 6 miles. Cross the canal and turn left into the park and the road leads to the single-lane ramp, where there is unimproved parking for eight vehicles.

Canals lead from Alligator Lake to the other lakes in this group, although neither the lakes nor the canals have launch sites. Like most of the lakes in the Upper Chain, there is not much development along the shorelines. The lakes do offer some solitude and a chance to catch small bass, crappie, and bream, but they don't have much in the way of properly-sized baitfish and do not lend themselves to good reproduction.

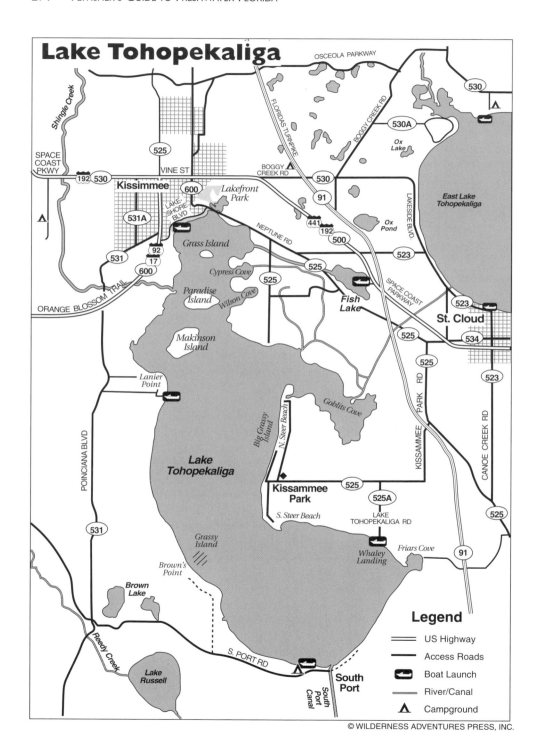

Lake Tohopekaliga

© WILDERNESS ADVENTURES PRESS, INC.

LOWER KISSIMMEE CHAIN OF LAKES: LAKE TOHOPEKALIGA, FISH LAKE, AND BROWN LAKE

By the time you read this, Lake Tohopekaliga (18,810 acres) may be recognized as the finest lake in the country for largemouth bass. I do not mean one of the top 10 in the country, or even one of the top 10 in the state (as it has been one of Florida's top lakes for quite some time). I said *numero uno* in the nation. I realize that is a pretty bold statement, but I think that I can back it up.

Often referred to as West Lake Toho, this lake is about 10 miles south of the Orlando International Airport, adjacent to and southeast of the town of Kissimmee. There are islands in the northern end, along with fingers, arms, points, coves, pockets and bays to offer shelter for both you and the fish. There is plenty of grass and cattails along the rim of the lake, although not many bonnets or lily pads. Marsh surrounds much of the lake, except at the extreme northern end. The lake averages about 8 to 10 feet deep, but it is a little less than that at the northern end. Lake Toho has a canal (South Port Canal) leading from the southern end, giving boaters access to lakes in the Lower Kissimmee Chain.

Several years ago, the water in Lake Toho was lowered and new vegetation grew where there had recently been shoreline muck. When water levels were returned to their normal levels, Lake Toho became one of the best bass fishing lakes in the state, yielding large stringers of 10-pound-plus bass. At a Bass Anglers Sportsman's Society (B.A.S.S.) tournament held in January 2001, pro angler Dean Rojas from Arizona weighed-in five largemouth bass at the end of the first day that had a total weight in excess of 45 pounds. That is an average of over 9 pounds per fish! This one-day total was the heaviest stringer ever brought to the scales for a 5-fish weigh-in in the history of all BASS tournaments. The tournament lasted three more days and he went on to win with a total weight in excess of 108 pounds, bringing his average catch for the 20 fish that he selected for weigh-in down to a little over 5 pounds each.

Flyfishers targeting largemouth bass should focus on Goblets Cove, Browns Point, North Steer Beach, Little Grassy Island, and larger clumps of vegetation in the extreme northern end. This is the place to get out your 8-weight rod and a large deer-hair popper or bass bug protected by a monofilament weedguard. Be on the water ready to fish at first light and be prepared for a fierce fight.

The best time of the year for shellcrackers is on the full moon during spring months, especially in April. Look toward areas with sandy bottoms in the open water close to vegetation around Makinson's Island, Browns Point, and North Steer Beach. Those targeting crappie will also want to look to Goblets Cove and the open water between Paradise Island and Makinson's Island. In spring, fish areas with vegetation, as this will likely be used for spawning activity.

Now the good news. Lake Tohopekaliga is scheduled for a drawdown to restore quality fish habitat. Lake levels are scheduled to be lowered beginning in November 2002 and will be at their lowest levels by February 2003. The fish will be concentrated and anglers should find lots of quality fish. This will present many new wading opportunities for flyfishers. Lake Toho will remain at the low pool levels until June 2003 and then begin to refill. This should be completed by September 2003. The next few years thereafter, fishing should be fantastic, especially for big bass.

To reach the launch site at the northern end of Lake Toho, get off I-4 at Exit 27 and go south on CR 535 for 3 miles. At the intersection with US 192, turn left and go 4 miles to the intersection with US 17/US 92 in Kissimmee. Turn right and go south on Main Street for 0.6 mile to Monument Avenue. Turn left onto Monument Avenue and go about 0.5 mile to Lakeshore Blvd. Turn right onto Lakeshore Blvd. and go south for 0.3 mile to the six-lane ramp at Lakefront Park on your left. There is paved parking for 84 vehicles and unimproved parking in the vacant lot across the street. The size of the ramp and number of parking spaces is a clear indication of how good the fishing is and the demand that anglers are placing on the waters. This is about as good as it gets.

There is another launch site in the southeastern corner of the lake. To get to this one, go south from Kissimmee on CR 525 for about 10 miles, twice crossing SR 91. Turn left onto CR 525A and go 1.5 miles to the launch site.

Brown Lake (about 150 acres) is a shallow marshy lake about two miles southwest of West Lake Toho. There is no boat access and water levels fluctuate. There are a few homes on the perimeter of the lake, and this is another small body of water that is best left to the locals. There is no reason to make Brown Lake a destination choice when world-class fishing is less than 5 miles away.

Three double-lane ramps at the launch site in Kissimmee demonstrate the popularity of Lake Toho (West Lake Tohopekaliga).

Fish Lake (about 200 acres) lies midway between East Lake Toho and West Lake Toho. The lake does not have the quality of fish that the Tohos have, but when the wind is blowing hard, it will not be as rough as either of these two larger lakes. I would save it for really inclement weather (and then think twice about going). To get to Fish Lake, go west on US 441/US 192 from the intersection of Canoe Creek Road in St. Cloud for 3 miles. Just past passing the Florida Turnpike, turn left onto Florence Road and go one block to Emerald Road. Turn right and go 0.1 mile along the side of the lake to the single-lane ramp on your left.

CYPRESS LAKE

Cypress Lake (4,097 acres) is next in line in the Kissimmee Chain of Lakes. It is located at the lower end of the South Port Canal leading from West Lake Tohopekaliga. The bottom of the lake has a very gentle slope when approached from the west where the canal enters, with an average depth of around 6 to 8 feet throughout most of the open water. The southeastern corner has the deepest water in the lake, a hole of about 10 feet. What is noteworthy, however, is that this hole is about one mile due south of the ramp and in front of the Short Canal leading toward Lake Kissimmee. As a result, the bottom slopes much more rapidly on the east side of the lake. From the southwestern corner, there is a second canal (Hatchineha Canal) leading away from Cypress Lake and on toward Lake Hatchineha.

Cypress Lake is rather remote, with no residential development along its shoreline. The surrounding area is very low and marshy, with numerous creeks feeding the lake, especially from the north. Cypress trees surround the rim and provide relief from an unwanted breeze.

This lake is not known for its largemouth bass fishing, as are some of the larger and more easily accessed lakes in the Kissimmee Chain. That doesn't mean they aren't there, however. Plenty of good-sized bass are take from Cypress Lake by anglers willing to drive a little farther to get away from the crowds. Try the northern end of the lake during early spring using a deer-hair popper to search around vegetation that extends out into the lake.

In winter, look for crappie (often called "specks" in Florida) to be suspended over the hole in the southeastern corner. Tie a Clouser on a sink-tip line and make note of the depth at which the fish are holding when you catch one. During spring and summer, both bluegills and shellcrackers provide reliable action on small poppers and terrestrial patterns.

You can get to Cypress Lake by launching in West Toho or Lake Hatchineha and motoring through the connecting canals. There is also one launch site on Cypress Lake. From US 441/US 192 in St. Cloud (see the southern ramp for East Lake Tohopekaliga), go south on CR 523 (Canoe Creek Road) for 11.2 miles. Turn right onto Lake Cypress Drive and go west for 2.3 miles to the single-lane ramp.

Lake Hatchineha

Lake Hatchineha (6,665 acres), like Cypress Lake, is remote and lacks any residential development along its shoreline except near the immediate vicinity of the launch site. And what a beautiful shoreline it is, with stands of cypress trees creeping out of the marsh and into the lake. The cypress offer shade and cover for bass, crappie, and bream, while affording flyfishers relief from wind. Hydrilla has frequently been a problem for navigation on Lake Hachineha. It does provide good habitat for fish, however. You might want to consider late fall and early winter when the hydrilla is not as dense.

Lake Hatcheneha is not bowl-shaped like so many central Florida lakes. Instead, it runs along an axis that goes northwest to southeast and averages about two miles wide. There is also an arm coming from Cypress Lake and Hatchineha Canal that runs along a northeast to southwest axis. The lake averages about 8 feet deep, although there is a 12-foot hole near the shore in the southeast corner that holds wintering crappie.

Largemouth bass fishing can be good, particularly in early spring in the northwest corner where three creeks flow into the lake from the marsh. Crappie also use this area to spawn, and by late spring and early summer, bluegill and shellcrackers can be found here.

Do not overlook the Hatchineha Canal connecting to Cypress Lake, as the slight current keeps the hydrilla at bay and is "user-friendly" for flyfishers. On average, the bass will not be as large as they are in the main lake, but there are plenty that seem to be more catchable. The Kissimmee River headwaters flow from the southeast corner of Lake Hatchineha and the large hole there. In addition to the current, there are numerous turns and bends in the river as it snakes its way for about 10 river miles to Lake Kissimmee. The river is a great place to get out of a stiff wind and still catch fish.

To get to the launch site, approach Lake Hatchineha from the west. From the center of Winter Haven (10 miles south of Exit 22 off I-4) go east on CR 542 for 18 miles to the single-lane launch site at the road's end.

Lake Rosalie and Tiger Lake

Lake Rosalie (4,597 acres) is the template from which bowl-shaped lakes are made. The lake slopes uniformly to 15 feet with almost no shoreline irregularities. As a result, you have to search for fish, as there are no prominent depth changes or islands to concentrate them.

Tiger Lake (2,200 acres) has an average depth of 9 feet at the northern end and only 7 feet in the southern end. A creek flows out of Lake Rosalie just east of the launch site and into the northwest corner of Tiger Lake. Tiger Creek flows from the northeast corner of Tiger Lake for about two miles to Lake Kissimmee. The southern end of Tiger Lake can have substantial hydrilla problems because of a lack of water movement.

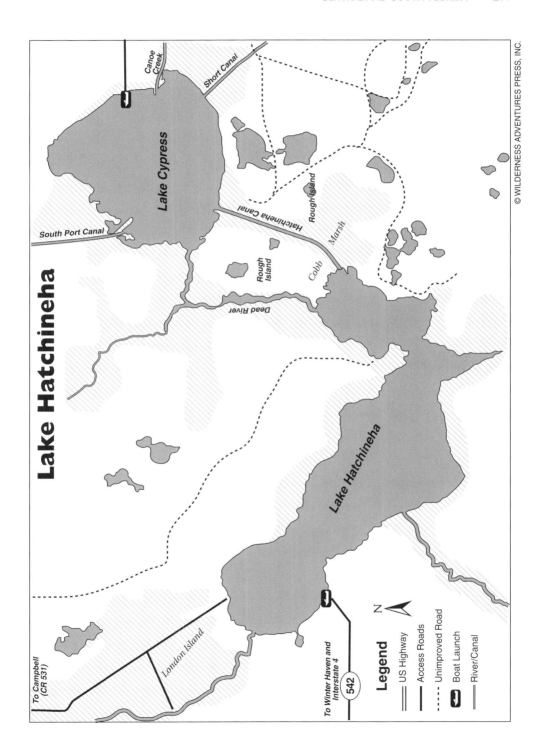

© WILDERNESS ADVENTURES PRESS, INC.

Lake Hatchineha

Lake Cypress

Canoe Creek

Short Canal

Hatchineha Canal

Rough Island

South Port Canal

Rough Island

Cobb Marsh

Dead River

Lake Hatchineha

London Island

To Campbell (CR 531)

To Winter Haven and Interstate 4

542

Legend

N

═══ US Highway

─── Access Roads

········· Unimproved Road

◪ Boat Launch

─── River/Canal

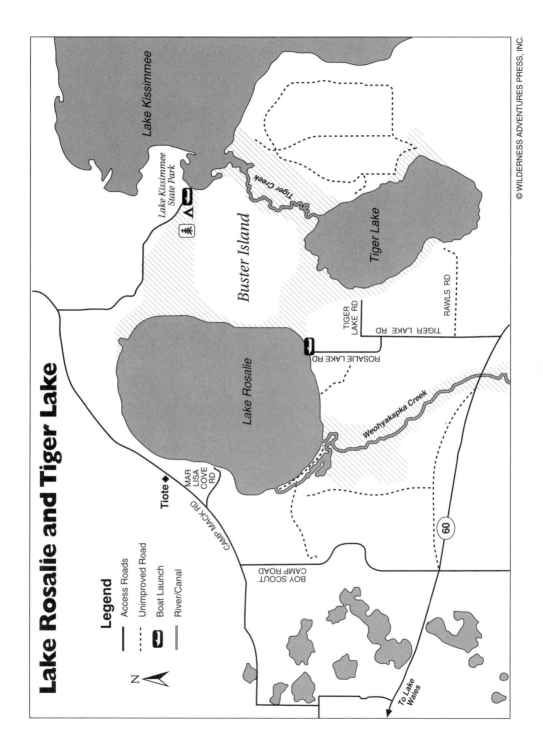

Lake Rosalie and Tiger Lake

Both of these lakes can be difficult to fish, and the creeks that lead into and out of them have some of the most consistent water. In the creeks, cast your popper toward shoreline vegetation; or in areas where there is open water due to flow, try a subsurface baitfish pattern next to vegetation for largemouth. Assorted bream will be most easily caught in the main lakes using small grass shrimp patterns, terrestrials, and small poppers. The panfish in these lakes get quite large and are fun to fight on a light fly rod.

To get to the only launch site on Lake Rosalie, take SR 60 east from the US 27 intersection in Lake Wales. Go east for 14 miles to Tiger Lake Road and turn left. Go north for 1.9 miles to Rosalie Lake Road and again turn left. Go 1 mile to the single-lane ramp where there is unimproved parking for 30 vehicles.

LAKE KISSIMMEE

Lake Kissimmee (34,948 acres) has long been regarded as one of Florida's top 10 lakes. With over 55 square miles of surface area, it is Florida's third largest lake (after Lake Okeechobee and Lake George). Kissimmee means "Heaven's place" in the Calusa Indian language and the name is an apt description of this beautiful body of water. Lake Kissimmee is about 13 miles long and nearly 5 miles across at its widest point, with a bottom that is mostly sandy. The water is clearer than it is in most of the lakes in the Kissimmee Chain, with grass and hydrilla growing up towards the surface and bonnets and lilies growing out into the lake from the shoreline. The land surrounding Lake Kissimmee is mostly marsh, and there is very little development around the edges. The lake is shallow, averaging about 10 feet deep. There are several large islands and some deeper water (up to 17 feet) between them in the middle of the lake. The islands at the northern end are in shallower water. When the wind picks up, the lake gets whitecaps in a hurry. Keep an eye out for storm clouds, as it can go from a rough ride to a dangerous ride in short order.

Much of Lake Kissimmee's fame comes as a result of a large drawdown in 1977, which removed muck and sediment from about 52 miles of shoreline. These areas quickly grew new vegetation and the bass, crappie, and panfish flourished in shallow waters rich with bait. The strong 1978 year-class of fish yielded great numbers and many went on to become 10-pound-plus fish in the next 10 years. These areas were also easily fished, and the hard sandy bottom that had previously been muck could be waded, as well.

As vegetation thickened, causing sediment to settle to the bottom, a layer of muck once again covered the sand. The wadeable area became smaller and smaller; by 1996, only 2 miles remained. The drawdown of 1996 removed over 1.5 million cubic yards of organic material from 971 acres. As a result, another 22 miles of shoreline have been cleaned and can again be waded by flyfishers. Recall the warnings elsewhere in this guidebook about alligators, however.

The results of the 1996 drawdown, so far, have been similar to those of the 1977 drawdown. Electrofishing surveys conducted in 1999 showed that both the 1997 and

Kissimmee State Park offers a beautiful launch area
with a canal leading to Lake Kissimmee.

the 1998 year-class of fish were exceptionally strong. The last survey prior to the drawdown had yielded 13 bass per hour that were less than 12 inches in length. The 1999 survey conducted in the same area yielded an astonishing 86 bass per hour that were between 4 and 12 inches in length. This will be the perfect lake to fly fish for numbers of quality bass in the 2003-2005 timeframe, with some really big bass after 2005. Fisheries biologist Mike Hulon headed the crew that conducted the electrofishing survey for Florida's Fish and Wildlife Commission, and he reports, "These size classes are showing the anticipated results of the project and will be the basis for a tremendous quality sportfishery for years to come."

Bass are not the only game in town, however. Most anglers who fish Lake Kissimmee are doing so for crappie. Florida has a generous limit (25 crappie per day per angler) for these tasty fish, which readily take a Clouser, especially in early spring when they move to the shallows to spawn.

By late spring and early summer, the primary target is bream, which use the same areas to spawn as crappie. Fishing is especially productive around the full moon. Another generous limit (50 panfish per angler per day) make these scrappy fighters the object of most angler's interest. A small popper, terrestrial, or freshwater shrimp pattern cast around the bonnets will be quickly seized.

In addition to several fish camps, there are public launch sites on the east, west, and south shores of Lake Kissimmee. In the northwestern corner, Lake Kissimmee

Lake Kissimmee

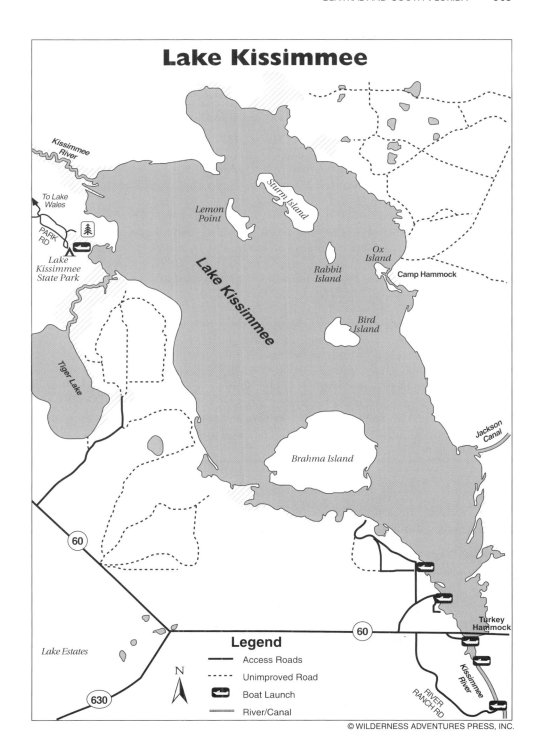

Kissimmee River

To Lake Wales

PARK RD

Lake Kissimmee State Park

Lemon Point

Sturm Island

Lake Kissimmee

Rabbit Island

Ox Island

Camp Hammock

Bird Island

Tiger Lake

Brahma Island

Jackson Canal

60

Lake Estates

630

Turkey Hammock

Kissimmee River

RIVER RANCH RD

Legend

N

—— Access Roads

- - - Unimproved Road

Boat Launch

River/Canal

60

© WILDERNESS ADVENTURES PRESS, INC.

State Park offers 60 campsites with electrical and water hookup, making a good base for the camper. To get to the state park, take Exit 23 off I-4 and go south on US 27/SR 25 for 23 miles to the town of Lake Wales. At the intersection with SR 60 in Lake Wales, turn left and go east for 9.2 miles to Boy Scout Camp Road. Turn left and go north on Boy Scout Camp Road for 3.2 miles to the end. Turn right onto Camp Mack Road and go 5.2 miles to the state park on your right. Follow the signs to the single-lane ramp with paved parking for 20 vehicles.

To launch on the east side of Lake Kissimmee, go south from the town of St. Cloud (see directions to East Lake Tohopekaliga) on CR 523 (Canoe Creek Road) for 20.8 mile. Turn right onto Overstreet Road and go west for 5.5 miles to the single lane ramp at the end of the road.

At the extreme southern end of the lake, a lock separates Kissimmee Lake to the north and the Kissimmee River to the south. There are several launch sites that can be reached off SR 60 near the southern end of the lake. To approach the area from the east, get off Florida's Turnpike at Yeehaw Junction (milepost 193) and go west on SR 60 for 20 miles to where SR 60 crosses Kissimmee Lake. If approaching from the west, start from the town of Lake Wales (see the directions to Kissimmee State Park above) on SR 60 for about 28 miles to where SR 60 crosses Kissimmee Lake. Turn onto Grape Hammock Road 1.5 miles west of the lake crossing and go north for a mile. Turn left onto Shady Oak Drive and go 1.2 miles to the single lane ramp on your right.

There is another single-lane ramp about a mile south of this one. Again, exit SR 60 onto Grape Hammock Road and go north for 1.6 miles to the launch site.

At the lock south of the SR 60 crossing, there are two ramps. The northern one yields access to Lake Kissimmee and the southern one will be discussed with the Kissimmee River. To reach the lock and these two ramps, turn south onto Levee Road at the west end of the SR 60 Bridge and go 0.5 mile to the single-lane ramp. There is unimproved parking for 30 vehicles.

LAKE JACKSON AND LAKE MARIAN

Lake Jackson (1,020 acres) and Lake Marian (5,739 acres) are about 5 miles east of Lake Kissimmee and their waters drain into the southeastern corner of Kissimmee through the 2-mile-long Jackson Canal.

Lake Jackson is between Lake Marian and Lake Kissimmee. At the shallow, southern end of Jackson, the stream from Lake Marian enters from the east. Directly across, Jackson Canal leads to Lake Kissimmee. Remember this canal if the wind picks up and waters start to get rough. The southern end of Lake Jackson is also a good area to prospect for spawning fish in the spring. Jackson is smaller than most other lakes in the Lower Kissimmee Chain and does not share their reputation. That does not mean that bass, bream, and crappie fishing on Lake Jackson is not good, though. Because of its small size and the fact that fishing tournaments are discouraged, it merely lacks the same national reputation.

The launch site to Lake Jackson is in the northeast corner. To get there, go south

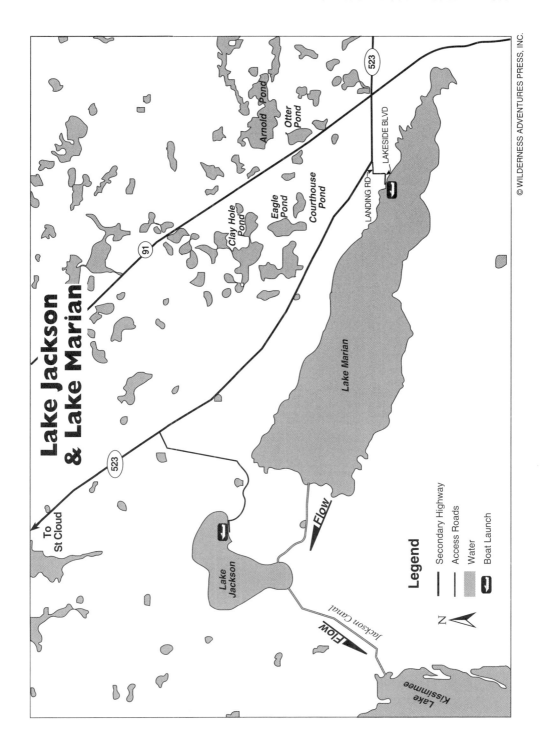

Lake Jackson
& Lake Marian

To
St Cloud

523

91

Arnold Pond

Otter Pond

Eagle Pond

Clay Hole Pond

Courthouse Pond

523

LAKESIDE BLVD

LANDING RD

Lake Marian

Lake Jackson

Flow

Jackson Canal

Flow

Lake Kissimmee

Legend

N

Secondary Highway
Access Roads
Water
Boat Launch

from the town of St. Cloud (see directions to East Lake Tohopekaliga) on CR 523 (Canoe Creek Road) for 25.8 miles. Turn right into the main entrance (this is the second entrance) of the Three Lakes Wildlife Management Area and follow the unpaved road for 2 miles. Turn right again and go 1.1 miles to the single-lane ramp. There is unimproved parking for eight vehicles.

Lake Marian is a deep lake for this area, with mid-lake depths of 20 feet. The lake is oriented so that it lays east/west, and the ends are typically shallow as they merge into the marsh. Grass and bonnets grow out from the surrounding shorelines and provide excellent cover for fish. Lake Marian has a reputation for being one of the best crappie lakes in the entire state. That is easily overlooked when the surrounding larger lakes in the Kissimmee Chain get so much national attention for their tremendous fishing opportunities for a variety of species. In midsummer and midwinter, look to the open water and let your Clouser sink, counting down to increasing depths until you locate the crappie. These fish like to suspend, but rarely rise to take a fly. Once the depth at which they are holding is determined, return to that depth and you should be able to catch more fish. Look for crappie to move toward shoreline cover (bulrush, cattails, Kissimmee grass, and lily pads) by early January. Flyfishers using Clousers or fly patterns that imitate small baitfish can easily catch them. Lake Marian has a good population of bass but it is not on par with the other excellent lakes in the southern part of the Kissimmee Chain. Bream fishing can be excellent on Lake Marian, especially from March to April, in and about the same shoreline vegetation.

The public ramp is at the northeast corner of Lake Marian. To get there from the town of St. Cloud, go south (see directions to East Lake Tohopekaliga) on CR 523 (Canoe Creek Road) for 30 miles. Turn right onto Landing Road and go 0.6 mile. Turn right onto Lakeside Blvd. and go 0.3 mile to the single-lane ramp.

Lake Jackson is the largest lake in the Avon Park/Sebring area and has a good population of largemouth bass.

LAKE WEOHYAKAPKA (WALK-IN-WATER)

Lake Weohyakapka (7,528 acres) is more commonly referred to as Lake Walk-in-Water. This lake is another lake in the Lower Kissimmee Chain of Lakes that is ranked as one of Florida's top 10. It is known nationally for its largemouth bass fishing and is highly regarded for large numbers of bass and the really big bucketmouths that are mixed in.

You already may be having difficulty deciding whether to fish Lake Toho and Lake Kissimmee at this point, but the decision may be even tougher. Lake Walk-in-Water regularly yields catches of 25 to 30 bass per day, with most fish weighing 2 to 4 pounds and a generous number of 5- to 7-pound fish joining the bag. An angler also has a very realistic shot at catching a largemouth weighing in excess of 8 pounds. In support of the big fish prediction, I offer the following: Florida has a citation program that recognizes anglers who catch exceptionally large fish by awarding them a certificate. For example, in the first half of 2001, there were 244 certificates issued statewide for largemouth bass. Of this number, 75 came from Lake Walk-in-Water. Another 31 came from the Stick Marsh/Farm 13 in Region 1. Almost half of the citations awarded statewide for bass came from these two bodies of water, and Lake Walk-in-Water had two and a half times as many of the next most productive lake. Looking at it another way, one-third of all bass qualifying for a citation from around the state came from this one lake.

Lake Walk-in-Water is another soup-bowl-shaped lake with depths that reach a maximum of 10 to 12 feet. The lake averages about 5 or 6 feet deep, and the bottom is usually visible in the clear water. There is little development along the shoreline and, hence, few pollutants. Vegetation includes hydrilla, bulrush, cattail, and eelgrass. Tiger Creek, located in the southwest corner, is the major feeder creek, and the lake drains onward to the Kissimmee Chain by way of Weohyakapka Creek and Lake Rosalie. The primary forage in the lake is shad, glass minnows, and grass shrimp. Try casting a fly that imitates one of these forage foods near the edge of hydrilla for your best shot at a lunker largemouth.

There are special regulations on Lake Walk-in-Water for anglers fishing for largemouth bass. A slot limit is in place that requires all bass between 15 and 24 inches be immediately released. There is also a daily bag limit of three bass, only one of which may be greater than 24 inches.

In addition to the outstanding bass fishing, Lake Walk-in-Water yields impressive stringers of crappie, bluegill, and shellcrackers. Fishing techniques are the same here as they are in other lakes. The crappie will be suspended over the deepest water in midsummer and midwinter, moving toward the shallows to spawn in early January. These shallow spawning areas next hold bass, then bluegill and shellcrackers. Panfish can be caught well into summer.

There are two launch sites, both on the west side of Lake Walk-in-Water. To get to the lake, take Exit 23 off I-4 and go south on US 27/SR 25 for 23 miles to the town of Lake Wales. At the intersection with SR 60 in Lake Wales, turn left and go east for

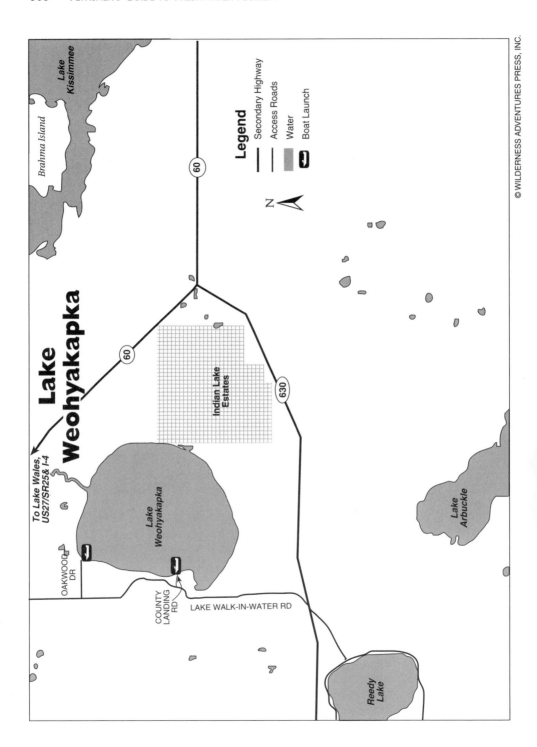

Lake Kissimmee

Brahma Island

Legend

— Secondary Highway
— Access Roads
Water
Boat Launch

N

60

60

630

Lake Weohyakapka

To Lake Wales, US27/SR25& I-4

Indian Lake Estates

Lake Weohyakapka

Lake Arbuckle

OAKWOOD DR

COUNTY LANDING RD

LAKE WALK-IN-WATER RD

Reedy Lake

© WILDERNESS ADVENTURES PRESS, INC.

8.8 miles. Turn right onto Lake Walk-in-Water Road and go south for 2 miles. Turn left and go east on Oakwood Drive for 1 mile to the single-lane fee ramp.

The other launch site is at a county park to the south. Continue on Lake Walk-in-Water Road for another 2.5 miles. Turn left onto Boat Landing Road and go east for 0.4 mile to the single-lane ramp.

Lake Weohyakapka (Walk-in-Water) currently yields more large bass than any other lake in the state.

Efforts are being made to restore the Kissimmee River (here, below the SR 60 Bridge) to its meandering ways.

KISSIMMEE RIVER

The Kissimmee River was once a great fishery whose fish-filled waters snaked slowly southward from central Florida on toward Lake Okeechobee. Although the straight-line distance between the headwaters and the river's end was substantially less, a canoeist would have covered more than 100 miles of wetland habitat that harbored countless bald eagles and migratory birds, along with more than 35 species of fish. The flow was sluggish and hundreds of square miles of marsh would frequently flood when the river rose even slightly.

Yielding to public pressure to provide more adequate flood control, as well as to make productive lands available for agricultural use, the U.S. Army Corps of Engineers channeled the Kissimmee River into a 56-mile-long, 30-foot-deep, 300-foot-wide ditch in the 1960s, known today as the C-38 Canal. Before its completion in 1971, the canal's negative impacts were already being observed. Water quality was deteriorating, and a 90 percent decline in waterfowl had been noted along the corridor. In addition, as lands were converted to agricultural use, nutrients from fertilizer-enriched soil seeped into the water and were delivered straight into Lake Okeechobee, the freshwater source of much of south Florida's drinking water. Water flow was negligible in Okeechobee and significant algae blooms covered much of the lake, depleting oxygen from the water and resulting in massive fish kills.

In the early 1990s Congress recognized that the only solution was to restore the

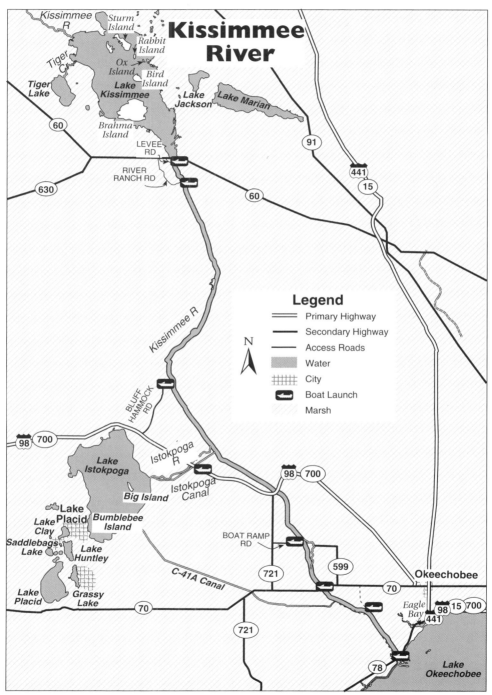

Kissimmee River

Legend

— Primary Highway
— Secondary Highway
— Access Roads
▓ Water
▦ City
⛴ Boat Launch
░ Marsh

N

© WILDERNESS ADVENTURES PRESS, INC.

Kissimmee River to its meandering ways. A massive restoration project was undertaken. Today, there are 43 miles of meandering river, and more than 25,000 acres of wetlands once again grace the river's shoreline. While it shows only a shadow of the beauty that was previously present, the river again can be fished and enjoyed.

Largemouth bass are present, with an occasional good-sized fish taking a fly. Assorted members of the panfish family also cooperate by taking small poppers and terrestrial patterns, especially near structure on the outside bends of turns.

Reminiscent of rivers in Region 2, there is not a good road system that permits easy access to the Kissimmee River. There is a launch site at the northern end of the river just below the lock at the southern tip of Lake Kissimmee. To get there, (see the last launch site for Kissimmee Lake) turn south onto Levee Road at the west end of the SR 60 Bridge and go 0.8 mile to the single-lane ramp. (You will pass the launch site above the lock leading back into Lake Kissimmee.) There is unimproved parking for 30 vehicles.

There is another single-lane ramp about a mile and a half downstream. To get there, about one mile west of the SR 60 Bridge crossing the southern tip of Lake Kissimmee, turn south onto River Ranch Road and go 3 miles to the launch site.

The next launch site is about 25 miles downstream. From the US 98 Kissimmee River Bridge at the community of Fort Basinger, go west on US 98 for 11 miles. Turn right onto Bluff Hammock Road and go north for 4.2 miles to the single-lane ramp at the end of the road.

The next launch site on the river is another 20 miles downstream at a county park. From the US 98 Kissimmee River Bridge, turn south on CR 721 and go 4.5 miles. Turn left onto Boat Ramp Road and go 1.9 miles to the single lane ramp at what is referred to as Nine Mile Grade. There is unimproved parking for 60 vehicles.

The next launch site downstream is only a river mile away, but you must approach it from the opposite (east) side of the river. From the SR 70 Kissimmee River Bridge, go east for 1.5 miles and turn left onto CR 599 (N.W. 128th Avenue/Gache Road). Go north on CR 599 for 5.7 miles (it makes a 90-degree left turn after 3 miles) to the single-lane ramp at Platts Bluff. There is unimproved parking for 20 vehicles.

The last ramp in the fishable part of the Kissimmee River is at the SR 70 Kissimmee River Bridge. Beyond this single-lane ramp, the river is basically a ditch for the last 10 miles south to Lake Okeechobee.

PARRISH LAKE

Parrish Lake (6,000 acres) is a manmade reservoir created to hold cooling water for the Manatee Power Plant. While it has a very good population of bass, bream, and crappie, they are only average in size (which is not a bad thing). This lake is not a place around which to plan a trip, however.

To get to Parrish Lake, take Exit 43 off I-75 near Bradenton and go north on US 301/SR 43 for 7 miles. Turn right and go east on SR 62 for 5 miles to the power plant entrance. Turn left into the power plant and go 0.5 mile, then go right along the lake's edge for 2.7 miles to the single-lane ramp.

LAKE BUFFUM

Lake Buffum (2,000 acres) is about 10 miles south of the Winter Haven Chain of Lakes and 15 miles west of the Kissimmee Chain of Lakes. It stands alone (not being part of any chain) and does not offer the outstanding fishing present in the aforementioned chains. The lake is irregularly shaped, with a small amount of residential development on the west end. Shallow coves on the east and west ends of the lake offer some escape from the wind and are favorite sunrise/sunset spots for bass and bream.

To get to Lake Buffum, get off I-4 at Exit 23 and go south on US 27/SR 25 for 25 miles. Turn right at the intersection with CR 640 (Cutoff Road) and go 4 miles west to the railroad tracks. Cross the tracks and turn left onto Lake Buffum Road. It will make a series of hard right and left turns as it skirts the lake about a mile away. Stay on Lake Buffum Road for 7.5 miles to Lindsey Road. Turn left and go 1.2 miles to the single-lane ramp on your right.

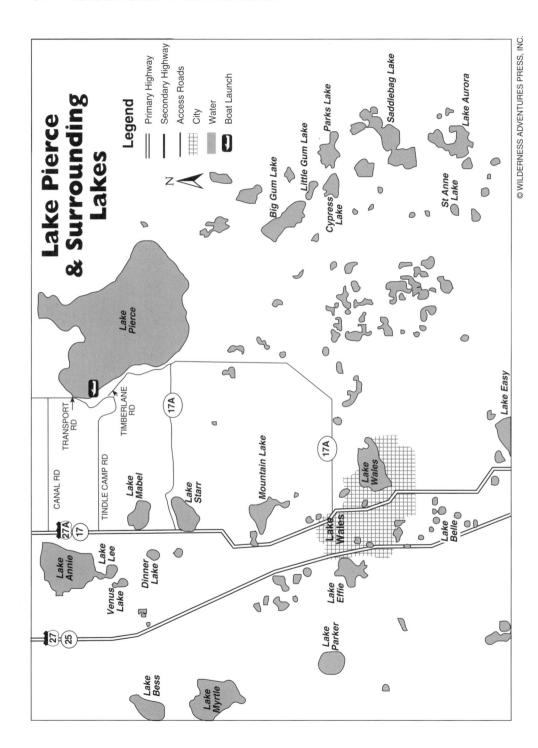

Lake Pierce & Surrounding Lakes

Legend

Primary Highway
Secondary Highway
Access Roads
City
Water
Boat Launch

N

Big Gum Lake
Little Gum Lake
Parks Lake
Saddlebag Lake
Lake Aurora
Cypress Lake
St Anne Lake

Lake Pierce

TRANSPORT RD
TIMBERLANE RD
CANAL RD
TINDLE CAMP RD

17A

17A

Mountain Lake

Lake Easy

Lake Mabel

Lake Starr

Lake Wales

Lake Wales

Lake Belle

27A
17

Lake Annie

Lake Lee

Venus Lake

Dinner Lake

Lake Effie

27
25

Lake Parker

Lake Bess

Lake Myrtle

LAKE PIERCE, LAKE ANNIE, LAKE MABEL, DINNER LAKE, LAKE STARR, MOUNTAIN LAKE, LAKE WALES, BIG GUM LAKE, LITTLE GUM LAKE, CYPRESS LAKE, PARKS LAKE, SADDLEBAG LAKE, AND LAKE AURORA

This group of lakes is about 5 miles north and east of the town of Lake Wales. They are small for the most part, with only Lake Pierce (3,729 acres) having a launch site. Pierce has quite a bit of development along its northern and western shorelines, with numerous docks extending out into the lake. It averages about 5 or 6 feet deep, sloping gradually to 10 to 12 feet in the middle. The lake has bonnets (lily pads) and peppergrass, which provide excellent habitat for largemouth bass and crappie. In early spring, pay close attention to the long arm in the northeast corner. This is a favorite spawning area for crappie, followed by bass, and finally bream. In summer, look to the shade of the docks for largemouth bass and get your fly close to the pilings. A cast that is two feet might as well be 20 feet away. Look for crappie to be suspended over the open water in summer and winter.

To get to Lake Pierce, leave I-4 at Exit 23 and go south on US 27/SR 25 for 17.5 miles. Turn left onto CR 540 (Waverly Road) and go east for 2 miles. Turn left onto US 27A/SR 17 and go north for 1.2 miles. Turn right onto Canal Road and go east for 3 miles. Turn right onto Timberlane Road and go south 1 mile along the edge of the lake. The single-lane ramp will be on your left.

*The sunrises are spectacular and so is the
fishing—ask angler Brian Penrose.*

CROOKED LAKE, LAKE EASY, BLUE LAKE, LAKE LEONORE, LAKE MOODY, LAKE CLINCH, REEDY LAKE, LAKE LIVINGSTON, LAKE STREETY, AND LAKE ARBUCKLE

This group of lakes is about 5 miles to the south and east of the town of Lake Wales. They offer very good bass fishing, as well as plenty of opportunities for bream and crappie. Each lake differs from the rest in residential development, bottom contour, and shoreline shape.

Crooked Lake (4,500 acres) is the largest in this group and has the most irregular shoreline. With a "dog-leg right," it has segments running north/south, as well as an arm that runs east/west. You should always be able to get out of the wind and fly fish a productive lee shoreline somewhere on this lake. The western side of the southern end is shallower, and fish spawn here in early spring. To reach the east side of Crooked Lake, get off I-4 at Exit 23 and go south on US 27/SR 25 (through the town of Lake Wales) for 25 miles. Turn left onto CR 640 and go east 1 mile. At the merger with US 27A/SR 17, go south on US 27A/SR 17 for 5 miles. Turn right onto West Cody Villa Road and go west for 1 mile to the one-lane ramp.

There is another launch site at the south end of Crooked Lake. Continue going south on US 27/SR 25 for another 5 miles (30 miles from I-4). Turn left onto CR 630 and go east for 1 mile. Turn left onto the dirt road (Keen Park Road) and go north for 0.4 mile to the single-lane ramp. There is unimproved parking for 45 vehicles.

Reedy Lake (3,486 acres) borders the west side of the town of Frostproof and has a lot of residential development. Nonetheless, it has a very good fishery, most notably for crappie. Try the fish attractors for suspended fish in midwinter and midsummer. You will need a sink-tip line to get your Clouser down. Make note of the level at which you find the slabsides. For largemouth bass, try fishing in the shade next to docks.

To get to Reedy Lake, continue as above for Crooked Lake (south from I-4 for 30 miles on US 27, then left onto CR 630). Go 4 miles east on CR 630 and continue straight onto North Lake Reedy Blvd. as CR 630 makes a sweeping left turn. The single-lane ramp is 0.5 mile straight ahead.

Lake Arbuckle (3,828 acres) is three miles east of Reedy Lake, and it is regarded as the area's most pristine body of water. There is no residential development or agricultural runoff into Lake Arbuckle, and the water is remarkably clear. Anglers fishing over submerged grass beds make excellent catches of bass, bluegill, and crappie.

To get to Lake Arbuckle, make the left turn off US 27/SR 25 onto CR 630 (30 miles south of Exit 23 off I-4). Go east on CR 630 for 3 miles and turn right onto US 27A/SR 17. Go south on US 27A/SR 17 for 2.1 miles, and turn left onto Wilson Road. Go east on Wilson Road for 4.5 miles (Reedy Lake is on your left). In the middle of a sweeping left turn, you make a right onto Lake Arbuckle Road and go 3.3 miles to the single-lane ramp.

Lake Livingston (1,450 acres) is still farther south, almost to Avon Park. It is sur-

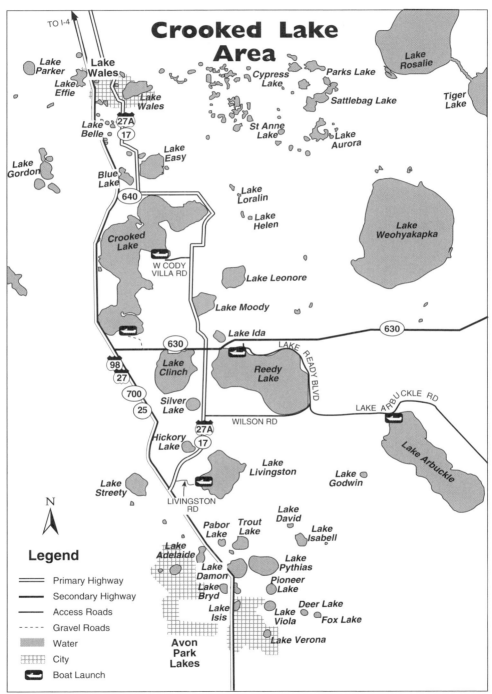

Crooked Lake Area

TO I-4

Lake Parker
Lake Wales
Lake Effie
Lake Wales
27A
17
Lake Belle
Lake Easy
Lake Gordon
Blue Lake
640
Crooked Lake
W CODY VILLA RD
Cypress Lake
Parks Lake
Sattlebag Lake
St Anne Lake
Lake Aurora
Lake Loralin
Lake Helen
Lake Leonore
Lake Moody
Lake Ida
630
Lake Clinch
630
Reedy Lake
LAKE READY BLVD
98
27
700
25
Silver Lake
Hickory Lake
27A
17
WILSON RD
Lake Livingston
Lake Godwin
LAKE ARBUCKLE RD
Lake Arbuckle
Lake Streety
LIVINGSTON RD
Pabor Lake
Trout Lake
Lake David
Lake Isabell
Lake Adelaide
Lake Damon
Lake Bryd
Lake Isis
Lake Pythias
Pioneer Lake
Deer Lake
Lake Viola
Fox Lake
Lake Verona
Avon Park Lakes

Lake Rosalie
Tiger Lake
Lake Weohyakapka

N

Legend

Primary Highway
Secondary Highway
Access Roads
Gravel Roads
Water
City
Boat Launch

© WILDERNESS ADVENTURES PRESS, INC.

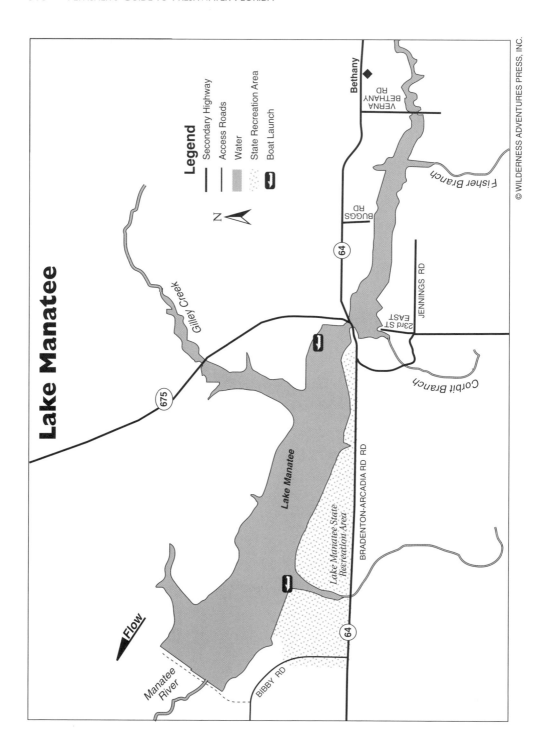

Lake Manatee

rounded by marsh and has no development on its shorelines. This is the shallowest lake in the group, and it can be rough when the wind blows, despite its smaller size. Lake Livingston has a good population of small bass and bream, but otherwise is not a "destination" lake.

To get there, continue south on US 27/SR 25 for 38 miles after leaving I-4 at Exit 23. Turn left onto US 27A/SR 17 and go north for 0.7 mile. Turn right onto Livingston Road and go 0.5 mile to the single-lane ramp.

LAKE MANATEE

Lake Manatee (2,500 acres) is a manmade lake created by damming the east fork of the Manatee River and it serves as a water reservoir for two counties. It is a narrow lake (barely a mile wide at the lower, western end) with a long, east/west axis that runs for nearly five miles. Numerous creeks deposit their waters into the lake. Lake Manatee Recreation Area stretches for three miles along the southern shoreline and includes a launch site and camping facilities. The lake offers good fishing for large-mouth bass, bream, and crappie. In midwinter and midsummer, look to the open water at the deep, western end of the lake for suspended fish. During the spawning period, move into shallow areas at the eastern end and along the northern arm of the lake. Sunshine bass have been stocked and fishing for them can be quite good, especially around the mouths of feeder streams. If you see birds diving on shad in open water, be sure to cast a white Gurgler or baitfish imitation into the mix. Outboard motors are restricted to 10 hp and less.

To get to the south side of Lake Manatee near the dam, take Exit 42 off I-75 and go east on SR 64 (Bradenton Arcadia Road) for 7 miles to the Lake Manatee Recreation Area entrance on your left. Follow the signs to the single-lane ramp and paved parking.

There is another launch site on the north side of the lake. Continue east on SR 64 past the park for another 3 miles. Turn left onto CR 675 (Rutland Road) after crossing the lake and go north for 0.5 mile. Turn left onto the old CR 675 and go 0.3 mile to the single-lane ramp.

LAKE MYAKKA AND LOWER MYAKKA LAKE

Impounding the small but beautiful Myakka River created Lake Myakka (2,400 acres) upstream and Lower Myakka Lake (1,200 acres) downstream, and they each flooded a wide expanse of marsh and prairie. While the fishing is good for largemouth bass and assorted bream, the fish lack size compared to those from the lakes of central Florida.

Myakka River State Park on the southern shoreline is one of Florida's largest and most diverse natural areas. The "Florida Wild and Scenic" Myakka River flows through 45 square miles of wetlands, prairies, hammocks and pinelands. The river and its two shallow lakes attract a myriad of wetland creatures making birding, canoeing, fishing and wildlife observation popular activities. Cabins are available for rent. In addition to the cabins and launch site, camping is available and canoes can be rented.

A 7-mile scenic drive winds through shady oak-palm hammocks and along the shore of the Upper Myakka Lake. Over 39 miles of hiking trails and many miles of dirt roads provide access to the remote interior.To reach the single-lane ramp at Myakka River State Park, get off I-75 at Exit 37 and go east on SR 72 (Proctor Road) for 10 miles. Turn left onto Myakka State Park Road and go north for 3 miles to the park entrance. Follow the signs to the ramp and paved parking.

Fishing is good for one species or another all year long in Florida.

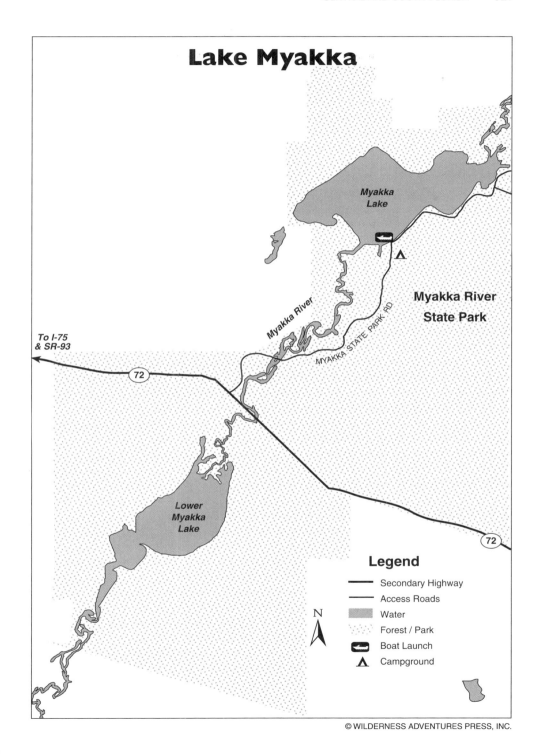

Lake Myakka

Myakka
Lake

Myakka River

Myakka River
State Park

MYAKKA STATE PARK RD

To I-75
& SR-93

72

Lower
Myakka
Lake

72

Legend

— Secondary Highway
— Access Roads
Water
Forest / Park
Boat Launch
Campground

N

LAKE LELIA, LAKE TULANE, LAKE ANOKA, LAKE GLENADA, LAKE PYTHIAS, PIONEER LAKE, LAKE VIOLA, LAKE VERONA, LAKE LOTELA, LAKE LETTA, LAKE DENTON, BONNET LAKE, LITTLE REDWATER LAKE, LAKE SEBRING, DINNER LAKE, LAKE JACKSON, HUCKLEBERRY LAKE, WOLF LAKE, RUTH LAKE, LAKE CHARLOTTE, AND RED BEACH LAKE

On the southwest side of the community of Avon Park (and all within five miles of town), there are several small lakes set close to one another. Many of the lakes are in the midst of orange groves, while others now have residential communities on their shorelines. These lakes have very good bass fishing, both for numbers of fish and size. Bream also grow big in these fertile waters. Given their small size, getting to a lee shoreline and out of the wind is never a problem. The lakes have sandy bottoms for the most part and many have deep holes going 20 feet and more. Shorelines tend to be bowl-shaped with subsurface grass and bonnets extending out into the lake for some distance. This area is worth considering, as you can try a different body of water in the morning and afternoon—fishing several days without hitting the same water. You always have the potential for catching a big bass, and you will likely have some success on each of the lakes. In midwinter and midsummer, be sure to visit the deep holes, as both bass and crappie like to suspend in the cooler water there.

To get to Avon Park, get off I-4 at Exit 23 and go south on US 27/SR 25 (through the town of Lake Wales) for 40 miles to Avon Park. I will give directions to each of the lakes from the intersection of US 27/SR 25 with SR 64 in the middle of the town, just east of the municipal airport.

Lake Lelia (165 acres): Go south on US 27/SR 25 for 1.5 miles. Turn left onto Martin Road and go 0.2 mile to the single-lane ramp.

Lake Glenada (177 acres): Go south on US 27/SR 25 for 2 or 3 miles. Turn right onto Ponce DeLeon Blvd. and go east for 0.1 mile. Turn left onto Bass Lane and go north for 0.2 mile to the single-lane ramp.

Pioneer Lake (93 acres): Go north on US 27/SR 25 for 1.3 miles to Stryker Road (CR 17A truck route). Turn right onto Stryker Road and go east for 1 mile. Turn left onto Oak Park Avenue and go north for 0.7 mile. Turn right onto Shockley Road and go east for 0.2 mile. Lastly, turn right and the single-lane ramp is at the end of the block.

Lake Lotela (802 acres): Go east on SR 64 for 1.7 miles. Turn right onto SR 17 and go south for 2 miles. Turn right onto Lake Lotela Drive and go around the southeast side of the lake for 1.3 miles to the single-lane ramp.

Lake Letta (478 acres): Go east on SR 64 for 1.7 miles to the intersection with SR 17. Turn right onto SR 17 and go south for 3 miles to the lake access road on your

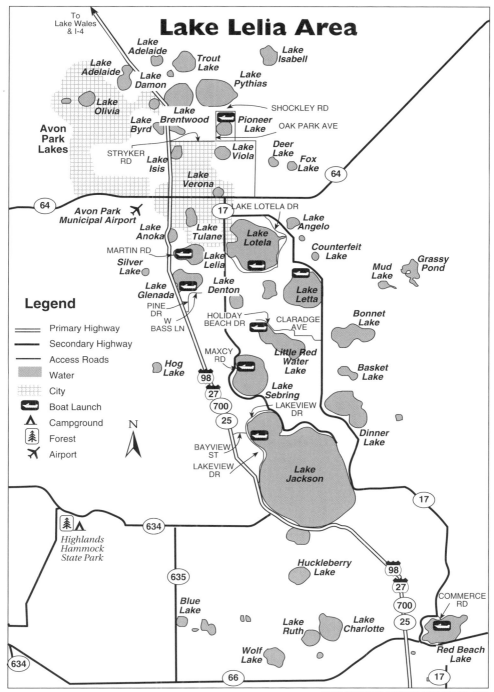

Lake Lelia Area

To Lake Wales & I-4

Lake Adelaide

Lake Adelaide

Lake Damon

Trout Lake

Lake Isabell

Lake Pythias

Lake Olivia

Avon Park Lakes

Lake Byrd

Lake Brentwood

SHOCKLEY RD

Pioneer Lake

OAK PARK AVE

STRYKER RD

Lake Isis

Lake Viola

Deer Lake

Fox Lake

64

Lake Verona

64

Avon Park Municipal Airport

17

LAKE LOTELA DR

Lake Anoka

Lake Tulane

Lake Lotela

Lake Angelo

Counterfeit Lake

Mud Lake

Grassy Pond

MARTIN RD

Silver Lake

Lake Lelia

Lake Glenada

Lake Denton

Lake Letta

Bonnet Lake

Legend

PINE DR

W BASS LN

HOLIDAY BEACH DR

CLARADGE AVE

— Primary Highway

— Secondary Highway

— Access Roads

Water

City

Boat Launch

Campground

Forest

Airport

Hog Lake

MAXCY RD

Little Red Water Lake

Basket Lake

98

Lake Sebring

27

LAKEVIEW DR

700

25

BAYVIEW ST

LAKEVIEW DR

Dinner Lake

Lake Jackson

17

634

Highlands Hammock State Park

Huckleberry Lake

98

635

27

COMMERCE RD

Blue Lake

700

Lake Ruth

Lake Charlotte

25

Red Beach Lake

634

Wolf Lake

66

17

N

right. The single-lane ramp is 0.1 mile ahead, with unimproved parking for 25 vehicles.

Little Redwater Lake (329 acres): Go east on SR 64 for 1.7 miles to the intersection with SR 17. Turn right and go south on SR 17 for 6 miles to Claradge Avenue. Turn right and go 1.2 miles to Sunset Lane. Turn right and go 0.2 mile and when the road becomes Holiday Beach Drive, go another 0.5 mile to the single-lane ramp. There is unimproved parking for 15 vehicles.

Lake Sebring (468 acres): Go south on US 27/SR 25 for 4 miles. Turn left onto Maxcy Road and go 0.6 mile to the single-lane ramp. There is unimproved parking for 10 vehicles.

Lake Jackson (3,412 acres): Go south on US 27/SR 25 for 5 miles. Turn left onto Bayview Street and go east for 0.4 mile to the single lane ramp. There is a second ramp 0.5 mile to the south. When you get to the side of the lake off Bayview Street, turn right onto Lakeview Drive (CR 634) and go south for 0.5 mile. The single-lane ramp will be on your left.

Red Beach Lake (335 acres): Go south on US 27/SR 25 for 11 miles (going around the south side of Lake Jackson in Sebring) to the intersection where US 98 goes to the left. Turn left onto US 98 and go east for 0.3 mile to SR 17. Turn left onto SR 17 and go north for 0.9 mile to Commerce Street. Turn right onto Commerce Street and go 0.2 mile to the single-lane ramp. There is unimproved parking for 15 vehicles.

LAKE JOSEPHINE, PERSIMMON LAKE, REDWATER LAKE, CENTER LAKE NELLIE, LAKE APTHORPE, LAKE SIMMONS, LAKE FRANCIS, LAKE HENRY, LAKE JUNE-IN-WINTER, LAKE CLAY, LAKE SIRENA, LAKE PEARL, LAKE McCOY, LAKE HUNTLEY, GRASSY LAKE, AND LAKE PLACID

Continuing south (15 miles) down US 27/SR 25 from Avon Park, and between the towns of Sebring and Lake Placid, there is another group of lakes that offers very good fly fishing. These lakes are bigger, on average, than those around Avon Park. Lake Francis and the smaller lakes without ramps are bowl-shaped, but the others offer irregular shorelines that are good for both fish and flyfishers. Some of the lakes have very deep holes, especially by Florida standards. Lake Placid has a hole in the southwest corner that is over 40 feet deep. The water temperature varies significantly from top to bottom in these holes, and you will need to methodically search for the depth at which fish are suspended. Except for the spring spawn, these holes are favorite haunts that should be probed on each visit. These lakes have some big bass, as well as good populations of crappie and bream. For the largemouth bass and crappie, look to the shallow pockets in early spring and put on a sinking line for deep, open water in midsummer and midwinter. The bream will move into the shallows in

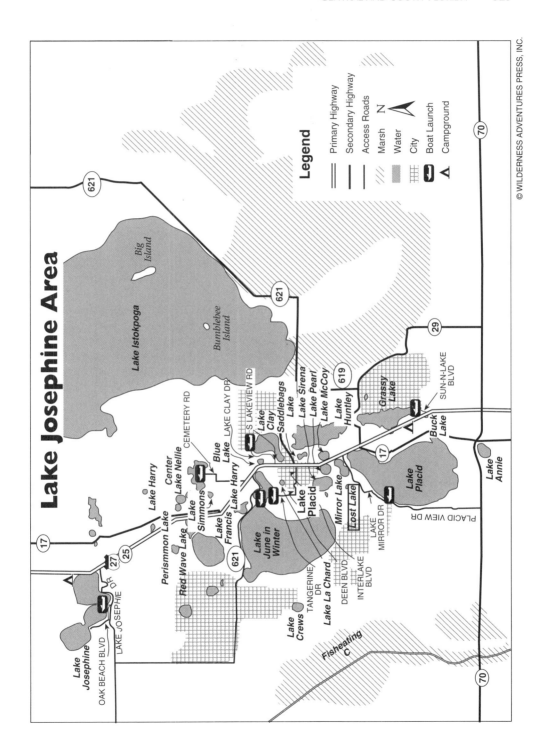

Lake Josephine Area

Legend

Primary Highway
Secondary Highway
Access Roads
Marsh
Water
City
Boat Launch
Campground

N

© WILDERNESS ADVENTURES PRESS, INC.

Big Island

Lake Istokpoga

Bumblebee Island

Lake Harry

CEMETERY RD

Center
Lake Nellie

Blue Lake

LAKE CLAY DR

S LAKEVIEW RD

Lake Clay

Saddlebags Lake

Lake Sirena

Lake Pearl

Lake McCoy

Lake Huntley

619

Grassy Lake

SUN-N-LAKE BLVD

Buck Lake

Lake Annie

Lake Placid

Lake Harry

Lake Simmons

Lake Francis

Lake June in Winter

Lake Placid

Mirror Lake

Lost Lake

LAKE MIRROR DR

MIRROR DR

PLACID VIEW DR

Lake Placid

Perismmon Lake

Red Wave Lake

LAKE JOSEPHIE

OAK BEACH BLVD

Lake Josephine

Lake Crews

TANGERINE DR

Lake La Chard

DEEN BLVD

INTERLAKE BLVD

Fisheating C

17

25

27

621

621

621

17

29

70

70

A

late spring and stay there on into summer. The deeper lakes, especially Lake June-in-Winter and Lake Placid, definitely require a sink-tip or sinking line to get down to where fish will be holding.

I will give directions to these lakes from the intersection of SR 621 with US 27/SR 25 in downtown Lake Placid. To get to Lake Placid, take Exit 23 of I-4 and go south on US 27/SR 25 (through the towns of Lake Wales and Avon Park) for 60 miles to Avon Park.

Lake Josephine (1,236 acres): Go north on US 27/SR 25 for 7 miles to Lake Josephine Drive. Turn left and go west for 2.8 miles to Gresham Road. Turn right and go north for 0.8 mile to Oak Beach Blvd. Turn right and go 0.1 mile to the single-lane ramp. There is unimproved parking for 15 vehicles.

Lake Apthorpe 219 acres): Go north on US 27/SR 25 for 1.5 miles to Cemetery Road. Turn right onto Cemetery Road and go north for 1.5 miles to the single-lane ramp.

Lake Francis (539 acres): Go north on US 27/SR 25 for 3 miles to Clover Leaf Road. Turn left and go east on Clover Leaf Road for 0.8 mile to the single-lane ramp. There is unimproved parking for 15 vehicles.

Lake June-in-Winter (3,504 acres): Go north on US 27/SR 25 fro 1.2 miles. Turn west on CR 621 and go 0.5 mile to the entrance to H.L. Park on your left. Follow the signs to the double-lane ramp inside the park where there is paved parking for 30 vehicles. There is a second launch site to the south on the same arm of Lake June-in-Winter. Go west on Interlake Blvd. for 0.6 mile. Turn right onto Park Drive and go 0.2 mile to Deen Blvd. Turn right and go 0.2 mile to Tangerine Drive. Turn right and go 0.6 mile to City Park. Follow the signs to the single-lane ramp where there is unpaved parking for 30 vehicles.

Lake Clay: Go north on US 27/SR 25 for 1 mile and turn right onto South Lakeview Road. Go 0.3 mile to the lake and turn left onto Lake Clay Drive. Go north around the lake for 0.6 mile to the single-lane ramp at the downtown lake.

Grassy Lake (517 acres): Go south on US 27/SR 25 for 4 miles to Sun-n-Lake Blvd. Turn left and go east for 0.3 mile to the single-lane ramp.

Lake Placid (3,320 acres): Go south on US 27/SR 25 for 1.5 miles to Lake Mirror Drive. Turn right and go 2.2 miles (Lake Mirror Drive becomes Placid View Drive) to the single-lane ramp.

Lake Istokpoga is a shallow lake with a sandy bottom
that can be waded in many places.

LAKE ISTOKPOGA

Lake Istokpoga (27,692 acres) arguably has the best year-round fishing of any lake in Region 3. I realize that we have yet to discuss Lake Okeechobee, that Lake Toho will be coming on strong in a couple of years, that Lake Walk-in-Water is the place right now for big bass, and that Lake Kissimmee will be very strong once again, but Lake Istokpoga may be the place to start fishing on your visit to Florida.

Istokpoga is a shallow lake lying between Lake Okeechobee and Lake Kissimmee. It is the fifth largest lake in the state and averages about 6 to 8 feet deep. Hydrilla is frequently a problem, especially for boats with small motors. Efforts are being made to control the hydrilla and when it is reduced, look to the shorelines for bass and bream. However, when the lake has a lot of hydrilla, it becomes a favorite hangout for bass, and they will be found mid-lake in the vegetation. Because the lake is so shallow and big, it is often quite rough. Know where the nearest marina or canal is located in the event that you need to get out of inclement weather quickly. The shorelines have few trees to knock the wind down, with mostly citrus groves, pastureland, and swamps surrounding the lake. The eastern shoreline has several caladium (a flowering bush) farms, while residential development grows out from the north and southwest corners.

Two feeder creeks enter Lake Istokpoga. Josephine Creek comes from the west and Arbuckle Creek from the north. The areas where these creeks enter the lake

Lake Istokpoga

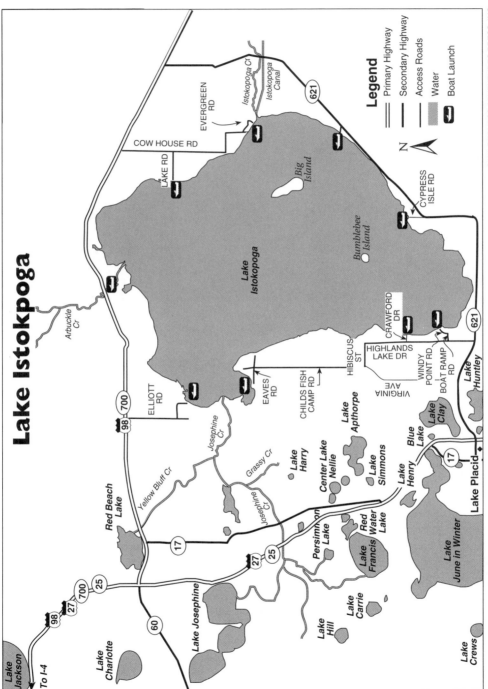

Legend

Primary Highway
Secondary Highway
Access Roads
Water
Boat Launch

N

© WILDERNESS ADVENTURES PRESS, INC.

EVERGREEN RD

COW HOUSE RD

LAKE RD

Istokpoga Cr

Istokpoga Canal

621

Big Island

CYPRESS ISLE RD

Bumblebee Island

Lake Istokpoga

Arbuckle Cr

CRAWFORD DR

621

HIBISCUS ST

HIGHLANDS LAKE DR

WINDY POINT RD

BOAT RAMP RD

Lake Huntley

700

98

ELLIOTT RD

EAVES RD

CHILDS FISH CAMP RD

VIRGINIA AVE

Lake Apthorpe

Lake Clay

Lake Placid

17

Josephine Cr

Lake Harry

Center Lake Nellie

Lake Simmons

Lake Henry

Blue Lake

Red Beach Lake

Yellow Bluff Cr

Grassy Cr

Josephine Cr

Persimmon Lake

Red Water Lake

Lake Francis

Lake June in Winter

17

25

27

Lake Jackson

To I-4

98

27

700

25

60

Lake Charlotte

Lake Josephine

Lake Hill

Lake Carrie

Lake Crews

should be fished in the spring. Water leaves the lake by way of the Istokpoga Canal, going on to the Kissimmee River and the S-68 canal, then to the Kissimmee River and Lake Okeechobee.

The lake gained its original fame for crappie, shellcracker, and bluegill. With a firm sandy bottom, it can be waded. Flyfishers can take numerous panfish on small poppers early and lake in the day. A particularly good wading area is in front of the launch sites off Cow House Road. Recently, the lake has gained quite a reputation for its big bass, and the Florida Game and Freshwater Fish Commission now ranks Lake Istokpoga as one of the top 10 bass lakes in the state. Numerous bass tournaments are held on the lake and bass up to 8 pounds are caught frequently (with 10- to 12-pound fish not uncommon). In March of 1998, a 16-pound largemouth bass was caught. Look for pods of threadfin shad and other baitfish, as these may have been corralled by a school of fish. Often the bass will go on a sudden feeding binge and then turn off without warning. Avoid weekends, if possible, as numerous fishing tournaments are held on Lake Istokpoga.

As is the case in most Florida lakes, bass spawn in the shallows in bulrush and cattail stands near the shoreline. Lake Istokpoga has two large islands in the southeast quadrant, and the waters surrounding them are early spring favorites for crappie and largemouth bass. By April and May, these areas hold large numbers of bream. During summer and winter, look for bigger bass holding in mid-lake areas of submerged vegetation, as well as some schooling bass in the open water in the north end of the lake.

*The southwest corner of Lake Istokpoga is
an excellent area to search for bream.*

There are nine public ramps spread out pretty evenly around the perimeter of Lake Isokpoga. That should be a not-so-subtle indication of how good the lake can be on a year-round basis. I'll give directions starting at the north end and work clockwise around the lake. From I-4, take Exit 23 and go south on US 27/SR 25 (through the town of Lake Wales and south around Lake Jackson) for 50 miles. At the intersection where SR 98 goes to the left (east), turn left onto SR 98 and go east for 7.4 miles. There is a single-lane ramp at Arbuckle Creek that leads south for about a mile to the northernmost part of Lake Isokpoga.

In the northeast corner, there is another launch site. Continue east on SR 98 past the Arbuckle Creek launch site above for another 3.2 miles. Turn right and go south on Cow House Road for 1.3 miles. Turn right again and go east on Lake Road to the single-lane ramp. There is unimproved parking here for 10 vehicles.

The next site is on the eastern shoreline. Continue south (see above) on Cow House Road past the Lake Road turnoff for another 2 miles (Cow House Road will make 90-degree left and right turns). Continue straight onto Evergreen Road (as Cow House Road makes another 90-degree turn to the left) for 0.5 mile to the single-lane ramp. Bird Island is about a mile and a half out into the lake heading southwest.

The last launch site on the eastern shoreline will also give you good access to Bird Island. From the Arbuckle Creek ramp above, continue east on SR 98 for 5.5 miles. Turn right onto CR 621 and go south for 4 miles. Turn right on the unnamed paved road and go 0.3 mile to the single-lane ramp.

The next launch site is in the southeast corner, about 3.5 miles farther south on SR 621, but it is best reached by coming from the south on SR 621. Return to the directions above for Arbuckle Creek. From the US 27/SR 25 intersection with US 98, continue south on US 27/SR 25 for another 10 miles (you are now about 60 miles south of Exit 23 off I-4) to the town of Lake Placid. Turn left onto CR 621 and go north on CR 621 for 7.5 miles. Turn left onto Cypress Isle and go 0.3 mile to the single-lane ramp.

The next two launch sites give access to the southwest corner of Lake Istokpoga from the town of Lake Placid. In Lake Placid, turn left off US 27/SR 25 onto CR 621 and go east for 2.8 miles. Turn left onto CR 619 (Highland Lakes Drive) and go north for 0.7 mile. Turn right onto Windy Point Lane and go 0.3 mile to the single-lane ramp, where there is unimproved parking for 11 vehicles.

Continuing north on CR 619 (Highland Lakes Drive) for another 1.5 miles will get you to the other launch site in the southwestern quadrant of the lake. Turn right onto Crawford Avenue and go 0.1 mile to the single-lane ramp.

To get to the northwest corner, let's go back to the town of Lake Placid. Turn left again onto CR 621 as you did for the previous two sites and go east for 1.5 miles to Virginia Avenue. Turn left onto Virginia Avenue and go north for 3 miles to where it turns into Child's Fish Camp Road. Continue north and go another 3 miles to Eaves Road. Turn left and go 0.2 mile west to the single-lane ramp.

The last access point to Lake Istokpoga is also in the northwest corner. Going back to the Arbuckle Creek directions, turn left off US 27/SR 25 onto US 98 and go east for 4.1 miles. Turn right onto Elliott Road and go south for 1.3 miles to where it makes a 90-degree left turn. Turn left and go another mile to the single-lane ramp.

*Lake Okeechobee is more than 30 miles wide
and long, with numerous grass islands.*

LAKE OKEECHOBEE

Many seasoned anglers from around the country regard Lake Okeechobee (448,000 acres) as the outstanding largemouth bass lake in the world. It has been that good over the years. I believe that praise, once well deserved, now overstates the quality of the fishery, but only by a little. Lake Okeechobee would clearly have to be near the top of any top 10 list of Florida fishing lakes, whether the targeted species is largemouth bass, crappie, or bream. There have recently been some pollution issues (excessive nutrient enrichment), but efforts to return the Kissimmee River (the primary water source for Lake Okeechobee) to its more natural meandering ways, coupled with a good drawdown, will have the Big O back to the very top of the list within a couple of years.

Lake Okeechobee gets its name from the Seminole Indian language. The word "aoki" means water, and "achubi" means big or large. The literal translation of "big

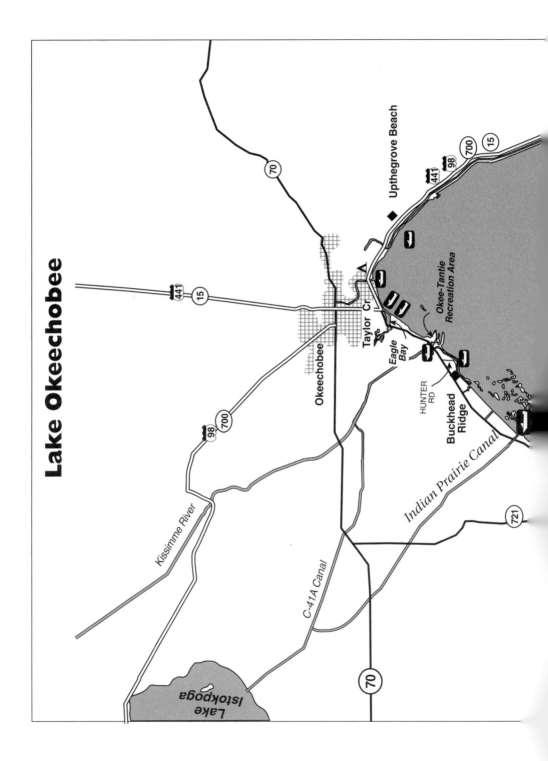

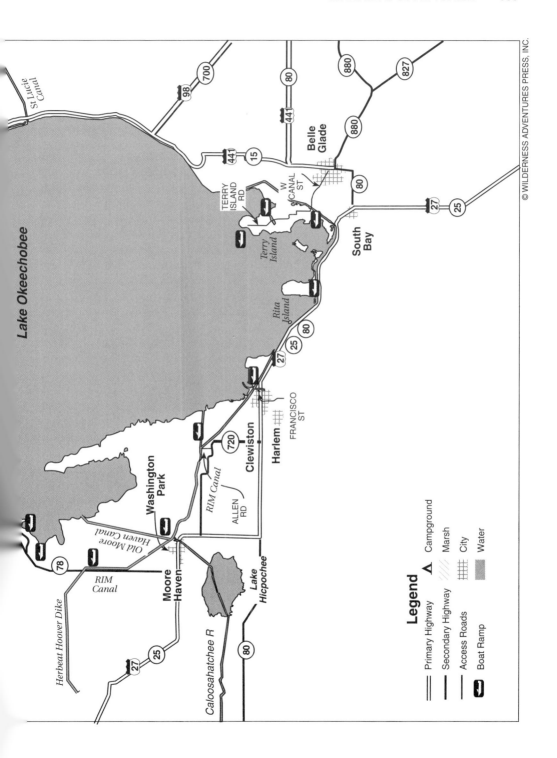

Lake Okeechobee

Belle Glade

South Bay

TERRY ISLAND RD

W CANAL ST

Terry Island

Rita Island

Harlem

FRANCISCO ST

Clewiston

720

RIM Canal

ALLEN RD

Washington Park

Old Moore Haven Canal

Moore Haven

RIM Canal

Herbeat Hoover Dike

Lake Hicpochee

Caloosahatchee R

St Lucie Canal

Legend

△ Campground

Primary Highway

Secondary Highway

Access Roads

Boat Ramp

Marsh

City

Water

water" is quite appropriate, as the lake is more than 30 miles wide and long, with a surface area in excess of 730 square miles. It is the chief component of southern Florida's watershed, holding most of the drinking water for several large coastal communities in the area and providing irrigation water for massive farming operations on reclaimed swampland. Lake Okeechobee averages only about nine feet deep, and when winds come across the wide expanse of open water, it can get rougher here than on any other lake in Florida.

While there are now no communities on the lake's shoreline, that was not always the case. In the late 1920s, a pair of hurricanes crossed southern Florida and Lake Okeechobee. Water was blown out of the lake, flooding much of the surrounding area and killing over 5,000 people. To preclude such a disaster in the future, then-President Hoover approved the building of a dike around the massive lake. When construction was completed, it averaged 34 feet in height and was in excess of 140 miles in length. There is a navigable channel (about 8 feet deep) outside the dike and alongside the highways from which fill was dredged to build the dike. Flyfishers often fish this rim canal for assorted freshwater species, as well as for acrobatic juvenile tarpon and snook. You will likely see several cars pulled off the side of the road and anglers fishing the canal. Watch your backcast, as a large truck hauling farm produce can get you into your backing before you can say "oops" (or whatever else comes to mind). When the wind blows and the open water is not safe, get on the lee side of the lake and the shelter of the dike will provide a break so that you can continue to fly fish.

The primary source of water for Lake Okeechobee (70 percent) is from tributaries, canals, backwater pumping from sugarcane fields, and runoff, while rainfall accounts for the balance. Water escapes primarily by evaporation (70 percent) and the remainder through engineered outflows that regulate lake water levels. Prior to the dikes being built, the water moved out through the south end of the lake and flowed like a sheet into the Everglades. The dikes reduced the size of the lake to its present configuration and made it more stagnate, causing sediment to settle to the previously sandy bottom. After the Kissimmee River was straightened in the late 1960s, agricultural runoff was deposited into Lake Okeechobee in great quantities. By the early 1990s, the lake had reached its capacity to hold the ever-rising level of nutrients and the oxygen depletion caused by algae blooms led to severe fish kills. The lake is recovering nicely now that the Kissimmee River has been somewhat restored so that it no longer carries such a high nutrient level into Okeechobee.

Historically, bulrush growing in shallow water near the shoreline has held the greatest concentration of adult game fishes. With years of intense wave action pounding these shorelines, much of that vegetation had been uprooted. However, submerged vegetation such as hydrilla, eelgrass, and peppergrass still provides important habitat for forage such as minnows, shiners, and small bream, and fish have relocated to mid-lake locations. In the year 2000, the lake level was lowered, and coupled with drought conditions that were then present, the lake's bottom near the shoreline was exposed for quite some distance out into the lake. Much of the sediment and muck dried out and new plant growth has taken hold around the outer edges of the lake. With a cleaner bottom around the edges, new plant growth in the preferred range of the game fish, and less nutrients suspended in the water, the Big O should be back in national prominence very shortly.

Fishing for crappie remains excellent on Okeechobee, and the lake is regarded as the best crappie lake in the state, if not the country. Many anglers from across the country make a spring pilgrimage to the Big O to fish for the tasty slabsides. Although they can be caught year-round, the best time is January and February, when crappie move into the shallows to spawn. A Clouser Minnow cast near shoreline vegetation is likely to yield a strike on any cast. If not, keep moving, as the key is to locate a school. Once found, you will likely catch several in a row. With the lake being so shallow, it is possible to catch crappie at other times of the year, too. Look to canals that have deeper water and get your sink-tip line down to where they are located. A two-pound crappie is quite common.

Largemouth bass in Lake Okeechobee have the fastest growth rate in the state's natural water bodies, with an average gain of 1.3 pounds per year. Add to this the fact that the bass population is dominated by young fish (over 90 percent of bass recently sampled were less than five years old), the potential for fly fishing success is certain for years to come.

Largemouth are going to spawn in February and March. They are opportunistic feeders and will take both deer-hair poppers and flies that resemble forage fish. While bait fishermen using live shiners catch most of the 10-pound-plus fish, a fly-fisher can catch quality fish, too. In summer, look to open water for schooling activity on the surface as bait pods get corralled. This is a good time for a white foam Gurgler (size 1). Be sure to visit the areas around the rim canal that open into the lake, as the flowing water holds bait and largemouth like to congregate in these areas, as well.

Bream spawn around the full moon in March and April. Look again to the shoreline vegetation and try a small popper or a dark terrestrial fly. Often, their crater-like beds can be spotted from a distance. These panfish are scrappy fighters on 5- and 6-weight tackle. Do not overlook the rim canal if you are fishing for bream.

There are several launch sites that give flyfishers access to Lake Okeechobee from every side of the lake. Your best bet is to check wind conditions and launch from the lee side of the lake if at all possible. As an overview, the town of Okeechobee is at the northern tip of the lake. US 441 skirts the east side of lake from Okeechobee to the town of Belle Glade. US 27 runs along the southwestern side of the lake between Belle Glade and the extreme western tip of the lake near the intersection with SR 78. SR 78 runs along the northwestern side of the lake between US 27 and back to the town of Okeechobee. I'll describe access points in a clockwise direction from the intersection of US 98/US 441 and SR 78 (about 2.5 miles south of the town of Okeechobee) with these major routes as the primary arteries of travel.

The first launch site on Okeechobee is at Taylor Creek. Go south on US 98/US 441 for 2.5 miles to the Taylor Creek Bridge. Immediately after crossing the bridge, turn right onto Taylor Creek Lock and Access Road. Go 0.2 mile to the single-lane ramp. There is unimproved parking for 10 vehicles.

Continuing south on the Levee Road (running on top of the dike) for 4 miles, there is another single-lane ramp across from the community of Upthegrove Beach.

It is a long way to the next public launch site on the east side of the lake. From the Taylor Creek Bridge on US 98/US 441 continue south on US 98/US 441 for about 26 miles to the West Palm Beach Canal where US 98 and US 441 split. Continue south on US 441 for 7.5 miles and when it veers to the left, continue straight onto SR 80 (west) for 2.5 miles to the town of Belle Glade. In Belle Glade, turn right onto West Canal Street and go west for 1.5 miles. Bear right onto West Lake Road (CR 717) and continue west for another 1.5 miles to the single-lane ramp on the rim canal.

West Lake Road (CR 717) crosses the rim canal and goes onto Torry Island, where there are two additional launch sites at the southeast corner of the lake. Go 0.2 mile on West Lake Road after crossing the rim canal and turn right onto Torry Island Road. The first launch is 2.5 miles ahead and the second is another 1.5 miles farther ahead at the end of the road. Both sites are one-lane ramps.

There is a launch site behind Ritta Island at the southern end of the lake by Miami Canal. From Belle Glade, continue west on SR 80 for 10 miles (it will join with US 27). Just before crossing the Miami Canal, turn right and go 0.2 mile to the single-lane launch on your left.

Continuing clockwise, the town of Clewiston is 7 miles west on US 27/SR 80. There is a good public launch in Clewiston on the west side of the canal. Turn right onto Francisco Street and go 0.2 mile. Turn right onto Okeechobee Blvd. and continue 0.1 mile to the launch site.

By continuing west on US 27/SR 80 for 2 miles after leaving Clewiston, you can again gain access to the rim canal. Turn right onto CR 720 and go west for 3 miles. Turn right onto Allen Road and go north 0.7 mile to the single-lane ramp. You will need to go (east) through the marsh using the rim canal and not the Okeechobee Waterway (southeast) for about 2 miles to reach the lake.

The next launch on our clockwise route around the lake is off US 27. Go west for 6 miles on US 27/SR 80 and go right (north) on US 27 at the intersection where US 27 and SR 80 divide. Go north for 5 miles and just before crossing the Caloosahatchee Canal in the community of Moore Haven, turn right onto Herbert Hoover Dyke Road and go 0.3 mile to the single-lane ramp. You will need to go north through the marsh for about 6 miles using Old Moore Haven Canal to reach the lake.

Two miles west of the Caloosahatchee Canal is the intersection of US 27 and SR 78 (going east to the town of Okeechobee). Turning right onto SR 78 and going east for 5.5 miles leads to a launch site just before crossing the rim canal. Turn right and go 0.2 mile to the single-lane ramp. There is marsh in front of you for over 4 miles before you reach the open water of the lake.

SR 78 crosses the rim canal about 3 miles to the north of Caloosahatchee Canal and there are single-lane launch sites to your right before and after crossing the bridge over the canal.

Immediately after crossing the bridge, turn right onto CR 721 (Loop Road) and go north for 1.8 miles. There is a single-lane ramp on your right.

You can continue north on CR 721 (Loop Road) for 1.5 miles, or go east on SR 78 for 3.1 miles after crossing the bridge over the rim canal to reach three more launch sites set close together. Turn right onto Mertie Road and go 0.1 mile to the single-lane ramp at the northern end of this segment of the rim canal. The dike extends out into the lake for about half a mile, and there is a double-lane ramp at the end of this finger-like projection called Harney Pond, where there is unimproved parking for 50 vehicles. In addition, by going east on SR 78 for another 0.2 mile, you can turn right and go 0.1 mile on the levee road to the single-lane ramp on the southern end of the next segment of the rim canal. Three ramps in one small area is a strong indication that this is a portion of the lake that is either highly regarded or easily accessed from a metropolitan area. I would suggest that the fishing is good in this area.

By continuing east on SR 78 for another 7.5 miles, you come to Indian Prairie Canal. Turn right at the canal and go 0.5 mile to the single-lane ramp. There is unimproved parking for 50 vehicles.

The town of Okeechobee is about 15 miles east on SR 78. The next ramp, however, is only 7 miles east of the Indian Prairie Canal in the community of Buckhead

A dike more than 30 feet high surrounds Lake Okeechobee
and the rim canal also holds fish.

Ridge on the right side of SR 78. Turn right onto Hunter Road as you enter Buckhead Ridge and go 0.6 mile to the single-lane ramp.

The Kissimmee River enters Lake Okeechobee as you leave Buckhead Ridge. Continue east on SR 78 for 2 miles to the Okee-Taintie Recreation Area on your right. There is a double-lane ramp with parking for 50 vehicles. There are numerous facilities located here.

There are two launch sites in the area of Eagle Bay, which can be reached by continuing east on SR 78 for 0.2 mile after the bridge over the Kissimmee River. Turn right and go over the dike, heading north on the levee road for 3.5 miles. At what is referred to as Culvert 7, there is a three-lane ramp with paved parking for 75 vehicles. The other ramp is 0.5 mile ahead on the levee road. The town of Okeechobee is to the north, so we have completed the loop of the lake.

CALOOSAHATCHEE RIVER

While numerous canals move water from Lake Okeechobee to cities along the southern coast of Florida, the major outflow of water from the lake is the Caloosahatchee River, which flows from the western tip of Okeechobee west to the Gulf of Mexico. This channelized waterway is controlled by a series of locks, and there often can be quite a bit of boat traffic, especially in the lower portions of the river as you approach Ft. Myers. Freshwater species are available in the upper reaches of the river while the lower section near Charlotte Harbor has a good mix of saltwater game fish.

About three miles downstream from the rim canal at Lake Okeechobee, the river widens into a very shallow marsh referred to as Lake Hicpochee (whose size varies greatly depending upon the discharge from Lake Okeechobee). Some fly fishing for largemouth bass and bream can be done as water overflows the river into the marsh, where the river is no longer a straight ditch.

The fishing quality varies greatly in Lake Hicpochee, and water flow is the key. While hardly discernible, if the water level is being raised or lowered, you can catch good numbers of largemouth and bream along shoreline cover. On the other hand, if the water is not flowing, you might think that there is not a fish to be had.

The rest of the Caloosahatchee River has the same need for water movement in order for the fishing to be considered good. In the upper reaches, it is the discharge from Lake Okeechobee that causes movement, while in the lower regions it is tidal flow. Look for largemouth bass and bream to be along shorelines, especially where a drainage ditch joins the river. Cast a small popper or baitfish pattern to the drainage ditch and strip it back into the river. The largemouth will not be as big as those in the Big O, but they often school nicely in front of these ditches.

There are several launch sites along the 50-mile course of the river, but I do not recommend it for freshwater fishing. If the wind is howling from either the north or south, the narrow river would offer a lee side to wet a line, but with the Big O as a neighbor, I'd certainly look to the rim canal for shelter. I'll give directions from Clewiston on the southeastern banks of Lake Okeechobee and move west along the

Caloosahatchee River

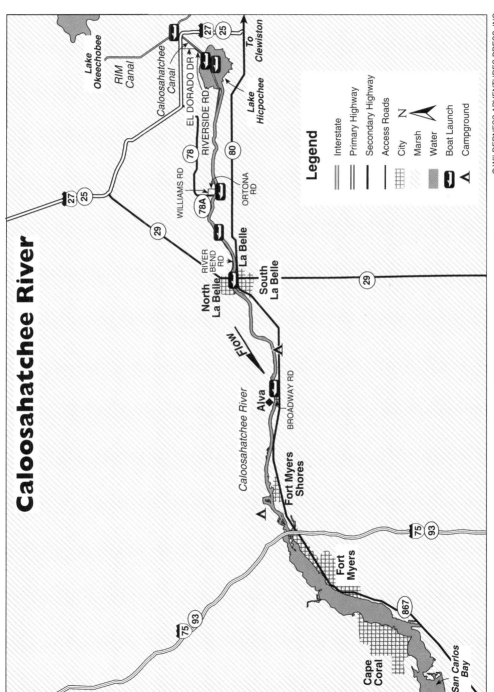

Lake Okeechobee

RIM Canal

Caloosahatchee Canal

To Clewiston

EL DORADO DR

RIVERSIDE RD

Lake Hicpochee

78

80

27 25

27 25

29

WILLIAMS RD

78A

ORTONA RD

La Belle

RIVER BEND RD

North La Belle

South La Belle

29

FLOW

Caloosahatchee River

Alva

BROADWAY RD

Fort Myers Shores

Fort Myers

75 93

Cape Coral

867

San Carlos Bay

75 93

Legend

Interstate	City
Primary Highway	Marsh
Secondary Highway	Water
Access Roads	Boat Launch
N	Campground

Caloosahaatchee River as SR 80 moves west across the southern part of the state. The launch at the rim canal where the river leaves the lake was previously described (see the launch described above for Lake Okeechobee in the community of Moore Haven).

The next launch downstream (about 3 miles) is at the point where the river widens to form Lake Hicpochee. From Clewiston, go west for 6 miles on US 27/SR 80 and turn right (north) on US 27 at the intersection where US 27 and SR 80 divide. Go north on US 27 for 6 miles and after crossing the Caloosahatchee Canal (and as you are about to leave the community of Moore Haven), turn left onto El Dorado Drive and go south for 1.8 miles. Turn right onto Riverside Road and go 1 mile to the single-lane ramp.

There is another single-lane ramp in the middle of Lake Hicpochee. Continue on Riverside Road for another mile on top of the dike extending out into the marsh to the launch on your left.

The next launch is near the Ortona Lock about 10 miles downstream from the previous launch site. To get there, continue north on US 27 after leaving the community of Moore Haven for 5 miles. Turn left onto SR 78 and go west for 9 miles to the intersection with SR 78A. Turn left and go 1 mile on SR 78A and then turn left again onto Williams Road and go east for 0.5 mile. Turn right onto Ortona Road and go 0.6 mile to the single-lane ramp.

The next launch site, although also accessed from the north side of the river, is

Kids from La Belle use the ramp near SR 29 on the
Caloosahatchee River as a swimming hole.

best reached by going west on US 27/SR 80 from Clewiston (and staying on SR 80 after they split about 6 miles west of town) for 28 miles to the town of La Belle. Turn right onto SR 29 and there is a single-lane ramp 0.7 mile north where SR 29 crosses the river.

There is also a single-lane launch about 4 miles upstream from here that can be reached by turning right onto River Bend Road immediately after crossing the SR 29 Bridge in La Belle.

Continuing west another 11.5 miles on SR 80 from La Belle, there is a single-lane ramp to your right just after CR 884 intersects SR 80 from the south but before Broadway Road leading to Alva on the north side of the river. Turn right onto the ramp road and go one block to the launch site. This site can also be reached by going east on SR 80 from Exit 25 off I-75 for 11 miles and making a left onto the ramp road just after passing Broadway Road.

As you continue west and downstream on the Caloosahatchee River, it loses its freshwater characteristics and becomes a coastal river with brackish water and salt-water opportunities. This is a very good thing, as what was previously marginal freshwater fishing now gets quite exciting with the addition of snook, spotted seatrout, and tarpon.

LAKE TRAFFORD

Lake Trafford (1,494 acres) is a natural lake with a reputation for giving up big bass. The deepest water is only about 9 feet and submerged grass provides most of the cover for fish. The bowl-shaped lake is surrounded mostly by marsh (there is a bit of high ground to the west). Shellcrackers (redear sunfish) can also be very good, especially during the late spring spawn.

The launch site is at the northern end of Lake Trafford. To get there, take Exit 14A off Interstate 75 and go north on SR 29 for 17 miles to the town of Immokalee. Turn left onto Lake Trafford Road in Immokalee and go west for 3 miles to the single-lane ramp.

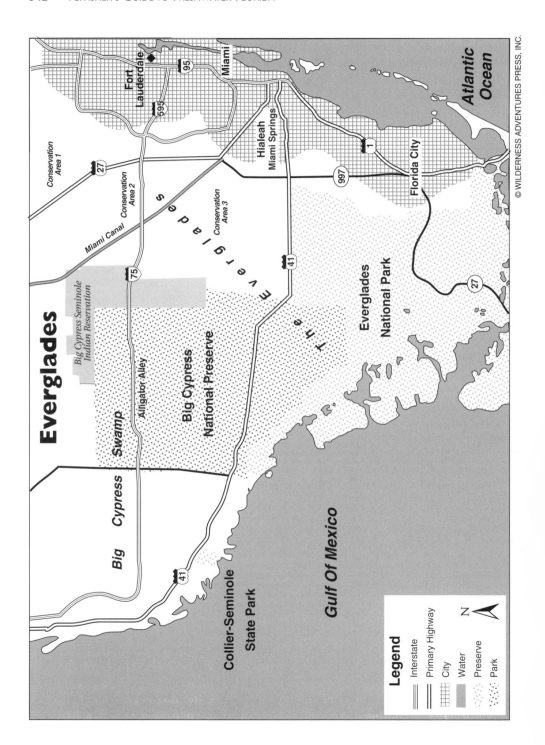

© WILDERNESS ADVENTURES PRESS, INC.

Atlantic Ocean

Fort Lauderdale

Miami

95

595

Hialeah
Miami Springs

1

Florida City

997

Conservation Area 1

27

Conservation Area 2

Conservation Area 3

Miami Canal

75

41

Everglades National Park

27

Everglades

Big Cypress Seminole Indian Reservation

Big Cypress National Preserve

Alligator Alley

The Everglades

Swamp

Big Cypress

41

Collier-Seminole State Park

Gulf Of Mexico

Legend

Interstate
Primary Highway
City
Water
Preserve
Park

N

THE EVERGLADES

(including Everglades National Park)

Saw grass reaches up both sides of that lake (Lake Okeechobee) in great enclosing arms, so that it is correct to say that the Everglades are there also. But south, southeast and southwest, where the lake water slopped and seeped and ran over and under the rock and soil, the greatest mass of the saw grass begins. It stretches as it always has stretched, in one thick enormous curving river of grass, to the very end. This is the Everglades.

Marjory Stoneman Douglas,
The Everglades, River of Grass, 1947

Lake Okeechobee's discharge once served as the headwaters for a broad sea of saw grass known as the Everglades. Over the years, canals were dug to move water to large coastal communities and lands surrounding the lake were drained so that they could be farmed and irrigated. Such things were done in the name of progress. In 1947, 1.5 million acres were set aside as the Everglades National Park, but even this vast area protected only 12 percent of what was the Everglades—the world's largest salt marsh. Volumes have been written, and many more could be penned, describing the importance and natural beauty of the Everglades. I'll try to focus on the fly fishing opportunities offered by the vast area, but first a little about the Everglades…

The area referred to as the Everglades reaches for 120 miles from Lake Okeechobee to Florida Bay in the Gulf of Mexico. The river of grass was once 50 miles wide, while the water averaged less than a foot deep as it moved across the area. The Everglades National Park encompasses 1,509,000 acres, or 2,358 square miles, and the largest remaining subtropical wilderness in the United States has numerous prehistoric and historic cultural sites. More than 400 species of birds have been identified in the park, along with 25 species of mammals, and 60 species of amphibians and reptiles. In addition, there are over 120 species of trees.

Today, canals and levees have captured and diverted water for human needs such as drinking water, irrigation, and flood control. Frequently (in an effort to maintain a bit of balance), too much water is released into the Everglades during a dry season or too little is sent that way during a wet season, disrupting the natural cycle of highs and lows (and dry and wet) necessary for nesting birds and other animals, as well as interfering with the ability of seed-bearing plants to reproduce. Nature's regular cycles over the years have permitted the Everglades to become what they are; and the loss of habitat, the disruption of water flow, and the invasion of non-native species has dramatically reduced the number of some animals, while virtually eliminating others.

If the population of south Florida continues to grow, the problems described above will only get worse. A change of only a few inches in water elevation in an area means the difference between wet marsh and dry ground in this vast, flat landscape.

There are fish in the canals and natural lakes of the Everglades, as well as in the coastal rivers and wet marshlands. In all, 125 species of fish have been identified from 45 different families. Recall that this once pristine area is, as President Truman described it, "serving not as the source of water, but as the last receiver of it." Hence, with all of the farming and mining that has occurred from Orlando south to the Everglades, minerals get into the water, and in turn, show up in the higher-ordered species. In the freshwater fish family, the largemouth bass is at the top of the food chain, and there is a fish advisory against eating this superior predator when caught in the Everglades because of high mercury levels contained in the flesh.

You should seriously consider getting a guide to fish the Everglades area. It is very easy to get lost when everything looks the same and the canals begin to look like a maze. Area guides know fish locations and seasonal patterns and can save you a great deal of time and expense in the long run, while providing a wealth of information.

Conservation Area 2 (about 10 miles west of Ft. Lauderdale) has 210 square miles of Everglades marsh that is connected by perimeter canals. It was originally designated to receive floodwaters from adjacent areas and store them for potential municipal, urban, and agricultural use. The Florida Fish and Wildlife Conservation Commission manages the area for recreational use (including fishing). These canals hold bass, bluegill, redear sunfish, and warmouth in great numbers, especially in the winter and spring when the area's dry season causes water levels to drop and concentrates fish in the canals. Snook and tarpon occasionally can be found in the canals, as well. Most of the fishing takes place in L-35B and L-38E canals, each about 12 miles long. The main access for this area is at the Sawgrass Recreation Area, 2 miles north on US 27 after getting off Interstate 75 (Alligator Alley) at Exit 13. Another launch site is available 3 miles north on US 27. These two sites give access to the west side of Conservation Area 2.

Conservation Area 3 is to the west and south of CA-2 (north of Everglades National Park). It has 915 square miles, with many canals running through and around the area. Bass and assorted bream are the favorite fish targeted by flyfishers, and this is also the northern range for peacock bass. This bass is an aggressive daytime feeder willing to take big, brightly colored poppers, as well as streamers (size 1). Peacock bass are strong, acrobatic fish imported from the tropics. The east side of CA-3 also can be accessed from the Sawgrass Recreation Area. Additional launch sites on the east side are located 6 miles and 13 miles to the north off SR 27. Access to the south side of CA-3 is gained off US 41 (Tamiami Trail). From the intersection of US 41 with the Palmetto Expressway in Miami, go west on US 41 for 10.5 mile. The first launch site is on your right about 0.4 mile after crossing SR 997. There are additional launch sites 3 miles, 8 miles, 11 miles, 12 miles, and 15 miles west of the SR 997 intersection with US 41 (Tamiami Trail). Canals lead to the north into the marsh from each of these launch sites, although an airboat may be required for all but the highest water conditions.

The Everglades National Park is to the south and offers very good freshwater fishing for bass and bream. Only canoes may be launched in freshwater areas and you are cautioned not to overestimate your ability to paddle a canoe, as tides and wind can make it difficult to return to your launch site. In addition, the subtropical nature of the climate can make physical exertion more difficult. Nonetheless, this area offers a unique fly fishing experience, even more so for the scenery and wildlife than for the quality of the freshwater fish that can be caught. If you want a truly quality fishing experience while getting a taste of the park, launch from a coastal area (Everglades City or Chockoloskee from the Gulf side or from one of the Keys into Florida Bay from the east side) and motor into one of the coastal bays and up into a river. You will have an opportunity to catch snook, tarpon, redfish, seatrout, and an assortment of saltwater species along the way as the saltwater "sweetens" in the upper reaches.

*Airboats are the best means of transportation in the
Everglades and on skinny-water lakes.*

Region 3 Hub Cities

The listings that follow are only a small sampling of the facilities available in the major hub cities.

CENTRAL FLORIDA
Kissimmee

ACCOMMODATIONS
Clarion Hotel Maingate, 7675 W. Irlo Bronson Memorial Hwy., Kissimmee, FL 34747; 407-396-4000
Holiday Inn Express-Kissimmee East, 2456 E. Irlo Bronson Memorial Hwy., Kissimmee, FL 34747; 407-846-4646
Radisson Resort Parkway, 2900 Parkway Blvd., Kissimmee, FL 34747; 407-396-7000

CAMPING
Kissimmee/Orlando KOA, 2643 Alligator Lane, Kissimmee, FL 34746; 407-396-2400

RESTAURANTS
Damon's, A Dining Event, 5770 W. Irlo Bronson Memorial Hwy., Kissimmee, FL 34746; 407-397-9444
Kissimmee Steak Company, 2047 E. Irlo Bronson Memorial Hwy., Kissimmee, FL 34744; 407-847-8050
Pacino's Italian Restaurant, 5795 W. Hwy. 192, Kissimmee, FL 34746; 407-396-6210

FLY SHOPS AND SPORTING GOODS
The Sports Authority, 2599 W. Vine St., Kissimmee, FL 34741; 407-932-4444

HOSPITALS
Florida Hospital - Kissimmee, 2450 N. Orange Blossom Trail, Kissimmee, FL 34741; 407-846-4343

AIRPORTS
Kissimmee Airport, 301 N. Dyer Blvd., Kissimmee, FL 34741; 407-847-4600

AUTO SERVICE
Smitty's Auto Repair, 2639 N. Orange Blossom Trail, Kissimmee, FL 34744; 407-846-6767

FOR MORE INFORMATION
Kissimmee/Osceola County Chamber of Commerce, 1425 E. Vine St., Kissimmee, FL 34744; 407-847-3174

Orlando

ACCOMMODATIONS

Holiday Inn Express, 1853 McCoy Road, Orlando; 407-851-1113
Red Roof Inns, 5621 Major Blvd., Orlando, FL 32819; 407-313-3100
Travelodge, 6263 Westwood Blvd., Orlando, FL 32821; 407-345-8000

CAMPING

Disney's Fort Wilderness Resort and Campground, 4510 No. Fort Wilderness Trail, Lake Buena Vista; 407-824-2900
Hidden River RV Park & Canoe Rental, 15295 E. Colonial Dr., Orlando; 407-568-5346

RESTAURANTS

Barney's Steak & Seafood, 1615 E. Colonial Dr., Orlando; 407-896-6864
Café Italiano, 565 N. Semoran Blvd., Orlando; 407-277-6840
Cheng's Chinese Restaurant, 4004 S. Semoran Blvd., Orlando; 407-249-4180
Gains German Restaurant, 5731 S. Orange Blossom Tr., Orlando; 407-438-8997
Linda's La Cantina, 4721 E. Colonial Dr., Orlando; 407-8894-4491

FLY SHOPS AND SPORTING GOODS

Al's Fishing Tackle, 1718 N. Goldenrod Road, Orlando; 407-380-6787
Amanda Bait and Tackle, 2300 S. Crystal Lake Dr., Orlando; 407-894-5200
Bass Pro Shops Outdoor World, 5156 International Drive, Orlando, FL 32819; 407-563-5200
Denton Hardware's Gone Fishin', 3408 S. Orange Ave., Orlando; 407-859-4550
Downeast Sporting Classics, 538 Park Ave. So., Orlando, FL 32789; 407-645-5100
Fish-N-Pole, 1416 N. Mills, Orlando; 407-894-2020
Lake Conway Bait & Tackle, 655 Hoffner Ave., Orlando; 407-857-7040
Reel McCoy Bait & Tackle Center, 14180 E. Colonial Dr., Orlando; 407-282-3130
The Fly Fisherman, 1213 North Orange Avenue, Orlando, FL 32804; 407-898-1989
The Sports Authority, 993 N. Semoran Blvd, Orlando; 407-277-1994
The Sports Authority, 881 W. Sand Lake Road, Orlando; 407 857-1611
The Sports Authority, 380 SR 434, Altamonte Springs; 407-774-8088
The Sports Authority, 7500 W. Colonial Dr., Orlando, FL 407-291-6653
West Marine, 5135 Adanson St., Orlando, FL 32804; 407-644-8557

HOSPITALS

Orlando Regional Medical Center, 1414 Kuhl Ave., Orlando, FL 32806; 407-841-5111

AIRPORTS

Orlando International Airport, One Airport Blvd., Orlando; 407-825-2001

AUTO SERVICE

Mobicare, 10747 Rocket Blvd., Orlando, FL 32824; 407-859-9966

FOR MORE INFORMATION

Greater Orlando Chamber of Commerce, P.O. Box 1234, Orlando, FL 32802; 407-425-1234

Tampa Bay Area
(Tampa, St. Petersburg, Sarasota, and Bradenton)

ACCOMMODATIONS

Banyan Tree Motel, 610 4th St. No., St. Petersburg, FL 33701; 727-822-7072

Belleview Biltmore Resort & Spa, 25 Belleview Blvd., Clearwater, FL 33756; just north of St. Petersburg, there is quite a bit of history in this nicely renovated, large wooden structure; 727-373-3000

Courtyard Sarasota-Bradenton by Marriott, 850 University Parkway, Sarasota, FL 34234; 941-355-3337

Days Inn Historical Bradenton, 1819 Main St., Sarasota, FL 34236; 941-746-1141

Doubletree Guest Suites - Tampa / Busch Gardens, 11310 N. 30th St., Tampa, FL 33612; 813-971-7690

Econo Lodge Midtown, 1020 S. Dale Mabry Hwy., Tampa, FL 33629; 813-254-3005

CAMPING

Hillsborough River State Park, 15402 US 301 No., Thonotosassa, FL 33592; Canoeing and fishing, along with campsites; 813-987-6771

Lake Manatee State Park, 2007 SR 64, Bradenton, FL 34202; in addition to the campsites, the lake has a ramp for smaller boats; 941-741-3208

Little Manatee River State Park, 215 Lightfoot Road, Wimauma, FL 33598; canoeing and fishing are available; in addition to the normal campsites with hookups, there are 4 equestrian campsites; 813-671-5005

RESTAURANTS

Beach Bistro, 6600 Gulf Dr., Holmes Beach, FL 34217; 941-778-6444

Bern's Steak House, 1208 S. Howard Ave., Tampa, FL 33606; outstanding aged beef; 813-251-2421

Cosimo's Brick Oven, 201 Southgate Plaza, Sarasota, FL 34239; 941-363-0211

Grace O'Malley's Irish Pub & Restaurant, 250 75th Ave., St. Pete Beach, FL 33706; 727-363-4117

St. Petersburg Ale House, 7901 9th St. N., St. Petersburg, FL 33702; 727-217-9206

FLY SHOPS AND SPORTING GOODS

CB'S Saltwater Outfitters, 1249 Stickney Pt. Rd., Sarasota, FL 34242; 941-346-2466

Discount Tackle Outlet, 3113 1st St., E., Bradenton, FL 34208; 941-746-6020

The Sports Authority,
201 Cortez Road W., Bradenton, FL 34207; 941-752-0331
4092 Cattlemen Road, Sarasota, FL 34233; 239-377-4301
4900 W. Kennedy Blvd., Tampa, FL 33609; 813-282-1180
4340 W. Hillsborough Blvd., Tampa, FL 33614; 813-875-2220
1730 E. Fowler Ave., Tampa, FL 33612; 813-632-9091
12601 Citrus Plaza Dr., Tampa, FL 33625; 813-792-1550
3700 Tyrone Blvd., St. Petersburg, FL 33710; 727-343-2088

West Marine,
3905 W. Cypress St., Tampa, FL 33607; 813-348-0521
5001 34th Street S., St. Petersburg, FL 33711; 727-867-5700
2800 34th St. N., St. Petersburg, FL 33713; 727-327-0072
3979 S. Tamiami Trail, Sarasota, FL 34231; 941-924-6777
3130 N. Tamiami Trail, Sarasota, FL 34234; 941-351-3431
4569 14th St., Bradenton, FL 34207; 941-753-3585

HOSPITALS
Memorial Hospital, 2901 Swann Ave., Tampa, FL 33609; 813-873-6400
Palms of Pasadena Hospital, 1501 Pasadena Ave., S., St. Petersburg, FL 33707;
727-341-7575
Sarasota Memorial Hospital, 1700 S. Tamiami Trail, Sarasota, FL 34239;
941-917-1300

AIRPORTS
Tampa International Airport, 5507 West Spruce St., Tampa, FL 33607; 813-870-
8700
St. Petersburg/Clearwater International Airport, 14700 Terminal Blvd.,
Clearwater, FL 33762; 727-453-7800
Sarasota / Bradenton International Airport, 6000 Airport Circle, Sarasota, FL
34243; 941-359-5200

AUTO SERVICE
Independent Auto Repair, 1890 University Pkwy., Sarasota, FL 34243; 941-955-
3282
Downtown Auto Service, 855 Burlington Ave. N., St. Petersburg, FL 33701;
727-823-5503
Gulf Auto Clinic, 807 18th Ave. W., Bradenton, FL 34205; 941-741-0042
Long Tire & Auto Center, 601 N. Morgan St., Tampa, FL 33602; 813-273-0988

FOR MORE INFORMATION
Greater Tampa Chamber of Commerce, P.O. Box 420, Tampa, FL 33601;
813-228-7777
St. Petersburg Area Chamber of Commerce, 100 Second Ave. North, Suite 150, St.
Petersburg, FL 33701; 727-821-4069
Sarasota Chamber of Commerce, 1819 Main St., Ste. 240 Sarasota, FL 34236; 941-
955-8187
Bradenton Area Convention & Visitors Bureau, P.O. Box 1000, Bradenton, FL
34206; 941-729-9177/800-4-MANATEE

US 27 Central Corridor
(Haines City, Lake Wales, Avon Park, and Sebring)

ACCOMMODATIONS

G. V. Tilllman House Bed & Breakfast, 301 Sessoms Ave. E., Lake Wales, FL 33853; 863-676-5499

Holiday Inn - Winter Haven, 1150 Third St. SW, Winter Haven, FL 33880; 863-294-4451

Lake Brentwood Motel, 2060 US 27 N., Avon Park, FL 33825; 863-453-4358

Quality Inn & Suites Conference Center, 6525 US Hwy 27 N., Sebring, FL 33870; 863-385-4500

CAMPING

Camper Village of Lake Wales, 4616 US Hwy 27 S., Lake Wales, FL 33853; 863-638-1908

RESTAURANTS

Chalet Suzanne Inn & Restaurant, 3800 Chalet Suzanne Dr., Lake Wales, FL 33853; 863-676-6011

Crazy Cuban Café, 120 East Park Ave., Lake Wales, FL 33853; 863-679-3934

Outback Steakhouse, 921 US Hwy 27 N., Sebring, FL 33870; 863-385-4329

Red Lobster, 721 US Hwy. 27 N., Sebring, FL 33870; 863-382-2200

Sandwich Depot, 21 W. Main St., Avon Park, FL 33825; 863-453-5600

Scuttles New England Seafood Restaurant, 343 W. Central Ave., Lake Wales, FL 33853; 863-676-7547

FLY SHOPS AND SPORTING GOODS

Andy Thornal Company, 336 Magnolia Avenue, Winter Haven, FL 33880; 863-299-9999

HOSPITALS

Lake Wales Medical Center, 410 S. 11th St., Lake Wales, FL 33853; 863-676-1443

Highlands Regional Medical Center, 3600 S. Highlands Ave., Sebring, FL 33871; 863-385-6101

AIRPORTS

Avon Park Municipal Airport, 1545 SR 64 W., Avon Park, FL 33825; 863-453-5046

AUTO SERVICE

Bucks Body Shop, 500 N. Scenic Hwy., Lake Wales, FL 33853; 863-676-2354

Cross Country Automotive Services, 3310 US 27 S., Sebring, FL 33870; 863-402-2700

Yarbrough Tire & Service, 2306 S. Highlands Ave., Sebring, FL 33870; 863-385-1574

FOR MORE INFORMATION

Haynes City Chamber of Commerce, 908 U.S. Hwy. 27, Haines City, FL 33844; 941-422-3751

Lake Wales Chamber of Commerce, 340 W. Central Ave., Lake Wales, FL 33853; 941-676-3445

Avon Park Chamber of Commerce, 28 E. Main St., Avon Park, FL 33825; 941-453-3350

Greater Sebring Chamber of Commerce, 309 S. Circle, Sebring, FL 33870; 941-385-8448/800-255-1711

*A wood stork keeps a watchful
eye in the Everglades.*

South Florida—Ft. Lauderdale

ACCOMMODATIONS

Sheraton Suites Plantation, 311 N. University Dr., Plantation, FL 33324;
954-424-3300

Doubletree Guest Suites, 2670 E. Sunrise Blvd., Ft. Lauderdale; 954-565-3800

Doubletree Oceanfront Hotel, 440 Seabreeze Blvd., Ft. Lauderdale, F; 33316;
954-524-8733

Hilton, 1870 Griffin Rd., Dania Beach / 954-920-3300

Sheraton, 1825 Griffin Rd., Dania Beach / 954-920-3500

Best Western Marina Inn, 2150 SE 17 St. Causeway / 800-528-1234

Ramada Inn, 2275 State Rd. 84 / 954-4000 / 800-Hol-iday

FT. LAUDERDALE PROPER

Bahia Cabana Resort, 3001 Harbor dr. / 954-524-1555

Doubletree–Oceanfront, 440 Seabreeze Blvd. 954-8733

Holiday Inn, 999 Ft. Lauderdale Beach Blvd. / 305-563-5961

Clarion, 4660 N Ocean Dr. / 954-776-5660

CAMPING

Kozy Kampers Travel Trailer Park, 3631 W. Commercial Blvd., Ft. Lauderdale, FL
33309; 954-731-8570

RESTAURANTS

Castaways's Seafood Co., 4599 S. University Dr., Davie, FL 33328; 954-434-5445

Gibby's Steak & Seafood, 2900 NE 12th Terrace, Ft. Lauderdale, FL 33334;
954-565-2929

Martha's on the Intracoastal, 6024 N. Ocean Dr., Hollywood, FL 33019; 954-923-
5444

California Cafe Bar & Grill, 2301 SE 17th St., 954-728-3500, Views of the
Intracoastal Waterway and yacht harbor, Award-winning wine list, full bar

Margarita Café, 221 South Atlantic Blvd., 954-463-6872, Fine Mexican dining

Oasis Cafe, 600 Seabreeze Blvd., 954-463-3130

Pastabilities on the Beach, 201 S. Atlantic Blvd., 954-463-7209, Excellent Italian
cuisine as well as brick oven pizzas

Sloppy Joe's, 17 S. Fort Lauderdale Beach Blvd., 954-522-7553, Popular night-spot
with American bar menu

Sloop John B. Raw Bar & Saloon, 239 South Atlantic Blvd., 954-463-3633, Excellent
local seafood menu

Bahia Mar at the Radisson Hotel, 801 Seabreeze Blvd., 954-764-2233

Bistro Mezzaluna, 741 SE 17th St., 954-522-6620

15th Street Fisheries, 1900 SE 15th St., 954-763-2777, High-end fantastic seafood
restaurant

La Marina @ the Marriott, 1881 SE 17th St., 954-463-4000, Fine Florida-style
Caribbean fare

Shirttail Charlie's, 400 SW 3rd Ave., 954-463-3474, 954-463-9800

FLY SHOPS AND SPORTING GOODS
Bill Boyds, Tackle Shop, 508 N. Andrews Ave., Ft. Lauderdale; 954-462-8366
Bass Pro Shops Outdoor World, 200 Gulf Stream Way, Dania; 33004;
954-929-7710
Carl's Bait & Tackle Shop, 2510 Davie Blvd., Ft. Lauderdale; 954-581-8890
Competition Tackle & Marine, 4620 Griffin Road, Ft. Lauderdale; 954-581-4476
Kingsbury & Sons Tackle, 1801 S. Federal Hwy., Ft. Lauderdale; 954-467-3474
Lauderdale Marina, 1900 SE 15th St., Ft. Lauderdale; 954-523-8507
Les Wills Bait, Tackle & Gun Shop, 217 SW 27th Ave., Ft. Lauderdale;
954-583-7302
LMR Fly Shop, 1495-F SE 17th St, Ft. Lauderdale; 954-525-0728
Lou's Tackle & Marina, 3463 Griffin Road, Ft. Lauderdale; 954-989-9219
Ole Florida Fly Shop, 6553 No. Federal Hwy, Boca Raton; 561-995-1929 or
877-653-3567
Tanner Tackle, 701 NW 57th Place, Ft. Lauderdale; 954-776-6773
T & R Tackle Shop, 228 Commercial Blvd., Ft. Lauderdale; 954-776-1055
The Fly Shop of Ft. Lauderdale, 5130 N. Federal Way, Ft. Lauderdale; 654-772-5822
The Sports Authority,
1901 N. Federal Hwy., Fort Lauderdale; 954-568-6226
3203 N. SR 7, Lauderdale Lakes, FL 33319; 954-484-5232
West Marine
2300 S. Federal Hwy., Ft. Lauderdale, FL 33316; 954-527-5540
1201 N. Federal Hwy., N. Ft. Lauderdale, FL 33304; 954-564-6689

HOSPITALS
Broward General Medical Center, 1600 S. Andrews Ave., Ft. Lauderdale, FL 33316;
954-355-4400

AIRPORTS
Ft. Lauderdale, Hollywood International Airport, 320 Terminal Dr., Ft.
Lauderdale, FL 33315; 954-359-6100
Ft. Lauderdale Executive Airport, 6000 NW 21st Ave., Ft. Lauderdale, FL 33309;
954-828-4966

AUTO SERVICE
Autologic, 608 W. FLagler Ave., Ft. Lauderdale, FL 33301; 954-462-6631

FOR MORE INFORMATION
Greater Ft. Lauderdale Chamber of Commerce, 512 NE Third Ave., Ft. Lauderdale,
FL 33301; 954-462-6000

Miami

ACCOMMODATIONS
Biscayne Bay Marriott Hotel & Marina, 1633 N. Bayshore Dr., Miami, FL 33132; 305-374-3900

Courtyard by Marriott Miami Downtown, 222 SE 2nd Ave., Miami, FL 33131; 305-374-3000

Crowne Plaza Hotel Miami International Airport, 950 NW LeJune Road, Miami, FL 33126; 305-446-9000

Marriott, Courtyard 1201 NW 42nd Ave., 305-642-8200

Days Inn, 7250 NW 11st St., 305-261-4230

Hilton, 5500 Blue Lagoon Dr., 305-261-3335

Comfort Inn & Suites, 5301 NW 36th St., Miami Springs, 305-871-6000

MIAMI PROPER (within 15 minutes of Miami International Airport)
Travelodge Royalton, 131 SE First St., 305-374-7451

Hyatt Regency Miami, 400 SE 2nd Ave., 305-358-1234

Holiday Inn Downtown, 200 SE 2nd Ave., 305-374-3000

Ramada Inn, 300 Biscayne Blvd. Way, 305-531-5771

CAMPING
KOA-Miami, 20675 SW 162nd Ave., Miami, FL 33187; 305-233-5300

RESTAURANTS
Lombardi's Miami, 401 Biscayne Blvd., Miami, FL 33132; 305-381-9580

Monty's on the Beach, 300 Alton Road, Miami Beach, FL 33139; 305-673-3444

Pollo Tropical, 7300 N. Kendall Drive (8th FLoor), Miami, FL 33156; 305-670-7696

MIAMI (DOWNTOWN & AIRPORT AREA)
Bayview Grille @ the Biscayne Hotel, 1633 North Bayshore Drive/Miami/ 305-536-6414, Specializing in seafood

Blue Water Café @ Inter-Continental Hotel, 100 Chopin Plaza/ 305-577-1000, Great gourmet pizzas at moderate prices with view of Biscayne Bay.

Cheescake Factory, 7497 Dadeland Mall, 305-665-5400

Capital Grille, 444 Brickell Ave., Downtown Miami, 305-374-4500, One of the best steakhouses in town, Cigar lockers available

Garcia's Seafood Grille, 398 NW North River Dr. /305-375-0765, A casual, friendly, family-run eatery with a great atmosphere, In and outdoor dining

Tobacco Road, 626 S. Miami Ave., 305-374-1198, A casual bar atmosphere, popular with locals – hamburgers & bar menu

FLY SHOPS AND SPORTING GOODS
Atlantic Bait & Tackle, 1690 SW 27th Ave., Miami; 305-444-7101

A Fisherman's Paradise
3800 NW 27th Ave., Miami; 305-634-1578
17730 South Dixie Hwy., Miami; 305-232-6000

Biscayne Bay Fly Shop, 8243 So. Dixie Hwy., Miami, FL 33143; 305-669-5851 or 877-291-6746

Boaters World Discount Marine Center, 13617 S. Dixie Hwy., Miami;
305-278-9878
Capt. Harry's Fishing Supply, 100 NE 11th St., Miami; 305-374-4661
Charlie Richter's Fly Shop, 472 NE 125th St., Miami; 305-893-6663
Complete Angler Fishing, 6827 SW 40th St., Miami; 305-266-2028
Crook & Crook Fishing, 2795 SW 27th St., Miami; 305-854-0005
El Capitan International, 1590 NW 27th ST., Miami; 305-635-7500
Fishing Tackle Unlimited, 10786 SW 188th ST., Miami; 305-234-3410
Florida Keys Outfitters, 81880 Overseas Highway, Islamorada, FL 33036;
305-664-5423
Jet's Florida Outdoors, 9696 SW 40th St., Miami; 305-221-1371
Haulover Maine Center, 15000 Collins Ave., Miami; 305-945-3934
Kendall Bait and Tackle, 94022 S. Dixie Hwy., Miami; 305-665-0215
Marlin's Bait & Tackle, 6911 Collins Ave., Miami Beach; 861-9959
Ocean Reef Outfitters, 31 Ocean Reef Drive, Suite C-300, Key Largo, FL 33037;
305-367-2611
Oshman's, 11521 NW 12th St., Miami; 305-716-0229
Reef Bait & Tackle, 760 NE 79th ST., Miami; 305-757-4373
River Maine Supply, 260 SW 6th St., Miami; 305-856-0080
Scott's Bait & Tackle, 8241 SW 124th ST., Miami; 305-278-7007
The Fishing Line Bait and Tackle, 9379 SW 56th ST., Miami; 305-598-2444
The Sports Authority
200 E. FLagler St., Miami, FL 33131; 305-538-1598
8390 S. Dixie Hwy., Miami, FL 33143; 305-667-2280
18499 Biscayne Blvd., Miami, FL 33160; 305-591-0622
10688 N.W. 12th St., Miami, FL 33186; 305-270-0622
11910 S.W. 88th St., Miami, FL 33186; 305-270-9762
West Marine
19407 S. Dixie Hwy., Miami, FL 33157; 305-232-0811
8687 SW 24th St., Miami, FL 33155; 305-263-7465
3635 S. Dixie Hwy., Miami, FL 33133; 305-444-5520
16215 Biscayne Blvd., N. Miami Beach, FL 33160; 305-947-6333
7286 Bird Road, Miami; 305-267-4400
81576 Overseas Highway, Islamorada, FL 33036; 305-664-4615

HOSPITALS
Jackson Memorial Hospital, 1611 NW 12th Ave., Miami, FL 33136; 305-585-6754
Mercy Hospital, 3663 S. Miami Ave., Miami, FL 33133; 305-285-2121

AIRPORTS
Miami International Airport, 4300 NW 21st St., Miami; 305-876-7000

AUTO SERVICE
Carfel, 15750 NW 59th Ave., Hialeah, FL 33014; 305-592-2760

FOR MORE INFORMATION
Miami/Dade Chamber of Commerce, 9190 Biscayne Blvd., Suite 201, Miami, FL
33138; 305-751-8648

Naples

ACCOMMODATIONS

Comfort Inn/Downtown on the Bay, 1221 5th Ave., S., Naples, FL 34102; 239-649-5800

Courtyard by Marriott - Naples, 3250 Tamiami Trail N., Naples, FL 34103; 239-434-8700

The Cottages of Naples, 370 11th Ave. S., Naples, FL 34102; 239-450-0776

CAMPING

Naples/Marco Island KOA, 1700 Barefoot Williams Road, Naples, FL 34113; 239-774-5455

RESTAURANTS

Buca Di Beppo Italian Restaurant, 8860 Tamiami Trail N., Naples, FL 34108; 239-596-6662

Kelly's Fish House Dining Room, 1302 5th Ave. S., Naples, FL 34102; 239-774-0494

Yabba Island Grill, 711 5th Ave. S., Naples, FL 34102; 239-262-5787

Maxwell's On the Bay, 4300 Gulf Shore Blvd, North Naples, FL, 941-263-1662

Snook Inn, 1215 Bald Eagle Dr., Marco Island, FL 31145, 941-394-3313

America Railroad Grill and Saloon, 8939 Tamiami Trail, N. Naples, FL, 941-597-0800

Brass Pelican, 475 Seagate Dr., Naples, 941-597-3232

FLY SHOPS AND SPORTING GOODS

Everglades Angler, Inc., 810 Twelfth Ave. So., Naples, FL 34102; 800-573-4749

Mangrove Outfitters Fly Shop, 4111East Tamiami Trail, Naples, FL 34112; 941-793-3370/888-319-9848

The Sports Authority, 2505 Pine Ridge Road, Naples, FL 34109; 239-598-5054

West Marine, 2025 Davis Blvd., Naples, FL 34104; 239-793-7722

HOSPITALS

The Willough at Naples, 9001 Tamiami Trail E., Naples, FL 34113; 239-775-4500

AIRPORTS

Naples Municipal Airport, 160 Aviation Drive N., Naples, FL 34104; 941-643-0733

AUTO SERVICE

John Collins Auto Parts, 5598 Shirley St., Naples, FL 34109; 239-597-1725

FOR MORE INFORMATION

Naples Area Chamber of Commerce, 895 5th Ave. S., Naples, FL 33940; 941-262-6141

Clewiston/Okeechobee

(http://www.floridaguide.com/chambers/cities.html)

ACCOMMODATIONS

Angler's Waterfront Motel, 6th St., Okeechobee, FL 34974; 941-763-4031

Budget Inn, 201 S. Parrott Ave., Okeechobee, FL 34974; 941-763-3185

Days Inn of Okeechobee, 2200 Hwy. 441 SE, Okeechobee, FL 34974; 941-763-8003

CAMPING

Okee-Tantie Recreation Area, 10430 W. Hwy. 78, Okeechobee; 309 waterfront campsites with direct access to both Lake Okeechobee and the Kissimmee River; 863-763-2622

RESTAURANTS

Branding Iron, Hendry Isles Resort, Clewiston, FL 33440; 863-902-1102

Skips Bar-B-Q, 104 SE 6th St., Okeechobee, FL 34974; 863-763-8313

FLY SHOPS AND SPORTING GOODS

Southern Angler, 3585 SE St. Lucie Blvd., Stuart, FL 34997; 407-223-1300

Nix's Fishing Headquarters, Hwy. 441, Okeechobee, FL 34974; 941-763-2248

HOSPITALS

H. H. Rraulerson Memorial Hospital, Okeechobee, FL 34972; 941-763-2151

Hendry General Hospital, Sugarland Highway, Clewiston, FL 33440; 863-983-9121

AIRPORTS

(See Ft. Lauderdale.)

AUTO SERVICE

A & H Automotive, SR 832, Rte. 121, Clewiston, FL 33440; 863-902-0204

E 7 E Automotive Clinic, 3585 N. Hwy. 441, Okeechobee, FL 34973; 863-763-2666

FOR MORE INFORMATION

Clewiston Chamber of Commerce, P.O. Box 275, Clewiston, FL 33440; 941-983-7979

Okeechobee County Chamber of Commerce, 55 South Parrot Ave., Okeechobee, FL 34972; 941-763-6464

Florida's Top Ten Freshwater Fisheries

Selecting Florida's top 10 freshwater fly fishing destinations is quite a subjective undertaking. Fortunately, I have had some help. Expert biologists from Florida's Fish and Wildlife Conservation Commission (FWC) have previously selected their pick of Florida's top lakes by various species, and their opinions were very helpful. With over 7,700 named lakes and 12,000 miles of rivers, we are not all going to agree on what are the best bodies of water. There are large lakes, small lakes, urban ponds, rivers, streams, and reclaimed phosphate pits that all have fish of one type or another willing to take your fly.

The species that you want to catch weighs heavily in choosing the waters you will ultimately fish. In addition, the type of water you prefer to fish will be a significant selection criterion. Many species can be caught in differing types of water, while others have a much narrower range. If I only had limited time and opportunity to sample Florida's freshwater, I would start with this list.

I. ST. JOHNS RIVER, MIDDLE BASIN

My pick as the top fishing destination in all of Florida is not a lake at all. I believe that the middle (central) basin of the St. Johns River in Region 1 is the premier place to fly fish. If this were a horse race, it would be like placing a bet not on a single horse, but on "the field." No single lake in this mid-portion of the river may be the very best, but collectively, the many lakes in close proximity to one another and the outstanding fishing that some of them offer for selected species, makes this an easy selection. Lake George is one of the top bass lakes in the state, offering fine striper and sunshine bass fishing, as well. Nearby, Lake Jessup has some of the state's best bream fishing for assorted panfish, while Lake Monroe consistently yields both big numbers and large-sized crappie early each spring. In addition, the spectacular scenery and abundant wildlife contribute greatly to making this my top fly fishing destination in the state.

2. LAKE WEOHYAKAPKA (LAKE WALK-IN-WATER)

Lake Walk-in-Water, part of the Kissimmee Chain of Lakes in Region 3, is my choice as the second most desirable place to fish. This lake appears on the FWC list as one of the top bass lakes, top panfish lakes, and top crappie lakes. There are a couple of other lakes that also have the distinction of being on all three lists, but Lake Walk-in-Water stands ahead of the others in this group because of the number of oversized largemouth bass that are currently being caught.

3. Lake Istokpoga

Lake Istokpoga, lying between the southern end of the Kissimmee Chain of Lakes and Lake Okeechobee in Region 3, is my third choice among the top lakes in Florida. The lake has outstanding bass, bream, and crappie fishing throughout its waters, along with several good access points to ensure that you can launch and fly fish in an area that has favorable wind conditions.

4. Lake Okeechobee

Lake Okeechobee follows as the next top destination. The Big O in Region 3 is well on its way to returning to its rightful position at the top of everyone's list as the water quality continues to improve now that nutrient levels coming from the Kissimmee River are back to normal and periods of low water have improved shoreline habitat. For years, anglers who came to Florida to fish went to Lake Okeechobee, and it remains one of the best bass, panfish, and crappie lakes in the state. Because of its enormous size, it can absorb several hundred fishermen who will not get in one another's way.

5. Lake Kissimmee

Lake Kissimmee, at the southern end of the Kissimmee Chain in Region 3, has cycles between good and great. There is a period of "greatness" coming after the most recent drawdown and you will not want to miss it. Its number five position on the list is a ranking of its present quality, but I anticipate that like Lake Okeechobee it will continue to improve and move up higher on the list. The drawdown will result in increased numbers of fish in succeeding year classes and make the shorelines easier to fish. Catch rates will be going up, while at the same time, more and bigger fish will be present. The already outstanding bream and crappie fisheries will benefit, but the largemouth bass fishing may become legendary.

6. Tenoroc Fish Management Area

The Tenoroc Fish Management Area near Lakeland is the FWC's opportunity to experiment and see just how good a fishery can become. These phosphate pits in the northwestern part of Region 3 are managed to enhance the fishery and some of the very best fishing for a selected species can be found there. Only a limited number of boats and anglers can be on a body of water (there are presently fourteen pits, with more being prepared for public use) and size and harvest restrictions are also in place. Call for reservations to get on one of these small bodies of water.

7. STICK MARSH/FARM 13 RESERVOIR

Stick Marsh/Farm 13 Reservoir and Lake Kenansville in the southwestern part of Region 1 are not related to the St. Johns River system, nor or they a part of the Kissimmee Chain of Lakes. Located close to Lake Okeechobee, they are the product of the flooding of recently irrigated farmland. With old ditches and dikes present, there is some interesting bottom contours over some very fertile soil. These bodies of water are in their infancy (about 10 years old) and may not be able to sustain their present lofty position. For the time being, however, you should consider giving their big bass and vast numbers of crappie and bream a visit.

From here, my list becomes more subjective. The lakes included up to this point have made the list because they are the very best for each of several species. The last three lakes on my top 10 list have good populations of very large bass, and one fish could make the fly fishing memory of a lifetime.

8. WEST LAKE TOHOPEKALIGA

West Lake Tohopekaliga at the upper end of the Kissimmee Chain in Region 3 is undergoing a drawdown in an effort to improve the fishery. How you make such a good lake even better is hard to imagine, but that is what the FWC is trying to do. The fishing will, in fact, get better. There are obviously plenty of fish with strong genetics swimming in Lake Toho's waters, and they are going to spawn more fish than ever before on the lake's improved shorelines. These shorelines will become easier to fish with more open areas. There will soon be a fantastic mix of both big numbers of smaller fish and several really large fish, too. In a few years, these small fish will become big, too. This lake deserves to be on the list, just for its bass fishing alone.

9. RODMAN RESERVOIR

Rodman Reservoir, near the end of the Oklwaha River before it adds its waters to those of the St. Johns River in Region 1, produced the last two 17-pound largemouth bass caught in the state. Rodman gets regular drawdowns at very frequent intervals to ensure that vegetation does not get out of hand and that the fishery remains at its historically high level. Hence, bass fishing is good now and will be long into the future.

10 LAKE TARPON

Rounding out the list is Lake Tarpon at the northwestern edge of Region 3. I realize that this near-urban lake may be past its prime, but I believe that it is well on the way to a significant comeback. For years, Lake Tarpon produced some of the state's largest bass and the water quality is improving with the addition of some nutrient-rich runoff.

OTHER NOTABLE FRESHWATER FISHERIES

One additional body of water is included from each region as an "honorable mention," and you will certainly want to consider these waters if you happen to be in the area. From Region 1, Lake Harris deserves mention for its outstanding panfish angling. Both bream and crappie are plentiful on this lake that, like Rodman Reservoir, is located on the Oklawaha River before it flows into the St. Johns River system.

In Region 2 (and the north-central part of the state had no lakes in my top 10 list) try Lake Talquin. This lake has a good population of striped bass and sunshine bass to complement the fine bream and crappie that can also be caught. There are good numbers of black bass, as well, although their size does not rival largemouths found in the Kissimmee Chain of Lakes to the south. If you find yourself near Tallahassee, be sure to make a visit here.

Finally, Lake Marian in Region 3 offers an outstanding crappie fishery, along with some very good bream and bass. The bass have consistently failed to reach the size of those found in the larger neighboring lakes of the Kissimmee Chain, though.

It is seldom more than a short boat ride to outstanding fly fishing on the St. Johns River.

Flies for Freshwater Florida

IMPORTANT PATTERNS

Terrestrials
    Dave's Hopper (tan or green; size 8-12)
    Dave's Cricket (black or brown; size 8-12)
    Hard Body Ant (black or brown; size 10-16)

Poppers
    Swimming Frog (size 2)
    Peeper Popper (green/yellow, size 8)
    Bluegill Bug (black or yellow; size 8-12)
    Foam Poppers (white, yellow or chartreuse; size 1/0-2)
    Pencil Poppers (white, yellow or chartreuse; size 1)

Clousers (white, yellow, chartreuse or pink; size 4-6)
Streamers (blue/white or chartreuse/white; size 1-2/0)
Peterson's Baby Bunker (olive/white; size 2/0)
Lefty's Deceivers (green/white, olive/white, or blue/white; size 1-2/0)
Foam Gurgler (white, size 1-4)
Grass Shrimp (tan; size 2-6)
Shad Flies (white, yellow, pink or chartreuse; size 8-12)
Epoxy Minnow (white, yellow, chartreuse, light blue, light green; size 1-4)

Matt Socha selects a fly to tie onto the fighting end of his 5-weight fly rod.

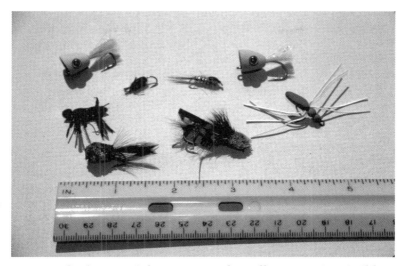

Bream find terrestrial patterns and small poppers irresistible.

BREAM

Anglers looking for bream should use a small topwater popper (Bluegill Bug, black or yellow, size 8-12, or a similarly-sized foam popper) or a terrestrial pattern (Hard Body Ant, black or brown, size 10-16; Dave's Hopper, tan or green, size 8-12; or Dave's Cricket, black or brown, size 8-12). In the lakes and ponds, move toward the shorelines and cast to any available structure. Look around bonnets and lilies that are in about three to four feet of water. Seasonally, the best opportunities for bream are late in the spring and throughout the summer, especially around the full moon in May and June. Bream are fond of feeding early and late in the day. Often, afternoon rains in the summer wash insects into the water, and there is a period of active feeding after a storm front passes. This is a pleasant time to be on the water, as both the temperature and humidity will have dropped. You should not miss this opportunity. In the rivers and streams, bream will be along grass beds and shoreline structure. If you find an area of slower moving water, bream are likely to be present.

BLACK BASS

When black bass are your target, consider one of the larger foam poppers (white, yellow or chartreuse) or a deer-haired pattern (Swimming Frog, size 2). On lakes and ponds, these topwater flies should be fished around any available shoreline cover. As the lakes and ponds age, lilies and bonnets will begin to grow away from the shoreline in water that is three to four feet deep. These areas become prime habitat for largemouth bass, as small bream and other baitfish take up residence there. Do not become fixated on casting to the shoreline when there is vegetation growing several feet up from the bottom. In addition, if you find bass schooling in open water, be sure to try a baitfish pattern such as Peterson's Baby Bunker (olive and white; size 2/0) or a white foam Gurgler (size 1). In streams, black bass will be smaller and likely feeding on minnows or crustaceans. A small Clouser (size 6) or a grass shrimp pattern (size 4) should be at the top of the list. Look to the downstream side of any structure, as bass like to lie below it, using it to break the flow of water and feed on forage brought to them by the moving water. When there is a midstream island, be sure to explore the eddy immediately downstream, too.

CRAPPIE

Crappie will primarily feed on minnows, but they are not going to rise in the water column to do so. You will need to get your fly down to where they are holding, and there is no better fly than a Clouser (size 6) to do this. Bright colors, especially chartreuse, should be selected. Count your fly down as it sinks so that you can return to the same level with your next cast. Crappie school in prolific numbers, and once they are located, it's not hard to catch several by returning to the same depth. Some crappie weigh upwards of two pounds, and they all have paper-thin mouths, so do not try to horse these fish.

Primarily found in lakes and ponds, crappie move out of the deep holes where they winter and begin to move toward the shorelines to spawn as soon as the water begins to warm around the end of January. By mid-February, they will be along any available shoreline structure and remain there until the end of the month. By March, you again need to look towards the deeper holes, and a sink-tip line will assist you getting to them the rest of the year.

Small poppers cast around the shoreline will take both
bream and bass.

*A baitfish or grass shrimp imitation will be readily
seized by any member of the striper family.*

STRIPERS

Stripers feed primarily on baitfish, and a pattern that imitates a small shad should be your first choice. Peterson's Baby Bunker (olive/white, size 2/0) will take both sunshine bass and white bass. For the larger striped bass, the same pattern or a Deceiver pattern (green/white, olive/white, or blue/white; size 1 to 2/0) would be an excellent choice. Stripers tend to school in large numbers and feed voraciously on pods of baitfish. During the fall in late afternoons, they are noted for moving out of a channel and onto a flat where topwater action can be hot. Often, schools of gulls will flock overhead and dive into the fray. If you see this activity going on, race over to them and join in. You should consider a topwater fly like a white foam Gurgler (size 2) since the stripers are shallow and pushing baitfish toward the surface. These same patterns work for stripers below dams, where they congregate in the tailrace to feed on baitfish that have been cut or stunned by blades of turning turbines. Lastly, many of Florida's lakes have springs feeding them and stripers tend to gather near them in large numbers. While the traditional baitfish patterns will work, you should also try a freshwater shrimp fly (size 2) in these springs.

OTHER SPECIES

American shad readily take small shad flies (white, yellow, pink or chartreuse; size 8 to 12) and spoon flies (gold or chrome, size 8 to 12) in the cooler months far upstream in the St. Johns River (between Sanford and Melbourne). Look for breaks in the current behind bridges or downstream from an island, and fish along the edge of the channel. Shad are game fighters and the lighter tackle necessary to cast small flies has made the winter shad fishery quite a sport in recent years.

Peacock bass feed primarily on small baitfish, and streamers (white, size 2), epoxy minnows (white, yellow or chartreuse; size 2), and pencil poppers (white, yellow or chartreuse; size 2) are the preferred patterns. These imported, tropical fish are primarily located in the canals of Miami and because they cannot tolerate cooler temperatures, they have a very limited range.

Pickerel are seldom a targeted species, but they are frequently encountered by flyfishers searching for largemouth bass around weedy areas in lakes and in sluggish areas of streams. Baitfish is the primary food for chain pickerel, but they also eat insects, frogs, mice, crayfish, and a wide variety of other foods. They are not going to be particularly selective in either the pattern or size of fly they will take. You can use any of the patterns that you might for largemouth bass. Pickerel have a pretty good set of molars and their teeth might make a mess of a good fly. If you are encountering a large number of pickerel, switch to a streamer (white, yellow or chartreuse; size 2) and save your better flies for another day.

Oscars are carnivorous and prey on small fish, insects and amphibians. As such, they are perfect targets for flyfishers. Their size tends to be small (the average size is about 10 inches) and their range is limited to the southern half of Region 3, especially in marsh-type habitats with man-controlled water levels. The same patterns that you would cast for bream will take these tropical imports.

Deer-hair flies in olive and brown are excellent
choices for largemouth bass.

Florida Freshwater Game Fish

(The following information is reprinted with permission from the Florida Fish and Wildlife Conservation Commission (Division of Freshwater Fisheries) website, http://floridafisheries.com. Mark Trainor, Bob Wattendorf, and Paul Shafland wrote the descriptions for Florida's game fish species.)

Florida Largemouth Bass

(*Micropterus salmoides floridanus*)

Common Names

black bass, Florida bass, Florida (or southern) largemouth, green bass, bigmouth, bucketmouth, linesides, Oswego bass, and green trout.

Description

The largemouth is the largest member of the sunfish family. It generally has light greenish to brownish sides with a dark lateral line that tends to break into blotches towards the tail. Often confused with smallmouth and spotted bass, it is easily distinguishable because the upper jaw extends beyond the rear edge of the eye. Also, its first and second dorsal fins are almost separated by an obvious deep dip, and there are no scales on the soft-rayed second dorsal fin or on the anal fin.

Subspecies

Two are recognized, the northern largemouth (*M. s. salmoides*) and the Florida largemouth (*M. s. floridanus*). The two look much the same, but the Florida largemouth has 69-73 scales along the lateral line compared to the northern largemouth's 59-65 scales. Florida bass grow to trophy size more readily than northern largemouth in warm waters.

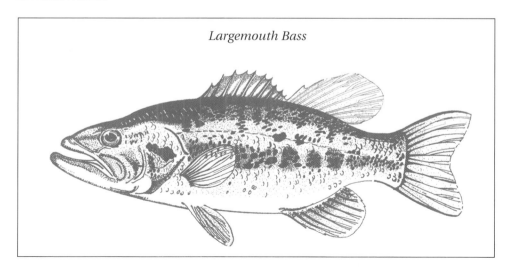

Largemouth Bass

Range

Originally, the Florida largemouth was found only in peninsular Florida, but they have been stocked in several other states, including Texas and California. Pure northern largemouth bass are not found in Florida. Genetic intergrades between the subspecies, however, occur throughout north Florida.

Habitat

Prefers clear, nonflowing waters with aquatic vegetation where food and cover are available. They occupy brackish to freshwater habitats, including upper estuaries, rivers, lakes, reservoirs, and ponds. Also, they can tolerate a wide range of water clarities and bottom types, prefer water temperatures from 65 to 85 degrees, and are usually found at depths less than 20 feet.

Spawning Habits

Spawning occurs from December through May, but usually begins in February and March in most of Florida when water temperatures reach 58 to 65 degrees and continues as temperatures rise into the 70s. The male builds saucer-shaped nests 20 to 30 inches in diameter by placing its lower jaw near the bottom and rotating around this central location. Bass prefer to build nests in hard-bottom areas along shallow shorelines or in protected areas such as canals and coves. Depending on her size, the female can lay up to 100,000 eggs, which are fertilized as they settle into the nest. After spawning is completed, usually 5 to 10 days, the male guards the nest and eggs and later the young (sometimes called fry) attacking anything that approaches the nest. The female bass stays near the nest or may swim a short distance and remain listless for up to a day. After hatching, the fry swim in tight schools, disbanding when the small fish reach a length of about one inch.

Feeding Habits

The diet of bass changes with its size. Young fish feed on microscopic animals (zooplankton) and small crustaceans such as grass shrimp and crayfish. Fingerling bass feed on insects, crayfish, and small fishes. Adult bass will eat whatever is available, including fish, crayfish, crabs, frogs, salamanders, snakes, mice, turtles, and even birds.

Age and Growth

Growth rates are highly variable with differences attributed mainly to their food supply and length of growing season. Female bass live longer than males and are much more likely to reach trophy size. By age two or three, females grow much faster than male bass. Males seldom exceed 16 inches, while females frequently surpass 22 inches. At five years of age females may be twice the weight of males. One-year-old bass average about seven inches in length and grow to an adult size of 10 inches in about 1½ to 2½ years. The oldest bass from Florida whose age has been determined by fisheries biologists was 16 year of age. Generally, trophy bass (10 pounds and larger) are about 10 years old. The formula used by Florida scientists to estimate weight based on length and girth is: log(weight, in grams) = -4.83 + 1.923 x log(total length, in mm) + 1.157 x log(girth, in mm).

Eating Quality

The meat is white, flaky and low in oil content. The flavor depends upon the way the fish are cleaned and prepared. The strong weedy taste of bass caught in some waters may be eliminated by skinning the fish and salting and peppering the fillets before battering. Fillets usually are fried, while larger ones may be baked.

World Record:

22 pounds, 4 ounces, caught in Montgomery Lake, Georgia in 1932.

Certified State Record

17 pounds, 4¼ ounces, caught in an unnamed lake in Polk County in 1986.

Uncertified State Record

20 pounds, 2 ounces, caught in Big Fish Lake (private pond) in Pasco County in 1923.

Suzy Reihl's big bass came from the stump fields of Rodman Reservoir.

Redeye Bass
(*Micropterus coosae*)

Common Names
Coosa bass, shoal bass, Flint River smallmouth, Chipola bass, black bass.

Description
The red color of eyes and fins easily separates this species from other bass. Suwannee and shoal bass also have red eyes, but generally have less red on their fins. Redeye bass generally are brownish to greenish in color with vertical bars with light centers along their sides and are bronze-olive above, dark olive mottling, yellow-white to blue below. It has a prominent dark spot on the gill cover, and scales on the base portion of the soft-rayed dorsal fins, clearly connected first and second dorsal fins, and an upper jaw bone that does not extend beyond the eyes.

Subspecies
No known subspecies. There were two widely recognized forms: the Apalachicola form, now separately described as the species shoal bass, and the Alabama form, which remains classified as a redeye bass.

Range
Has been recorded from the Apalachicola and Chipola River systems in Florida. The shoal bass is common in the Chipola River where shoals exist. However, the redeye bass of Alabama and Georgia is so rare in Florida that it is not considered a resident fish.

Habitat
Likely to be found in rocky runs, pools of creeks, and small to medium rivers close to main-channel habitat. They are seldom found in natural lakes, ponds, or impoundments. They prefer a water temperature of about 65 degrees. Shoal bass in the Chipola River are closely associated with rock shoals and is uncommon in other habitats.

Spawning Habits
Redeye bass spawn in coarse gravel at the heads of creek pools in late May to early July. They will not spawn in ponds or lakes and prefer spawning temperature of 62 to 69 degrees. Like the largemouth, the male prepares the nest and guards the eggs and fry.

Feeding Habits
Redeye bass feed mainly on aquatic insects on the surface. They also feed on larval insects, crayfish, and fish.

Age and Growth
The growth rate of redeye bass is slow when compared to other species of black bass. Growth is fast the first year but decreases as the fish becomes older. Shoal bass

grow much faster than redeye bass.

Eating Quality
Good. It has white, flaky meat and tends to be drier than that of a largemouth.

World Record
8 pounds, 3 ounces, caught in the Flint River, Georgia in 1977. This fish was actually a shoal bass.

State Record
7 pounds, 13¼ ounces, caught in the Apalachicola River in 1989.

Shoal Bass (*Micropterus cataractae*)

Common Names
shoal bass.

Description
Until October 1999, this species was variously considered to be a redeye bass or subspecies of the redeye bass. James Williams and George Burgess published the official description of the new species in Volume 42, No. 2 of the "Bulletin of the Florida Museum of Natural History," which was printed on October 8, 1999. The red color of eyes associates this species with the redeye and Suwannee bass at first glance. However, it is more closely related to the spotted bass morphologically. Shoal bass generally are olive green to nearly black along the back. A dusky dark blotch about 50-67 percent of the size of the eye occurs on the back edge of the gill cover. Three diagonal black lines radiate along the side of the head looking like war paint. Ten to 15 vertical blotches appear along the sides with tiger-stripes often appearing in between. The belly is creamy or white and wavy lines may appear slightly above the white belly on the sides. The dorsal, caudal, and anal fins are dark olive green to grayish black. Pelvic fins may have a cream colored leading edge with dark spots. The shoal bass has scales on the base portion of the soft-rayed dorsal fins, clearly connected first and second dorsal fins, and an upper jaw bone that does not extend beyond the eyes.

Subspecies
No known subspecies.

Range
The shoal bass is common in the Apalachicola and Chipola Rivers where shoals exists. It is also known in the Chattahoochee and Flint River drainages.

Habitat
Shoal bass are closely associated with rock shoals and are uncommon in other habitats.

Spawning Habits
Shoal bass spawn in coarse gravel at the heads of creek pools in April and May, to early June. They prefer spawning temperatures of 64 to 73 degrees. Like the largemouth, the male prepares the nest and guards the eggs and fry.

Feeding Habits
Shoal bass feed mainly on aquatic insects on the surface. They also feed on larval insects, crayfish, and fish.

Age and Growth
Shoal bass grow much faster than redeye bass.

Eating Quality
Good. It has white, flaky meat that tends to be drier than that of a largemouth.

World Record
8 pounds, 3 ounces, caught in the Flint River, Georgia in 1977. This fish was a shoal bass but originally reported as the Apalachicola form of redeye bass.

State Record
7 pounds, 13¼ ounces, caught in the Apalachicola River in 1989.

Small poppers can be used to take spotted bass feeding along shorelines.

Spotted Bass (*Micropterus punctulatus*)

Common Names
Kentucky bass, Kentucky spotted bass, northern spotted bass, Alabama spotted bass, Wichita spotted bass, black bass, smallmouth bass, and spot.

Description
Is similar in appearance to the largemouth bass. It has green to olive-green hue; white, mottled belly; and a broad stripe of broken blotches, usually diamond-shaped, along the midline of the body. Unlike the largemouth, the spotted bass has scales on the base portion of the second dorsal fin; its first and second dorsal fin are clearly connected, and its upper jaw does not extend past the eye. Above the lateral line there are dark markings, and below the lateral line the scales have dark bases that give rise to the linear rows of small spots, which are responsible for the common name.

Subspecies
Three are recognized: the northern spotted bass (*M. p. punctulatus*) has 60 to 68 scales along the lateral line, the Alabama spotted bass (*M. p. henshalli*) has 68 to 75 scales along the lateral line, and the Wichita spotted bass (*M. p. wichitae*) usually has 13 dorsal rays and often lacks rows of black spots along lower side of body. Spotted bass can be found from Texas to the Florida panhandle, including Georgia, Alabama, Tennessee, and Kentucky. The Wichita spotted bass (thought by some to be extinct) is limited to West Cache Creek, Oklahoma. The Alabama spotted bass has been introduced into California.

Range
While widely distributed outside Florida, the spotted bass is restricted to streams of the panhandle from the Perdido River to the Apalachicola River. Abundance is limited in this area, but the fish primarily occurs in and west of the Choctawhatchee River.

Habitat
Prefers small to medium streams and rivers with clear, slow-moving water, gravel or rock bottoms. Spotted bass may occupy reservoirs, but are seldom found in natural lakes. They do not enter brackish water.

Spawning Habits
Spawns very much like the largemouth. Spawning occurs in the spring when water temperatures reach 60 to 65 degrees. Sexually mature males build saucer-shaped nests on a soft, clay bottom or on gravel bars generally near brush, logs, or other heavy cover. The eggs hatch in four or five days, yielding up to 3,000 fry per nest.

Feeding Habits
The principal food items are crayfish, fish, and aquatic insects. The species is less

piscivorous than other black basses and seems to be more selective in its feeding habits.

Age and Growth

Tends to grow slower than largemouth bass and does not attain as large a size as other species. The young grow to 1½ to 4 inches the first summer. Maturity is reached at about seven inches. Average lengths for fish aged 1 to 8 years are 4, 8, 12, 14, 15, 16, 17, 18 inches.

Eating Quality

White, flaky meat with good flavor. Generally considered better eating than largemouth.

World Record

9 pounds, 4 ounces, caught in Lake Perris, California in 1987.

State Record

3 pounds, 12 ounces, caught in Apalachicola River in 1985.

Suwannee Bass (*Micropterus notius*)

Common Names

No other common names are known. It is sometimes incorrectly identified as a smallmouth bass, redeye bass, or a spotted bass.

Description

A heavy-bodied bass seldom exceeding 12 inches long. The most unique characteristic of a mature Suwannee bass is its bright turquoise blue coloring on the cheeks, breast, and ventral parts. The upper jaw does not extend beyond the eye. Also, there is a shallow notch between the dorsal fins with a distinct connection between the spiny and soft-rayed dorsal fins. A pattern of dark vertical blotches occurs along the lateral line. There is generally a distinct dark blotch where the lateral line meets the caudal fin. Scales are present on bases of dorsal, anal, and caudal fins.

Subspecies

It is a distinct species with no known subspecies.

Range

Restricted to the Suwannee and Ochlockonee River systems of Florida and Georgia. Also occupies spring-fed lower reaches of the Santa Fe and Ichetucknee Rivers, tributaries of the Suwannee River.

Habitat

Generally prefers more rapidly flowing water along rocky shoal areas but is not restricted to these areas. Also found in large springs and spring runs. The Suwannee bass is designated a "Species of Special Concern" because of its limited range. Degradation of habitat or water quality in the Suwannee and Ochlockonee Rivers could threaten this species.

Spawning Habits

Spawning occurs from February to June when water temperatures reach 65 to 68 degrees. Reproduction is similar to the largemouth bass, including nest construction.

Feeding Habits

Young fish feed on aquatic insects and small crustaceans. Larger fish feed heavily on crayfish and also take small fishes.

Age and Growth

Suwannee bass are generally smaller than largemouth bass. A two-pound fish is considered large. It seldom exceeds a length of 10 inches or a weight of 12 ounces.

Eating Quality

White, flaky meat with a good flavor and may be prepared like other freshwater bass.

State and World Record

3 pounds, 14¼ ounces caught in the Suwannee River in 1985.

Black Crappie (*Pomoxis nigromaculatus*)

Common Names

Speckled perch, specks, papermouth, bachelor perch, calico bass, strawberry bass, or white perch.

Description

The black crappie is a silvery-green to yellowish fish with large dorsal and anal fins of almost identical shape and size. The sides are marked with black blotches that become more intense towards the back. The dorsal, anal, and caudal fins also are marked with rows of dark spots. Crappies have compressed bodies, small heads and arched backs. It has a large mouth with an upper jaw extending under the eye.

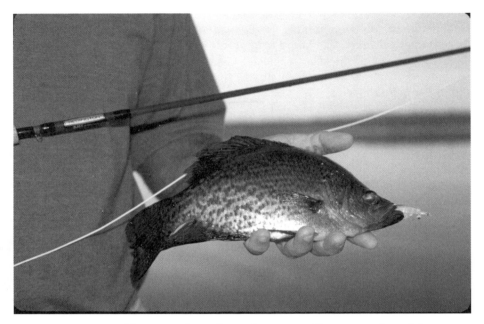

Crappie seldom rise for a fly. A chartreuse Clouser sank to this one's level in the water column.

Subspecies

There are no recognized subspecies. They are closely related to the white crappie found in Alabama and Georgia. However, the white crappie is not found in Florida.

Range

Found statewide except in the Florida Keys.

Habitat

Black crappies thrive in clear, natural lakes and reservoirs with moderate vegetation. They are also found in large, slow-moving, less turbid rivers, provided the water is not too murky. Crappies prefer water from 70 to 75 degrees but will tolerate water over 80 degrees. It is gregarious and often travels in schools.

Spawning Habits

Spawning occurs from February to April when water temperatures reach 62 to 65 degrees. They nest in colonies. Circular nests are fanned by males over gravel or soft muddy bottoms and frequently around submerged vegetation in waters from three to eight feet deep. After spawning, males guard the eggs and fry. Females may produce between 11,000 and 188,000 eggs.

Feeding Habits

Primary food items are crustaceans, aquatic insects, and small fishes. Adults mainly eat small fish, particularly open-water forage fish, like threadfin shad.

Age and Growth

Sexual maturity is reached in the second or third year, with few fish surviving beyond their fifth year in Florida waters. The oldest crappie aged in Florida, to date, has been 11 years old.

Eating Quality

Considered to be excellent eating by many anglers. The meat is prepared by rolling in cornmeal or dipping in pancake batter and deep frying and can also be baked or broiled.

World Record

4 pounds, 8 ounces, caught in Kerr Lake, Virginia, in 1981.

State Record

3 pounds, 13.25 ounces, caught in Lake Talquin, in 1992.

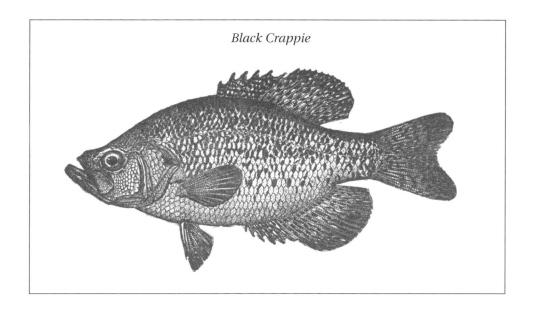

Black Crappie

Bluegill (*Lepomis macrochirus*)

Common Names
Bream, blue bream, sun perch, blue sunfish, copperhead, copperbelly, roach.

Description
Bluegills have small mouths and oval-shaped, almost rounded, bodies. Body coloration is highly variable with size, sex, spawning, water color, bottom type, and amount of cover. In general, they are somewhat lavender and bronze with about six dark bars on their sides. Males tend to have a copper-colored bar over the top of the head behind the eyes. The breast is silver to slightly blue most of the year, with some yellow or orange during spawning season. Females are generally lighter colored than males. Two distinctive characteristics are the prominent black spot on the rear edge of the gill-cover and a black spot at the base of the posterior portion of the dorsal fin.

Subspecies
Two are recognized, the northern bluegill (*Lepomis macrochirus macrochirus*), found in northwest Florida; and the Florida bluegill (*Lepomis macrochirus mystacalis*), found throughout Florida except the panhandle. The bluegill also hybridizes with other members of the sunfish family.

Range
Found throughout Florida and the United States because of widespread stocking.

Habitat
Bluegills prefer quiet, weedy waters where they can hide and feed. They inhabit lakes and ponds, slow-flowing rivers and streams with sand, mud, or gravel bottoms, near aquatic vegetation.

Spawning Habits
Bluegills are well known for "bedding" in large groups, with their circular beds touching one another. Bedding occurs in water two to six feet deep over sand, gravel, or mud bottom, often among plant roots. Spawning occurs from April through October with the peak in May and June, when water temperature rises to about 67 degrees. A female may lay 2,000 to 63,000 eggs that hatch 30 to 35 hours after fertilization.

Feeding Habits
Insects, insect larvae, and crustaceans are the dominant foods of bluegills, with vegetation, fish eggs, small fish, mollusks, and snails being of secondary importance, although they may dominate their diet during certain times of the year.

Brian Penrose looks for red-breast sunfish in the upper St. Johns River marsh.

Age and Growth

Growth is rapid in Florida. A one-year-old fish may be four inches long. Spawning may occur the first year. Bluegills can live up to 11 years. The rate of growth varies considerably in different bodies of water. However, a six-inch bluegill in Florida is typically two to four years old.

Eating Quality

Excellent; the flesh is white, flaky, firm, and sweet. They are generally rolled in cornmeal or dipped in pancake batter before frying. Many rank the bluegill as the most delicious of all freshwater fish.

World Record

4 pounds, 12 ounces, caught in Ketona Lake, Alabama, in 1950.

State Record

2 pounds, 15.25 ounces, caught in Crystal Lake, Washington County, Florida, in 1989.

Redbreast Sunfish (*Lepomis auritus*)

Common Names
Redbelly, robin, yellowbelly sunfish, bream, river bream, longear sunfish, sun perch, and redbreast bream.

Description
The redbreast is one of the brightest colored sunfishes. Males have yellow, orange, or red breast, olive upper sides, blending into blue-tinged bronze on the lower sides and blue streaks on the cheek. Females are less colorful; their breasts are yellowish or pale red. The most distinguishing characteristic of this species is a long, narrow (no wider than the eye) extension of the gill cover. These flaps, which may reach a length of one inch or more, are entirely black.

Subspecies
There are no recognized subspecies. They are known to hybridize with other members of the sunfish family.

Range
The redbreast is found throughout northern Florida. It is the most dominant sunfish in such streams as the Oklawaha, Ochlockonee, Suwannee, and Santa Fe Rivers. This species has been introduced into the Blackwater and Yellow Rivers in northwestern Florida.

Habitat
Redbreasts inhabit sand-bottom areas as well as rocky areas of coastal-plain streams, rivers, and lakes. They frequently concentrate around boulders, limestone outcroppings, logs, aquatic vegetation, or in undercut tree roots.

Spawning Habits
They reproduce in typical sunfish fashion by constructing circular beds (but not clustered like bluegills), in water from one to three feet deep usually adjacent to underwater objects such as stumps and snags. They often occupy beds that have been abandoned by other sunfishes. Spawning occurs from May through August when water temperatures range from 68 to 82 degrees. Males are the nest builders and guard the eggs and larvae for a short period after hatching. The number of eggs laid in a season ranges from about 1,000 to 10,000, varying with the age and size of the female.

Feeding Habits
The redbreast's diet is probably the most varied of any of the sunfishes. Principal food organisms are bottom-dwelling insect larvae, snails, clams, shrimp, crayfish, and small fish.

Age and Growth
Compared to most other sunfish, redbreasts grow slowly. They seldom live beyond seven years and commonly reach a length of six inches.

Eating Quality
The sweet, flaky, white flesh is excellent eating. They are most often fried after dipping them in seasoned cornmeal or pancake batter.

World Record
1 pound, 12 ounces, caught in the Suwannee River, Florida, in 1984.

State Record
2 pounds, 1.25 ounces, caught in the Suwannee River, in 1988.

Shellcracker or Redear Sunfish (*Lepomis microlophus*)

Common Names
Widely known as shellcracker because of its fondness for snails. Also called bream, stumpknocker, yellow bream.

Description
The redear is similar in shape to the bluegill, but lacks the dark spot at the base of the posterior portion of the dorsal fin and has a red or orange border around the "ear" flap. The body coloration is light olive-green to gold, with red or orange flecks on the breast. The breast of a mature redear is typically a rather bright yellow. The body is heavily spotted, and they have long, pointed pectoral fins. Five to 10 vertical bars are more or less evident on the sides, depending on the size of the fish. Males and females are similar in appearance, although the male is generally more colorful.

Subspecies
There are no recognized subspecies. They are known to hybridize with other members of the sunfish family.

Range
Found throughout Florida and the southeastern United States. They are also one of the dominant sportfish in the vast Everglades marshes.

Habitat
The redear prefers large, quiet waters and has a tendency to congregate around stumps, roots, logs, and in open water offshore. They are common in lower, more slowly flowing reaches of rivers. Rarely are they found in swiftly moving water. They tolerate brackish water better than other sunfish but are intolerant of cool water. Like

black bass and spotted sunfish, they may be abundant in tidal areas near the mouths of rivers.

Spawning Habits

Spawning occurs during May, June, and July (March through August in central Florida) when water temperatures reach 70 degrees. They prefer water three to four feet deep and a firm, shelly bottom. Nesting sites are often near aquatic vegetation such as water lilies, cattails, lizardtails, and maidencane. Breeding behavior is similar to other sunfish, with the males doing the nest building and guarding the young. A female may lay between 15,000 to 30,000 eggs during a spawn.

Feeding Habits

Redears are opportunistic bottom feeders, foraging mainly during daylight hours on a variety of invertebrates. Important food items include snails and clams, which are crushed by grinding teeth in the throat, larval insects, fish eggs, small fish, and crustaceans. In some areas snails may be secondary to insects as a food preference.

Age and Growth

Redears grow faster than any other true sunfish. The maximum age is about eight years old. Nine- to 10-inch redears are common throughout Florida.

Eating Quality

Similar to that of bluegill, with white, flaky, sweet-tasting meat. They are prepared the same as bluegill.

State and World Records

4 pound, 13 ounces, caught in Merritt's Mill Pond, Florida, in 1986.

Stumpknocker or Spotted Sunfish (*Lepomis punctatus*)

Common Names

Stumpknocker and bream.

Description

Spotted sunfish tend to be olive-green to brown in color, with black or reddish spots on the base of each scale to form rows of dots on its sides. On some fish there is a red bar in front of many of the black spots, particularly below the lateral line. These bars give the fish a reddish hue. Body shape is thick and ovate, with the length about twice the depth. Some fish have blue on the lower portion of the eye.

Subspecies

Two are recognized. *L. p. punctatus* is found from North Carolina to Florida. *L. p. miniatus* is found in Mississippi and in Gulf coast drainages. Intergrades are found in northwest Florida.

Range

It is found throughout the Florida peninsula and west to the Perdido River.

Habitat

The preferred habitat is slow-moving, heavily vegetated streams and rivers with limestone, sand, or gravel substrates. They are virtually ubiquitous, inhabiting large rivers to very small creeks.

Spawning Habits

A nest-building sunfish that tends to be more solitary than some of the other members of the sunfish family. Males are very aggressive and antagonistic toward other fish in its nesting area. The beds are about one foot in diameter and are fanned out by the male, who also stands guard over the eggs and larvae. Concentrations of beds are found where suitable habitat is limited. Spawning takes place from May through November.

Feeding Habits

This species is very aggressive and will take almost anything they can attack and catch. They generally feed on the bottom, but sometimes will rise to the surface to take food. Spotted sunfish will feed on invertebrates, insects, and small fishes when they are easy to catch. The bulk of their diet consists of a variety of plants and animals that are usually associated with aquatic vegetation, brush, or rubble.

Age and Growth

Very little information is available on age and growth. A four-year-old fish averages about six inches long.

Eating Quality

The flesh is excellent. Preparation is the same as the redbreast sunfish.

World Record

None exists due to its small size.

State Record

13.25 ounces, caught in the Suwannee River, in 1984.

Warmouth (*Lepomis gulosus*)

Common Names
Warmouth bass, warmouth perch, goggle-eye, redeye, and goggle-eyed perch.

Description
The warmouth closely resembles a bass or a bream. It has a stout, deep body similar to that of a bluegill or redear sunfish, yet has a large bass-like mouth. The red eye and large mouth are the first conspicuous field marks of mature warmouth. They vary from brassy to dark-olive green and often have a purple tint overall. Broad, irregular dark bars give it a mottled appearance. The soft-rayed portions of the dorsal and anal fins are marked with rows of dark spots. Three or four conspicuous dark stripes radiate back from the eye across to the cheek and gill cover.

Subspecies
There are no recognized subspecies. However, warmouths readily hybridize with other members of the sunfish family.

Range
Found throughout Florida.

Habitat
Warmouths inhabit swamps, marshes, shallow lakes, slow-moving streams, and canals with soft, muddy bottoms. They prefer to stay around aquatic vegetation, stumps and snags, and under the banks of streams and ponds. They have more tolerance for muddy water than most species.

Spawning Habits
Warmouths are solitary nesters that prefer to build their nest adjacent to some submerged object. Nests are found over a wide range of water depths. They often spawn more than once a year, usually between April and August. Females may produce 3,000 to 23,000 eggs.

Feeding Habits
Warmouths are carnivorous. Crayfish, shrimp, insects, and small fishes make up the bulk of its diet. Most of its feeding is done in the morning, as it seems to sleep at night.

Age and Growth
Warmouths are capable of living up to eight years and may reach a length of 12 inches and a weight of approximately one pound.

Eating Quality
The warmouth has little food value; however, they are good to eat when caught

from clean water. Like other panfish they are small and bony. The flesh is usually prepared by deep-frying after rolling it in seasoned cornmeal.

State and World Records
2 pounds, 7 ounces, caught in Guess Lake (Yellow River), Florida, in 1985.

Peacock Bass (*Cichla ocellaris*)

Common Name
Butterfly peacock.

Description
The body shape is similar to that of a largemouth bass. Body color is generally golden with three black vertical bars and a black spot with a silver halo on the caudal fin but have highly variable color patterns. In older fish, the bars tend to fade and may be completely absent in fish larger than 3 pounds.

Subspecies
It is a distinct species with no known subspecies.

Range
Butterfly peacocks were first stocked into the main coastal canal systems of southeast Florida in 1984. Low water temperatures prevent this species from becoming abundant outside of eastern Dade, Broward, and Palm Beach counties. The native range of butterfly peacock lies within the Amazon River basin of South America.

Habitat
Butterfly peacock were stocked in the freshwater sections of the major coastal canals in southeast Florida and support good fisheries. The many lakes, small ponds, rock pits, and lateral canals in eastern Dade and Broward Counties also provide excellent opportunities to catch butterfly peacock. They are frequently found in shady areas around bridges, culverts, and other structures. Canal junctions, bends, dead ends and fallen trees are also areas that concentrate butterfly peacock.

Spawning Habits
Spawning occurs in Florida from April through September with a peak in May and June. A female will select a flat, hard surface near shore and spawn between 4,000 and 10,000 eggs. Both parents care for the eggs and guard the young for several months. Male butterfly peacock develop a hump on their forehead while spawning and guarding young.

Feeding Habits
Butterfly peacock prey primarily on fish. They feed only during daylight hours and rely on their exceptional speed to capture food.

Dan Limbaugh enjoys a misty morning fly fishing for peacock bass.

Age and Growth
Butterfly peacock grow rapidly to 12-14 inches after which they become much heavier with each inch they add in length. A 17-inch fish will weigh approximately 3 pounds while a 19-inch fish will weigh up to 5 pounds. The largest butterfly peacock caught in Florida weighed 103 pounds and measured 23.3 inches. It is not known how long butterfly peacock typically live.

Eating Qualities
This is an excellent tasting fish with white, flaky meat and mild flavor.

State and World Records
The state record is 98 pounds and the current world record (caught in Florida) is 9.5 pounds. The International Game Fish Association recently added butterfly peacock to its list of world record game fishes eligible for line class records. This provides Florida anglers with one of the best opportunities ever to catch a world record fish.

Oscar (*Astronotus ocellatus*)

Common Name
Oscar.

Description
Young fish have wavy white and orange bars and spots on black head, body, and fins. The body and fins of adults are olive blue-green in color with large black blotches. A black spot surrounded by red is at base of upper caudal fin. The second dorsal, caudal, and anal fins are large and rounded. Some have orange or red on the body.

Subspecies
It is a distinct species with no known subspecies.

Range
The distribution of oscars in Florida is restricted to the area south of Tampa. The native range of oscars lies within the Orinoco, La Plata, and Amazon River basins in South America.

Habitat
Marsh-type habitats with man-controlled water levels have the largest oscar populations, although they are found in lesser numbers in most permanent aquatic habitats in southern peninsular Florida.

Spawning Habits
Oscars spawn when water temperatures range between 82 and 91. The preferred spawning site is a flat, solid surface parallel or slightly raised off the bottom. The female will lay up to 3,000 eggs and both parents care for the eggs and guard the young.

Feeding Habits
Oscars are carnivorous, preying on small fish, insects and amphibians.

Age and Growth
An average-sized oscar caught in the Everglades is 10 inches long and weighs ¾ of a pound. A two-pound fish is considered large. Biologists do not know how long oscars typically live.

Eating Qualities
White, flaky meat with good flavor.

State Record
The state record weighed 2.34 pounds and was caught in Lake Okeechobee.

Chain Pickerel (*Esox niger*)

Common Names
Pike, river pike, grass pike, jack, jackfish, eastern pickerel, chainsides, mud pickerel, black chain pike, duck-billed pike.

Description
Chain pickerels are deep olive-green on the back, shading to a creamy yellow on the belly. Olive green blotches are present within distinct black chain-like or interwoven markings on the sides. There is a distinct dark, vertical bar below the eye. The cheek and gill covers are completely covered by scales. The underside of the lower jaw has 14-17 branchiostegal rays.

Subspecies
There are no recognized subspecies. However, they hybridize readily with redfin pickerels.

Range
They are found statewide.

Habitat
Normally found in vegetated lakes, swamps and backwaters, and small to large rivers. They prefer water temperatures from 75 to 80 degrees.

Spawning Habits
Chain pickerels are random spawners rather than nest builders. Spawning occurs in late winter to spring among heavy aquatic weed growth or flooded grasses, in water from a few inches deep to several feet deep. Large number of adhesive eggs are scattered over vegetation. No nest is constructed and no parental care is given to the eggs or fry. About three to four weeks after hatching, they begin cannibalizing other fry.

Feeding Habits
The chain pickerel's diet is mainly fish. They also eat insects, frogs, mice, crayfish, and a wide variety of other foods.

Age and Growth
Sexes are similar. Sexual maturity is reached in the first to fourth year, and maximum life span is probably eight to nine years. Females grow faster than males. In Florida, chain pickerels can reach lengths of up to 30 inches.

Eating Quality
The white, flaky meat tastes good but is quite bony.

World Record
9.38 pounds, caught in Guest Millpond, Georgia, in 1961.

State Record
80 pounds, caught in Lake Talquin, Gadsden County, in 1971

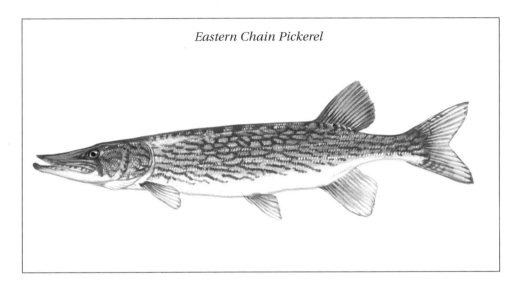

Eastern Chain Pickerel

Redfin Pickerel (Esox americanus)

Common Names
Little pickerel, mud pickerel, grass pickerel, banded pickerel, redfinned pike.

Description
Redfin pickerels have 15 to 36 dark, wavy vertical bars and reddish-orange lower fins. Otherwise, the coloration is much the same as that of chain pickerels. There is a dark, backward slanting bar below the eye. The snout is shorter and broader than that of a chain pickerel. Normally there are 11 to 13 branchiostegal rays on the underside of the lower jaw. The cheek and gill covers are completely scaled.

Subspecies
Two are recognized: the redfin pickerel (*Esox americanus americanus*) and the grass pickerel (*Esox americanus vermiculatus*). Both subspecies hybridize with chain pickerels in the Florida panhandle. Most of the redfin pickerels in Florida are intergrades between (*Esox americanus americanus*) and (*Esox americanus vermiculatus*). The former occurs in extreme northeast Florida.

Range
They are widely distributed in Florida but diminish in numbers south of Lake Okeechobee.

Habitat
Usually found in among heavy growths of aquatic plants in sluggish streams, in shallow coves of lakes, or in ponds. They prefer water from 75 to 80 degrees. Redfin pickerels may be the dominant predator fish in small creeks.

Age and Growth
This species grows much more slowly than other members of the pike family. The maximum age is about eight years, but the usual life span is seven to eight years. There is little difference in growth between males and females, although females live longer. Redfin pickerels rarely exceed 12 inches long.

Eating Quality
White, flaky, sweet-tasting meat, but quite bony.

World Record
1.50 pounds, caught in Bluff Lake, South Carolina, in 1984.

State Record
15 pounds, caught in Jr. Walton Pond, Okaloosa County, in 1986.

Kayaker Pete Elkins can attest to the fight of largemouth bass caught from coastal streams

American Shad

American Shad (*Alosa sapidissima*)

Common Names
   White shad.

Description
   Green or greenish blue with metallic luster on back; silvery sides; body compressed; upper jaw with a smaller or larger median notch; lower jaw not protruding beyond upper jaw, teeth missing in examples greater than 8 inches; adipose eyelid present, chest and abdomen with bony sautes; pectoral fin without a free axillary process; cheek deeper than long; sometimes with a few spots on sides behind shoulder spot.

Subspecies
   None; very similar to hickory shad (*Alosa mediocris*), which also occur in the St. Johns River, Florida.

Range
   St. Lawrence River, Canada to St. Johns River, Florida. In Florida, it occurs only in the northeast, mostly in the St. Johns River and Nassau River.

Habitat
   Anadromous; lives most of its life at sea.

Spawning Habits
   Most spawning occurs between late December and early April in the stretch of the St. Johns River from Sanford to Melbourne. Eggs are spawned directly into the

river where they drift freely for 2-3 days. Juveniles leave the river when it cools in late fall or early winter. Juveniles mature into adults in the Atlantic Ocean and do not return to the St. Johns River until they are ready to spawn, two to five years later. In the St. Johns River and all other rivers below Cape Fear, North Carolina, shad die after they spawn.

Feeding Habits
Plankton feeders, but strike small, bright spoons and flies.

Age and Growth
Two to four inches long when they leave the river (6 to 10 months), although they can grow up to 30 inches.

Eating Quality
Flesh good, especially smoked; roe is excellent.

State Record
5.19 pounds from the St. Johns River, Seminole County in 1990. St. Johns River, Volusia County in 1992.

Largest on Record
13.5 pounds.

Striped Bass (*Morone saxatilis*)

Common Names
Striper, rockfish, rock, linesides.

Description
The striper is the largest member of the temperate bass family. Body coloration is olive-green to blue-gray on the back with silvery to brassy sides and white on the belly. It is easily recognized by the seven or eight prominent black uninterrupted horizontal stripes along the sides. The stripes are often interrupted or broken and are usually absent on young fish of less than six inches. The striper is longer and sleeker and has a larger head than its close and similar looking relative, the white bass, which rarely exceeds three pounds.

Subspecies
There are no recognized subspecies.

Range
The striper on the Atlantic Coast has a range from the Gulf of St. Lawrence, N.Y.

to the St. Johns River in northern Florida and in the Gulf of Mexico from western Florida to Louisiana.

Habitat

All Florida populations of striped bass are river dwellers rather than anadromous (normally living in salt or brackish waters, but entering freshwater streams to spawn). The species has been widely introduced in numerous lakes, rivers, and impoundments throughout the world. Stripers prefer relatively clear water with a good supply of open-water baitfish. Their preferred water temperature range is 65 to 70 degrees.

Spawning Habits

Spawns in March, April, and May when water temperatures reach 60 to 68 degrees. Stripers are river spawners that broadcast millions of eggs in the water currents without affording any protection or parental care. During spawning, seven or eight smaller males surround a single, large female and bump her to swifter currents at the water surface. At ovulation, ripe eggs are discharged and scattered in the water as males release sperm. Fertilized eggs must be carried by river currents until hatching (about 48 hours) to avoid suffocation. Fry and fingerlings spend most of their time in lower rivers and estuaries. Because striped bass eggs must remain suspended in a current until hatching, impoundments are unsuitable for natural reproduction. Freshwater populations have been maintained by stocking fingerlings, and, despite initial difficulties in hatchery procedures for obtaining females with freely flowing eggs, a modern technique of inducing ovulation with the use of a hormone has been successful.

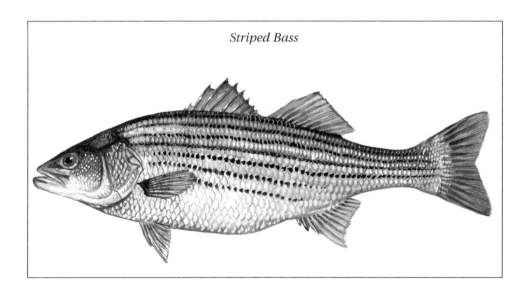

Striped Bass

Feeding Habits

Stripers are voracious feeders and consume any kind of small fish and a variety of invertebrates. Preferred foods for adults mainly consist of gizzard and threadfin shad, golden shiners, and minnows. Younger fish prefer to feed on amphipods and mayflies. Very small stripers feed on zooplankton. Like other temperate bass, they move in schools, and all members of the school tend to feed at the same time. Heaviest feeding is in early morning and in evening, but they feed sporadically throughout the day, especially when skies are overcast. Feeding slows when water temperatures drop below 50 degrees but does not stop completely.

Age and Growth

Stripers are fast growing and long-lived and have reached weights of over 40 pounds in Florida. Sexual maturity occurs at about two years of age for male stripers and at four years of age for females. They can reach a size of 10 to 12 inches the first year.

Overcast mornings are great for catching stripers that congregate around bridges and below dams.

Eating Quality

Stripers are excellent eating fish and may be prepared in many ways. Smaller fish are usually fried and larger ones are baked.

World Record (landlocked)

66 pounds, caught in O'Neill Forebay, California, in 1988.

World Record

78 pounds, 8 ounces, caught in Atlantic City, New Jersey, in 1982.

State Record

38 pounds, 9 ounces, caught in Lake Seminole, in 1979.

Sunshine Bass (*M. chrysops x M. saxatilis*)

Common Names

Striped bass hybrid, wiper, whiterock, palmetto bass.

Description

The sunshine bass is a hybrid produced by crossing a female white bass with a male striped bass. Sunshines closely resemble both striped bass and white bass, making identification difficult, particularly for young fish. When comparing adult fish, the sunshine has a deep body and an arched back similar to the white bass. Sunshines can often be distinguished by broken or irregular stripes on the front half of the body and straight lines on the rear half of body. A mid-body break in line pattern occasionally occurs.

Subspecies

There are no recognized subspecies since the sunshine bass is an artificial hybrid. Some states, including Florida, produce a hybrid called palmetto bass that is a cross between a female striped bass and a male white bass.

Range

Sunshines are stocked throughout Florida. The largest fish are from northwest Florida, but sunshine bass have produced fisheries as far south as Lake Osborne in West Palm Beach.

Habitat

Sunshines appear to prefer areas within lakes and rivers similar to striped bass and white bass. Older sunshine bass require cooler water during summer months.

Spawning Habits

Sunshines do not reproduce naturally. They are hatchery-produced by Florida Game and Fresh Water Fish Commission biologists and stocked in selected river and lakes. Sunshine bass were developed by the Commission with two goals in mind. The first was to control abundant gizzard shad populations in nutrient-rich lakes. The second goal was to create and maintain a new fishery that would supplement existing native species. The sunshines have served those functions in the Apalachicola River system, one of only a few northwest Florida rivers containing enough shad and thermal refuges to ensure optimal growth of sunshines. In most years since 1975, sunshine bass have been stocked in Lake Seminole and the Apalachicola River.

Feeding Habits

Like stripers, sunshines are voracious feeders and consume any kind of small fish including threadfin and gizzard shad. Young fish also feed on mayflies and crustaceans. Sunshines also travel and feed in schools with peak activity in the early morning or evening.

Age and Growth

Sunshines are probably best known for their rapid growth. They have attained weights of six to seven pounds by three years of age.

Eating Quality

Similar to striped and white bass.

World Record-

24 pounds, 3 ounces, caught in Leesville Lake, Virginia, in 1989.

State Record

16 pounds, 5 ounces, caught in Lake Seminole, in 1985.

White Bass (*Morone chrysops*)

Common Names

Stripe, silver bass, striper, sand bass, barfish.

Description

The white bass looks similar to a shortened version of its larger relative, the striped bass. It is silvery-white overall with five to eight horizontal dusky black stripes along the sides. Stripes below the lateral line are faint and often broken in an irregular pattern. It differs most noticeably in being shorter and stockier with a smaller head, and the dorsal fins are set closer together. The white bass has a deep body, strongly arched behind head and is deepest between the dorsal fins.

Subspecies
There are no recognized subspecies.

Range
General boundaries are the St. Lawrence River in the east; Lake Winnipeg in the north; the Rio Grande in the west; and northwest Florida and Louisiana in the south. It has been stocked within and outside its natural range. In Florida, white bass are found only in the Apalachicola and Ochlockonee River systems.

Habitat
White bass are found in large lakes and streams connected to major river systems and in rivers with moderate current. They prefer clear water with a temperature range of 65 to 75 degrees. Manmade impoundments have greatly favored the white bass, but the species is one that can become overabundant and stunt.

Spawning Habits
Male white bass migrate upstream in large schools to a dam or other barrier in early spring, followed shortly by schools of females. Spawning occurs in moving water over gravel shoals or a hard bottom. Large females may lay as many as half a million adhesive eggs that stick to rocks and gravel. If no water current is present white bass have been known to spawn on wind-swept sandy beaches. After spawning, they abandon their eggs and provide no parental care. Fry hatch in only two to three days.

Feeding Habits
White bass are primarily piscivorous. Fry feed on zooplankton first and within a few weeks larger crustaceans and insects are eaten. Larger fish prefer to feed on minnows and thrive on open- water baitfish like gizzard and threadfin shad. Like the striper, white bass move in schools and feed most heavily around dawn or dusk.

Age and Growth
Although white bass may live up to 10 years, few live beyond three to four years. Females grow slightly faster and probably live longer than males. The average size is one pound with fish over two pounds considered large.

Eating Quality
The flesh is similar to that of the striped bass and may be prepared by frying, baking, broiling, or stewing.

World Record
6 pounds, 13 ounces, caught in Lake Orange, in Orange, Virginia, in 1989.

State Record
4 pounds, 11 ounces, caught in Apalachicola River, in 1982.

Other Freshwater Species

Although there are numerous other freshwater species in Florida, a flyfisher is not likely to target them because they do not readily take flies. Among the more common species of freshwater fish in our lakes and rivers are the bowfin, catfish (channel, white, flathead, blue, brown, and yellow), common carp, gar (Florida, longnose, alligator and spotted), and tilapia.

Pete Elkins took this snook from brackish water in the lower portion of a coastal river.

FRESHWATER FISHES PREFERRED TEMPERATURES

Please note that feeding temperatures only refer to preferred ranges and are subject to wide variations.

SPECIES	FEEDING TEMPTURE	SPAWNING TEMPERATURE
American Shad	45-70	50-65
Striped Bass	55-75	55-71
Spotted Bass	65-80	60-70
Redbreast	70-85	60-82
Black Crappie	70-75	62-65
Redeye Bass	65-80	62-69
Largemouth Bass	65-80	62-75
Shoal Bass	65-80	64-73
Suwannee Bass	65-80	65-68
Redear Sunfish	65-80	70-80
Bluegill	70-85	75-85
Oscar	70-90	82-91

(Temperature ranges are from the USFWS Fish Culture Guidelines or from subjective recommendations by FWC biologists.)

Saltwater Species

The primary saltwater species that you are likely to encounter as you move downstream on a coastal river where fresh water begins to turn brackish are flounder, redfish, snook, spotted seatrout, and tarpon. Freshwater flyfishers should be prepared to encounter these species on the lower sections of most coastal rivers.

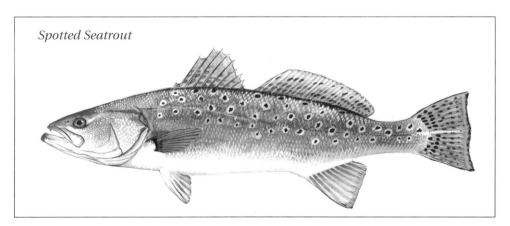

Spotted Seatrout

Getting In Gear

Most of the flies that you will be using in Florida's freshwater can be easily cast with a 5-or 6-weight rod. The larger deer-haired patterns and Deceivers for largemouth or striped bass might warrant an 8-weight rod. These two rods will adequately cover most situations that you will encounter, whether it be a stream or river or a lake, pond, pit, or puddle.

*A well-equipped fly angler can fish
comfortably for many hours.*

The reel that you select should match the rod size and have a good drag. A spring and pawl drag will be fine for bream and crappie, but if you are going to tackle a striper or largemouth bass, you may want to consider using a reel with a disc drag system. If there is any chance that you will be fishing in salt water or even at the lower end of a coastal river where there is a mix of both fresh and salt water, choose a reel that has an anodized finish. The corrosion that takes place will ruin an unprotected reel in very short order. Be sure to wash and wipe down your rod and reel after using them under these conditions.

Most of the water that you will be fishing is shallow, and a floating line will work fine. If you are after crappie in the summer or stripers in a spring, you may want to use an intermediate or full sink-tip line. Florida's waters are often exposed and susceptible to wind. A weight-forward line helps punch through the wind to get a little more distance. Many anglers also load their reel with a line that is one weight more than the rod is intended to handle in order to cheat just a bit on the wind.

Much has been written about building leaders, but in this regard, our fish are more forgiving than the wary trout. I have found that a 20-pound butt section of fluorocarbon, followed by a tippet of fluorocarbon matched to the species you will likely encounter makes a good leader. For bream and crappie, I use 6-pound fluorocarbon for the tippet. In streams and rivers (excepting the St. Johns River), I like a 10-pound fluorocarbon tippet. If I anticipate the possibility of a big bass or a testy striped bass, I will use 14-pound fluorocarbon for my tippet.

Before moving on to gear that you might wear and carry, I must digress and follow up on the need to be able to cast for distance despite some degree of wind. The water in which you will be fishing will likely be gin clear and moving slowly, if at all, and the fish will not feed if they are aware of your presence. You will not be drifting a slot or short run of fast moving water and making roll casts back to the top to start another drift. Nor will you likely have to mend your line because of drag. To be successful, you are going to have to remain at some distance from your quarry and make a long cast, ideally preceded with only one or two false casts. How far must you be able to accurately cast? A good benchmark would be 50-60 feet with only two false casts. This may require a technique to which you are not accustomed.

I strongly suggest that if you are not proficient at casting with a double-haul (loading the rod both as you lift line out of the water and once again as you begin to move the line back toward the water after it is straight behind you), you practice this technique. You may be using a fly rod and reel with which you are not familiar while fishing in Florida and your distance might be less than it would otherwise be. A couple of hours spent practicing the double-haul with the fly rod and reel that you will have in your hands while in Florida will pay enormous dividends.

You are going to need to protect your skin from the sun's ultraviolet rays to avoid getting sunburned. Don't try to take any short cuts here, or you may miss a couple of days fishing while you wait for a new layer of skin. The obvious choice is a sunblock or sunscreen lotion applied liberally to exposed skin. You may have to do this a couple of times during the day to make sure that you have complete protection. Don't overlook the backs of your hands, as they will likely be turned up towards the sun, as well as frequently in and out of the water. You may wear a hat that shields your face from direct sunlight, but the reflected rays off the water compound the sun's effect. Keep your lips protected, too. Another area often overlooked is the top of the ears. A baseball cap will leave them exposed all day long, so you may want to consider another style of hat that offers greater protection. Polarized sunglasses are a must. Nothing cuts down on the reflection off the water any better. They help you to see into clear water and can go a long way in preventing a headache caused by squinting and peering into the sun all day.

You will appreciate having the lightweight, supplex shirts and pants that dry so quickly. The shirts have numerous pockets and the vents allow for air circulation when the boat is moving. The long sleeve version provides that much more sun protection. Avoid the darker colors, however, as they are warmer. Shoes are a matter of personal choice. I wear sandals and take them off while fly fishing so that I can feel the line when I step on it on the deck of the boat. If you choose to do the same, put some sunscreen on the top of those dogs, too.

You will not likely need a vest if you are fishing out of a boat with any amount of storage room. The exception to this is when fishing from a kayak, and I have found that a "shorty" vest is perfect for holding several hours' worth of fly fishing necessities while casting from a seated position. Another common item that you are not likely to need in Florida's freshwater are waders. Most of your fishing will have to be done from a boat, and they will be unnecessary. There certainly are exceptions, such as wading out from the shoreline to fish the tailrace below a dam in the winter for stripers. If you are fishing a stream in the summer, the cool water might be quite refreshing.

Hopefully, you will not encounter mosquitoes or the smaller, but even more annoying, "no-see-ums." A prudent angler will be prepared with some repellant to spray on if needed. I even go so far as to carry a small squirt bottle of 100 percent DEET in my tackle bag. I find that I only need it about once a year, but when I do, there is no substitute for it short of getting off the water. (With the West Nile virus becoming more prevalent, I won't ever be without insect spray.) Try to keep the spray off your flies and terminal tackle.

Lastly, bring water. In fact, bring more water than you need. You can continue to fish after running out of food, but you need to rehydrate your body at regular intervals if you find that you are perspiring extensively. Do not wait until you are thirsty; drink some water every hour.

Each person's needs and wants will be different, but if you begin making your trip list by including the items I have mentioned, you should find that you are well equipped for a good day on the water.

Tips on Traveling to Florida

If you plan to fly into Florida, there are a number of large, international airports to which you can usually get a direct flight, such as Jacksonville, Miami, Tampa, and Orlando. Lodging in and around these areas is nearly unlimited. There are also numerous smaller airports at places like Daytona Beach, Melbourne, Ft. Lauderdale, Ft. Myers, Sarasota, Gainesville, and Tallahassee that can easily be reached with connecting flights from around the country. In addition, there is a good system of regional airports serving intra-state travelers.

Fortunately, Florida is a popular destination and in addition to frequent air service, there usually are good rates to be had. Be sure to check with your travel agent or check airline websites. In the post-9/11 era, what you can carry onboard an airplane is severely limited. You will not be able to hand-carry any hooks (no flies) and when your reels are x-rayed, they are sure to cause your luggage to be opened and hand checked. Rod tubes are now suspicious, too, and cause for scrutiny. This is the price we pay for added security, and airline employees have little discretion in how they enforce new regulations. Heed the warning to arrive at the airport early, as a fly-fisher's gear attracts more than casual attention.

Competition for the tourist dollar keeps rental car prices down and rental agencies near airports are well stocked with air-conditioned cars. Florida probably has the best rates for car rentals in the country.

Just another day in paradise.

If you are driving, the interstate highway system is quite good and well maintained, so travel by road should be relatively easy. Note that the exit numbers are in the process of being changed from consecutive numbers to a system that corresponds to the mile-marker at that exit. I have provided a table showing both numbers, but the book uses the older, consecutive numbering system in describing how to get to various bodies of water.

Lodging is also competitive, and there are vacancies most of the time. Competition also keeps the rates in check.

I have provided the address and phone number of the chamber of commerce for numerous cities. Check with them not only about places to stay, car rentals, and places to eat, but inquire about any "special events." You may be surprised to learn of planned programs that you will want to attend, or find that crowds are anticipated in numbers you cannot imagine. For example, in February and July, Daytona Beach attracts 200,000 NASCAR race fans, and Interstate 95 (between Jacksonville and Daytona) and Interstate 4 (between Orlando and Daytona) get more than a little crowded with the extra traffic.

Be prepared for the humidity. Florida does not have oppressively hot temperatures, but the humidity can make you uncomfortable. Drink plenty of fluids and wear light, well-ventilated clothing. The dress in Florida is probably more casual than you may be accustomed to. Being comfortable seems to be more important than being stylish. In the section on Florida facts at the front of this book I provided temperature charts for various locations to help you decide what clothing to bring. If you add some raingear, you will likely be prepared for whatever you may encounter.

The onshore breezes that keep Florida's temperatures in check also produce heavy, late-afternoon rains in the summer. These make for pleasant evenings, but you are advised to seek cover when you see the sky darken. The winds can be intense as a front approaches, lightning strikes are frequent, and the rain locally intense. It is a great time to get off the water or road and relax for an hour or so.

Fishing licenses can be obtained from most tackle stores, as well as from major retailers like Wal-mart and K-mart. You may also obtain your license by phone by calling 888-FISH-FLORIDA (888-347-4356) and selecting the day that you want your license to begin. Out-of-state licenses are only available for seven days or a full year.

Florida's State Parks

The Florida State Park system is an award-winning collection of over 150 sites spread throughout the state offering a variety of opportunities for flyfishers and their families. After being a finalist in 1999, the Florida State Park system went on to win the National Gold Medal Award the following year for being the best in the nation.

You may wish to make a state park your base camp while you venture out to fly fish. Most of the parks have camping facilities with electrical hook-up and water, many have boat ramps giving access to lakes and rivers, several have cabins that can be reserved as far ahead as eleven months in advance, and some have canoes and kayaks for rent. There is an excellent guide available (*The Florida State Parks Guide, The Real Florida*) that provides a description of activities and facilities available at each state park, as well as including the address and phone number for the site. To obtain a copy, write: Department of Environmental Protection Park Information, Mail Station #535, 3900 Commonwealth Blvd., Tallahassee, FL 32399-0300; call: 850-488-9872; or visit the website: www.dep.state.fl.us/parks and link to "park guide request."

The state parks are generally located on sites of historic, cultural, or ecological significance and offer resource-based recreation. Among the special features and facilities that are available at differing sites include: camping (full facility, primitive, group and youth); picnic areas; canoeing; fishing; hiking and nature trails; beaches; boating; boat ramps; interpretive exhibits; visitor's centers; bicycling; swimming; scuba; snorkeling; campfire circles; horse trails; showers; concessions and restaurants; cabins and lodging; boat tours; tubing; rollerblading; and wildlife viewing.

Among the many interesting sites in the state park system is Edward Ball Wakulla Springs State Park, which has been described as having the largest and deepest single spring in the world. It is 185 feet deep and discharges 600,00 gallons of water per minute. In addition, Fakahatchee Strand Preserve State Park has the largest variety of wild orchids in the United States, while Ft. Zachary Taylor Historic State Park has the largest collection of Civil War armaments in the country. Looking for an underwater state park? Florida had the first one in the nation. John Pennekamp Coral Reef State Park even has camping available, although all campsites are above ground. The list could go on and on, and you should consider taking advantage of this inexpensive opportunity to see what is uniquely Florida.

Florida's state parks offer over 3,300 campsites and more than 100 cabins (with another 100 cabins under construction). Pets are permitted at most campsites, but they are not allowed in cabins. You may make reservations for cabins and campsites up to eleven months in advance by calling 800-326-3521 or online at www.dep.state.fl.us/parks (link to "reservations").

Florida's State Park system was recently voted the best in the nation. The scenic parks offer excellent lodging and recreational opportunities.

Why Drawdown?

Throughout this guidebook I have referred to lakes that were being "drawn down," often accompanied by a prediction of better fishing soon to come. The reasons for both the drawdowns and my predictions can be easily understood.

THE PROBLEM

In the 1950s and 1960s, many lakes and waterways throughout central and southern Florida were modified for the purpose of flood control. Usually, meandering waterways were straightened and made deeper, allowing water to rush onward to the lakes and not spill their banks onto rich, fertile flatlands. The result, however, was that organic material that naturally washed into the streams was swept onward to the lakes without the opportunity to be filtered out of the water. The lakes, with their slow moving water and aquatic plant life, trapped tons and tons of organic material and became holding basins for the sediment as it continued to pour in on a daily basis. Hard, sandy bottoms gave way to a thick layer of muck and unnatural plant growth. As the organic material decayed, oxygen was depleted and the lakes were no longer capable of supporting marine life to the same degree as they had before. When the problem got really bad, algae would cover the surface and consume nearly all the oxygen. The result was often an extensive kill of the remaining fish.

THE SOLUTION

The long-term solution is to return the waterways to their natural state. Perhaps you are aware of organizations attempting to reclaim portions of trout streams in northern states so that they may be productive once again. In Florida, the problem is the same, but on a much bigger scale. The midsection of the state is flat, and flooding has been quite extensive at times. In the past 50 years, much of the reclaimed land has become populated. Numerous communities now line these waterways. The costs associated with putting the bends back into the rivers is staggering at a time when money is not readily available. Fortunately, efforts are being made, but it is a slow process fraught with political and economic considerations.

The short-term solution, however, is to drawdown a lake. The process requires the level of a lake to be lowered several feet so that bottom sediments are allowed to consolidate, dry, and become compacted. The layer of muck that has accumulated over the years is then removed and desirable native aquatic plants are replanted on the substrate. Along with better understanding of the drawdown process have come reduced costs and quicker completion times. Presently, the cost to remove the bottom sediment is about $10 per cubic yard, down from more than twice that amount, as contractors have established a market for the removed material to be used as "fill." Projects can now be completed in about 4 months, and they are typically done in the winter when the lakes see less use and rain seldom occurs.

After completion, lakes have historically had a couple of strong year classes of fish, especially in the areas that have been renovated. This surge soon begins to decline, however, as a lake once again starts to deteriorate from the continued influx of organically rich water. For example, Lake Kissimmee in Region 3 had a drawdown in 1977 and the lake quickly became on of the best fisheries in the state, if not the nation. The highly successful spawns that followed resulted in a decade of quality fishing with many bass growing to trophies exceeding 10 pounds. Twenty years later, though, more than 52 miles of shallow habitat had been reduced to less than two miles of productive water. Electrofishing surveys collected only 13 bass per hour that were less than 12 inches, indicating that spawning conditions were once again poor. Another drawdown was done in 1996 and 1,500,000 cubic yards of organic material was removed from 971 acres along 22 miles of shoreline. As before, the following two year classes of fish were exceptional, and subsequent electrofishing surveys revealed that bass less than 12 inches were being collected at the rate of 86 fish per hour. Do the math and you will see that with growth rates being what they are for Florida strain largemouth bass, Lake Kissimmee has a huge number of quality fish right now, and it will continue to produce exceptional catches of big fish for many years to come.

Lake Kissimmee is only one example of the drawdown process, but it is no different than lakes around the rest of Florida. The cycle will repeat and lakes will be "hot" for several years and then they will no longer support the fishery they recently did. Fortunately for informed flyfishers, the results are predictable and I have noted scheduled drawdowns on major lakes throughout this guidebook. When one is completed, add three years for catch rates that will be staggering. Give the lake about six years and it will yield fantastic catches of assorted sizes, many of them quality fish. Wait nine years and the number of small fish caught will begin to decline, but there will be trophy fish to be had like nowhere else in the country. When they are gone, however, a declining fishery continues to worsen, and the drawdown process must be repeated.

A hefty Lake Kissimmee largemouth bass
goes into an angler's livewell.

Freshwater Fishing Regulations

For a complete listing of the most current fishing regulations, go to the Florida Fish and Wildlife Commission website: http://floridafisheries.com/rules.html.

GENERAL STATEWIDE BAG AND LENGTH LIMITS

Special bag and length limits apply to some lakes, river, and Fish Management Areas. Other fishes considered to be nongame fishes have no daily bag or possession limits, except as noted in individual Fish Management Area regulations.

5 **Black Bass:** (largemouth, Suwannee, redeye, spotted, and shoal bass, individually or in total), only one of which may be 22 inches or longer in total length. In south Florida: only one bass may be 14 inches in total length or longer. South and east of the Suwannee River: black bass less than 14 inches in total length must be released immediately. In the Suwannee River: areas north and west of the Suwannee River, and in any tributary river, creek or stream of the Suwannee River: black bass less than 12 inches in total length must be released immediately.

50 **Panfish**: including bluegill, redear sunfish (shellcracker), flier, longear sunfish, mud sunfish, shadow bass, spotted sunfish (stumpknockers), warmouth, and redbreast sunfish, individually or in total.

25 **Black Crappie:** (speckled perch) and/or white crappie, individually or in total.

20 **Striped bass, white bass, and sunshine bass:** (individually or in total), of which only 6 may be 24 inches or longer in total length.

2 **Butterfly peacock bass:** only one of which may be 17 inches or longer in total length.

Possession limit is two days' bag limit. It is illegal to transport or possess more than two days' bag limit of fish per licensed angler without a commercial license.

SPECIAL BAG AND LENGTH LIMITS

(See Fish Management Area regulations for bag and length limits for lakes in the Fish Management Area system.)

Jim Woodruff Reservoir, Lake Seminole: 10 black bass, all of which must be at least 12 inches in total length; 15 striped bass, white bass and sunshine bass (individually or in total), of which no more than 2 may be 22 inches or longer in total length; 30 black or white crappie (speckled perch), in total; 50 panfish (does not include black crappie); 15 pickerel (chain, grass and redfin). Possession limit is 50 fish total, regardless of species.

St. Marys River: 10 black bass, all of which must be at least 12 inches in total length; 2 striped bass, both of which must be at least 22 inches in total length; 15 sunshine bass or white bass (individually or in total); 30 black or white crappie (speckled perch), in total; 50 panfish (does not include black crappie); 15 pickerel (chain, grass and redfin). Possession limit is 50 fish total, regardless of species.

Lake Talquin, Leon and Gadsden Counties: Black bass caught that are shorter than 18 inches in total length and black crappie that are less than 10 inches in total length must be released immediately.

Lake Jackson, Leon County: Black bass caught that are shorter than 18 inches in total length must be released immediately.

Ocala National Forest Lakes, Marion County: Lakes Crooked, Wildcat, Grasshopper, Lou, Echo, Quarry Fish Pond, and Hopkins Prairie: all black bass must be released immediately.

Lake Monroe, Volusia and Seminole Counties: Black crappie less than 12 inches in total length must be released immediately.

St. Johns River Water Management Area (Farm 13, including the Stick Marsh), Indian River County: All black bass must be released immediately.

S.N. Knight Tract, Indian River County: All black bass must be released immediately.

Lake Weohyakapka (Walk-in-Water), Polk County: Black bass from 15 to 24 inches in total length must be released immediately. Black bass daily bag limit is 3, only one of which may be 24 inches in total length or longer.

Lake Okeechobee, including Harney Pond Canal (C-41) north of S.R. 78 to water control structure S-71; Indian Prairie Canal (C-40) north of S.R. 78 to water control structure S-72; all of Taylor Creek and Nubbin Slough; C-38 Canal/Kissimmee River south of water control structure S-65E to S.R 78, Okeechobee County: Black bass from 13 inches to 18 inches in total length must be released immediately; bass less than 13 inches or bass 18 inches or longer may be kept.

FISHING LICENSE FEES

Licensing requirements follow the species of fish you are fishing for, regardless of where you are fishing. For example, anglers fishing for and possessing large-mouth bass in brackish water need a freshwater license; anglers fishing for saltwater species in fresh water (e.g., spotted seatrout, red drum, snook, American shad) need a saltwater license to possess these species if fishing from a boat.

Resident

For the purpose of fishing in Florida, a person is a resident if he or she has lived in Florida for six continuous months prior to applying for licenses and claims Florida as his or her primary residence. Active military personnel stationed in Florida, including their spouses and dependent children residing in the household, are considered residents when purchasing fishing licenses. (Resident licenses are valid for 12 months from specified beginning date.)

Resident 12-Month Freshwater Fishing: $13.50

Resident Freshwater Fishing/Hunting Combination: $23.50

Resident Freshwater/Saltwater Combination: $25.50

Resident Freshwater/Saltwater/Hunting Combination: $35.50

64 or Older Hunting and Fishing Permit: $13.50 (Includes Freshwater Fishing and Hunting licenses; and Type I Wildlife Management Area, Archery, Muzzleloading Gun and Turkey permits.)

Sportsman's License: $67.50 (Includes Hunting, Freshwater Fishing and permits for Wildlife Management Area, Archery, Muzzleloading Gun, Turkey and Florida Waterfowl.)

Gold Sportsman's License: $83.50 (Includes all licenses and permits in the Sportsman's License, plus saltwater fishing, Crawfish and Snook permits.)

Nonresident

7-Day Freshwater Fishing: $16.50
(Valid for seven consecutive days from specified beginning date.)

12-Month Freshwater Fishing: $31.50
(Valid for 12 months from specified beginning date.)

Licenses may be purchased from county tax collectors or their subagents, who are generally located at tackle shops, fish camps, and sporting goods stores. In addition to license and stamp fees listed above, subagents are entitled to an additional 50 cents. License fees are set by the Florida Legislature and are subject to change.

FRESHWATER FISHING LICENSE EXEMPTIONS

• Florida residents 65 years of age or older who possess either a Resident Senior Citizen Hunting and Fishing Certificate or proof of age and residency. A Florida Senior Citizen Hunting and Fishing Certificate is accepted in Georgia, but a trout stamp may be required.

• Georgia residents 65 years of age or older who have in their possession a Georgia Honorary Combination Hunting and Fishing License and proof of age.

• Florida residents certified as totally and permanently disabled, who possess a Florida Resident Disabled Person Hunting and Fishing Certificate. Applicants need to provide a certification of total and permanent disability from the United States Armed Forces, Railroad Retirement Board, Florida Worker's Compensation or the United States Veterans Administration. Alternatively, current documentation from the Social Security Administration for Supplemental Security Income (SSI) or Supplemental Security Disability Income (SSDI) benefits also will be accepted.

• Any person who has been accepted by the Florida Department of Health as a client for developmental services, with proof (e.g., retardation).

• Children under 16 years of age.

• Any resident who is a member of the U.S. Armed Forces and is not stationed in Florida, home on leave for 30 days or less, upon submission of orders.

• Anyone fishing in a private fishing pond less than 20 acres. A private pond is a manmade pond constructed for the primary purpose of fishing, entirely within the property lines of the owner and with no surface water connection to public waters.

• Anyone fishing in a private pond of 20 acres or more where the pond owner has purchased a fish pond license at a fee of $3 per surface acre.
• Any person fishing in their county of residence on the homestead of their spouse or minor child, or any minor child fishing on the homestead of their parent.

• Anyone fishing in the St. Marys River or Lake Seminole (but not including tributary creeks in Florida), who has a valid Georgia fishing license.

• Anyone fishing during Free Fishing Weekend.
(Note: A valid Fishing License is required to fish by any method in a Fish Management Area.)

Although the above exemptions apply, individuals may always choose to purchase a license as a way to contribute to fish and wildlife conservation. Purchasing a license also helps the FWC receive more of the excise taxes spent on fishing tackle and motor boat fuels under Federal Aid in Sportfish Restoration.

Methods of Taking Freshwater Fish

Game fish and nongame fish may be taken with pole and line or rod and reel. There is no limit on the number of rods an angler may use.

Freshwater fish may not be taken by use of any free-floating, unattached device, or by use of firearms, explosives, electricity, spear gun, poison, or other chemicals. The taking of fish by underwater swimming or diving is prohibited. It is unlawful to sell, offer for sale or transport out of the state any freshwater game fish unless specifically permitted by the FWC, except that licensed anglers may transport two days' bag limit of legally harvested game fish.

It is illegal to possess any freshwater fish along with gear that cannot legally be used to take freshwater fish, including gear types listed above and below for taking nongame fish or bait. An exception is game fish may be possessed together with cast nets having a stretched mesh size not greater than 1 inch; minnow dip nets not more than 4 feet in diameter; minnow seines having a stretched mesh size not greater than 1 inch, a length not more than 20 feet and a depth not more than 4 feet; and minnow traps not more than 24 inches in length and 12 inches in diameter, with a funnel entrance not more than 1 inch in spread.

It is illegal to fillet or remove the head or tail fin of black bass, striped bass, white bass, sunshine bass, peacock bass, black crappie, and panfish (where special black crappie or panfish size or bag limits are in effect) until after you have completed fishing for the day.

Freshwater Game Fish and Nongame Fish

Game Fish—black bass, black crappie, bluegill, redear sunfish, warmouth, redbreast sunfish, spotted sunfish, flier, mud sunfish, longear sunfish, shadow bass, peacock bass, white bass, striped bass and sunshine bass.

Nongame Fish—bowfin, common carp, catfish, pickerel, eels, gar, threadfin shad, gizzard shad, shiners, tilapia (Nile perch), killifish, suckers, topminnows, and fishes not listed as freshwater game fish and not taken for sport.

FISH MANAGEMENT AREA REGULATIONS

A Fish Management Area (FMA) is a pond, lake, or other body of water established for the management of freshwater fish as a cooperative effort with the local county. The FWC's Division of Freshwater Fisheries manages about 80 water bodies throughout the state that are designated as Fish Management Areas. Examples include most urban fishing lakes and Commission-constructed impoundments. In many cases, these lakes are stocked with channel catfish, largemouth bass, and sunshine bass. Automatic feeders and fish attractors concentrate sportfish for bank anglers. Because of their small size or the lack of a boat ramp, many of these lakes and ponds have not been included in the regional discussion of bodies of water in this guidebook.

A freshwater fishing license is required for all Fish Management Area lakes. Also, special bag limits and methods apply on these lakes. A list of FWC Fish Management Areas and regulations pertaining to each of them is included below. For a complete listing of the most current fishing regulations, go to the Florida Fish and Wildlife Commission website: http://floridafisheries.com/rules.html.

Suzie Reihl admires a largemouth that fell
to a deer-hair popper on a FMA pond.

GENERAL REGULATIONS FOR FISH MANAGEMENT AREAS

1. A fishing license is required for residents from 16 to 64 years of age, and for non-residents 16 or more years of age, to fish by any method, including cane poles, on a Fish Management Area.

2. The possession of fishing tackle is prohibited on any Fish Management Area that is closed to fishing.

3. Daily bag limits and methods of taking freshwater fish apply except as provided for a particular Fish Management Area. The daily bag limit for channel catfish is 6, unless otherwise specified in a Fish Management Area rule. The possession of nets (other than legal minnow seines, cast nets or dip nets), fish traps, trotlines or setlines is prohibited unless specifically authorized by rules established for a particular Fish Management Area.

4. Persons entering or leaving Fish Management Areas that have designated entry points shall enter or leave only at such designated points.

5. Any vehicle, boat, or other transportation device may be searched while in, entering, or leaving a Fish Management Area.

6. Fish Management Areas may be temporarily closed to accommodate management projects (e.g., drawdowns), or if unsafe conditions exist, or as otherwise specified in a specific Fish Management Area rule.

7. Intentional release of wildlife or freshwater fish on Fish Management Areas is prohibited.

SPECIAL REGULATIONS FOR DESIGNATED FISH MANAGEMENT AREAS

Lake Piney Z (193 acres), Leon County: open to fishing.
- All black bass must be released immediately.
- Panfish daily bag limit: 20
- Swimming, possession of firearms, and possession of alcoholic beverages are prohibited.
- Watercraft shall be allowed only as authorized by the City of Tallahassee.

Lake Victor (130 acres), Holmes County: open to fishing.
- Gasoline motors may not be used on boats.
- No motor vehicles on dams, spillways and fishing fingers.

Merritt's Mill Pond (202 acres), Jackson County: open to fishing.
- No rifles or gigs.
- Redear sunfish (shellcracker) daily bag limit: 5
- All redear sunfish less than 14 inches in total length must be immediately released.

Hurricane Lake (318 acres), Okaloosa County: open to fishing.
- Black bass less than 18 inches in total length must be released immediately.
- Gasoline motors may not be used on boats.
- No motor vehicles on dams, spillways and fishing fingers.

Karick Lake (58 acres), Okaloosa County: open to fishing.
- All black bass must be released immediately.
- Gasoline motors may not be used on boats.
- No motor vehicles on dams, spillways and fishing fingers.

Lake Stone (130 acres), Escambia County: open to fishing.
- Gasoline motors may not be used on boats.
- No motor vehicles on dams, spillways and fishing fingers.

Bear Lake (107 acres), Santa Rosa County: open to fishing.
- Gasoline motors may not be used on boats.
- No motor vehicles on dams, spillways and fishing fingers.

Camp Blanding Area, Clay County: Magnolia (205 acres) and Lowery (1,263) Lakes are open to fishing from 30 minutes before sunrise until 30 minutes after sunset, except during National Guard training encampments.
- Picnicking and boat launching are permitted only at designated areas.
- Camping is prohibited.
- All watercraft shall be operated at idle speed only.

Ronnie Vanzant Park (3 acres), Clay County: open to fishing from 30 minutes before sunrise until 30 minutes after sunset.
- Boats or any floating vessel apparatus are prohibited.
- No swimming or camping.
- No person between the ages of 16 years and 64 years shall fish unless accompanied by an angler less than 16 years of age.
- Fishing permitted only with hook and line or rod and reel.
- Nets are prohibited, except for dip nets.
- Black bass less than 16 inches in total length must be released immediately.
- Panfish daily bag limit: 20

Lake Lochloosa (8,350 acres), including Tadpole and Lochloosa Creeks; Orange Lake (12,700 acres), including Orange Lake proper, and waters south and east of CR 346, and west of U.S. Highway 301; and Cross Creek; Alachua and Marion counties: open to fishing.
- All black bass 15 inches or more total length and less than 24 inches must be released immediately.
- Black bass daily bag limit: 3
- No daily bag limit for channel catfish.

Captain Brian Clancey admires a largemouth bass taken from a coastal river's dark water.

Suwannee Lake (63 acres), Suwannee County: open to fishing.
- Black bass less than 18 inches in total length must be released immediately.
- All black crappie less than 10 inches in total length must be released immediately.
- No camping or discharge of firearms.
- No motor vehicles on dam and fishing fingers.
- Possession of alcoholic beverages is prohibited.
- Access to the area from 30 minutes after sunset until 30 minutes before sunrise for any use other than fishing and the launching and loading of boats is prohibited.

Koon Lake (125 acres), Lafayette County: open to fishing.
- No discharge of firearms.

Montgomery Lake (36 acres), Columbia County: open to fishing.
- Black bass less than 16 inches in total length must be released immediately.
- Black crappie daily bag limit: 10
- All black crappie less than 10 inches in total length must be released immediately.
- Panfish daily bag limit: 20
- Boats are restricted to idle speed, no wake.

Watertown Lake (46 acres), Columbia County: open to fishing.
- Black bass less than 16 inches in total length must be released immediately.
- Black crappie daily bag limit: 10
- All black crappie less than 10 inches in total length must be released immediately.
- Panfish daily bag limit: 20
- No discharge of firearms.
- Watercraft shall be operated at idle speed only before 10:00 a.m. and after 4:00 p.m. daily.

Lang Lake (86 acres), Hamilton County: open to fishing from 30 minutes before sunrise until 30 minutes after sunset.
- Gasoline motors may not be used on boats.
- Panfish daily bag limit: 20
- Black bass less than 18 inches in total length must be released immediately.
- All black crappie less than 10 inches in total length must be released immediately.

Lake Jackson (1,020 acres), Osceola County: open to fishing.
- All black bass must be released immediately.
- All black crappie less than 12 inches total length must be released immediately.

Lake Marian (5,739 acres), Osceola County: open to fishing.
- Minnow lift nets and trotlines may be used.

Lake Lorna Doone (14 acres), Orange County: open to fishing.
- Swimming, possession of firearms or possession of alcoholic beverages is prohibited.
- Boats are prohibited.
- Panfish daily bag limit: 20

Lake Richmond (38 acres), Orange County: open to fishing.
- Swimming, possession of firearms or possession of alcoholic beverages is prohibited.
- Boats are prohibited.
- Panfish daily bag limit: 20

Lake Ivanhoe (125 acres), Orange County: open to fishing.
- Swimming, possession of firearms or possession of alcoholic beverages is prohibited.
- Panfish daily bag limit: 20

Clear Lake (339 acres), Orange County: open to fishing.
- Swimming, possession of firearms or possession of alcoholic beverages is prohibited.

Kirkman Pond, Orange County: open to fishing.
- Swimming, possession of firearms or possession of alcoholic beverages is prohibited.
- Panfish daily bag limit: 5
- All bluegill less than 12 inches in total length must be released immediately.
- All black bass must be released immediately.

Lake Lawne (156 acres), Orange County: open to fishing.
- Swimming, possession of firearms or possession of alcoholic beverages is prohibited.

Turkey Lake (323 acres), Orange County: open to fishing.
- Swimming, possession of firearms or possession of alcoholic beverages is prohibited.
- Panfish daily bag limit: 20

- All black bass must be released immediately.

Lake Underhill (147 acres), Orange County: open to fishing.
- Swimming, possession of firearms or possession of alcoholic beverages is prohibited.
- Panfish daily bag limit: 20
- All black bass must be released immediately.

Saddle Creek (321 acres), Polk County: open to fishing.
- All black bass 1 inches or more in total length and less than 18 inches in total length must be released immediately.
- Black bass daily bag limit: 3

Webb Lake (395 acres), Charlotte County: open to fishing.
- Gasoline motors may not be used on boats.
- Gasoline motors may not be used on boats.
- Panfish daily bag limit: 20
- All bluegill and redear sunfish less than 8 inches total length must be released immediately.
- All black bass caught must be released immediately.
- Vehicles may be used only on designated roads.
- Fishing is allowed only during posted hours.

Dan Limbaugh gets into a motorized, square-backed canoe as he prepares to fly fish a WMA lake.

Marl Pits 1 and 3 (6 acres total, including Marl Pit 2), Charlotte County: open to fishing.
- Panfish daily bag limit: 20
- All bluegill and redear sunfish less than 8 inches total length must be released immediately.
- All black bass caught must be released immediately.

Marl Pit 2 (6 acres total, including Marl Pits 1 and 3), Charlotte County: open to fishing.
- All bluegill and redear sunfish less than 12 inches total length must be released immediately.
- Bluegill and redear sunfish combined daily bag limit: 5
- All black bass caught must be released immediately.

Tenoroc Fish Management Area; Lake A (23 acres), Lake B (206 acres), Lake C (27 acres), Lake D (35 acres), Lake F (33 acres), Hydrilla Lake (48 acres), Lake 2 (25 acres), Lake 3 (76 acres), Lake 4 (43 acres), Lake 5 (228 acres), Lake 6 (13 acres), Picnic Lake (59 acres), East Pasture (5 acres), West Pasture (5 acres), Cemetary lake (7 acres), Derby Lake 17 acres), Pasco County.
- Fishing, hunting or trapping is allowed only by permit issued by the Commission. All anglers and hunters must check in and out at the Tenoroc Fish Management Area headquarters and deposit their valid fishing or hunting license with the custodian unless otherwise instructed.
- Days and hours of operation and quotas shall be as designated by the Commission and posted at area headquarters. Quotas will be established for each lake, and fishing is permitted in designated lakes only. Any lake may be closed to public access for management purposes or if access to the lake exposes the public to danger, by posting notice at the Tenoroc check station office. Quotas for open lakes may be temporarily increased to accommodate anglers during times when other lakes are closed due to management construction projects, road repair, unsafe access or special recreational events.

Unless otherwise specified, harvest restrictions are as follows:
- Black crappie daily bag limit: 10
- All black crappie less than 10 inches must be released immediately.
- Sunshine bass daily bag limit: 6
- All black bass caught must be released immediately.
- Fish may not be filleted, nor their head or tail fin removed, until the angler has completed fishing for the day.
- Firearms are prohibited during closed hunting seasons except at the shooting range or on the access road to the shooting range. Guns transported to and from the shooting range shall be unloaded and cased.

- No person shall have any gun under his/her control while under the influence of alcohol or drugs.
- Dogs are prohibited unless leashed.
- Public access is prohibited in areas posted as "Restricted" for protection of threatened or endangered species, or environmentally sensitive areas.
- Motor vehicles may be operated only on named roads, designated parking areas, and fishing ramps as designated in the area use brochure.
- Vehicles may not obstruct designated roads, boat ramps and fire lanes.
- Swimming and float tubes are prohibited.

Regulations for individual water bodies are as follows:

Lakes A, C, D, Shop 2, 3 and 4:
- Gasoline motors may not be used on boats.

Lakes B and 5:
- Outboard motors more than 10 hp May not be used.
- All black bass greater than 15 inches in total length must be released immediately.
- Black bass daily bag limit: 2

Picnic Lake:
- Gasoline motors may not be used on boats.
- Black bass daily bag limit: 2
- Black bass less than 16 inches in total length must be released immediately.
- No person 16 years or more of age may fish unless accompanied by an angler less than 16 years of age.

Lakes East Pasture, West Pasture and Derby:
- Boats may not be used.
- Closed to fishing unless authorized by permit issued by the Commission for Commission-sanctioned events.
- No person shall fish unless that person has been certified by the U.S. Veterans Administration, U.S. Social Security Administration, by any branch of the U.S. Armed Services, or by a licensed physician in this State to be totally and permanently disabled and has obtained a permanent license issued pursuant to S. 373.561 (5)(b); or unless that person presents proof of acceptance as a client for retardation services by the Department of Health.
- One properly licensed person may also be allowed to fish if accompanying or assisting a permitted individual as described above.
- Panfish daily bag limit (Derby Lake only): 20
- All bluegill and redear sunfish less than 8 inches in total length must be released immediately (Derby Lake only).

Cemetery Lake:
- Boats may not be used.
- Panfish daily bag limit: 20
- All bluegill and redear sunfish less than 8 inches in total length must be released immediately.

Hydrilla Lake:
- Hydrilla Lake is a Special-Opportunity fishing lake. Fishing is authorized only by special-use permit.
- No person shall obtain a permit to fish more than once in any of the four-month periods, January through April, May through August, September through December, unless unused permits are available.
- No gasoline motors are allowed.
- Panfish daily bag limit: 20
- All bluegill and redear sunfish less than 8 inches in total length must be released immediately.

Lake Istokpoga (27,692 acres), Highlands County:
- All black bass 15 inches or more in total length and less than 24 inches must be released immediately.
- Black bass daily bag limit: 3
- Only one black bass may be 24 inches or greater in total length.

Lake Okeeheelee (150 acres), Palm Beach County:
- Gasoline motors may not be used on boats.
- All black bass caught must be released immediately.
- Panfish daily bag limit: 20
- All bluegill and redear sunfish less than 8 inches total length must be released immediately.

Florida Fly Shops

SHOP	ADDRESS	CITY/ZIP	PHONE
Forgotten Coast Outfitters	94 Market St.	Apalachicola 32320	850.653.9669
Tidewater Outfitters	Amelia Village #10	Amelia Island 32035	904.261.2202
Boca Grande Outfitters	375 Park Ave	Boca Grande 33921	941.964.2445
Fishing Unlimited	431 Park Ave	Boca Grande 33921	941.964.0191
Ole Florida Fly Shop	6353 N. Federal Hwy	Boca Raton 33487	561.995.1929
Sunshine Ace Hardware	9090 Bonita Beach Rd	Bonita Springs 34116	941.262.2940
Olde Park Down East	75 Bloom St.	Celebration 34747	407.566.0000
Saltwater Flyfisherman	623 Cleveland St	Clearwater 34615	727.443.5000
Xstream Outfitters	1416 West Lakeshore	Clermont 34711-2941	352.243.0140
Backcountry Concepts	1580 N. Meadowcrest Blvd	Crystal River 34429	352.563.5001
Leisure Time Fly Shop	614 NW Highway 19	Crystal River 34429	800.771.2202
Swann's Fly Shop	13650 US Highway 98 Bypass	Dade City 33525	352.567.6029
Half Hitch Tackle	1601 Front Beach	Destin 32541	850.230.5936
Sockeye Beach & Sport	20011 Emerals Coast Pky	Destin 32541	850.654.8954
Blue Bay Outfitters	41 East Highway 98	Destin 32541	877.321.3474
Bass Pro	200 Gulf Stream Way	Ft. Lauderdale 33004	954.929.7710
Fly Shop of Ft. Lauderdale	5130 N. Federal Way	Ft. Lauderdale 33308	954.772.5822
Lee Island Outfitters	17699 Summerlin Rd	Ft. Myers 33909	239.437.5488
Lehr's Economy Tackle	1366 N. Tamiami	Ft. Myers 33909	239.995.2280
Grand Slam Fishing Center	101 A Seasway Dr	Ft. Pierce 34950	561.746.0526
The Tackle Box	1490 Hawthorne Rd	Gainesville 32641	352.372.1791
Brasington's	2331 NW 13th Street	Gainesville 32641	352.372.1791
Fisherman's Edge Tackle	4425 Placida Rd	Grove City 34224	941.697.7595
Fisherman's World	1312 US Highway 19N	Holiday 34691	727.942.8944

SHOP	ADDRESS	CITY/ZIP	PHONE
Florida Keys Outfitters	81888 Overseas Hwy	Islamorada 33036	305.664.5423
Worldwide Sportsman	81576 Overseas Hwy	Islamorada 33036	305.664.465
The Salty Feather	3733 Southside Blvd #9	Jacksonville 32216	904.645.8998
Ocean Reef Outfitters	31 Ocean Reef Dr	Key Largo 33037	305.367.2611
Saltwater Angler	243 Front Street	Key West	800.223.1629
Harry Goode's Outdoor Shop	1231 East New Haven Ave	Melbourne 32901	321.723.4751
Florida Sportsmen	2771 W. New Haven Ave	Melbourne 32901	407.956.3474
Jet's Florida Outdoors	9696 Nird Rd	Miami 33165	305.221.1371
Capt. Harry's Fishing Supply	100 N.E. 11th St	Miami 33132	305.374.4661
Fishing Line Bait & Tackle	9379 SW 56th St	Miami 33165	305.598.2444
Complete Angler	6827 SW 40th Street	Miami 33155	305.665.2771
Biscayne Bay Fly Shop	4805 Cherokee Ave	Miami 33140	305.669.5851
Crook & Crook Fishing	P.O. Box 109	Miami 33133	305.854.0005
Kingsbury & Sons Tackle	1801 South Federal Hwy	Ft. Lauderdale 33316	954.467.3474
Fisherman's Heaven	101 1st Street	Moore Haven 33471	863.946.3441
Charlie Richter's Fly Shop	472 N.E. 125th St	N Miami 33161	800.866.0763
Murray Brothers	804 Is Highway 1	N. Palm Beach 33408	561.626.7840
Mangrove Outfitters	4111 Tamiami Trl E.	Naples 34112	888.319.9848
Everglades Angler	810 12th Av South	Naples 34102	941.262.8228
Anglers Answer	11387 Tamiami Trail East	Naples 34113	941.775.7336
Scudder & Sons	2709 SW 27th Ave	Ocala 34474	352.628.7103
Garrards Tackle Shop	4259 Hwy 441 S	Okeechobee 34974	800.600.3474
Nix's Fishing Headquarters	3235 Hwy. 441 SE	Okeechobee 34974	813.763.2248
Bass Pro	5156 International Drive	Orlando 32819	407.563.5200
Down East Sporting Classics	538 Park Ave S	Orlando 32789	407.645.5100
Fly Fisherman Orlando	1213 N Orange Ave	Orlando 32804	407.898.1989
The Fly Fisherman	1213 N. Orange Ave.	Orlando 32804	407.898.1989
East Coast Outfitters	385 S US Highway 1	Ormond Beach 32174	386.672.5003

SHOP	ADDRESS	CITY/ZIP	PHONE
The Tackle Box Pro Shop	619 Hwy 19 South	Palatka 32177	386.328.9311
Half Hitch Tackle	2206 Thomas Dr	Panama City 32408	850.234.2621
Fisherman's Corner	13486 Perdido Key Dr	Pensacola 32507	850.492.5574
St. Andrew's Lt. Tackle & Fly	2303 W. 15th St.	Pensacola 32507	850.769.5873
Bill Jackson's	9501 US Hwy 19 N.	Pinellas Park 33782	727.576.4169
Compleat Angler II	11 SE 20TH Ave	Pompano Beach 33060	954.788.8686
Fisherman's Center	56 E. Blue Heron Blvd	Riviera Beach 33404	561.844.5150
Griggs Bros. International	207 E. Blue Heron Blvd	Riviera Beach 33404	561.863.9864
Sanibel Fly Shop	2340 Periwinkle Way	Sanibel 33957	941.472.8485
CB's Saltwater Outfitters	1249 Stickney Rd	Sarasota 34242	941.346.2466
Avid Angler	3101 North Ponce De Leon Blvd	St. Augustine 32084	904.824.8322
Austin & Gunn Outfitters	8487 4t St N	St. Petersburg 33702	727.577.9898
Southern Angler	3585 S.E. Old Lucie Blvd	Stuart 34996-5116	407.223.1300
Kevin's Guns & Sporting Goods, Inc.	3350 Capital Circle N. E.	Tallahassee 32308	850.386.5544
The Fly Fisherman, Inc.	1114 S Washington Ave	Titusville 32780	321.267.0348
The Back Country	2855 Ocean Dr Ste A-1	Vero Beach 32963	561.567.6665
Dewing's Fly & Gun Shop	123 Datura St.	West Palm Beach 33401	561.655.4434
Outdoor Sports World	3415 S Dixie Hwy	West Palm Beach 33405	561.833.7539
Andy Thornal \ Expedition Outfitter's	336 Magnolia Ave. S W.	Winter Haven 33880	800.499.9890

Florida Guides

The following list is just a sampling of the many guides who fish Florida's freshwater. Guides who cater exclusively to freshwater fly fishers in Florida are few and far between, but many light-tackle guides are also equipped to deal with fly fishers.

The area they fish most often is included. When contacting any of these guides, ask for references and referrals to other guides. The following websites have additional listings for other guides, both freshwater and saltwater:

http://www.florida-fishing-guide.com/ or

http://www.fishingworks.com/fishing_guides/location.cfm/FL

Region 1
- Capt. Randy Camps, 877-213-4777 (Stick Marsh / Farm Pond 13)
- Capt. James Hillman, 386-837-3465 (middle St. Johns River)
- Joe and Jean Middleton, 800-258-5002 (Blue Cypress Lake)
- Bob Stonewater, 1-800-835-2851 (middle St. Johns River)
- Capt. John Turcot, 321-267-9818 (lower St. Johns River)
- All Pro Guide Service, 407-260-1862 (Rodman Reservoir)

Region 2
- Capt. Ken Daubert, 352-624-1878 (kayak fishing in the Ocala National Forest)
- Capt. Ned Maxwell, 850-663-2149 (Lake Seminole)
- Dave Mock, 850-576-7614 (Lake Jackson, Lake Talquin, and Lake Miccosuckee)
- Steve Williams, 904-397-2945 (Suwannee River)

Region 3
- Capt. Bill Hunter, 407-290-1593 (Orlando / Kissimmee area)
- Capt Carl Kindberg, 863-467-8844 (Lake Okeechobee)
- Capt. Rob Murchie, 1-800-347-4007 (Lake Kissimmee)
- Capt. Brian Murphy, 954-926-3300 (Everglades/Ft. Lauderdale area)
- Capt. Bill O'Bry, 352-447-0439 (Withlachochee River)
- Capt. Harry Simmons, 873-467-0039 (Lake Okeechobee/Lower Kissimmee chain)
- HawgHunter Guide Service, 954-658-4568 (Lake Okeechobee, Everglades, Miami)
- Stave Kantner, 954-761-3570 (Everglades) www.landcaptain.com

Resources

Florida Fish and Wildlife Conservation Commission
620 South Meridian Street
Tallahassee, FL 32339
850-488-4676
www.floridaconservation.org
(This division oversees fishing in Florida and has an outstanding website.)

Department of Environmental Protection
Division of Recreation and Parks
Mail Station #535
3900 Commonwealth Blvd.
Tallahassee, FL 32399
850-488-9872
www.dep.state.fl.us/parks
(Publishes an excellent guide, "Florida State Parks, The Real Florida.")

Florida Sportsman Magazine
2700 So. Kanner Hwy.
Stuart, FL 34994
561-219-7400
www.floridasportsman.com
(Florida's largest fishing magazine with regular features on freshwater and
    fly fishing opportunities. Check out their website.)

International Game Fish Association
300 Gulf Stream Way
Dania Beach, FL 33004
954-927-2628
www.igfa.org
(World record game fish and very interesting museum near Ft. Lauderdale.)

Coastal Conservation Association (CCA) - Florida Chapter
3333 S. Orange
Ste. 103
Orlando, FL 32806
407-854-7002
www.ccaflorida.org
(Conservation issues related mostly to Florida's coastline.)

Florida Guides Association
P.O. Box 7146
Wesley Chapel, FL 33544
941-695-4421
www.florida-guides.com
(A listing of professional guides.)

Fly Fishing Clubs
North Florida Fly Fishers (Gainesville), www.nfff.netfirms.com
First Coast Fly Fishers (Jacksonville), www.fcff.org
Marco Island Flyrodders (Marco Island), www.marco-island-florida.com/flyrod/home.htm
Back Country Fly Fishers (Naples)www.naples-florida.com/back/country.htm
Central Florida Flyrodders (Orlando), home.cfl.rr.com/cffr
Fly Fishers of Northwest Florida (Pensacola), sites.gulf.net/flyfish
St. Augustine Fly Fishing Club (St. Augustine), www.oldcity.com/flyclub
Florida Big Bend Fly Fishers (Tallahassee), www.fbbflyfishers.com
Tampa Bay Fly Fishing Club (Tampa), scfn.thpl.lib.fl.us/menus/production/flyfish.html

DeLorme Maps
PO Box 298
Yarmouth, ME 04096
207-846-7000
www.delorme.com
(The Florida Atlas and Gazetteer is a collection of maps showing good detail of the interior of the state.)

MapTech
888-839-5551
www.maptech.com
(Custom designed maps for locations that you choose.)

National Oceanic and Atmospheric Administration (NOAA)
301-436-6990
www.noaa.gov
(Up-to-date weather information.)

Florida Chambers of Commerce and Visitor's Centers
http://www.2chambers.com/florida2.htm
http://www.flausa.com/

Sporting Goods Stores & General Fishing Supplies

SHOP	ADDRESS	CITY/ZIP	PHONE
The Sports Authority	380 S State Road 434	Altamonte Sprngs 32714	407.774.8088
Robinson & Sons Outfitter	PO Box 248	Apalachicola	805.653.9669
Big Bass Bait & Tackle	55522 Front St	Astor 32102	352.759.2795
Fishin Stuff	12105 SE US Hwy 441	Belleview 34420	352.307.9811
Big Bend Sporting Goods	1407 N Hwy 71	Blountstown 32424	850.674.5115
Fishing Unlimited Outfitters	PO BOX 1407	Boca Grande 33921	800.482.7766
7 Seas Bait & Tackle	47 E Blue Heron	Boca Raton 33432	561.842.7190
The Sports Authority	20851 State Road 7	Boca Raton 33428	561.488.5754
Boynton Fisherman's Supply	618 N Federal hwy	Boynton Beach 33435	561.736.0568
Florida Native Bait & Tackle	1824 N Federal Hwy	Boynton Beach 33435	561.738.2246
The Sports Authority	363 N. Congress Ave.	Boynton Beach 33426	561.731.2353
Turner Marine Supply	826 13th St W	Bradenton 34208	941.746.3456
West Marine	4569 14th Street	Bradenton 34207	941.753.3585
Island Discount Tackle	2219 Gulf Dr	Bradenton Bch 34217	941.778.7688
Bait Box	37095 Canal Street	Canal Point 33438	561.924.7500
Angler's Outlet	4404 Del Prado Blvd S	Cape Coral 33904	941.549.7555
Chiquita Bait & Tackle	3816 Chiquita Blvd	Cape Coral 33914	239.540.0052
West Marine	1012 Cape Coral Pkwy E	Cape Coral 33904	239.540.7300
Tom's Tackle Shop	1625 N. Ft. Harrison Ave	Clearwater 33755	727.447.5247
West Marine	18891 US Hwy 19 N	Clearwater 34624	727.536.4002
West Marine	1231 Cleveland Street	Clearwater 34615	727.443.2280
Clearwater Bait & Tackle	2999 Gulf to Bay Blvd	Clearwater 33759	727.669.5455
Clermont Bait & Tackle	1730 Hwy 27	Clermont 34711	352.394.7000
Angler's Marina	910 Okeechobee Blvd	Clewiston 33440	941.983.2128

SHOP	ADDRESS	CITY/ZIP	PHONE
Ed's Tackle Shop	983 N Suncoast Blvd	Crystal River 34429	352.795.4178
West Marine	160 SE Highway 19	Crystal River 34429	352.563.0003
Everglades Prof. Bass Ctr	8246 Griffin Road	Davie 33328	954.434.4495
Hinkle Bait and Tackle	5790 Griffin Road	Davie 33314	954.583.2189
Fishin Hole	450 N. Beach Street	Daytona 32114	386.252.9804
West Marine	125 Basin Street	Daytona Bch 32114	386.226.9966
Fishin' Bait & Tackle	3514 S. Atlantic Ave	Daytona Bch Shrs 32127	386.788.2120
The Sports Authority	3810 West Hillsboro Blvd	Deerfield Bch 33442	954.426.4360
West Marine	110 N. Federal Highway	Deerfield Bch 33441	954.427.6165
Sockeye's Beach & Sport	20011 Emerald Coast Pkwy	Destin 32541	850.654.8954
West Marine	862-B Highway 98 East	Destin 32541	850.269.0636
Destin Sunrise Marine	331 Hwy 98E	Deston 32541	850.650.6530
Estero River Outfitters	20991 S Tamiami Trail	Estero 33928	239.992.4050
Amelia Island Tackle	1925 South 14th Street	Fernandina Bch 32034	904.277.0775
West Marine	1875 North US Highway 1	Fort Pierce 34946	772.460.9044
West Marine	248 Eglin Oarkway NE	Fort Walton Bch 32547	850.664.2254
Competition Tackle	4620 Griffin Rd	Ft. Lauderdale 33314	954.581.4476
The Sports Authority	1901 N. Federal Hwy	Ft. Lauderdale 33305	954.568.6226
West Marine	2300 South Federal Hwy	Ft. Lauderdale 33316	954.527.5540
Bill Boyd's Bait & Tackle	508 N Andrews Ave	Ft. Lauderdale 33301	954.462.8366
Captain Ted's Tackle	2510 Davie Blvd	Ft. Lauderdale 33312	941.627.6800
Deep Water Cay Club	1100 Lee Wagener Blvd	Ft. Lauderdale 33315	954.359.0488
West Marine	1520 Colonial Blvd	Ft. Meyers 33907	239.275.6077
Lee Island Outfitters	17699 Summerlin Rd	Ft. Myers	239.437.5488
The Sports Authority	2317 Colonial Blvd	Ft. Myers 33907	239.418.0281
White's Tackle Shop	521 N 2nd St.	Ft. Pierce 34905	561.561.6909
The Sports Authority	7400 West Newberry Rd	Gainesville 32605	352.331.2235

SHOP	ADDRESS	CITY/ZIP	PHONE
Brasington's Trail Shop	2331 Northwest 13th St	Gainesville 32609	888.438.4502
Gulf Breeze Bait & Tackle	825 Gulf Breeze Pkwy	Gulf Breeze 32561	850.932.6789
The Sports Authority	3895 West 20th Ave	Hialeah 33012	305.826.5599
Fishing Hut	585 E 49th Street	Hialeah 33013	305.769.9878
West Marine	3346 US 19 North	Holiday 34691	727.846.1903
Bait & Tackle Shop	1054 Sout h 56th Ave	Hollywood 33023	954.961.1474
West Marine	3350 N 28th Terrace	Hollywood 33020	954.921.1800
Don's Bait and Tackle	30710 S Federal Hwy	Homestead 33030	305.247.6616
Blue Water Bait & Tackle	4065 S Suncoast Blvd	Homosassa 34446	352.628.0414
D & D Bait, Tackle & Marine	439 Highway 40 West	Inglis 34449	652.447.2677
Black Creek Outfitters	10051 Skinner Lake Dr	Jacksonville 32246	904.645.7003
First Coast Fisherman's Supply	4853 Waller St	Jacksonville 32254	904.388.2125
Julington Creek Bait & Tackle	12807 San Jose Blvd	Jacksonville 32223	904.262.8826
The Sports Authority	9292 Arlington Exp	Jacksonville 32225	904.725.9181
The Sports Authority	6000 Lake Gray Blvd	Jacksonville 32244	904.771.9001
West Marine	14180 Beach Blvd	Jacksonville 32250	904.821.5033
West Marine	5951 University Blvd	Jacksonville 32216	904.737.4360
West Marine	4415 Roosevelt Blvd	Jacksonville 32210	904.388.7510
Fish Tales Bait & Tackle	887 NE Jensen Bch Blvd	Jensen Bch 34957	772.232.0002
The Sports Authority	3101 NW Federal Hwy	Jensen Bch 34957	561.692.1771
West Marine	3523 NW Federal Hwy	Jensen Bch 34957	772.692.3092
Fishing Headquarters	633 N. A1A	Jupiter 33477	561.743.7335
The Sports Authority	2599 W. Vine Street	Kissimmee 34741	407.932.4444
Wilderness Outfitters Inc.	1690 Starfish Street	Kissimmee 34741	407.935.1829
West Marine	1401 Old Dixie Highway	Lake Prk 33403	561.863.1440

Shop	Address	City/Zip	Phone
Tuppens Marine	1002 N. Dixie Hwy	Lake Worth 33460	561.582.9012
Phillips Bait & Tackle	3780 Hwy 92 East	Lakeland 33801	863.667.0049
The Sports Authority	3530 US Highway 98 North	Lakeland 33809	863.859.4680
Capt. John's Bait & Tackle	312 East Ocean Ave	Lantana 33462	561.585.4456
The Sports Authority	3203 North State Rd 7	Lauderdale Lakes 33319	954.484.8232
Custom Rod & Gun	1835 NE 25th Street	Lighthouse Point 33064	954.781.5600
Bitters Bait & Tackle	165 N US Hwy 17/92	Longwood 32750	407.699.6619
Marco River Marine	951 Bald Eagle Dr	Marco Island	941.597.3549
West Marine	1085 North Collier Blvd	Marco Island 34145	239.642.7060
The Sports Authority	1750 Evans Road	Melbourne 32904	407.722.0150
West Marine	1509 Harbor City Blvd	Melbourne 32965	321.242.9600
West Marine	1024 S Harbor City Blvd	Melbourne 32901	321.723.1878
Baitmasters of S. Florida	6911 Northeast 3rd Ave	Miami 33138	305.751.7007
Carl's Bait & Tackle Shop	2510 Davie Blvd	Miami 33312	954.581.8890
Fishing Tackle Unlimited	10786 S.W. 188th St	Miami 33157	305.234.3410
Kendall Bait & Tackle	9402 S. Dixie Hwy	Miami 33156	305.670.3474
Scott's Bait & Tackle	8241 SW 124th Street	Miami	305.278.7006
The Sports Authority	200 East Flagler Street	Miami 33131	305.358.1598
The Sports Authority	10688 Northwest 12th St	Miami 33172	305.591.0622
The Sports Authority	8390 South Dixie Highway	Miami 33143	305.667.2280
The Sports Authority	11910 SW 88th Street	Miami 33186	305.270.9762
West Marine	19407 S Dixie Highway	Miami 33157	305.232.0811
West Marine	3635 S Dixie Hwy	Miami 33133	305.444.5520
West Marine	8687 SW 24th Street	Miami, FL 33155	305.263.7465
The Sports Authority	18499 Biscayne Blvd	Miami Beach 33160	305.682.0717
Alvin's Bait&Tackle Shop	100 S. Florida Ave	Moore Haven 33471	863.946.0661

SHOP	ADDRESS	CITY/ZIP	PHONE
West Marine	12189 US Hwy 1	N Palm Beach 33408	561.775.1434
West Marine	1201 N Federal Hwy	N. Ft. Lauderdale 33304	954.564.6767
The Sports Authority	2505 Pine Ridge Rd	Naples 34109	239.598.5054
West Marine	2025 Davis Blvd	Naples 34104	239.793.7722
Fishin' Store	248 N. Causeway	New Smyrna 32169	386.427.4514
Dona Bay Outfitters	504 Tamiami Trail S.	Nokomis 34275	941.488.6411
Scudder & Sons Outfitters	2709 SW 27th Ave	Ocala 34474	352.628.7103
The Sports Authority	2400 SW College Rd.	Ocala 34474	352.873.1466
Bubba's Tackle Box	1268 Blanding Blvd	Orange Park 32065	904.276.3474
West Marine	311 Blanding Blvd	Orange Park 32073	904.276.4343
Al's Fishing Tackle	1718 N Goldenrod Rd #3	Orlando 32807	407.380.6787
The Sports Authority	7500 West Colonial	Orlando 32818	407.291.6653
The Sports Authority	881 Sand Lake Road	Orlando 32809	407.857.1611
The Sports Authority	993 N. Semoran Blvd	Orlando 32807	407.277.1994
West Marine	5135 Adanson St	Orlando 32804	407.644.8557
East Coast Outfitters	385 S. US Hwy 1	Ormond Beach 32174	386.672.5003
Palm Bay Fishing Outfitters	1663 Georgia Street NE	Palm Bay 32907	321.952.4436
Dave's Discount Tackle	3904 US 41	Palmetto 34221	941.729.8876
The Sports Authority	525 West 23rd Street	Panama City 32405	850.784.6059
West Marine	1388 West 15th Street	Panama City 32401	850.763.1844
The Sports Authority	11140 Pines Blvd.	Pembroke Pines 33026	954.447.9666
Buck and Bass	6827 Pine Forest Rd	Pensacola 32526	850.944.5692
Pearsons & Sons Outfitters	207 S Pala Fox St	Pensacola 32501	850.470.9626
Reel Fun One Stop Bait Shop	711 N. Pace Blvd	Pensacola, FL 32505	850.433.2962
The Sports Authority	1220 Airport Blvd	Pensacola, FL 32504	850.494.1611
West Marine	3500 Barancas Ave	Pensacola, FL 32507	850.453.0010

SHOP	ADDRESS	CITY/ZIP	PHONE
Holy Mackerel Tackle	8629 49th Street N	Pinellas Park 33782	727.576.4169
Atlantic Bait & Tackle	900 East Atlantic Blvd	Pompano Beach 33060	954.946.1040
The Sports Authority	18700 Veterans Hwy	Port Charlotte 33954	941.766.1993
West Marine	4265 Tamiami Trail	Port Charlotte 33980	941.625.2700
The Sports Authority	9560 US Highway 19	Port Richey 34668	813.846.1537
Billy Bones Bait & Tackle	10640 South Federal Way	Port St. Lucie 34952	772.335.3715
Bill's Tackle Shop	135 W Marion Ave	Punta Gorda 33950	941.639.1305
West Marine	915 Taylor Rd	Punta Gorda 33950	941.637.0000
The Sports Authority	100 North Entrance Rd	Sanford 32771	407.302.3704
Stanley & Livingstons	2340 Periwinkle Way	Sanibel 33957	941.472.8485
Bait Box	1043 Periwinkle Way	Sanibel 33957	941.472.1618
Economy Tackle	6018 S Tamiami Trail	Sarasota 34231	941.922.9671
The Sports Authority	4092 Cattlemen Rd	Sarasota 34233	239.377.4301
West Marine	3979 S Tamiami Trail	Sarasota 34231	941.924.6777
West Marine	3130 N Tamiami Trail	Sarasota 34234	941.351.3431
Bass Fishing Heaven	8801 Seminole Blvd	Seminole 33772	727.392.4817
West Marine	2400 S. Ridgewood Ave US1	S. Daytona Beach 32119	386.760.0660
Fishing Pad II	4249 13th Street	St, Cloud 34769	407.891.1003
Fore Casters	53 King Street	St. Augustine	904.827.0606
West Marine	1030 S Ponce de Leon Blvd	St. Augustine 32086	904.810.5353
Beau Tyed Flied Outfitters	1114 New York Ave	St. Cloud 34769	407.891.1332
Mastry's Bait and Tackle	1700 4th St. S	St. Petersburg 33701	813.896.8889
The Sports Authority	3700 Tyrone Blvd	St. Petersburg, FL 33710	727.343.2088
West Marine	2000 34th St. No. US 19	St. Petersburg, FL 33713	727.327.0072

SHOP	ADDRESS	CITY/ZIP	PHONE
West Marine	5001 34th Street South	St. Petersburg 33711	727.867.5700
West Marine	4545 SE Dixie Hwy	Stuart 34997	772.223.1515
The Sports Authority	12801 W. Sunrise Blvd	Sunrise 33323	954.846.9395
West Marine	4248 W Tennessee St	Tallahassee 32304	850.574.3476
Inshore Masters	15619 Premire Dr, Ste 201	Tampa 33624	813.961.8669
Rodbenders Inc	207 N 11th Street	Tampa	813.223.7754
The Sports Authority	1730 East Fowler Ave.	TAMPA 33612	813.632.9091
The Sports Authority	4340 W. Hillsborough Blvd	Tampa 33614	813.875.2220
The Sports Authority	4900 W. Kennedy Blvd	TAMPA 33609	813.282.1180
The Sports Authority	12601 Citrus Plaza Dr	Tampa 33625	813.792.1550
World Class Outfitters	13911 N. Dale Mabry Hwy	Tampa 33618	813.968.3736
West Marine	3905 W Cypress St	Tampa 33607	813.348.0521
Inlet Bait & Tackle	140 Bridge Rd	Tequesta 33469	561.743.2248
Florida Fishing Outfitters	4260 S Washington Ave	Titusville 32780	407.868.0000
Eustis Outdoor Shop	37826 State Road 19	Umatilla 32784	352.669.1224
Hook Line & Sinker	472 Colgate Rd	Venice 34293	941.493.7637
West Marine	1860 Tamiami Trail South	Venice 34293	941.408.8288
Outcast Bait and Tackle	3520 Barrancas Ave	Warrington 32507	850.457.1450
The Sports Authority	2601 Okeechobee Blvd	West Palm Bch 33409	561.688.9501
The Sports Authority	3350 Northlake Blvd.	West Palm Bch 33403	561.622.7203

Index